ARTIFICIAL INTELLIGENCE IN MAINTENANCE

JOINT SERVICES WORKING GROUP ON ARTIFICIAL INTELLIGENCE IN MAINTENANCE

ARTIFICIAL INTELLIGENCE IN MAINTENANCE

Edited by

J. Jeffrey Richardson

Denver Research Institute
University of Denver
Denver, Colorado

Sponsored by

Air Force Human Resources Laboratory
Army Research Institute for the Behavioral and Social Sciences
Naval Training Equipment Center
Navy Center for Applied Research in Artificial Intelligence
Navy Personnel Research and Development Center
Rome Air Development Center
U.S. Army Project Manager for Training Devices

np

NOYES PUBLICATIONS
Park Ridge, New Jersey, U.S.A.

Library of Congress Catalog Card Number 85-15394
ISBN: 0-8155-1042-X
Printed in the United States

Published in the United States of America by
Noyes Publications
Mill Road, Park Ridge, New Jersey 07656

10 9 8 7 6 5 4 3 2 1

Library of Congress Cataloging-in-Publication Data
Main entry under title:

Artificial intelligence in maintenance.

"The Joint Services Workshop on Artificial Intelligence in Maintenance was held October 4–6, 1983 in Boulder, Colorado, sponsored by seven Department of Defense research agencies"--Pref.
Bibliography: p.
Includes index.
1. Artificial intelligence--Military applications--Congresses. 2. United States--Armed Forces--Equipment--Maintenance and repair--Congresses. 3. Expert systems--Congresses. 4. Problem solving--Congresses.
I. Richardson, J. Jeffrey. II. Joint Services Workshop on Artificial Intelligence in Maintenance (1983 : Boulder, Colo.)
UG479.A78 1985 623'.028'563 85-15394
ISBN 0-8155-1042-X

Foreword

Theoretical and practical research and development, and applications issues in the use of artificial intelligence in maintenance are identified here. Based on a Joint-Services sponsored workshop, this book provides an exchange of technical information for managers, engineers, and other personnel involved in on-going R&D in artificial intelligence applicable to automatic testing, maintenance aiding, and maintenance training.

AI research in problem solving and expert systems provides us with new tools and techniques to be refined for practical applications. The material presented covers the state of the science of artificial intelligence, specific efforts in expert systems and knowledge engineering, the psychologies of technical devices and fault diagnosis, and the future of AI as related to maintenance. This is an excellent presentation of an important application for artificial intelligence.

The information in this book is from *Artificial Intelligence in Maintenance: Proceedings of the Joint Services Workshop* edited by J. Jeffrey Richardson of the Denver Research Institute, University of Denver for the Air Force Human Resources Laboratory, June 1984.

The table of contents is organized in such a way as to serve as a subject index and provides easy access to the information contained in the book.

Advanced composition and production methods developed by Noyes Publications are employed to bring this durably bound book to you in a minimum of time. Special techniques are used to close the gap between "manuscript" and "completed book." In order to keep the price of the book to a reasonable level, it has been partially reproduced by photo-offset directly from the original report and the cost saving passed on to the reader. Due to this method of publishing, certain portions of the book may be less legible than desired.

NOTICE

The materials in this book were prepared as accounts of work sponsored by the Air Force Human Resources Laboratory. Publication does not signify that the contents necessarily reflect the views and policies of the sponsoring agencies or the publisher, nor does mention of trade names or commercial products constitute endorsement or recommendation for use.

When Government drawings, specifications, or other data are used for any purpose other than in connection with a definitely Government-related procurement, the United States Government incurs no responsibility or any obligation whatsoever. The fact that the Government may have formulated or in any way supplied the said drawings, specifications, or other data, is not to be regarded by implication, or otherwise in any manner construed, as licensing the holder, or any other person or corporation; or as conveying any rights or permission to manufacture, use, or sell any patented invention that may in any way be related thereto.

Preface

The Joint Services Workshop on Artificial Intelligence in Maintenance was held October 4-6, 1983 in Boulder, Colorado, sponsored by seven Department of Defense research agencies. The specific objectives of the workshop were:

- To provide an exchange of technical information among personnel involved in ongoing R&D in artificial intelligence applicable to automatic testing, maintenance aiding, and maintenance training.
- To identify both theoretical and practical R&D and applications issues in the use of AI in maintenance.

This volume includes most of the papers presented and is organized into four major sections. Rather than organizing the papers chronologically, we elected to gather them topically to reflect the contributions of the scientific community, the Department of Defense community, and the industrial community. Therefore, a section that presents an Overview of AI technology is followed by The Science, DoD Programs and Projects, and Commercial and Industrial Development Projects.

This book includes workshop papers and presentations, some of which are transcripts that have been edited, significant papers previously published, and contributions from workshop participants who were precluded from presenting in Boulder because of time constraints. We are grateful to the presenters and authors for their cooperation in gathering materials for the proceedings.

This workshop could not have been conducted were it not for the leadership and support of the Air Force Human Resources Laboratory, in particular, Dr. Earl Alluisi, Chief Scientist; Mr. Brian Dallman and Major Hugh Burns of the Training Systems Division; and Mr. Russell Genet of the Logistics and Human

Factors Division. We wish to acknowledge the support of Dr. Ken DeJong of the Navy Center for Applied Research in Artificial Intelligence for his assistance in developing the workshop program. Many others deserve credit for their help in making this workshop a success, especially Ms. Bonita Moul, Administrative Editor of this report, without whose tireless effort there would be no permanent record of these proceedings.

J. Jeffrey Richardson
Program Organizer
Denver Research Institute

Organization of the Workshop

Program Organizer:	J. Jeffrey Richardson Denver Research Institute
Air Force Program Monitor:	Brian Dallman Air Force Human Resources Laboratory Lowry Air Force Base, Colorado
Workshop Moderator:	Major Hugh L. Burns Air Force Human Resources Laboratory Lowry Air Force Base, Colorado
Administrative Editor:	Bonita L. Moul Denver Research Institute
Boulder Host:	Institute of Cognitive Science University of Colorado

Contents and Subject Index

Part I

Overview

KEYNOTE ADDRESS

Dr. Bernard Kulp

Air Force Systems Command

It is a pleasure to have this opportunity to come and discuss with you some of my thoughts on artificial intelligence in general and artificial intelligence as applied to maintenance and training in particular. If you'll pardon me, I don't like to read a speech, but I'm going to try to read a lot of this because--while I'm very flattered at the program committee's setting aside 45 minutes for my talk--I assure you I don't know that much about AI, especially in maintenance and training. But I'll shoot the bull a little bit with you, and I certainly have some firm ideas of what I want out of AI, and what I want out of AI in maintenance and training.

You have the advantage of being the first of a series of AI workshops or meetings within the DoD, and particularly in the community of "people" research. Coming up soon is a conference by our Aerospace Medical Division, sort of an in-house, in-Air Force kind of thing to get their thoughts organized in AI. They were involved in the very early days of AI--it's kind of interesting to look back in history, and I'm going to talk a little bit about history. Many of you probably know it a lot better than I do and have participated in it, but reviewing it has been interesting for me.

Back in the days when we were thinking about how to make machines that think, we liked to duplicate the human thought process, and so there's a lot of work on how humans think and how to model that in a computer and how to build software on that. Our Aerospace Medical Research Laboratory at Wright-Patterson had quite a bit of work in that in 1965, which is a date that is kind of famous in AI. They were told to get out of the business, and now they're struggling to get back into it.

Commander Paul Chatelier of DoD is planning an AI conference in spring 1984 on personnel and training which promises to be an interesting kind of a thing. There is clearly a major interest in AI in the DoD research and development community, not only in the personnel and people-oriented communities, but in the other areas of research within DoD. I'd like to tell you a little about the origin of that and how it came about.

We also ought to look back at the history of AI, how we got where we are and what are our accomplishments. I have said in the topic of my discussion that the time for artificial intelligence has come. I think we'd better make sure that that's true, because it's been said before. I'll tell you a little bit about the origin of AI and why it hasn't developed before. In the early days of my interest in AI, I would go into the general officers' meetings and say "We really ought to open up a research program in AI," and that's about all I'd get to say. Then I was asked to leave the room--"Thank you, we don't have time for such nonsense at these very high powered meetings." It took awhile before I was invited to say what I had to say in 5 minutes, and then 10 minutes, and then an hour. I'm sure there are other people at this workshop who have had a similar experience. So, we want to examine that at this time AI is here for real.

People really began thinking about intelligent machines back in 1937, back when the old computers were made with vacuum tubes. I'm sure there are a lot of people in this room who remember those. Ten thousand of them in a computer with a thousand-hour mean time to failure meant you worked fast when you had that thing up, because it was going to go down fast.

Even in those days, the late 1930s and early 1940s, we began to see novels and stories about intelligent machines that would rule human beings. I recall a very interesting episode of Star Trek that pointed out one of the problems we're going to have as we go into AI. These people presented a computer with a situation that they knew the computer had not seen before--a totally illogical situation to a human being. The computer didn't know what to do with it and crashed. Of course, that meant that people had won the battle.

Now, we're talking about presenting computers, computer programs, and computer systems to people on the flight line, in the trenches, and on the ships. It's not clear that these people are totally logical in their approach to the job that the computer wants to help them do. We in the high technology area often look at the world a little bit differently than those poor recruits down there. They come out of high school, go into the army, get 6 weeks training in electronic repair, and have to go out there and repair very sophisticated radar equipment.

The first major work about machines that think was published by Norbert Wiener of MIT in 1940, entitled Cybernetics: Machines that Think. If you haven't read that book, you ought to read it; it's a fascinating book. He coined the word cybernetics from a Greek word meaning helmsman. I don't really know why he picked that word. I've never been able to figure it out, and the two or three books that I've read on the subject didn't know either. But he defined it as the mathematics of information processing and its technical realization. It was a very popular word for a long time. It was replaced by the term artificial intelligence somewhat later, as we began to get a little bit more feeling that indeed we could get these machines to do at least some of the things that intelligent beings do.

In the early days, those included in AI recognized that there were two processes that human beings master which represent our thought processes and intelligence: natural language understanding and image understanding. An almost immediate application was machine translation. They dreamt of a machine into which you would put a printed page of English, turn a dial to German, French, Russian, or what have you, and out would come the document, all translated at a million words a minute or some similarly unreasonable number.

In fact, in 1952, there was a Frenchman who, referring to these machine translators, said that if a human being can do it, a suitably programmed computer can also do it. That was in 1952, and it's interesting to look at what machine translation capability is today. I talked to our people at Rome Air Development

Center (RADC) who are the Air Force experts in this field. They said, in scientific literature, where there are fairly well-structured expressions and words, we get between 60-85 percent fidelity in translation--depending on the particular system you have and the particular difficulty of the passage that is being translated. But when you go to newspapers and attempt to get the thought process, we're lucky to get 50 percent fidelity in translation of the ideas of the reporter into the translated document. Finally, if we go to poems, novels, and fiction, where idiosyncracies of the language become most evident, we're down to 30-40 percent fidelity. Thus, we have not accomplished the kind of challenge that the early AI researchers thought would reflect the development of a machine which has artificial intelligence.

I'd like to comment on one other thing before I go on. The United States is not alone in the field of AI, and I think all of you realize that. For example, toys and games were not neglected by the early researchers, and games of checkers and chess were a favorite pastime of the research community. In fact, this led some people, particularly critics, to say that artificial intelligence may be only useful in the design of the toys of the future. There was a chess match in Russia in 1966 or 1967 between the Russians and the United States. The United States took over a very fine program--a single, fairly sophisticated program designed to play chess with another computer. They were pretty proud of it. The Russians, on the other hand, came in with two programs. One was a rather simple program with which they started out the match. Then they switched to a much more sophisticated program that they had developed. In fact, the approach the Russians had was to use the simplistic one to get some things out of the way, get some of the excess pieces off the board, if you will, to where they could really work, then use the more sophisticated program. This approach proved to be decisive in the match and the Russians won.

In the newspaper within the last 6 months, there was a report of some very sophisticated computer equipment that was confiscated because it was being shipped to Russia. That was on the front page. About 2 weeks later, on the back page of the newspaper it was reported that this was a computerized chess machine that was going over to Russia to replay the earlier match. I have not seen any releases, at least in the Washington Post, about whether or not they did get that equipment cleared and went over there and played.

So, the U.S. is not alone in this. The Russians, French, Germans, and English are very old in this field of artificial intelligence. Certainly we must respect their position in the world, particularly if we're going to assess it in relationship to the economic value or the war fighting capabilities that it might give them. In particular the Japanese have embarked on a very large computer program--a fifth generation computer based on artificial intelligence. They make it clear that this is not a number cruncher. It is clearly an artificial intelligence implementing machine. DARPA has a next generation computer program that is also very interesting. When I first heard of the program, it was a 200 million dollar program over 5 years. It is now passing 750 million dollars in 8 years and going up rapidly. It will be an artificial intelligence based machine.

Well, I've talked about some of the problems of the early researchers, but there were also some successes in the 1950s and early 1960s. The community learned from these that the most successful programs were in fact those that were based on very large data bases and played in a machine that could organize, store, and manipulate data at a reasonable speed. They also recognized that it was a very labor-intensive project to get to this state of usefulness. Among the machines that were considered best were those which did not attempt to duplicate human thought processes. In fact, they were based upon information processing (indeed list processing) and did not necessarily try to emulate or duplicate human thought processing.

This is sort of a shock to the purists in AI, I think, because they believe that when you talk about artificial intelligence, it ought to be an artificial person. There is no question that the objective of the earlier phase of artificial intelligence research has not yet been accomplished. Even in expert systems, which are here today and very successful, there still seems to be, in the judgment of most researchers, some exciting research to be done--enough research for a sizeable effort in the university kind of environment for at least the next 10 years. This work would have to be done before we'll be ready to say that expert systems are mature and we have a technology, rather than a science, that's ready for routine applications.

In recent years, we've seen the recognition on the part of the research community that these so-called expert systems are indeed real and practical. We've seen researchers break off from their university associations and develop small companies. There is an industry called knowledge engineering, that's what I call it at least, that's developing rapidly. We're seeing the industrial applications being developed and used. We're very proud of that, and we in the DoD are beginning to take steps to transform that science into a technology of use to the military and get it finished and applied to many diverse problems.

For those of you who want a good review of the present state-of-the-art of AI, I could name a whole list of these programs that have been developed and are rather successful, but if you're like me, you won't remember them after the workshop is over. However, in AI Magazine (Fall 1983), there is an excellent review of the general state-of-the-art of expert systems and of AI in general--a result of the annual artificial intelligence conference which was held in Washington.

Now I'm going to move into a part of my talk that says, how did I get here, why am I here today, and what my thoughts are on the subject. Just like telling a war story, and indeed, I find that all of a sudden war stories seem to be fun to tell. I was first exposed to artificial intelligence in a study called Computer Technology 2000 in 1978. I had read Wiener's book back in the 1940s, but I had long since forgotten it. This particular study was part of a larger study called Look Forward 20 Years. It was performed for the Director of Laboratories at Air Force Systems Command (AFSC) and took a look at the technologies that the Air Force laboratories ought to be working on in the 15 to 20 year time period, that is in 1988 to 1990. The computer section of the study was run under Walt Beam and had a group in it made up of some prominent figures in artificial intelligence. That study predicted that AI techniques applied to inference, planning, and pattern recognition would enhance the generation of plans, and present and evaluate alternates to those plans in the general exploitation of reconnaissance and intelligence information in the late 1980s.

As a result of that prediction, and a number of other recommendations in the context of the 2000 study, the Director of Laboratories of AFSC put two million dollars into Rome Air Development Center (which had been given the charter for basic computer science development in the Air Force). Rome was to develop a program which would implement these recommendations, and one of the recommendations they chose to implement was indeed artificial intelligence. We also asked the Air Force Office of Scientific Research (AFOSR) to begin to take a look at this field and they responded with a program which has expanded continually over the years in the basic science of artificial intelligence.

The AFOSR program complemented quite an aggressive program by Defense Advanced Research Projects Agency (DARPA) and by the Office of Naval Research in this area. In about 1981, the Defense Science Board (DSB) held a summer study on technology and its implication for the military art. It was headed by George Heilmeier. He's a Vice President of Texas Instruments, spent a tour at USDR&E as the Deputy Undersecretary for Research and Advance Technology. Before that he'd been at DARPA for some time and was there when they got involved in the AI business.

The DSB study dedicated a whole day to artificial intelligence. A series of speakers from various organizations discussed the state-of-the-art of AI and its potential. It was during that particular series of discussions that I became convinced that AI was indeed ready for the conversion into a technology that would be useful to the military. We began to pick that up within the three services and talk about it, decide how to get into the area, and how to encourage our people to investigate AI, but there are some very severe constraints. I'll talk about a couple of them and how the Air Force is accommodating them in a few moments.

As a result of the DSB summer study which identified 17 major technologies which would contribute an order-of-magnitude increase in military capability in the 1990s, the Joint Directors of Laboratories established seven technical initiative panels in 1982. The objective of these panels was to take a look at the state of research in these technical areas within the services and to propose joint programs that would be of a fundamental nature applicable to all three services. This would give us a higher probability of creating a center of mass that was big enough to expand and absorb the technologies that we are involved with and also to accumulate some more money in each particular area.

The AI panel proposed three joint service programs, one of them to be executed in-house at the Navy Center for Applied Research in Artificial Intelligence (NCARAI) in maintenance, diagnostics, and training. It is initially a six-person effort, with two people from each of the services co-located at the Center.

The second program, also to be executed in-house at the Navy Center, is electronic warfare information fusion and resource management. We think that each service contributing two people to a program like this will result in a team which will, together with some contract help as needed, create a center of mass where the state-of-the-art can be advanced, particularly with reference to the military. This is the core in-house capability which many of us in the government think is absolutely necessary if we are going to understand and to rapidly advance the state-of-the-art in any area. We recognize that our general personnel policies are such that we cannot do all our work in-house (and in fact that we should not) because we depend on industry to build the systems and we depend on the universities to do the basic research. But we do have to know enough to be smart buyers. We have to know enough to evaluate the potential of a technology and the time in which we might exploit it. Thus, we think that in-house capability is very important and it's being established at the Navy.

This Navy Center will have approximately 25 principal researchers. They are very well equipped and in this tri-service program, the Army and the Air Force will contribute to the equipment. I think they have established an excellent atmosphere for productivity. In Figure 1, you'll see the three major areas on which they'll focus.

One of the other recommendations of the AI panel was that there be a DoD Information Center for AI and that will be housed at the Naval Research Laboratory and at the Navy Center. It will provide library services for ongoing programs in AI in all three service laboratories and a general background library of AI literature. We hope to get it in a position that it will also have the plans of the three services. We look forward to this as being a major initiative and a way to get a running start on understanding and transitioning artificial intelligence science into a technology of use to us in the services.

The third program that was proposed in this joint service arena was in software productivity. The DoD has a major problem in software. That is, it's very expensive to develop and we don't know how to judge the expense of it, a priori, before we start a program. As a result, generally speaking, our software programs overrun and you can figure an average overrun of 2 or 3 years. At any rate, the committee recommended that the software program be executed at Rome because they already had a good start. The Army and the Navy will probably not be asked to contribute any money to it.

Figure 2 shows Rome's view of their AI program and it is going strong. My first trip up there to see what they were doing was, in my estimation, a total disaster. However, my most recent trip up there was very gratifying. They'll have an in-house laboratory. I think it's clearly essential that the Air Force have a couple of these--not one in every laboratory, we can't afford that--but a place where people can go and work with the machines and live with people applying AI techniques and, in fact, developing them if we're able to develop that kind of capability.

In developing this AI capability, we recognize the staff problem that exists, both in our services and in industry. And so RADC has developed a relationship with a number of universities in the area, including the Air Force Institute of Technology. We expect these universities to (1) do research for us, (2) supply consultants who are knowledgeable of our interests and our business, and, of course, (3) train people, both for the services and for industry.

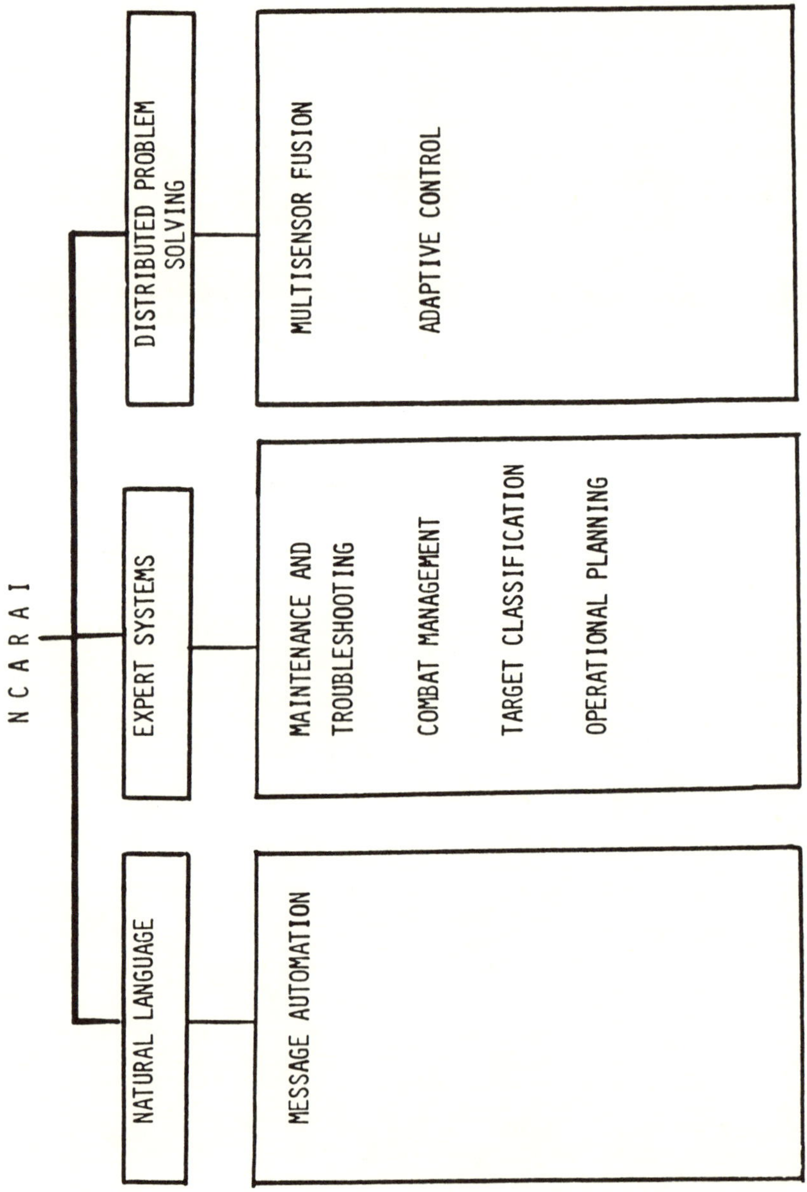
N C A R A I
NATURAL LANGUAGE
EXPERT SYSTEMS
DISTRIBUTED PROBLEM SOLVING
MESSAGE AUTOMATION
MAINTENANCE AND TROUBLESHOOTING
COMBAT MANAGEMENT
TARGET CLASSIFICATION
OPERATIONAL PLANNING
MULTISENSOR FUSION
ADAPTIVE CONTROL

Figure 1.

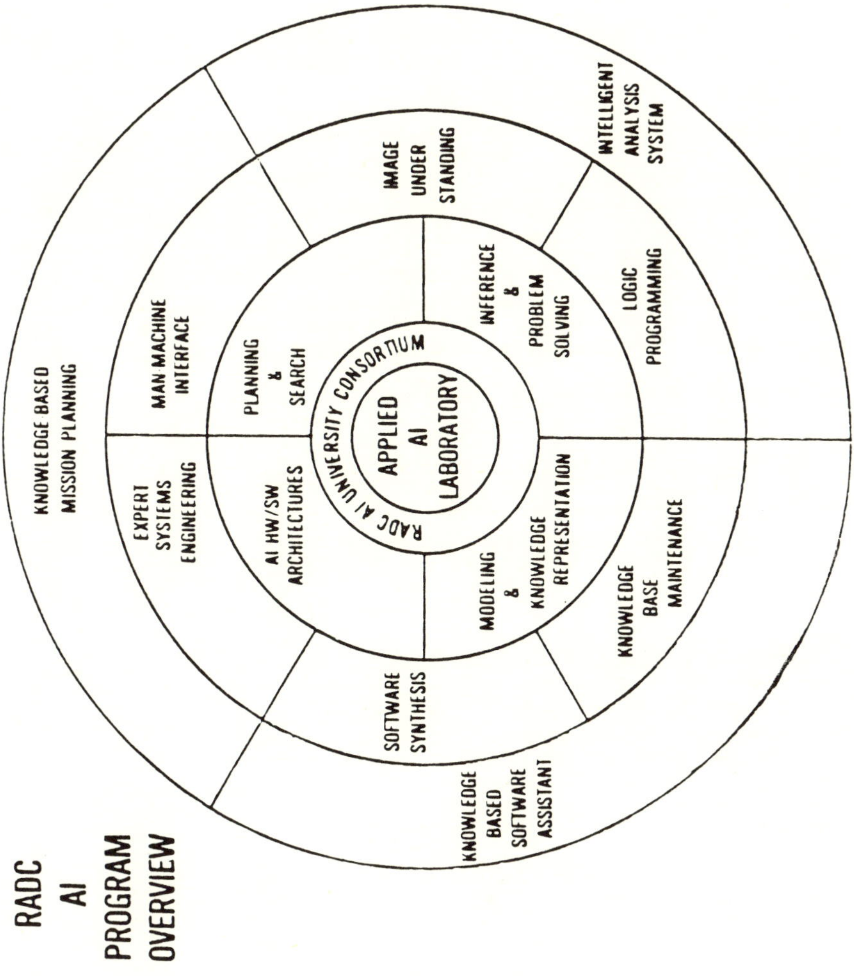
RADC
AI
PROGRAM
OVERVIEW
APPLIED
AI
LABORATORY
RADC AI UNIVERSITY CONSORTIUM
PLANNING
&
SEARCH
INFERENCE
&
PROBLEM
SOLVING
MODELING
&
KNOWLEDGE
REPRESENTATION
AI HW/SW
ARCHITECTURES
MAN-MACHINE
INTERFACE
IMAGE
UNDER
STANDING
LOGIC
PROGRAMMING
KNOWLEDGE
BASE
MAINTENANCE
SOFTWARE
SYNTHESIS
EXPERT
SYSTEMS
ENGINEERING
KNOWLEDGE BASED
MISSION PLANNING
INTELLIGENT
ANALYSIS
SYSTEM
KNOWLEDGE
BASED
SOFTWARE
ASSISTANT

Figure 2.

Some of the basic things RADC is working on are the tools for use by people developing a system based on AI techniques. At the level of exploratory development, we move into an actual systems development or demonstration. The three major systems areas that RADC is working on are the knowledge-based software assistant (which is that software productivity program), knowledge-based mission planning (in which one takes a look at various information coming into a central decision making authority from various sources), and the intelligent analyst system. In the intelligent analyst system, we get reams and reams of photographs, miles and miles of recordings of voice intercepts, and we need some help to separate the things we should look at more carefully. In the second area, knowledge-based mission planning, RADC takes a look at the input coming into the central decision making authority. For example, input from reconnaissance resources--space, airplanes, radars, and intercept information. All of this information is organized and pre-digested and then presented to a decision maker who says, "I have certain resources at my disposal (electronic jammers, bombers, fighters, aircraft, other communication systems, etc.) and here is why I want to use these resources to advance my goals in this particular arena." So it's sort of a commander's assistant, if you will, which will organize the input data, communicating and analyzing the kinds of alternatives to use with various equipment. Right now we do that numerically. We consider when we wish to send a bomber against a target and say, "Hey, here's the bombers we've got, here's the weapons, and now you can take the weapons or calculate your trajectories or calculate the attrition of the aircraft, etc." All of this is presently in beautiful long programs that take a month or more to run. We expect AI techniques to perform the analyses in near real time.

Finally, we would like to establish a second center of R&D in artificial intelligence and its techniques at Air Force Avionics Laboratory at Wright-Patterson (see Figure 3). They're about 3 or 4 years behind Rome in their implementation, but they're eager and they're looking forward to a rapid kind of build-up. You can see the four areas that they're interested in, and again, underlying this is an in-house laboratory for artificial intelligence. I strongly suspect that we'll use data links to Rome so we can take advantage of both of the computer systems. Again, we see the need for close ties with a university in order to get the kind of expertise and people that we think are necessary to help us organize our thoughts and pursue this very high technology program.

Other laboratories are also involved, for example, Flight Dynamics Laboratory. Flight Dynamics Laboratory has been looking at integrated systems for the last several years. They are responsible for flight control systems. They've integrated the fire and flight control of an airplane so that the two very diverse functions of avionics and flight control begin to talk to each other. They find that when you do that, it is quite interesting the kinds of capabilities you can develop in a modern airplane. Flight Dynamics Laboratory says that what they'd really like to develop is a flight control system that controls the trajectory of the aircraft. That, in fact, is what the pilots do when they design their intercept, for they control the trajectory to put them in a position of maximum advantage. That maximum advantage may be one in which they have the shortest time to intercept, or it may be the intercept that gives them the highest energy remaining in their aircraft at time of intercept, or in other cases, it may give them the minimum fuel consumption so they'll have enough fuel to stay in fight longer.

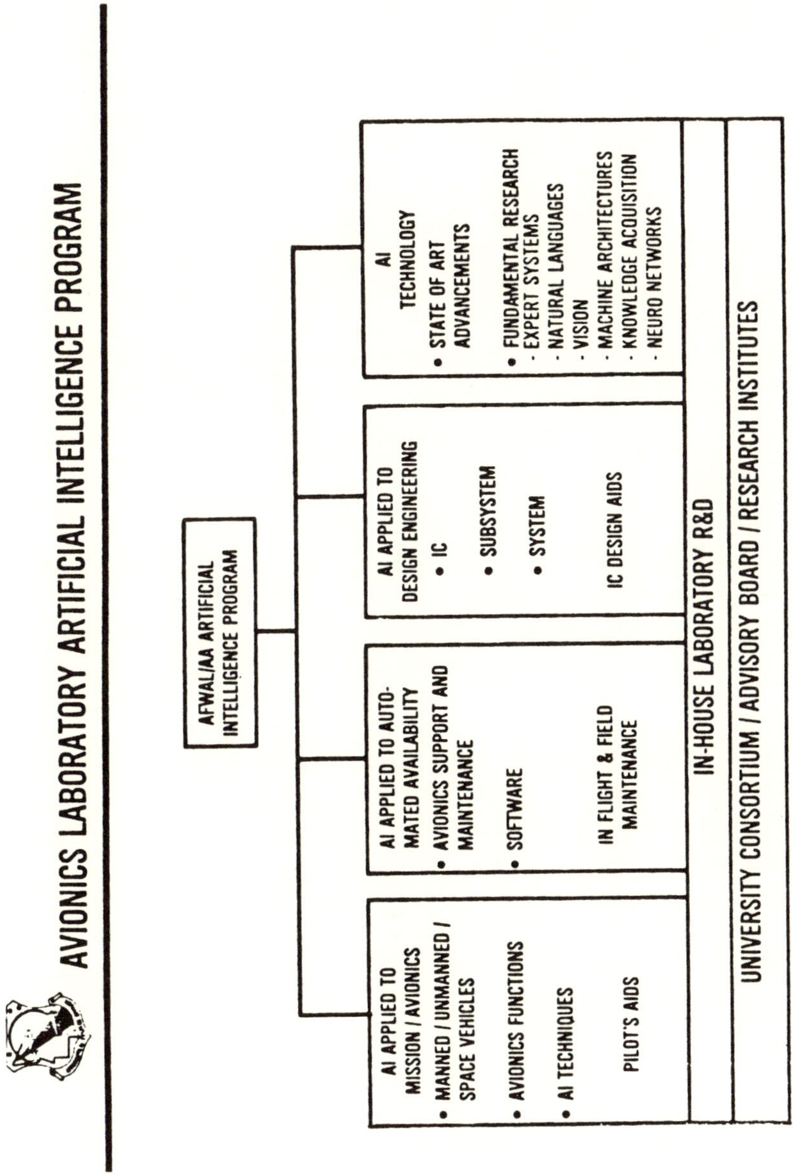
AVIONICS LABORATORY ARTIFICIAL INTELLIGENCE PROGRAM
AFWAL/AA ARTIFICIAL INTELLIGENCE PROGRAM
AI APPLIED TO MISSION / AVIONICS
• MANNED / UNMANNED / SPACE VEHICLES
• AVIONICS FUNCTIONS
• AI TECHNIQUES
PILOT'S AIDS
AI APPLIED TO AUTO-MATED AVAILABILITY
• AVIONICS SUPPORT AND MAINTENANCE
• SOFTWARE
IN FLIGHT & FIELD MAINTENANCE
AI APPLIED TO DESIGN ENGINEERING
• IC
• SUBSYSTEM
• SYSTEM
IC DESIGN AIDS
AI TECHNOLOGY
• STATE OF ART ADVANCEMENTS
• FUNDAMENTAL RESEARCH
- EXPERT SYSTEMS
- NATURAL LANGUAGES
- VISION
- MACHINE ARCHITECTURES
- KNOWLEDGE ACQUISITION
- NEURO NETWORKS
IN-HOUSE LABORATORY R&D
UNIVERSITY CONSORTIUM / ADVISORY BOARD / RESEARCH INSTITUTES

Figure 3.

So, Flight Dynamics Laboratory believes that artificial intelligence techniques can greatly aid in the solution of that problem. But they've got another problem. If a radar goes out, you can't see very well, but you're still in the air. If a radio goes out, you can't talk to anybody, but you're still in the air. If your flight control system goes out, you fall out of the sky. So reliability is the problem--electronic reliability in the sense of flight control is probably about three orders of magnitude more rigid than that demanded of a high reliability avionics system.

We expect Avionics Laboratory to look at equipment reliability, too. But the differences in thresholds of the two suggest that it's useful for the Air Force to attack both areas. Finally, other laboratories will probably be involved in pattern recognition, voice understanding, navigation, weapon guidance, and resource management applications of AI.

Thus far, I've spent most of the time talking about the Air Force, but I should not neglect the other services. You'll hear a lot about the Navy's work, an overview from the Center for Applied Research and NPRDC. But others that should be recognized include the Naval Ocean Systems Center, the Navy Undersea Systems Center, Surface Weapons Center, Air Development Center, and Weapons Center, and NTEC. The Army Research Institute is here and presenting. There is a major effort in the Army, in-house at the Engineering Topographic Laboratory at Fort Belvoir, in autonomous navigation. The kinds of unique understanding that are available today using artificial intelligence techniques seem to be quite adequate to start as the basis for autonomous navigation. Army Human Engineering Laboratory at Aberdeen is going into this field heavily. And I would say that an excellent overview of the state-of-the-art in AI in the military is going to be presented at the AIAA Conference in Computers in Aerospace in Hartford, Connecticut the 24th through the 26th of October.

There's one final thing I want to talk about--the Joint Directors of Laboratories (JDL). DARPA has been involved in artificial intelligence research and development for a long time. In order to adequately exploit the research, and indeed the researchers, that DARPA has spent many millions of dollars on, we requested that DARPA support efforts in the service laboratory with their researchers and their technologies. In this way, technology transfer to the services can be accelerated rather than relying on the usual process of osmosis that is more common between DARPA and the service laboratories. I'll be talking to Commander Ron Olander, the AI person at DARPA, to discuss some of the things he thinks are ready for application in the services. In fact, the three services will all be represented and we'll be back to our laboratories sometime within the next 2 or 3 weeks requesting them to take a look at DARPA programs and see which ones they would like to pick up. We hope to get an introduction to the DARPA researchers, who are among the outstanding researchers in the world in this area, and get them interested in looking at our problems and helping us transition their results into application in the services.

In summary, I'll have to say that my general attitude and enthusiasm for AI is evidence that I believe it's here. I'm particularly pleased with the maintenance community and their interest and aggressiveness in this area. There's no question in my mind that our systems will continue to become more complicated and more sophisticated. They will become more reliable but not that much faster. Labor will be more expensive and harder to come by. Our potential enemies will continue to become more sophisticated and more capable. Our equipment must be ready to fight and be able to sustain the fight without warning. Maintenance capability will be the key to our success and indeed our deterrence for a long time to come. I believe there are two principal aspects of AI which are going to be the cornerstone of the applications to maintenance. Those are expert systems and natural language understanding. The role of image understanding is not so clear in my mind yet. But one thing is very clear--the systems which ultimately are made from the technologies that are going to be developed in the laboratories presenting at this workshop must be very user friendly. A user that will be subjected to very inclement weather, dressed in very unwieldly gear (especially if chemical warfare becomes a reality or a possibility), and working at night or whatever. The user's education won't be that of a graduate engineer or a graduate mathematician. It'll be that of an eighth grader--hard as we may try to upgrade our educational system so that everybody has a strong education in mathematics and science at the end of the 12th grade.

I don't think we should kid ourselves that the application of this new science is going to be easy. It will be labor intensive; it will take some very sophisticated and very capable personnel to develop the systems that we're talking about. We need to plan and program our resources carefully.

I am not interested in seeing a step function in the support of AI if it's a step up and then a step down. I think we need to plan for the continuity of funding, both in our contractors and in our laboratories in this important and yet very sophisticated area.

Above all, we've got to be realistic in our expectations. It's going to take a while before we have a system out there on the flight line. We can't afford not to be demanding, and I've told you one of my demands of the system--user friendliness. But we've got to be realistic and accumulate knowledge and skills so that we can produce the kinds of systems that we high technologists (as I proudly call myself, and I'm sure all of you feel you are also) expect of ourselves and of our scientific endeavor.

ABOUT THE AUTHOR

Dr. Bernard A. Kulp is Chief Scientist, Director of Science and Technology, Air Force Systems Command, Andrews AFB. As Chief Scientist, he is responsible for evaluating and securing optimum effectiveness in all phases of research and development under the cognizance of the Director. He assists the Director in establishing technical realism, balance, and time lines of exploratory development in the areas of propulsion, aerospace mechanics, materials, and nuclear weapons. Dr. Kulp furnishes broad program guidance to all echelons of the Director's staff. He holds a Ph.D. in physics from Ohio State University.

THE NEED FOR IMPROVEMENTS IN WEAPON SYSTEM MAINTENANCE: WHAT CAN AI CONTRIBUTE?

Michael McGrath

Office of the Secretary of Defense

Good morning. When I first heard about this workshop I was enthusiastic about the opportunity to come out here. Not just because Boulder is a beautiful place to be in October, although that did have something to do with it, but because I think AI applications in maintenance is an important topic and an important subject on which to get a dialogue going. And I think the time is right for that dialogue to start. What I'd like to do is go briefly through why I think it is important--why I think the time is right. I'd like to cover very briefly the need as we see it from an Office of the Secretary of Defense (OSD) perspective, both current maintenance problems and future trends; look at some of the initiatives DoD-wide that have been instituted to deal with this need; look at some of the possible contributions of AI; and discuss some of the expectations that have been built.

The first thing I'd like to comment on is a large DoD and industry study that was undertaken as a result of a Defense Science Board (DSB) study in 1981. The DSB study recommended we undertake a comprehensive review of reliability and maintainability, looking both at the ingredients of successful programs in a case study mode and also doing an assessment of emerging technologies. That study started in 1982 and is winding up now. It had extensive involvement from all three services and from industry, and they're in the final throes in putting out a 30 volume report which I think will be a comprehensive reference work for us for the remainder of the 1980s. I recommend it to all of you. Tony Coppola, the next speaker, will talk more about that study, in particular the AI technology assessment.

Current Problems

When we talk about current problems in maintenance, the one that jumps out is diagnostics. I'm talking about built-in test and automated test equipment. All three services have some form of automated diagnostics on virtually all major weapon systems. The typical experience is that we see a long tail on the distribution of repair times. Some repairs take too long, keeping the weapon systems down, primarily due to troubleshooting problems. High "cannot duplicate" and "retest okay" rates account for over a third of the personnel hours expended on maintenance. On some systems such "no defect" maintenance actions account for over half of the maintenance events.

Diagnostic problems have a measurable effect on support and readiness. We see it in terms of increased downtime for the systems, and in low availability, because the automated systems don't do all the troubleshooting. We need highly skilled troubleshooters out there--an increasingly scarce resource. Because of the high false indication rate, we've put a lot of material into the repair pipeline (usually expensive avionics boxes) thereby creating a need for additional spares. Since there's never enough money for spares, that in turn causes readiness problems and low system availability.

Finally, because we can't, in all cases, rely on the indication from the built-in test, we have to bring along another piece of automated test equipment to confirm the BIT indications. Hence, we have a long logistic tail that follows the weapon system around.

Future Trends

When we look at future equipment trends, there are some things that I think are fairly predictable. It's apparent that equipment will continue to become more sophisticated. At the same time, some of the hardware technologies that we'll see in the new weapons systems bring with them promises of improved reliability and maintainability. A good example is VHISIC, very high speed integrated circuits. There we see promises of much greater performance capability because of the increased density of components. The VHSIC components themselves are advertised to be more reliable; yet they may bring a whole new set of problems. Testability of these dense electronics systems will be a problem, as will power supply reliability and built-in diagnostics. Unless we start to address those problems now, and get them worked into the technology demonstrations, we'll have a mixed blessing at best when those technologies hit the field. This is one of the primary messages of the Institute for Defense Analyses (IDA) study, and one that action will be taken on.

If you look at personnel projections, demographics show clearly that we're going to have a declining recruiting base. We don't see any upturn in aptitudes and education levels. We're not going to have graduate engineers out there doing the maintenance. And finally, if you look at the Service "Year 2000" operating scenarios, all of them are logistically more demanding. Maybe I can just illustrate those last two points.

Here's the well known demographic trend (see Figure 1). This chart shows all workers entering the work force--ages 18 to 24--including both males and females. You can see there's about a 20 percent decline in the period 1980 to the mid-1990s. If you look at males, age 17-21, which is a greater portion of the recruiting base, you can see the same phenomenon. It just shifts a little bit to the left (happens a little bit earlier).

All three services have done studies of operational requirements in the late 1990s and in the year 2000. In each of them we see a more capable threat which is going to lead to more complex systems. We see a scenario that calls for small, highly mobile units. Such units can't afford to carry a long support tail around with them. They probably cannot afford to carry a lot of maintenance experts around with them. They'll operate in a mode that calls for massing these small units to accumulate fire power and then dispersing them for survivability. Logistically, dispersed operations are hard to support. You don't have the economies of scale. A bag of spares doesn't support a whole squadron. Now you

WORKFORCE GROWTH

"THE WARNING SIGNS OF A LABOR SHORTAGE"

SOURCE: PROCEEDINGS, NATIONAL SECURITY INDUSTRIAL ASSOCIATION, FIRST ANNUAL CONFERENCE, MAY 1981, SAN DIEGO

Figure 1.

need smaller bags of spares. You need therefore to have logistics information systems at the unit level that will give you a better handle than we have today on where the support resources are, and what the status of maintenance and equipment is. The scenarios call for intense surge periods--some of them lasting more than 72 hours. During the surge period, we'd like the systems to be virtually maintenance free. Beyond the surge period, there's a higher sustained sortie rate than we see with current systems. That leads to a requirement for improved reliability, maintainability, and availability.

R&D and Acquisition Initiatives

In the face of these needs, there are a number of R&D initiatives that have been undertaken. Some of you may have heard of the Carlucci acquisition initiatives--the Defense Acquisition Improvement Program which the new administration initiated. It consisted of 32 initiatives, six of which were aimed at improving support and readiness. Action is complete on some of the original 32, and the new Deputy Secretary of Defense, Mr. Thayer, has consolidated the remainder into six high priority initiatives that continue to be pursued; improved support and readiness is one of those, and continues to get attention at the highest management levels in DoD.

A couple of years ago there was an in-house study done on independent research and development (IR&D) programs in industry; the conclusion was that less than 3 percent of the IR&D monies were being spent on logistics-related research. So a DoD policy letter went out stating that we wanted to increase the emphasis on IR&D for logistic research. That's been followed up in IR&D reviews and starting in 1985 there's a change in the form that industry will use to report on IR&D projects. This sounds like a bureaucratic triviality but it's one of the simple things that causes things to happen. There will be a block on the form for special interest items--the two areas of special interest that industry will be reporting on are interfaces with university affiliated research and logistics R&D implications of the project that they're proposing. I expect that new visibility to lead to increased emphasis by industry on logistics R&D.

Finally, we have a funded logistic R&D program initiative that started in fiscal 1984. This continued in the budgeting for fiscal 1985 this year. Initial objectives were to undertake technology demonstrations in five areas (see Figure 2). Concurrently, all three services are laying out longer range plans. These objectives are to be demonstrated in the fiscal 1985 through 1989 time frame. We want to move from a "paper" to a "digital" technical information system. I mentioned the need for logistics information systems at the unit level. The Army has an initiative going for automated battlefield material handling--fuel and ammo. The Navy has taken a lead on an automated parts-on-demand manufacturing (low volume spares production using robotics and AI). And, finally, there's an initiative for the next generation of weapon systems to eliminate or at least reduce the need for intermediate maintenance, thereby cutting that logistic tail.

WEAPON SUPPORT AND LOGISTICS R&D INITIATIVES

- ACQUISITION INITIATIVES TO IMPROVE SUPPORT AND READINESS IN WEAPONS PROGRAMS
- EMPHASIS ON LOGISTIC RESEARCH IN IR&D
- DOD WEAPON SUPPORT AND LOGISTIC R&D PROGRAM, INITIAL OBJECTIVES:
  - AUTOMATION OF TECHNICAL INFORMATION
  - LOGISTICS COMMAND/CONTROL
  - AUTOMATED BATTLEFIELD MATERIAL HANDLING
  - AUTOMATED "PARTS ON DEMAND" MANUFACTURING
  - ELIMINATE OR REDUCE INTERMEDIATE MAINTENANCE

Figure 2.

POSSIBLE CONTRIBUTIONS OF AI

- REDUCED DIAGNOSTIC ERRORS
  - "SMART" BIT
  - EXPERT SYSTEMS FOR TROUBLESHOOTING
- ENHANCED MAINTENANCE TRAINING TECHNOLOGY
- IMPROVED HANDLING OF TECHNICAL INFORMATION
- COMPUTER AIDED ENGINEERING
  - HARDWARE TESTABILITY AND FAULT TOLERANCE
  - BIT/ATE SOFTWARE DEVELOPMENT

Figure 3.

Favorable Climate for AI

So there's a climate that says we're ready to do some things to improve maintenance. Each of those initial R&D objectives has room for potential AI applications, but you'll notice that AI is not a separate topic area on the initial five demonstrations. Figure 3 shows some of the expectations that have been built for what AI might contribute in dealing with support problems. First and foremost, we'd like to see some reduction in the diagnostic areas. And so we're looking for smart built-in test systems and also for use of expert systems to assist the troubleshooters. We're expecting to see some contribution to both training technology and technical information presentation that will assist the maintenance people. And finally, we look for some contribution in the development of the weapon systems themselves. Software development, as Dr. Kulp mentioned, is an expensive and difficult process. Development of repetitive automated testing routines is one software area where we might gain substantially from AI applications. Similarly in the computer-aided design/computer-aided manufacturing (CAD/CAM) era of system design, we can look for some AI contributions in designing testability and fault tolerance into the systems themselves.

A Final Note of Caution

We have the ingredients: a well recognized need and a favorable climate for getting something done. But I'd like to end on a final note of caution. In the early 1970s there were a lot of promises made for built-in test and automated test equipment, and the benefits were overstated. A number of weapons systems were fielded with maintenance concepts that revolved around promises that never materialized. A lot of expensive and traumatic maintenance concept changes had to be made as a result. We don't want to repeat the mistakes of the past. I think that the benefits of AI can be modestly stated and yet still capture the resources that are needed to get the AI program well underway. Given that we do that, I think that the climate is right and now is the time to start.

ABOUT THE AUTHOR

Mr. Michael F. McGrath is a Staff Assistant in the Office of the Assistant Secretary of Defense, (Manpower, Reserve Affairs and Logistics). His responsibilities include the development of improved policies for the logistic support of weapon systems, and analysis of the application of these policies in DSARC reviews of major acquisition programs. Prior to joining the staff of the Office of the Secretary of Defense in 1980, he held logistic management positions in the Defense Logistic Agency and the Naval Air Systems Command. Mr. McGrath holds an M.S. in aerospace engineering and is a doctoral candidate in the Operations Research program at George Washington University.

ARTIFICIAL INTELLIGENCE APPLICATIONS TO MAINTENANCE

Anthony Coppola

Rome Air Development Center

EXECUTIVE SUMMARY

The maintenance of modern military systems employs a variety of automation. Built-In-Test (BIT) provides on-line fault detection and some isolation, Automatic Test Equipment (ATE) is indispensable at intermediate and depot repair stations, and automated maintenance aids and trainers abound.

These developments were designed to speed maintenance and to compensate for declining skill levels in the maintenance force. They are currently far from satisfactory. Modern maintenance is characterized by excessive false alarms and unnecessary removals at all levels of maintenance.

The results of these deficiencies are long maintenance times, resources wasted in unnecessary or inefficient maintenance actions, and systems out of action which need not be. Correcting these problems would therefore provide both an economic advantage and a force multiplier.

To create quantum improvements in maintenance will require the application of radical changes to the technology. One possibility is the application of Artificial Intelligence (AI) techniques to maintenance. AI is beginning to see application to practical problems in many disciplines, and hence is potentially capable of relatively rapid implementation into military systems.

At present, DoD efforts in applying AI to maintenance are small and exploratory.

The task of the Artificial Intelligence Applications committee was to examine the opportunities for applying AI to maintenance, assess the costs, risks, and development times required, and provide recommendations to the DoD for action.

The committee's recommendations are detailed in section 9 of this report. A summary follows:

1. The DoD should take advantage of the relative maturity of the technology for creating expert systems. Specific applications of maintenance expert systems should be started immediately and multi-application maintenance experts developed and standardized.

Develop maintenance expert systems immediately for current maintenance applications where the existing ATE has been inadequate. Permit these systems to be built in any convenient language and architecture, except that test programs generated for outside use would be in ATLAS.

Develop versatile maintenance experts for specific domains (eg digital electronics) capable of use in different systems. System specific data would be required for each application, but the knowledge base would remain the same.

Develop a tool to automate the creation of the system specific data required by the maintenance experts described in the preceding paragraph.

2. Develop "smart" built-in-test (BIT) systems to reduce false alarms, identify intermittent failures, improve BIT coverage.

3. Fund applied research in AI for maintenance to improve expert system designs and to develop other promising applications. Topics could include automating creation of maintenance manuals, applications to maintenance information systems, AI based automatic test pattern generation (ATPG), VHSIC design for testability, knowledge based computer aided instruction (CAI), and self-improving diagnostics.

4. Foster an integrated DoD-Industry approach. Coordinate DoD activity through a tri-service working group under the existing JLC panel on automatic testing. Encourage private avenues of development; continue to support industry IR&D in the area.

TABLE OF CONTENTS

1.0. INTRODUCTION

The maintenance of modern military systems employs a variety of automation. Built-In-Test (BIT) provides on-line fault detection and some isolation, Automatic Test Equipment (ATE) is indispensable at intermediate and depot repair stations, and automated maintenance aids and trainers abound.

These developments were designed to speed maintenance and to compensate for declining skill levels in the maintenance force. They are currently far from satisfactory. Modern maintenance is characterized by excessive false alarms and unnecessary removals at all levels of maintenance. Even with successful use of ATE, throughput is far from ideal. ATE too often fails to isolate a failure, requiring skillful human intervention, or expensive "shotgun" maintenance approaches.

The results of these deficiencies are long maintenance times, resources wasted in unnecessary or inefficient maintenance actions, and systems out of action which need not be. Correcting these problems would therefore provide both an economic advantage and a force multiplier.

It can be expected that normal evolution of testing technology will reduce the severity of these problems. However, quantum improvements will require radical changes in approaches. One possibility is the application of Artificial Intelligence (AI) techniques to maintenance. AI is beginning to see application to practical problems in many disciplines, and hence is potentially capable of relatively rapid implementation into military systems.

The task of the Artificial Intelligence Applications committee was to examine the opportunities for applying AI to maintenance, assess the costs, risks, and development times required, and provide recommendations to the DoD for action. This report presents their findings and recommendations.

2.0. COMMITTEE APPROACH AND MEMBERSHIP

From a variety of sources, 28 people were identified as potential contributors to the study. Each of these was informed of the study objectives and invited to contribute position papers describing their recommendations to DoD with their best estimates of costs, benefits, and technological risks. All responses were consolidated by the committee chairman into this report. Considered as a position paper was a copy of proposals submitted by the Air Force Human Resources Laboratory to a tri-service working group. Other inputs were a survey by the Rome Air Development Center on Artificial Intelligence applications to Testability and various articles in the literature. The chairmans consolidation was aided greatly by the technical advice of Mr. Robert Schrag, who reviewed each iteration of the draft.

The contributors to this report are:

- Anthony Coppola, Rome Air Development Center (chairman)
- Eric J.Braude, RCA
- R.P.Caren, Lockheed
- Marvin Denicoff, Office of Naval Research
- Leonard Friedman, Jet Propulsion Laboratory
- Russell M.Genet, Air Force Human Resources Laboratory
- 2lt Lorraine M.Gozzo, Rome Air Development Center
- John H. Hinchman, General Dynamics
- Robert Hong, Grumman
- Robert Schrag, Rome Air Development Center

3.0. ORGANIZATION OF THIS REPORT

The next section of this report will illustrate some of the problems with current maintenance of military equipment. Following it will be an introduction to Artificial Intelligence. The next section will discuss the extent of current applications of AI to maintenance, and the ultimate, though perhaps not realizable, implications of AI technology to maintenance. Following this will be a discussion of caveats and potential traps in applying AI. After a brief discussion of present AI research in maintenance applications, the final section will present a consolidation of the committees recommendations to DoD.

4.0. ILLUSTRATIONS OF MAINTENANCE PROBLEMS

Figure 1 shows a summary of information compiled by the Air Force Test and Evaluation Center during tests of the E-3A (AWACS) radar. Of the nearly 12,000 indications of malfunction, seven percent were excluded as not relevant to the test program (failures caused by external causes, etc.) Of the remainder, false alarms outnumbered failures (items on which maintenance was performed) by more than ten to one. Although these were recognized as false alarms before starting through the maintenance chain, they represent at the least a source of annoyance to a busy aircrew. Of those eight percent considered as valid indications of failure, 25% could not be duplicated at the first maintenance check (CND). These might be additional false alarms or, perhaps, intermittent failures which occur only under the flight environment. In either event, 25% of the first maintenance actions accomplished nothing.

Of the remaining maintenance actions, 98% of the failures were detected by the BIT, leaving two percent to be found by manual means. This is a creditable performance, but unfortunately not true of all systems.

When the attempt was made to isolate the failures detected by BIT, it was found that the automatic test equipment could not identify the failed component in half of the cases, which by necessity reverted to manual procedures. Also noteworthy is that 15% of the cases retested as apparently good (RETOK), requiring no maintenance.

The message of these figures is that there is too much unnecessary maintenance, that the automated techniques are contributing to unnecessary maintenance, that they are not sufficiently reducing manual troubleshooting, and, perhaps, that some failures are escaping the maintenance procedures.

The false alarm problems of AWACS are by no means unique. An on-board failure recorder for the F-111D proved ineffectual because a similar ratio of failure indications to actual failures. False alarms in the F-16 caused innovations in BIT mechanization which will be discussed later. Outside the military, a study by Lockheed for The Electric Power Research Institute (1977) found the same problem in Nuclear power plant control rooms. One rather frightening picture in their report shows a control room in which 65 warning lights could be seen. All were ignored by the operators as false alarms.

Another universal maintenance problem is the number of items which test good in maintenance. Figures gathered from the United States Air Force, the Canadian Air Force, the Navy avionics repair facilities and the commercial airlines all show that 30% or more of units in maintenance test good. Hence, a significant amount of maintenance is either unnecessary or ineffectual.

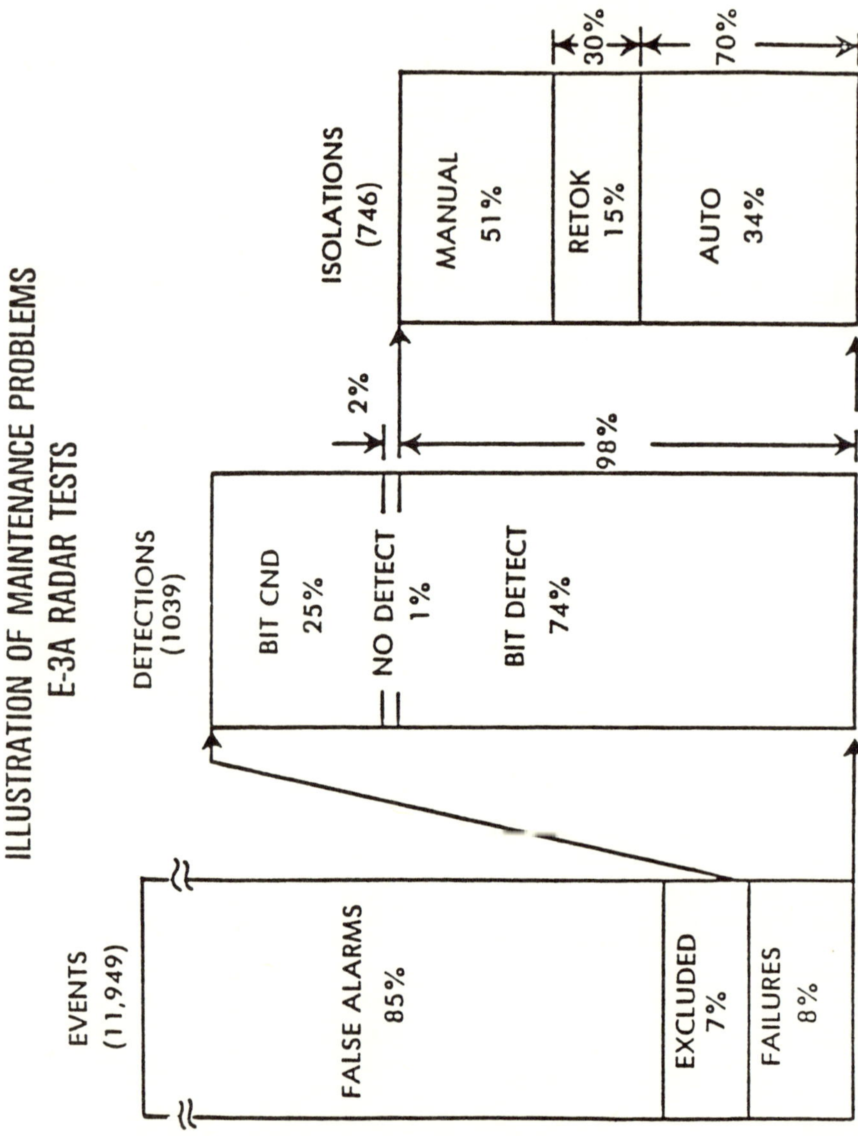
ILLUSTRATION OF MAINTENANCE PROBLEMS
E-3A RADAR TESTS
EVENTS
(11,949)
FALSE ALARMS
85%
EXCLUDED
7%
FAILURES
8%
DETECTIONS
(1039)
BIT CND
25%
NO DETECT
1%
BIT DETECT
74%
2%
98%
ISOLATIONS
(746)
MANUAL
51%
RETOK
15%
AUTO
34%
30%
70%

Figure 1.

In March 1983, the Warner-Robins Air Logistics Center provided the following list of maintenance problems:

- Test programs proceed in sequence until a failure is found. Some of these run as long as three and one-half hours. In one of these, the most common failure was detected in the last segments of the program.
- Memory devices are particularly difficult to test.
- The ATE does not isolate all the failures, leaving those not found to the ingenuity of the maintenance personnel.
- The fault isolation is too often ambiguous. For example, while the F-15 ATE normally isolates a failure to a single part, it can also return a list of suspect parts as high as 15. Memory devices are especially prone to high ambiguity in isolation.
- The test program may isolate to a string of components, which would all be replaced or further isolation performed by manual means. Some hybrid circuits cost from $300 to $3,000 making "shotgun" replacement an expensive proposition. Even a string of relatively cheap parts represents a significant maintenance cost in manhours if all are replaced.
- The ATE will not isolate chassis problems (eg broken wires)

These problems translate into overloaded maintenance facilities, increased requirements for spare units in the pipeline, and excessive costs for labor and consumables.

In summary, there is ample opportunity for increasing readiness significantly by alleviating these maintenance deficiencies. Significant improvements in new systems may be possible by merely designing the hardware to be easier to test. Another approach, applicable to both new and existing systems is to make the test equipment "smarter". Significant improvements will require significant changes in technology, incorporating the techniques of Artificial Intelligence.

5.0. INTRODUCTION TO ARTIFICIAL INTELLIGENCE

There is no standard definition of Artificial Intelligence. An often used definition is the capability of a machine to do a task which if done by a human would be considered to require intelligence. Thus an automobile would not be an example of AI, since walking is not considered to require intelligence. A chess-playing computer, on the other hand, is an example of AI.

This definition is, however, too simplistic. Under it, all BIT and ATE would be considered manifestations of AI, since locating faults requires intelligence. However, the brute force approach of a fixed sequence of stimulus-response comparisons to preestablished criteria cannot be considered an impressive show of intelligence in machine or man. Hence, a more sophisticated definition is called for.

To eliminate the trivial mechanizations falling under the simple definition, we shall add the criteria that the machine must have the capability of forming and manipulating abstractions. This would include such activities as forming hypotheses (eg the location of a failure), the testing of hypotheses, learning, and inference.

It should be noted that, for our purposes, it does not matter whether or not the machine solves a problem in the same manner a human would. While much research in AI is directed at understanding human intelligence, we will be completely indifferent to the processes involved, so long as they represent the most cost-effective solutions to the practical applications of interest.

5.1. AI FIELDS OF STUDY

There is also no standard breakdown of AI fields of study. For convenience we shall use a list of topics extracted from "Principles of Artificial Intelligence" by Nils J. Nilsson (1980,Tioga Publishing Co., Palo Alto, Ca.). In this section we will briefly describe the objectives of each topic. In the next section, their current and potential applications to Maintenance will be discussed. The fields of study are:

5.1.1. NATURAL LANGUAGE PROCESSING.

For our purposes, this field of study includes all attempts to make a machine capable of understanding inputs in natural language (i.e English) whether typed or spoken. We shall also include the synthesis of machine replies in written or spoken English.

It has been extremely difficult to give a machine the capability of "understanding" even subsets of natural language. This is because a message is understood not only by its text, but by the total experience of its receiver. For example, consider the following conversation:

"Hungry?"

"I've got a MacDonalds coupon."

"Keys?"

"Here. Let's go."

The many non-spoken portions of the conversation are readily understood by a human, and the message makes sense. To a machine, it is a sequence of non-sequitors.

This is not to say that useful language recognition has not been accomplished. A simulated robot manipulator called SHRDLU can carry on meaningful dialogs in the limited scope of its world of blocks on a table top. KNOBS, an expert system in development for tactical air mission planning, has an extensive natural language understanding capability.

Recognizing spoken speech compounds the problems of understanding the meaning of the message with problems of recognizing the message itself. Separating words in spoken sentences has proven a difficult chore. Practical use is being made of spoken cues to machines where a cue is a one word direction such as "back","next",or "two". Even here, the machine must be trained to the voice of its operator and may not respond to another speaker.

Synthesizing speech is much easier than understanding it as the plethora of talking computers indicates. The main problems in speech synthesis is giving the computer the ability to know what to say.

5.1.2. INFERENTIAL RETRIEVAL FROM DATA BASES.

The design of efficient data bases is a computer science field of interest. It becomes an AI consideration when the desired retrieval is a deduction rather than a stored fact. For example, an AI machine with intelligent retrieval could solve the logic puzzles which provide such facts as "John and the engineer went to Bermuda" and "Marie travelled by bus." with the reader required to deduce the occupation and vacation choice of all the names provided. Like language understanding, this requires a store of "common knowledge" pertinent to the problems of interest (eg Bermuda is not accessible by bus) as well as inferential mechanisms. A practical system will also have to understand queries, making natural language understanding ability a valuable adjunct feature.

5.1.3. THEOREM PROVING.

There are several programs which will automatically prove mathematical theorems. The techniques developed for these are of significant value to other AI applications. Theorem proving methods can be extended to information retrieval and failure location when these tasks are formalized as theorems to be proven. (eg a theorem to be proven could be that a failure is located in a given component.) Theorem-proving techniques attempt to establish a procedure for selecting from among possible rules to apply to the problem and to establish subproblems leading to the solution.

5.1.4. AUTOMATIC PROGRAMMING.

Strictly speaking, existing compilers are automatic programmers. They accept the higher order language and write an object code to do a specified job. In the AI sphere, the interest is in machines which will convert high level descriptions, the ultimate being an English input, to an executable program. This could include dialogue between machine and user to resolve ambiguities. Automatic programming systems can also provide the valuable added benefit of verifying that the program produced does the intended job. Contributions of work in the field include concepts of "debugging" as a strategy. It can be easier to modify a quickly generated erroneous program than to produce a perfect product on the first pass. Achieving the goals of automatic programming, will, however, require a long term effort.

5.1.5. COMBINATORIAL/SCHEDULING PROBLEMS.

The classic example of this class of problem is the "travelling salesman problem", in which the solver attempts to find a routing which will permit a salesman to visit a given number of cities with a minimum distance travelled. Solutions to these problems generate a "combinatorial explosion" of possibilities. The most efficient solutions known for this class of problem require solution times which grow exponentially with the size of the problem. AI efforts have been directed towards delaying and moderating the combinatorial explosion, using knowledge about the problem domain.

5.1.6. MACHINE PERCEPTION

Understanding of spoken speech is an example of machine perception. We have chosen to include this under natural language understanding; similarly, simulation of any of the human senses, and use of sensory inputs such as infra-red, radar returns, etc., can be considered machine perception. The problems can be represented by a discussion of the interpretation of visual images.

Detectors of light intensity can be constructed. AI programs exist to deduce geometric features such as straight lines and to separate the boundaries of various solid objects. The ultimate goal is to produce a high level description, such as "a house with three windows". Achievement of this goal is yet to come, but here again knowledge of the problem domain may be the key. (It should be easier to distinguish a tank from a truck in a convoy, for example, than to identify every object in a photograph of Times Square.)

5.1.7. EXPERT CONSULTING SYSTEMS

There now exist a number of automated consultants to aid in solving various problems, including fault diagnosis. One AI technique employed in such systems is rule based deduction. Specific domain knowledge and problem solving rules obtained from a human expert are used by the machine to formulate and test hypotheses. The system will create a dialog with its user to obtain data needed by its rules, and will use inferential procedures to work with incomplete or conflicting data.

Difficulties in creating expert systems arise in the reduction of the experts' knowledge to a set of rules. Even a willing expert may be unable to so reduce his knowledge. Representing the knowledge base is also a key problem.

Obviously, many developments in the AI fields described above will have their applications to expert systems.

5.1.8. ROBOTICS

Robots are the AI application most visible to the public, and thousands are in practical use. However, the typical application is far less sophisticated than the highly publicized experimental models. A presentation on General Motors robotic applications at the 1983 Annual Reliability and Maintainability Symposium pointed out that the robot in a work station is often virtually hidden behind a complex of automatic positioning machinery needed to assure the parts manipulated by the robot are always in the expected place. Developments in robotics are aimed at creating planning capabilities to elevate the robot from a mere manipulator of items in a structured situation, and at coupling machine perception to reduce its dependence on an orderly environment.

6.0. CURRENT AND POTENTIAL APPLICATIONS OF AI TO MAINTENANCE

This section will discuss the maintenance applications of each of the AI topics described above. Existing applications of AI in maintenance or in analogous fields will be described. Techniques on the fringes of AI or useful to AI applications will be also be covered. Potential near term applications will be identified. Finally, the ultimate implications of the field of study will be postulated. These are the applications which could be made if all the goals of the AI field were achieved. They are, of course, far out both in time and in imagination, and may never become possible. Nevertheless, they represent a set of goals against which progress can be measured.

6.1. NATURAL LANGUAGE PROCESSING.

As mentioned above, SHRDLU can carry on a conversation with its user about its limited domain. A medical diagnosis system, MYCIN, can do the same with a doctor about bacterial infections. Hence, it is certainly a near term possibility that a maintenance system can be made to converse with its user in a useful subset of English. This would be accomplished by the user typing in his side of the conversation. The machine could respond by printout, CRT display or synthesized speech.

Spoken interaction would be highly desirable as it would free the maintenance man from the terminal. He could then have both hands free and could operate in remote locations using a portable headset to consult his computer. At this time there exist maintenance trainers which respond to voice cues, which is certainly a step forward. However, verbal communication in near conversational style must be considered a far out application.

6.2. INFERENTIAL RETRIEVAL FROM DATA BASES

Current applications to maintenance of this topic must be considered only on the fringes of AI, with the possible exception of Automatic Test Pattern Generation (ATPG). ATPG is used to generate the test patterns for digital logic. At present, the machine is superior to the human in formulating tests for combinatorial logic, and inferior in sequential logic. Near term possibilities are the improvement of machine handling of sequential logic and development of ATPG for analog circuitry. The ultimate potential would be the complete elimination of the manual part of the process.

On the fringe of AI is the use of computerized models to direct the testing process. There are three existing programs which will use a stored representation of an equipment to reduce the number of tests needed to isolate a failure. The first of these was LOGMOD (DETEX Corp.). The LOGMOD data base is a user prepared logical model of the system. Using this model, a heuristic (rule following) procedure uses the results of each test made by the maintenance man to direct him to the next test such that each test eliminates half of the suspect components until the failed unit is isolated. The STAMP program (ARINC) uses a nodal representation of the system and provides various search options such as eliminating components with half the predicted failure rate. The third system, FIND, in development by Hughes, has similar features.

The Modular Automatic Test Equipment (MATE) office of the Air Force Aeronautical Systems Division has created a working example of a self-improving diagnosis (SID) system. This system would be used when a failure cannot be found by ATE. It would summon manual troubleshooting and request a record of the successful repair action. These records would be used to recommend repair actions on future occurrences of the same failure symptom. While the test model uses only the relative frequency of successful fixes for a particular symptom, inferential mechanisms could be added to detect trends which suggest revisions to the strategy dictated by frequency alone.

Also proposed by the MATE office is the recording by the SID of the serial numbers of all items repaired and the application of heuristics to identify items which return too often. These would be flagged as requiring special attention because of the possibility of a chronic problem not solved by the routine procedure. This feature now exists in a Marconi ATE system.

6.3. THEOREM PROVING

Theorem proving techniques, as mentioned, are used in AI applications in the other fields of interest listed, particularly in expert systems. Their contributions in these applications will be covered in the appropriate discussions. There is one application which is well worth noting here.

BIT signals are too often false alarms. In addition, intermittent failures are difficult to distinguish from false alarms. Theorem proving techniques could be employed to test BIT signals to discriminate against false alarms and to identify intermittent failures.

A simple procedure was used by the F-16 to evaluate BIT signals. Each signal was stored and the BIT checked again after a short time. If five out of seven checks agreed on a failure indication, the BIT latch was triggered. Smart bit would extend this to such actions as changing the decision threshold, adjusting the bit sensitivity, and identifying intermittent failures. Smart BIT systems on individual weapons systems could compare their memories to identify unusual circumstances. The comparison might, for example, show one system with more than expected failure indications indicating some problem with the platform (eg a faulty environmental control system). With incorporated environmental data, smart BIT could help locate an identified intermittent failure. The Boeing OBIT circuit and the Battelle stress meter are designed to record environmental data and could be added to the smart bit. Smart BIT is considered a near term possibility.

6.4. AUTOMATIC PROGRAMMING

ATPG, mentioned above,can be considered an example of automatic programming. There are also programs which assist a test engineer in creating ATLAS statements for test equipment, though these are not really sophisticated enough to warrant the title. The ultimate application of automatic programming will be the real time generation of ATLAS test vectors from a computerized representation of the system, as they are needed by an expert system isolating a failure. This is definitely not a short term goal.

6.5. COMBINATORIAL/SCHEDULING PROBLEMS

Work in this topic can be used in the near term to develop models for queuing maintenance for minimum impact on system down time. It can also be used to design for fault tolerance of distributed systems such as command and control systems or for fault tolerance in VHSIC chips.

The ultimate potential of the techniques would be in real time maintenance scheduling and in real time reconfiguration of networks around a failed component.

6.6. MACHINE PERCEPTION

Current AI programs can identify shapes. On a simpler level, the Marconi ATE mentioned above will read serial numbers marked in bar codes, and optical character readers are available to read stylized alphanumerics. We can thus easily produce systems which will read information printed on a board, but this will be of no use until the ATE is programmed to make use of the information. In the near term we can add automation to ATE letting it call its own test programs from its identification of the board. This could be of value in that it would eliminate some of the duller responsibilities of the maintenance man. In the long term, machine perception can be used to get full value from robot systems by recognizing rotations and displacements of items to be tested, which, with an appropriate control program, will eliminate the need for items to be fed to the robot in a rigidly controlled manner. Presuming a robot fed ATE system, the automatic identification features would become quite useful, as the human would be needed only when the machine required intelligent help. With ambulatory robots, perception could be used to locate particular boards in an equipment for removal by the robot and conveyance to the ATE.

6.7. EXPERT CONSULTING SYSTEMS

Expert systems are in practical use today for configuring computer systems (R1), and are available for medical diagnosis (MYCIN,CADUCEUS) and locating mineral deposits (PROSPECTOR). There are also expert systems in various states of development for fault isolation. These include DELTA for the maintenance of locomotives, REACTOR for nuclear reactors, CRITTER for digital circuits, IDT used on a computer, and DART designed for computer hardware. Hence, maintenance expert systems are relatively near term possibilities.

The diagnostic search programs (LOGMOD,STAMP,FIND), mentioned above, would seem to be a valuable adjunct to an expert maintenance program in that they can be used by the program to set up its strategy from the design of the unit under test.

An expert system requires a knowledge base of its domain. At present, this is provided by the user. LOGMOD, et al, require user layout of the system and user generation of appropriate tests. The ultimate expert system would use advances in automatic programming to perform fully automatic testing by deriving its knowledge from a machine read schematic, forming its strategy from that knowledge, and generating appropriate tests as it needs them.

Once the ATE has the knowledge it needs to operate as an expert system, it can also be used as a maintenance aid to direct a human when his intervention is necessary. It could also provide the interaction needed for training its operator. Thus the expert system would serve as ATE, maintenance aid, and training device. While probably not a short term effort, the integration of maintenance aids should not be a far out proposition. Integrating a training capability will be a long term proposition needing advances in computer aided instruction (CAI) techniques.

Computer aided design (CAD) programs can be considered a form of expert system, even though their current approaches may not be considered to be examples of AI. The Rome Air Development Center is studying the incorporation of ease of test considerations to CAD programs. From these can spring an expert system which will create a design with a minimum of maintenance problems. This will require the creation of a set of design rules for ease of maintenance and a set of rules to trade these off against other considerations such as thermal design, wiring constraints, etc. The design rules should be a near term possibility, but creating the trade-off rules will be a more difficult task.

6.8. ROBOTICS

Current use of robots is mostly as programmable manipulators. At least two companies have designed robot manipulators to feed test samples into ATE. Another immediate possibility is the handling of the adapters which form the interface between test samples and the ATE, relieving the human of the need to manually change adapters. Near term possibilities are the use of machine perception permitting the robot to work in an unorganized environment (eg correctly feed printed circuit boards piled randomly on a table.) The far out application is the use of an ambulatory robot with an expert system to perform completely automatic maintenance.

7.0. CAVEATS

Herbert Dreyfus, a critic of AI, divides intelligent activity into four classes. His lowest class, Associationistic (learned by memory) includes such examples as maze problems. The next higher class, Simple formal (learned by rule) includes games like tic-tac-toe and the proof of theorems using mechanical proof procedures. These problems are easily handled by AI techniques. The highest class, nonformal activities, (learned by example) includes problems which Dreyfus sees no possibility for solution by AI techniques. These include natural language translation and ill-defined games such as riddles. The remaining class is complex formal (learned by rule and practice) which includes uncomputable games like chess and proof of theorems where no mechanical proof procedure applies. Here AI is most difficult to apply and this is the realm of maintenance problems. Fortunately, as the many chess-playing programs attest, the difficulties are not insurmountable.

As with all new technology, applications of AI cannot be made carelessly. Besides the natural limitations and technical constraints, we must consider the impact of AI on the maintenance personnel. We shall now briefly discuss some potential traps.

The natural limitations of AI arise from the fact that we cannot build a machine which duplicates the intelligence of a human. Hence, we cannot create a machine which will understand natural language, because we cannot build in the total experience that a human uses to interpet a message. We can only hope to give it sufficient ability to communicate in its domain and some capability to add new words to its vocabulary.

It will be a long time, if ever, that a machine will have a true ability to learn. No plans should anticipate such a capability until evidence of significant progress is available.

In creating expert systems by reducing the expert's operation to a set of rules, we ignore the fact that expertise is a behavior rather than a set of rules. If the rules will suffice, the system will be successful. If not, we must provide for the human to take over as necessary.

Technical constraints on AI include processing time and memory requirements. AI programs are noted for filling up large machines. While higher speeds and larger memories are still being developed, practical applications must recognize the limits. As an example, ten factorial combinations is not a large number. Yet if the analysis of each took 23 milliseconds, the problem would require 24 hours of machine time. As another example, there are approximately 10 to the 50th power atoms in the earth. This is far smaller than the possible number of moves in a chess game. Hence, the combinatorial explosion is something to be avoided in AI programs, as the chess-players do by pruning their search trees.

AI programs are typically begun as small feasibility demonstrations. Trouble begins, however, when one attempts to scale up the program to handle real world complications. Hence, the technical limits to an available technique must be considered before its application to a new problem.

Finally, in applying AI to maintenance we must consider the man-machine relationship. Declining skill levels promote a temptation to follow a "smart machine-dumb man" philosophy. If the man is subject to direction by a machine which does not credit him with any capability, then:

- Any capability he has is wasted
- He will not improve in capability
- He will find no satisfaction with his job

The items listed above are not only demeaning to the man, they can create a dangerous working climate.

For this reason, AI applications to maintenance should to the greatest extent possible be designed to adapt to the skill of the user, and serve as a means to improve his skill. There are considerations which can be made. Intelligent trainers now exist which will adapt their mode of operation to the needs of the student. There is no need for an expert system to communicate by a fixed list of questions to the operator. It can begin by asking for the operators findings and conclusions.

AI systems must to the extent possible be designed so that the human will consider it as a partner rather than as an inanimate tyrant for which the human performs trivial functions.

8.0. PRESENT RESEARCH IN AI APPLICATIONS TO MAINTENANCE

A rough estimate of FY-83 funding in AI research is the range from $36 million to $46 million. Of this, DoD agencies account for $20 million, and other U.S. agencies, $6 million. The majority of these funds are 6.1. Industry will spend an estimated $10-20 million, which can be considered mostly 6.2.

Of these funds, we have identified $0.3 million being spent by DoD agencies in studies of AI applications to maintenance, and this amount is spread equally among three studies. These are:

(1). A study by the Rome Air Development Center to determine the opportunities and risks of AI applications to Testability, awarded April, 1983 to Boeing.

(2). A study by the Naval Air Engineering Center to develop AI applications to Navy ATE, award pending.

(3). A study by the Air Force Human Resources Laboratory to adapt medical expert systems to maintenance, awarded Feb. 1983 to Systems Exploration.

In addition, there are some other efforts, such as an AFHRL study of AI applications to training, which will provide results useful to maintenance.

In FY-84, The MATE office will continue its work on Self-improving Diagnostics, which was unfunded in FY-83. RADC will begin an effort to develop designs for Smart BIT. The Air Force Institute of Technology will be working with RADC and Warner-Robins Air Logistic Center to develop an experimental expert system for depot maintenance, aimed at specific problems of WRALC.

There is a significantly greater amount of Industry IR&D directed at applying AI to maintenance. A rough estimate is $3 million in FY-83. this does not include capital investments, such as GE's development of DELTA to aid in locomotive repair.

In summary, current DoD efforts are small and exploratory.

9.0. RECOMMENDATIONS TO THE DEPARTMENT OF DEFENSE

Despite the fact that the members of the committee worked completely independently, there is only one area of significant disagreement in the position papers. This is the recommended language in which AI programs should be written. An area of general agreement was that expert consultant systems can, and should, be applied to maintenance now. There was even a general consensus of the development resources required for an expert system: two years time, $200,000 in computer costs, and five to ten man-years per year. However, discussions after review of the position papers would cause these to be considered minimum projections, with perhaps double the computer resources and five years of time required. The following recommendations are the chairman's consolidation of the position papers, discussions with the RADC contributors, and his derivations from the information given above.

RECOMMENDATION NO. 1

The DoD should take advantage of the relative maturity of the technology for creating expert systems. Specific applications of maintenance expert systems should be started immediately, and multi-application maintenance experts developed and standardized.

The DoD should immediately develop expert systems for existing maintenance applications where maintenance is particularly troublesome. As an example, the AFIT-RADC-WRALC program would attempt to create a system to work with the F-15 analog printed circuit board test station. It would first be programmed with the knowledge required to troubleshoot only one board, the most troublesome of those the ATE handles. This would show the value of the approach and permit debugging of the system. More knowledge would be added incrementally until the system handled every board assigned to the original ATE. At this point, it would hopefully be cost effective to scrap the original system. If not, the expert system would still earn its keep by its superior handling of problem boards. Each service could pick a promising candidate (a system which is not handled well by the ATE, and for which expert maintenance personnel are both available and willing to cooperate in creating the expert maintenance system). As it builds and refines the maintenance expert system, the service would improve the operational readiness of the candidate system while it gains experience and confidence with the AI technology. No risk would be involved, since the existing ATE would still be in place. Resources would be two to five years calendar time, 10-20 manyears of effort and $200,000 to $500,000 in computer costs for each system. Each system would pay for itself in short order, by reducing maintenance time as much as 50%. However, the real value of these first efforts would be in the knowledge gained.

To permit immediate application, the first AI maintenance systems should be built in the language and architecture most convenient to the builder and user, with a blanket exemption from any current policies on languages. The only exception would be that any test sequence generated by the system for outside use would be in ATLAS. No cost involved. Will cause a proliferation of languages for first systems, but will permit earlier implementation, by years, and provide information needed for ultimate standardization. (Chairman's recommendation based on conflicting inputs in position papers.)

To improve cost-effectiveness in the longer term, the DoD should develop versatile maintenance experts for specific domains, such as digital electronics, which are used in many different systems. They would contain the necessary theory and diagnostic strategies for their specific domains. They must be user friendly (interact in a subset of English, explain their actions, and adapt to the skill of the user), and, presuming progress in computer aided instruction (CAI) techniques, each system could ultimately serve as an integrated ATE, maintenance trainer and training aid. One basic system (for one domain) could be built in two years with 10 manyears effort. System specific data bases would be incorporated during the development of the systems to be tested. Refinements would be added as developed. Benefit would be the elimination of the need for reinventing the engine for every application, easily worth millions in development and training savings. Technical risk is moderate.

Further improvements in cost-effectiveness would be made possible by developing a system building tool to automate the creation of the system specific data required by the expert system discussed in the preceding paragraph. The tool would extract the needed knowledge either from a human expert or, ideally, from a description of the system to be tested. This will minimize one of the major costs of the expert system. Cost would be about $200,000 a year in computer costs and ten manyears per year. A prototype could be available in two years, but it might take a five year program to complete a supportable product. Benefit would be significant savings in time and elimination of errors for every new system to which it is applied. No more than five applications, if that much, would repay the costs with a dividend in earlier test system availability and easier modification as the design of the system under test changes. Technical risk is presently considered high.

NOTE: The expert systems would eliminate the long test programs now used in conventional ATE. This feature can be incorporated into conventional ATE systems. To do so the DoD could prohibit all new ATE systems to use inflexible sequential test procedures. Instead require the use of segmented test programs which are called out in the order needed for most rapid fault isolation using the strategies now available in LOGMOD, STAMP, and FIND. Cost will be a significant increase in effort required to program the ATE and some additional memory. Will probably permit the elimination of one maintenance shift, paying for itself in one year or two. (Chairman's recommendation)

RECOMMENDATION NO. 2

Develop "smart" BIT for digital electronic systems to minimize false alarms, identify intermittent failures, improve coverage of BIT. An RADC proposed FY-84 effort hopes to provide design concepts which could be used by individual designers to construct smart BIT in their particular applications. A complete series of studies leading to the design of an on-board knowledge based monitoring system or the design and test of experimental BIT systems could run two to four years and one to six million dollars. Benefits are incalculable since they include the worth of reduced mission aborts due to false alarms. More tangible benefits could be a 90% reduction in false alarms, and the decrease of the portion of units sent to repair which test good, from the present 30% to perhaps 10%. A successful application should pay for itself in two years of operation on one system, and provide a measurable improvement in the ready rate of the system using it.

RECOMMENDATION NO. 3

Fund applied Research and Development of AI for maintenance, both to improve the capabilities of maintenance expert systems and to apply AI to other maintenance applications. Some specific topics are:

1. Automating the creation and presentation of Technical Manuals.

2. Applying AI to Maintenance Information Systems and databases.

3. Developing crisis alerting systems.

4. For expert maintenance systems, developing requirements for languages and computer systems, techniques for improving user friendliness, and more sophisticated approaches (eg means of forming rules from the circuit itself rather than from an expert familiar with the circuit).

5. Developing AI systems for Automatic Test Program Generation (ATPG). The current AI programs used to develop test patterns for digital combinatorial logic should be extended to sequential logic and analog circuits. Systems should work from the circuit description and provide test vectors in ATLAS.

6. Applying AI techniques to VLSI,VHSIC design for fault tolerance and testability. This should be incorporated into the VHSIC phase three study plans.

7. Developing knowledge based computer aided instruction (CAI) systems for maintenance training. Note: this could ultimately be incorporated into the ATE itself.

8. Developing self-improving diagnostics and test program sets.

Other topics will be identified by the FY-83 studies begun by RADC, NAEC, AFHRL. Recommend 6.2 programs be started by all three services, funded at one million dollars per service per year, to begin work. Promising developments should be followed by 6.3 · projects with appropriate higher funding.

RECOMMENDATION NO. 4

Foster an integrated DoD-Industry approach.

Coordinate the various efforts of DOD agencies through a tri-service group on AI applications to maintenance. Recommended group would be a committee under the JLC Automatic Testing Panel. It could also be under JDL working group for AI, but seems more appropriate for the Automatic Testing Panel because of its interface with other committees. Participants would include all service agencies involved to share responsibilities and avoid duplication of efforts. It would also provide a contact point for DoD and industry. (chairman's recommendation)

Encourage private avenues of development of AI applications to maintenance: continue to support industrial IR&D in the area, express DoD interest at appropriate meetings, provide copies of this report to Industry. The NSIA Testability Committee, which parallels the JLC panel, should be encouraged to create a subgroup on AI applications to serve as an industry focal point. The close working relationship of the NSIA committee and the JLC panel would be a natural avenue for creating a dialog on AI applications. (Chairman's recommendation.)

ABOUT THE AUTHOR

Mr. Anthony Coppola is Chief of the Reliability and Maintainability Engineering Techniques section of the Rome Air Development Center (RADC). His primary responsibility is developing methods for predicting, demonstrating, and improving the reliability and maintainability of Air Force electronic systems. He is also the Director of the RADC program to apply AI techniques to improve fault detection and isolation. He holds a Master's degree in engineering administration from Syracuse University.

ON APPLYING AI TO MAINTENANCE AND TROUBLESHOOTING

Dr. Ken DeJong

Navy Center for Applied Research in Artificial Intelligence

I'm really here wearing two hats today. The Director of the Navy AI Center, Jude Franklin, was unable to be here today, so I will be sitting in on some of the executive sessions and so forth for the AI Center. Let me say briefly for him that we're delighted, not only to be here participating in the workshop, but to be participating in the joint initiatives at the Joint Directors of Laboratories (JDL) level. We are really excited about it and looking forward to it, and we certainly invite any of you to stop by the next time you're in Washington, D.C. In the last couple of years we've put together a fairly nice collection of hardware, software, and a working environment which has kept me around. In fact, there's kind of a standing joke at the AI Center--"Name the visiting scientist who's been there longer than most of the staff."

Initially, when Jeff and I were planning the workshop, we thought maybe I would give a little bit of an overview of AI. We already know that there's no reason for that. We talked a little bit later about giving an overview of AI and ATE, but as the quality and number of presentations increased, it was pretty clear that you were going to get a very good overview of AI and ATE during the 3 days. So I'm going to take a little liberty and wax philosophical in hopes that some of the concerns, some of the issues, some of the experiences that we've had over the last 2 years will strike a common chord with you, and perhaps you will be able to avoid some of the tar pits we've seen in the last couple of years. Also, I'm a little bit concerned that this workshop has lapsed into a conference mode. There is a psychological barrier as soon as we set chairs out there and put a speaker up front; you become passive and I become the actor. So, I deliberately tried to include some controversial material in my talk, at least I think it is, to try to get a little real-time reaction out of you, rather than having you come up after lunch and say, "You know, during your talk, ..." Well, it's too late then, because I want to get you involved now.

We've been through a lot of agony over the last 2 years at the AI Center in deciding what in the world we are going to do with this emerging technology. What problems are of concern to the Navy? Which subsets of those problems, hopefully slightly larger than the null set, appear to be applicable to the AI techniques that are coming out of the AI laboratories? I've talked and visited with enough people from the other Navy labs and from the industrial areas to know that you are going through, or have gone through, these same kinds of agonizing discussions--trying to explain to managers what it is that AI can do for you.

The thoughts I would like to give you today are some of the issues that I've seen come up in the last couple of years. One that we've seen already (I think it's my pet peeve) is the AI hype. I'm really concerned about it because I think we've gone through a series like this once before. In the 1960s we had our rose-tinted glasses on; we could do no wrong; we were projecting rapid increases in the performance of our systems; and we found out, in fact, that we were on the bottom end of an exponential explosion in difficulty. There was a lot of negative feedback in the early and mid-1970s, but with our short-term memories, that's kind of been forgotten now. The pendulum has swung back. We're back again talking about dumb systems and smart systems in terms which carry a lot of emotional content, but have very little to do with the technical content of what's going on. Already a comment was made this morning to avoid terms like dumb and intelligent, and I really think that's important. I think we ought to talk more in terms of the deliverables of these systems. You look at a system and say it's dumb. Well, what do you mean by dumb? Dumb is a very vague word. It means it can't adapt. OK, so you want a system that's more adaptable? What does that mean? Well, it means it ought to be able to remember from one time to the next what has happened. And so on. The point here is that it is important to quickly get into the specifics of what you mean by making something "more intelligent." Another point of concern is that you've got a lot of people out there, operations research people, engineering people, and so forth, who have been attacking these problems from very legitimate points of view--totally different from AI. And so you take one of those systems and immediately label it as dumb. You've gained an enemy for life at that point. And of course, as soon as you deliver your system, you know what you're in for from the other side of the fence.

One of my concerns, particularly at the higher managerial levels, is that AI is viewed as some sort of a magic wand. And when you come and wave that magic wand, multi-sensor fusion goes away. Or very ill-structured problems like understanding natural language suddenly become simple and well-structured because of AI. It's tempting. It's both an advantage and a disadvantage being in the AI community. It's easy to hype and people somehow believe what you say. On the other hand, it's very difficult to deliver because their expectation level is built on nontechnical terms that we use to promise what we're going to deliver.

Point number two is watch out for tar pits. It's so easy to say things like, "Well, you know what this system needs. What I'm going to concentrate on for the next 6 months is to give it a natural language interface because it's not user friendly." And away we go with a simplistic view of what it means to add natural language. We build a dictionary and develop some primitive parsing techniques, maybe even something as simple as keyword based, and we go about trying to create the "Eliza" illusion. That is, being able to understand words or sentences or strings of things that look like natural language, but the deep semantic content behind them is totally missing. And so you build your "natural language" front end and demonstrate it with a few <u>well-chosen</u> examples. All of a sudden you've built up in the naive user's mind a model that this thing really does understand English, when in fact it's keyword based. It's picking out a few keywords that you've carefully chosen for your examples, and as soon as you leave the room, the system goes off into left field and the user can't make any headway at all with it. It's not that we shouldn't work in natural language--it's that it can be a tar pit. That is, to really handle the deep semantic meaning that you have to capture between the user and the system can involve years of intensive work. We're involved at the AI Center right now in looking at parsing military messages. The particular group that we've been focusing on for the last year is called casualty reports, for some reason, but they really are reports about equipment failures that get circulated in the Navy.

When you start to look at these messages, the amount of background information that's required to handle them properly is amazing. If you read something about fixing a piece of mechanical gear onboard ship, immediately what comes into your mind is a picture; that is, your model of what that mechanical gear is and what it means to fix it. You fill in all the blanks, all the missing material from the textual words using this model that you have in your head about what it means to fix that piece of gear. And to really do it right, that kind of deep understanding is frequently required--that's where the 6 months goes to 12, goes to 18, and so on.

Another tar pit that is quite easy to step into is the idea of common sense reasoning. We have this funny dichotomy that we're very impressed with programs that play chess, or programs that do medical diagnosis, or find oil wells or whatever. But we're not particularly impressed at all with our ability just to go out to lunch today, or to get up and walk out of this room. We use tremendous amounts of real-world knowledge without even thinking about it, and it's amazing how much of that kind of knowledge you have to build into some of these systems. Simple little things like child-parent relationships may come into play in a natural language interface, or relationships about commanders and their subordinates; things that we take for granted, but that have to be captured in order to understand the interface between the human and the system.

Question: Could you give an example of why it would need to know commander-subordinate relationships?

DeJong: For example with Navy reports, one of the issues had to do with routing of messages. Who should see what? Under what circumstances? You get into all kinds of protocol issues. Do we want him to see it? Should she see it? Is it politically required of me--those kinds of questions. You have to build up a whole model of the chain of command, as well as the politics behind the thing, to make decisions like that.

One of the areas that I'm interested in, but I believe right now should be considered one of the tar pits, is the area of learning. Many of you may have been through building an expert system or an AI system of some sort and realize what a difficult process it is injecting common sense, as well as technical expertise. It's a very seductive approach to say, "Hey, the way we can get out of this is to not have to hand-code all this stuff, but to get the machine to learn it. That is, we'll give it a few basic facts and some learning rules, and away we go." Well, that's true in a very superficial sense. However, even though our knowledge about capturing expertise in some formalism that we can convey to another person or another machine is still primitive, our understanding of how we learn that expertise or how someone else learns it is even more incomplete. And so, instead of improving the problem, you get sort of an infinite regress. Now you get involved in trying different learning techniques: Do they converge or don't they? What kind of deep knowledge about the world or about the subject do we need to know in order to implement these learning algorithms? And so we get farther and farther away from our original goals. It's not that learning is not important; it's just that it's not one of those up front deliverables that you should be promising right now.

Question: I'd like to say I strongly agree with you and think it's very unfortunate that we call these systems intelligent. What does it mean to call any system "intelligent" that doesn't learn, and how many systems that have been built throughout the whole history of the field have what one might call respectable, serious learning components? Maybe we should just shorten the whole thing to "AI" and let people think that it means "automatic inferencing"--something more modest.

DeJong: In the little biography that was read of me, I deliberately said that I was interested in adaptive systems. That's one useful way I think of avoiding this idea of dumb and smart. Another useful term is flexible, or something like that, to get away from some of the rigidness. Those aren't emotionally charged terms, and I tend to prefer that sort of thing.

Comment: I've always picked on the term "artificial" as being a wrong term. I always thought "pseudo" would be a lot easier to sell, because nobody feels that it's going to step on their territory.

DeJong: I guess I would prefer something like just "intelligence" or something like that. People claim they're really trying to build up models of human intelligence at the same time, that the two go hand in hand and are just two sides of the same coin. The question is, "At what point in time does it become artificial as opposed to real?"

Comment: John McCarthy, who coined the term artificial intelligence at a conference at Dartmouth in 1956, later realized the absurdity of the term and tried to replace it with the term "cognology," only to find out that just because you've coined a term doesn't mean you can retract it so easily.

DeJong: Another thing that concerns me a little bit is some misrepresentation or misunderstanding of the current state of AI. Largely because of the success we've seen in the expert systems area, one immediately says, "Gee, this whole AI field is something that's ready for immediate technology transfer." We've seen a few, highly visible examples, primarily in what you might call the expert system paradigm, that have moved successfully out of the labs and into more practical applications. But I don't think that that's true of the AI field in general. If you talk to many of the major practitioners in the field, they will tell you that right now we are an empirical science. We don't have a lot of strong theories yet about what we can or can't do or what kinds of problems are well structured in terms of solving AI techniques and what aren't. We have some specific data points which have suggested some theories, but we're primarily still empirical in nature. So if someone comes to me and says, "Here is a problem. Can you tell me if I should use AI or not?" I don't have a strong theory or even a good set of heuristics at this point that can answer that very well. I give them the classical answer, "Try it and see." That's what we do right now. We don't have theories to do strong forward predicting, but we've got some very strong tools for doing fast prototyping at a very high level. This allows us to get some feedback as to whether or not these kinds of things are feasible. It's very difficult to predict success or failure ahead of time, the kinds of things that people at very high decision making levels would like to see. They say, "Give me probabilities" and "What's the risk of this?" The answer in most cases is you're dealing with high risk, but high payoff. Can you live with that or not?

Question: What kind of high risk?

DeJong: An example of the kind of risk we're talking about is the area of applying ATE to maintenance and troubleshooting. A year and a half ago there were very strong arguments within the AI community as to whether or not the successes in building medical diagnosis systems would transfer to this particular area. We had no good data points as to whether or not that would happen. To a certain extent we still don't have strong data points. There were people who said, "It's a trivial transfer. It's exactly the same reasoning mechanisms; all you've got to do is just throw away all the domain dependencies. Give me an empty shell and shove the new knowledge base back in." Has it happened? No, it did not.

The questioner started out by saying what do you mean by "high risk?" What I mean is that we don't have any strong theories that will predict ahead of time whether or not that transition will take place. So risks are high in the sense of willingness to foot the bill for trying it and potentially failing. But if we win, we win big, in the sense that we've accomplished something that hasn't been done before.

Comment: Generally, there is a very simplistic notion of what it takes to build an AI system. You're throwing money at the problem and chances are you're not going to make it that way. However, there are people who realize this is too simple. And, there's a very small, not very visible group of people who are asking, "Can we characterize different types of problem solving in such basic way that you can look at a problem and if you are able to decompose it into the kinds of problem solving that you know how to do, then it's not that hard to build an expert system and it's no longer high risk." So the high risk comes from buying all these machines and spending months trying to build a system. You can go to an analytic state in which your risk is minimized.

DeJong: I'm with you 100 percent and we understand that that's a problem but the point is that that technology is not at the point of maturity yet that we can use it with high reliability. That's the current state right now. Now whether that's the case a year or 2 years from now, we don't know. We are still gathering those empirical points to help us build those theories which allow us to make those kinds of predictions. I, for one, don't believe that I can predict success or failure at this point. I have strong opinions, but you may or may not believe them.

Question: Another problem arises each time you get into a different domain and try to organize it in terms of artificial intelligence. Don't you find that you now have to solve problems that were inherent in that domain that those people have never solved? They really don't understand their own domain thoroughly and we have to.

DeJong: I think one of the major contributions, for example, of the expert system paradigm is not the systems that are built as much as the gaps in knowledge which are exposed during the building process. Attempting to codify knowledge in one form or another, whether it's in book form, or rules, or semantic nets tends to expose poorly understood areas.

Comment: There's a notion here that primarily empirical sciences work their way toward becoming strongly based theoretical sciences. It seems to me one thing that hasn't been elaborated on is that most of the other sciences that have done that have been much more formally and rigorously empirical than AI has. AI not only tends to study heuristically, it tends to do its empirical work heuristically. So that the learning is not codified in a way that would produce strong theories.

DeJong: I agree with you, but like the point that was brought up before, there is a silent majority or at a least a silent minority that is trying to do that kind of thing. Unfortunately, some of the visible stuff that you see in the Sunday Times doesn't. But in the field there is a strong subcomponent that believes very strongly that you have to advertise in order to advance the state-of-the-art.

Comment: I don't think we should beat our breasts too much about the fact that we don't have a strong theory in place right now. If you look at the history of most sciences, on the one hand, there have been alternating attempts to establish a strong theoretical base and, on the other hand, very empirically motivated attempts to get something put up and running. I think that you can't ignore either, frankly. They interact with one another, and I think that's been true in the history of AI.

Question: AI is not an empirical science like the other sciences are where you've got data that you collect in the lab and you have theories to account for that. What does a theory in AI look like?

DeJong: Well, certainly theories about problem solving--what kinds of mechanisms are involved there? We use mechanisms of analogy, inductive or deductive reasoning, and so forth. We are trying to somehow get a theory that is capable of predicting the success or failure of attacking a problem in a certain way; trying to capture the dimensions of problem solving in such a way that we can analyze. I don't mean to focus just on problem solving, but that is an example of the kind of theory that you'd like to have.

I'd like to reinforce the idea of the knowledge representation problem. It's come out here several times. We have lots of knowlege representation tools that have been tried and tested--semantic nets, frames, production rules, blackboard models, and so on--as ways of trying to capture the kind of knowledge that we need to do problem solving. They're tried and tested in the sense that they are known to be useful for certain things and they are known to have glaring weaknesses. I think the mature perspective is that these AI techniques may be useful in certain contexts, but none of them individually are capable of cutting down problems left and right. The evolving generation of AI systems is going toward complex combinations of such techniques. Our early hope that picking a simple approach, like a rule-based architecture, would allow us to really scale up and handle tough problems is a little bit naive. Now, maybe that's a controversial statement. I happen to be familiar with Harry Pople's work at the University of Pittsburgh. His medical diagnosis system has now gone through two, three, probably four generations. What's very clear is that the underlying knowledge representation is increasing in complexity with each go-round. He now has something called the "tangled hierarchy," which, if you've seen it diagrammed, is a tangled hierarchy, believe me. I think we're at the point now where that ought to be the perspective, rather than assuming a single tool will suffice.

Comment: That kind of view is being recognized. For example, there's a very substantial development at Xerox PARC. A system called LOOPS, which tries to integrate rules, procedures, data, and objects in a single coherent framework.

DeJong: Yes, there's no simple answer to the argument about whether knowledge should be procedural or declarative. LOOPS is a good example of a system which provides a collage of tools, and encourages the use of a particular subset that appears to be appropriate.

Even so, it's still an awesome task to even think about the problem of somehow building up a data base of common knowledge in a general format that we wouldn't have to reimplement with every system we build. I'm not even sure we know how to begin. We now have word processing dictionaries and the natural language people are passing around dictionaries. Anybody starting to build up a knowledge base of facts in a common format that we can pass around?

Comment: The truth is there's a project started at University of Massachusetts with about four other universities on that; it's a very large data base.

DeJong: Good. To go on, one of the things that very clearly came out of that first go-round with building expert systems is the knowledge acquisition problem. Where do you get that knowledge from and how in the world do you extract it? If you're extracting it from humans, that extraction process itself is an art. You ought to hear Harry Pople talk about how many agonizing hours he's spent trying to get problem solving information out of a cooperative expert. He says, "He doesn't deliberately mislead me; he just hasn't thought about it before." Performing an expert task and explaining how to perform it are two quite different things. Jim Slagle at the AI Center has been building a program to help the Marines with decisions on the battlefield. One artillery expert told him, "This is the way to do it." Then the expert got rotated out and the new artillery expert said, "That's not the way to do it. Throw it out and start over." We don't know how to reconcile these types of different points of view at all.

Question: If the problem is attacked by human experts in different ways, to what extent is there any kind of empirical verification behind developing a kind of meta-theory of problem solving?

DeJong: At this point, very little. We don't even have good intelligence tests after many years of trying.

Another thing that is really easy to trivialize is the complexity of the whole reasoning process. We're starting to build up little submodels of various facets of the reasoning process. But it's important not to get hung up on any one of these. A lot of work has been done in the areas of inductive and deductive reasoning. There has been interest, but not a whole lot of success, in temporal reasoning, i.e., how we integrate concepts of time into our problem solving, as well as spatial reasoning. What we're seeing more and more now are model driven reasoning systems. Let me give you an example of that. Some neurologists came along to Pople and said, "We would like to take this system of yours and move it out of internal medicine, and we'd like it to do diagnosis of neural diseases." Well, it turns out that, although there is a very large set of empirical rules for diagnosing neural problems, when somebody comes in with a neurological disorder, doctors are much more model-driven by a picture of the underlying neural network. As a consequence, they decided to solve that problem by building in up front, a very strong model of the neurological system and to use that as an underlying data base for the diagnostic process. I think the same thing is true with applying AI to ATE. A simple set of rules that is collected over time about the way this particular gear works is only going to provide a superficial solution to that problem. At some point in time, you're going to see a symptom you haven't seen before, and at that point you'd better have that underlying model.

We handle uncertainty well, but we don't know how to get machines to handle uncertainty. We're getting models now, like the Demster-Shafer theories of accumulating evidence, which give some hints along those directions. Another big problem is non-monotonicity. People can be working very hard on a problem and all of a sudden realize that something that was assumed to be true at some point in the process, isn't true. People will then back up, re-think, and undo all the incorrect implications that were drawn, but it is difficult (expensive) to get a machine to do likewise.

There are a number of human problem solving abilities that are not easily captured by AI systems. Without thinking about it, we shift points of view. We move from an electrical view of this box, to a mechanical view of this box, to a heat-related view of this box, to a view of how this thing fits into other boxes. In contrast, our expert systems right now don't do that very well. They can focus extensively on one point of view, but they don't move from one to another. The ability for self-assessment is also difficult. Current expert systems don't do that very well. The ability to explain and justify is another difficult area.

I don't mean to sound negative. I really think we're in an exciting area here, and these are exploitable technologies. I just think that you have to take that with a sense of caution--with a sense of high risk.

We are seeing rapid advancements in programming languages; the recent LOOPS development is a very good example of that. We are also seeing commercially available knowledge representation tools. They're not going to solve all the problems, but they have the potential of giving you a leg up. The expert system paradigm I think is a rather clever one; it avoids the broad problems of common sense in problem solving and focuses on a highly specialized area.

There is a delightful amount of hardware--every time you turn around there's another product announcement. That's one of the nice things about the Navy AI Center--we've had an equipment budget to bring in a variety of items from this emerging technology. Only one caution to that--I don't know who said it first, but it's been repeated many times, "You can tell the pioneers by the arrows in their backs." For example, we have both LMI machines and Dolphins in-house. In both cases there was a considerable time lag between their arrival and their use by the staff. So, although the hardware is there, be advised that you're on the front end of that technology, and there will be some pain and grief associated with it.

ABOUT THE AUTHOR

Dr. Kenneth DeJong is an Associate Professor of Computer Science at the University of Pittsburgh. He has spent the past 2 years as a visiting scientist at the Navy Artificial Intelligence Center at NRL. His primary interest is in the area of adaptive systems design and analysis. He is currently leading a project at the Navy AI Center in applying AI technology to the problem of troubleshooting reasonably general classes of electronic gear.

AN OVERVIEW OF THE JOINT LOGISTICS COMMANDERS AUTOMATIC TEST EQUIPMENT PANEL

Paul Gross

Naval Electronics Systems Command

Col. Howard Churchill from the Air Force Systems Command is the Panel Chairman for the Joint Logistics Commanders Panel on Automatic Testing. He's unable to be here today. The services in the last 3 or 4 months have had a lot of bad publicity, specifically in the area of the cost of our spare parts. Col. Churchill is serving right now on a board to determine some solutions to our problems with the cost of spare parts. I'm sure he'd rather be here.

Who are the Joint Logistics Commanders (JLCs) and what is their function in life? The four commanders are:

- General Donald R. Keith, Commander, Army Materiel Development and Readiness Command
- Admiral Steven A. White, Chief, Naval Materiel Command
- General James P. Mullins, Commander, Air Force Logistics Command
- General Robert T. Marsh, Air Force Systems Command

Why do we have a JLC and why do we have the panel structure? Basically, what we're trying to do is solve common problems among the services and share that solution among the services. There are many panels that span a wide spectrum of common programs, anywhere from depot maintenance interservicing to metrology and calibration and the area of automatic testing. Before we get started, I want to say one thing and make it perfectly clear, the JLC program is not a great big pot of money or a great big program in the true sense of a program. What we do is take the resources and projects that are available within the services and try to use the results and benefits and share them to everyone's advantage. Some of the people who will be talking during the workshop are part of the automatic testing panel tasks. The work that Tony Coppola is doing at Rome Air Development Center in testability and the work that Jerry Kunert is doing are all part of tasks that are defined and described in our subtask description book.

Figure 1 shows the JLC organization. The "four stars" are the key players in the services for developing, acquiring, maintaining, and disposing of most of the material we buy today in the services. The Panel on Automatic Testing falls under the heading "Panels" on the chart.

The players in our group are represented by all of the major commands: the Air Force Logistics Command, the Air Force Systems Command, The Army Materiel Development and Readiness Command, DARCOM, and Naval Material

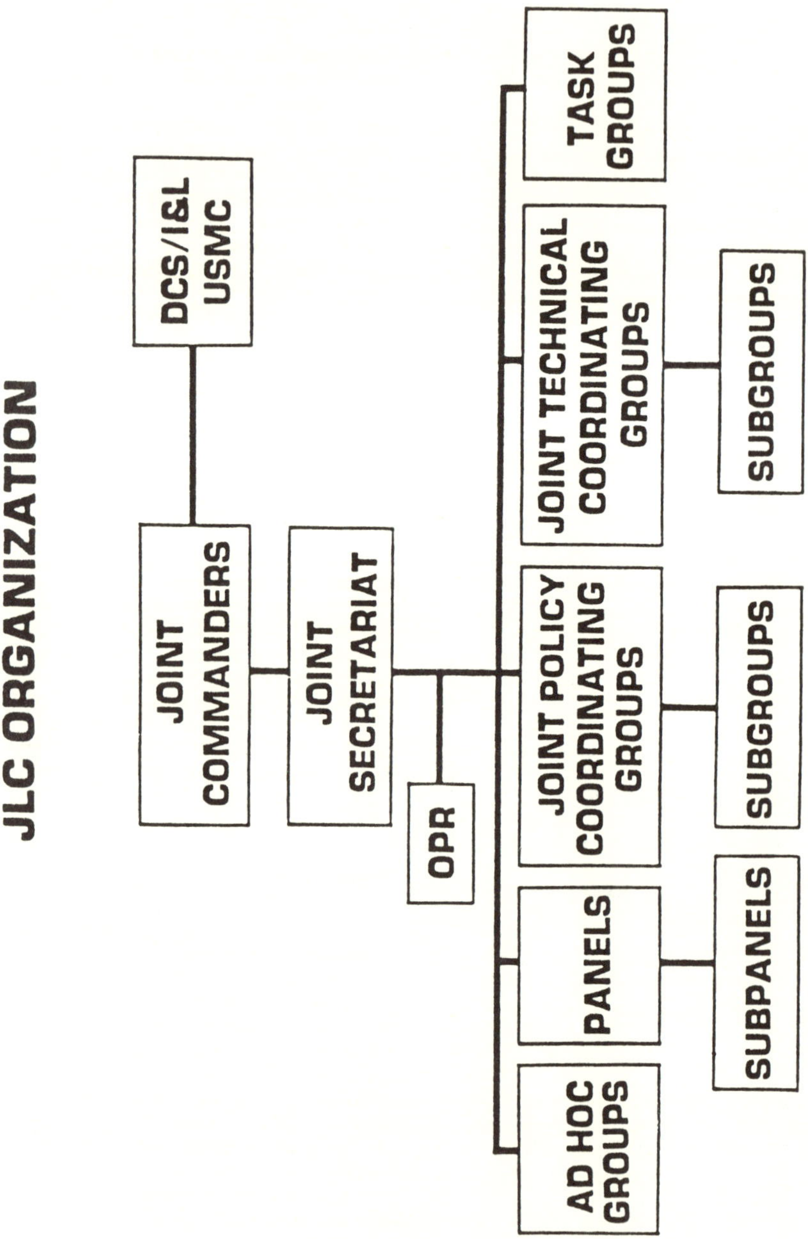
JLC ORGANIZATION
DCS/I&L USMC
JOINT COMMANDERS
JOINT SECRETARIAT
OPR
AD HOC GROUPS
PANELS
SUBPANELS
JOINT POLICY COORDINATING GROUPS
SUBGROUPS
JOINT TECHNICAL COORDINATING GROUPS
SUBGROUPS
TASK GROUPS

Figure 1.

Command. We also interface closely with the people at the National Bureau of Standards because automatic testing has a very close tie to the measurement sciences. Measurement is the bottom line, but maybe it won't be if we can get some AI injected into the program. Associate members of our panel are from Defense Logistics Agency (DLA) and the Marine Corps.

How do we define the scope of automatic testing? We take a broad view. It includes the built-in-test and on-line testing that we do on avionics and shipboard systems. It also includes off-line testing, the special purpose and the general purpose automatic test equipment which includes our test program sets and the software for the test stations themselves. There's a very extensive amount of software used to drive these test stations. We're also talking about testability from the standpoint of defining test point access, partitioning, and the general approach from which we design our electronics. I shouldn't really point out only electronics; we're interested in mechanical design, too.

The scope of automatic testing also includes new technology. Our primary interest here lies within the area of how we test these technologies. How do we test electro-optics and other emerging technologies? What are we going to be looking for in the next 5, 10, 15 years in our test requirements?

Let's go through more background on the Panel. From a Navy perspective, the origins of the Panel started in 1975. The then Assistant Secretary of the Navy, H. Tyler Marcy, initiated a study group that was worked on within the Navy, by the fleet, our hardware procurement systems commands, our laboratories, and a lot of people in our field activities. Basically, what the resulting report did was to define a series of problems and recommend solutions.

At about the same time, industry, in the form of five major industrial organizations, became interested in what we were doing with problems. They did a study for the Navy on our problems in automatic testing and they published a report. It had many of the same findings that were called out in the Marcy report. We began to realize that this automatic testing issue and the problems associated with it were not peculiar to the Navy. The same problems existed in the Army, the Air Force, and even in industry. At that time we laid the groundwork for setting up a panel on automatic testing.

In 1978, the Panel was chartered by the Joint Logistics Commanders. At the same time, the same five industrial groups initiated a joint services study to examine the problems and to come up with recommendations. In 1979, our study plan, which basically defined all of the tasking under that panel, was completed and approved by the JLCs. In 1980, the five major industrial organizations published a final report on the industry/joint service test project. Figure 2 lists, in priority order, the findings and recommendations that came out of that study panel. I think it's interesting that, if you look at it, you'll see the first two or three don't have anything to do with automatic testing. They have to do with management and the way we do business. We haven't done and still don't do a very good job in developing, acquiring and managing our automatic test systems. We've laid some groundwork, we've made some progress, but we're still striving to do a better job.

INDUSTRY/JOINT SERVICE AUTOMATIC TEST PROJECT

RECOMMENDATIONS

1. ORGANIZATIONS, PEOPLE & FUNDING
2. MILTARY EQUIPMENT DESIGN
3. SPECIFICATIONS, DIRECTIVES, CONTROLS & DELIVERABLES
4. NONELECTRIC TEST DEVELOPMENT
5. TEST PROGRAM SETS DEVELOPMENT
6. NEW TECHNOLOGY
7. DATA BANKS
8. SYSTEM SOFTWARE DEVELOPMENT & MAINTENANCE
9. METROLOGY & CALIBRATION
10. TRAINING
11. MAINTENANCE SHOP PRODUCTIVITY

Figure 2.

Figure 3 shows the current organization of the panel and the areas that we are trying to emphasize and consolidate. The people there are the points of contact for specific areas. In the policy and procedures area, we're trying to ensure that we manage our systems correctly. We want to be sure that policy is there to direct that certain techniques be used and that program managers are aware of their requirements in the acquisition of automatic testing for support of prime systems.

In the last 2 years, a lot of emphasis has been placed on standardizing test program languages. Right now, DoD is in the process of issuing 5000.31, which is applicable to Mission Critical Software. 5000.31 will be upgraded from a DoD directive to a DoD instruction. Basically, it calls for the use of ADA for mission critical equipment and also specifies special purpose languages such as ATLAS. We in the services have agreed to standardize on Common/ATLAS which is a pure subset of IEEE Standard-416-ATLAS.

We're also working to develop techniques and analysis tools to help us make tradeoffs in the testability area, and we're trying to assess the technology requirements for the future. We're tracking various technologies and trying to predict what the requirements will be for testing that technology.

I'm sure quite a few of you are familiar with the programs that each one of the services has in off-line ATE. The Air Force has the Modularized Automatic Test Equipment (MATE) program. It has established an acquisition process for acquiring and supporting automatic testing assets in the Air Force by standardizing interfaces and architecture. In the Navy we have the Consolidated Support System (CSS). What we're trying to do there is increase the productivity and through-put within intermediate maintenance and shore intermediate maintenance activities. We're placing a lot of emphasis on the reconfigurability of assets and resources and on modeling to better manage and utilize our assets at the intermediate maintenance level. The Army has the Direct Support-Automatic Test Support System, and the Marine Corps has their own program also.

The purpose of this group is to communicate what everyone is doing, share areas of common interest, share what's been developed, and transition that information to the other services. We don't want to reinvent the wheel. A lot of good work has come out of the Air Force MATE program, and there's going to be a lot come out of the CSS program in the Navy. We're trying to ensure that the communication lines are open, there's a free flow of information, a dialogue between the key players in the services and in industry.

Machinery testing is a disaster area, to say the least. This area offers the greatest potential for cost saving. If we can coordinate the efforts in the services, we won't squander our limited resources. There's little interest in putting R&D dollars in this area, but it has tremendous potential. It's not sexy I guess because it's not electronics. Ultimately, however, you're going to have to put some electronics in it to get the information out.

Let's take a look at the nature of the problem. When I was asked to give this presentation, I was asked to discuss some of the problems we're facing and

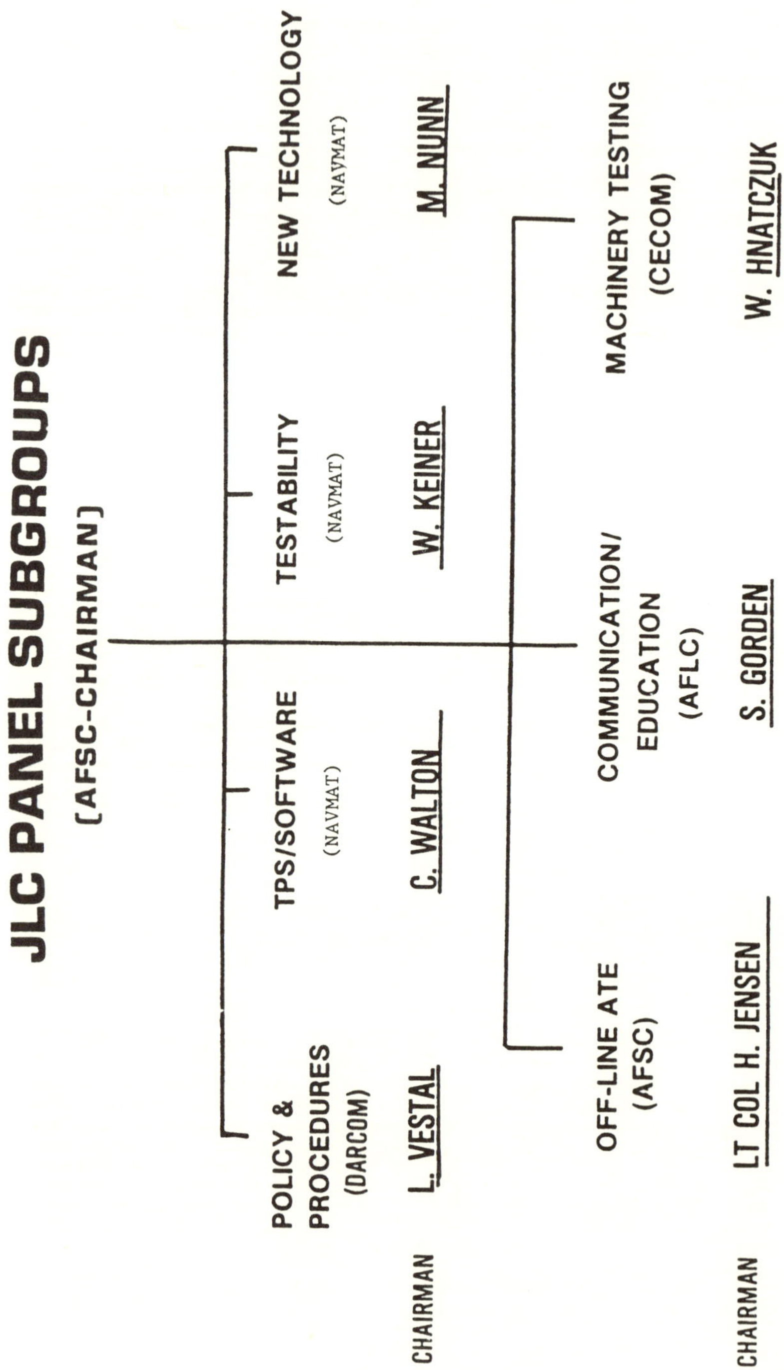
JLC PANEL SUBGROUPS
(AFSC-CHAIRMAN)
POLICY & PROCEDURES (DARCOM)
TPS/SOFTWARE (NAVMAT)
TESTABILITY (NAVMAT)
NEW TECHNOLOGY (NAVMAT)
CHAIRMAN
L. VESTAL
C. WALTON
W. KEINER
M. NUNN
OFF-LINE ATE (AFSC)
COMMUNICATION/ EDUCATION (AFLC)
MACHINERY TESTING (CECOM)
CHAIRMAN
LT COL H. JENSEN
S. GORDEN
W. HNATCZUK

Figure 3.

some of the areas where AI might be able to help us solve our problems. Basically, I think the waterfront is wide open. There are a lot of problems out there and a lot of areas where expert systems, knowledge-based systems, and other techniques can be used to help us solve our problems. Let's imagine a technician sitting in the middle of the Indian Ocean, standing watch and operating the surface search radar which is one of the critical systems on a ship. He knows where he is and who else is around and doesn't want to run into other people. He may be on the night watch, and playing pinochle with a couple of buddies, and all of a sudden, about midnight or 1:00 a.m., every amber light on the power panel lights up and someone says, "Holy cow, what's going on?" They've gone into a hard down situation. What does the technician do? Immediately, he picks up the maintenance manual, which is 9 inches thick and weighs about 15 pounds. He picks up about 7 or 8 pieces of general purpose electronic test equipment, walks over to the panel, starts playing with the built-in test, and goes through a routine of trying to fault isolate and detect what's wrong with that machine. Ultimately, if he's lucky, in a few minutes he fault isolates to an ambiguity group. Usually not a few minutes; believe me, sometimes it can be several hours. In the meantime, the CO of the ship is saying, "What the heck is wrong with my surface search radar? You took my eyes away." This poor technician is working with the tools we've given him which are, at best, barely adequate. If he's a smart tech or a super tech (and we do have some excellent technicians out there, believe me), he pulls out a little black book. If this thing has happened before, then he's got some information on it and he can go ahead and maybe solve the problem. If not, he's got a real problem. He's got to call the supply officer and say, "Hey, Mr. Porkchop, do you have 7 or 8 or 9 modules," whatever the ambiguity group is. "I need to replace them." If he's lucky, he might have what's called a maintenance assist module. This allows him to take a "golden module" and start "easter egging" by random trial and error to get down to a faulty card, or reduce that fault group to a smaller number.

In our example we'll say he's lucky and they have all the spares on board to solve this specific problem. So he pulls the specific module out, replaces it, runs through an operational test, and he's back on-line.

Well, what happens to the module? Right now, if we're talking about the surface Navy, they go back to either a shipyard or a contractor. That can be disastrous in some instances. If that was the only spare on the ship, you probably won't see another spare back on the ship for 4 or 5 months. In the meantime, you're probably going to experience a failure. So, if you're lucky, you have some capability on the ship to repair these modules. They are sent to the technician who starts running them on the ATE. The technician runs through all eight or nine modules and says, "Hey, I got two bad modules." The other ones are put back into the supply system as ready for issue and two modules must be tested. What's happened here is that we've lost a bit of information. There's been information from interrogating and isolating those modules that we haven't transferred to that technician. This technician now runs into the same problem that the person taking it out of the prime system does. It gets put on a piece of automatic test equipment, gets run through a test program set and a diagnostic procedure, and lo and behold the technician gets it down to two, three, maybe four devices. Unless there is an intelligent probe or some other technique, we're dead in the water. So all the chips get replaced. Well, I think that the example speaks for itself. We've got a real problem here, and it's not an easy problem to solve. I think we can do a better job. When you start thinking about what's coming down the line in the next 4 or 5 years, we're going to start inserting VHSIC. It introduces a lot of problems that require an upfront look, particularly in the area of testability.

So what is the nature of the problem? In the past we've failed to identify the maintenance requirements. We need to take a hard look at what we're doing, need to improve the reliability, need to improve the maintainability, and need to ensure that testability is in the design.

There's also a disparity between the maintenance requirements and the maintenance resources. We need to do a better job up front to make sure that these systems are testable and that the test systems are put out in the fleet on time. I've heard a lot of discussion this morning about not having the smart people out there with the skills. We need to train them and to maintain their skills. They're out there working on prime equiment and may not see the same problem week after week. Still, they have to maintain their proficiency.

It's also important to capture the information available from our supertechs. We need to have some way of pulling that information and getting it into a data base so we can reference it for later use.

Automatic testing is essential. You're just not going to get out there with general purpose manual test equipment and test these systems. Automatic testing is your only saving grace, and I think it's going to be more so in the coming years as technology advances.

Testing technology must not lag behind the technology we're putting in the prime system. We can't take a laboratory tester and put it out in the field; it doesn't work. When we're developing the system, we need to ensure that the test system will work in the field.

Finally, to catch your eye, we're spending about $3 billion annually on automatic testing; that's acquisition, ownership, hardware, software, and R&D. That's probably a conservative estimate, and it's a major expenditure that shouldn't be taken lightly.

One of our objectives in this program is to reduce proliferation and our dependence on off-line test equipment. When I first went to work for the Navy, the Naval Material Command, we'd just published an inventory. We had 280 unique pieces of ATE. One of the things we'd like to do in this area is embed more of the support in the avionics and electronics. We want to do this intelligently, not blindly.

Next, we really need to do a good job of applying management to acquiring automatic testing support and automatic testing systems to support our prime systems. We're making improvements in this area, but I don't think we've gone far enough. We have to use the tools available; the acquisition guides and policies should be followed more closely.

Third, we're trying to enhance the readiness of the weapons and the test systems. Remember, if the weapons system is down and your test system is down, you're down all over. There's no way you're going to fix it if your test system is down. We want to get the testability requirements up front in the acquisition process to ensure that we do an intelligent job. This testability should also be put in from the perspective of cost effectiveness.

A fourth objective is to improve communication, not only within the DoD and within the government, but with industry. We're spending a lot of money on R&D (I'm sure a lot of you think it's not enough money, and I agree) but we'd be foolish to duplicate what everyone is doing. We want to cut out redundancy. Communication can and has had a big payoff.

One of my biggest kicks is parochialism. We're very parochial in the Navy, and I think we have to overcome that. The "not invented here" syndrome is not acceptable in today's environment.

Next, we need to improve productivity and quality through more effective application of automatic testing technology. We need to grasp that technology and put it into our support systems and our automatic test systems. We're doing an awful job of transitioning the R&D out of the tech base. Two or 3 years ago we had two demonstration programs that weren't producing hardware. But they allowed us to develop, prove, and standardize a system to communicate information between various sytems on the ship. This improved communication among the CO, and the work centers on the ship and provided readiness information at the fingertips of the CO. That wasn't a high burner and it didn't win too many awards. It got cancelled at the Congressional level.

A sixth objective is to ensure the development, transition, and application of advancing testing technology to the solution of testing problems. Basically, we're saying one should use the technology that's there in the tech base. I don't think we've done that to the greatest extent possible.

Lastly, an objective is to enhance standardization of service automatic testing programs, including the development of appropriate standards and specifications. Standardization should be practical and sensible. We don't want to lock up technology or stop innovation.

Now I'd like to review some of the accomplishments of the JLC Panel.

- We've developed an automatic testing acquisition planning guide. This is a cookbook for the acquisition manager that explains what he should be doing in acquiring an automatic testing system when he buys his prime system. It discusses primarily off-line test systems.

- The panel has also developed a how-to guide for the built-in test area. It addresses getting the requirements into the contracts, defining the requirements, and provides engineering information, techniques, and practices to put built-in test in your system.

- We've developed an informational guide to provide a synopsis of many of the digital test generation systems on the market.

- Another handy tool is the weapon system acquisition review guidelines. It can be used by both the program manager and the person reviewing an acquisition program. It includes questions that program managers should be asking themselves while going through the acquisition process.

- We've also developed a reference guide of existing automatic testing information systems as part of our communications and education effort. There are a couple of data bases included: the Air Force has a lessons learned data base that a lot of people in the Navy didn't know about, and the Navy has a test technology information center where someone is on call to answer any and all questions in testing technology.

- The Sensor Handbook for Automatic Test Monitoring and Diagnostic Systems Applications to Military Vehicles and Machinery describes available sensors and state-of-the-art information on sensors used to monitor machinery systems. This was some very good work done for the Army by the National Bureau of Standards.

- Cross fertilization efforts started back in the Navy in about 1978 when we issued a newsletter to set up a means of communicating within the automatic testing community. This publication is open to anyone in industry and the services. If you'd like to be on the mailing list, write to: Betty Sponaugle, Editor, Naval Electronic Systems Command, ELEX 08TA, Washington, DC 20363.

A number of other projects are underway. Each one of the services has its own way of doing test requirements documents. We're trying to come up with a joint way of ordering test requirement data. This effort has taken about 2 years so far. Hopefully, next year we'll get a standard out on the street that everyone has agreed to and that addresses everyone's requirements. If we succeed, it's going to reduce the number of standards out there.

Something else we've been anxiously awaiting for the last 2 years is the issuance of a standard on testability. This standard was originally issued back in May 1983 for comment. All the comments are back from industry and the services; they're being integrated, and hopefully we'll have another version by February 1984. The approved version should be out by May 1984. When this happens, we can include requirements in our contracts to start incorporating testability in our systems. The standard was written to parallel the LSA standard, Mil-Std-1388, and it's got a direct interface. We've had some negative comments that pointed out that this should be system design oriented, so we have to work those problems out.

Other things we're doing in the testability area, a lot of which is coming out of the MATE project, are developing a testability design guide and a testability analysis handbook. These products, which we expect sometime before the end of the calendar year, will be applied across the services.

In the area of training, the panel sponsors two courses. One is on automatic testing acquisition management, and the other is a design for testability course. This is a 3-day course that addresses both management and design issues. Both have been taken all over the services and were well received. In industry, training has been sponsored by the National Security Industrial Association Automatic Testing Committee.

The panel has also gotten testability incorporated into the Defense Systems Management College curriculum. At the moment, we're developing a Common ATLAS course using IEEE Standard 716.

One other thing I want to bring up in terms of these accomplishments is that the Test Technology Office, which is located at the Naval Oceans Systems Center in San Diego, published a joint service assessment of testing technology. In this document, they have tried to focus R&D planning on developing testing technology to meet the emerging technology requirements in weapons systems.

For the future, we're going to keep doing what we've been doing. The question we always get when we go up to the JLC is "When is this panel going away?" Well, we'd like to go away in about 3 or 4 years. We don't know. Hopefully, we'll have a lot of the problems well in hand. What we'd like to do in the future is continue to have a good dialogue with industry, particularly to interface closely with the National Security Industrial Association Automatic Test Committee. We've had joint meetings. Let's face it, the services don't put hardware and weapons systems out in the field--it's really industry. So a lot of the knowledge in this area is in industry, and we would be remiss if we didn't try to tap it. Other future objectives include expanding training activities, implementing design for testability, developing the integrated diagnostics concept, and focusing on new technology, such as artificial intelligence.

About 2 years ago, the Air Force came out with a policy on integrated diagnostics. Some good things have resulted. You may or may not agree with the definition. Whether or not we achieve our objective depends on our ability to implement some of the things you're doing in AI. I see integrated diagnostics as doing business the way we ought to do business. We need a strategy to integrate these different test disciplines.

I also see integrated diagnostics as a useful tool to you. It may be a technique to insert AI into automatic testing. Some good news: the Air Force is in the process, at Aeronautical Systems Division (ASD), of establishing an integrated diagnostics Special Projects Office (SPO).

What do I envision for the JLC Panel? More emphasis on integrated diagnostics. You'll also see some tasking in the area of AI. We've already got one subtask described; it's a monitor task to see what we're doing in AI. We're going to make some inroads to apply AI to our automatic test systems and to solve some of our diagnostic problems.

ABOUT THE AUTHOR

Mr. Paul Gross is Technical Director of the Test and Monitoring Systems (TAMS) Program Office at the Naval Electronic Systems Command. He is also the Navy's panel member on the JLC Panel on Automatic Testing. In previous positions, Mr. Gross has served as a maintenance engineer on the F/A-18's F404 engine program and was responsible for overseeing the development of maintenance plans.

OVERVIEW OF TRAINING AND AIDING

Dr. Henry Halff

Office of Naval Research

Introduction

As with most of the presentations that I give, my remarks today will be determined more by my own current activities than by the guidance given me to prepare for this talk. Since I am a research psychologist working in the Personnel and Training Research Group at the Office of Naval Research, I will, therefore, be talking about the role that people play in maintaining systems and about psychological research which addresses that role. I believe that people will continue to play an important role in maintenance in the indefinite future. I realize that many of you in the audience do not share this belief and feel that people can be totally removed from the maintenance process (Coppola, this volume). Those of you whose sole interest is in peopleless maintenance should feel free to indulge in a half hour's nap. I must also beg the indulgence of people here who are not particularly concerned with the Navy. Since I work for the Navy, you may find that my remarks have a rather salty tang.

Two serendipitous events make this talk a good deal more enjoyable for me than I had thought it would be. First, in reviewing the presentations that follow my own today, I find that I will conform reasonably well to my instructions to prepare an overview of these talks, even though I totally ignored those instructions and simply put together a few opinions of my own for this presentation. Second, I had really planned on bringing out a few important facts about maintenance and then drawing some conclusions from those facts. The facts, fortuitously enough, were all revealed in yesterday's presentations, leaving me free to devote the rest of my time to the conclusions.

Let me begin with a summary of those conclusions--sources of maintenance problems in the military are widespread and their manifestations are widespread. Not all of the problems originate at the workbench and not all of the problems are seen on the workbench. Solutions, therefore, must be sought at a number of difference points and a concentration of effort on a single point, such as expert systems as troubleshooting aids, are bound to have a small or even negative impact.

The Military Problem

Sources

Much of what I have to say about sources of maintenance problems in the military was discussed yesterday by McGrath (this volume). We expect serious declines in the labor pool. In 1978, the prime recruit population, 17 year old males and females, numbered 4.25 million. In 1990, it will number less than 3.25 million.

Mental quality of this population, as I am sure you are aware, declined seriously in the late 1970s and has not significantly improved since then. According to a recent Navy study, the median Navy recruit reads at about a 10th grade level, and the average training and technical manuals are only readable at a 10th grade level. This means that the average technical manual is readable by only half of the personnel required to read it.

These problems are compounded by a problem not yet mentioned, namely, growth in the force. The Navy, for example, is expanding from a fleet of a little over 400 ships to one of about 600 ships. Although these figures should be taken with a grain of salt, it is clear to everyone that there will be more equipment to maintain and, therefore, a higher demand for maintenance personnel.

Finally, as was mentioned several times, military systems and hardware are becoming more complex. There are many ways of presenting data to illustrate this phenomena, but Figure 1 is one of my favorites. It plots the number of pages in the technical manuals for Navy aircraft as a function of time. It is easy to note that, starting in about 1950, the curve becomes quite steep. Nor should it escape your attention that the ordinate (manual size) is on a logarithmic scale so that technical manual size can be seen to double about every 10 years.

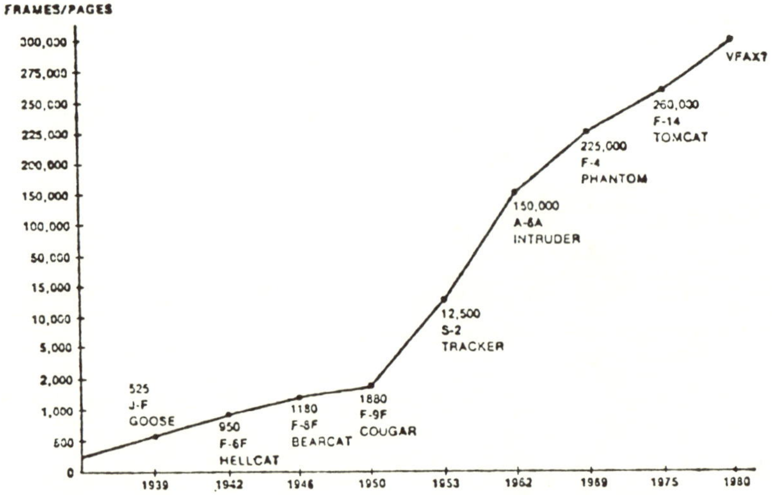

Figure 1. Technical Manual Growth Rate Within the Naval Air Systems Command.

Manifestations

One of the most devastating effects of these problems is on the resources available for training. I have noted the shortage of skilled personnel, a shortage compounded, by the way, by extremely attractive offers from industries competing with the Navy for those personnel. In addition to personnel shortages, the services with growth in the force experience equipment shortages. Both the training community and the operational forces have needs for people and equipment and in the competition for these resources, the operational forces should, and do, win. We, therefore, find our technicians being trained on obsolete equipment by overworked instructors with a subsequent decline in training effectiveness.

It is also possible to see manifestations of the maintenance problem in the fleet and field. (If this were not so, I don't suppose we would be here today.) For example, as Figure 2 shows, the ratio of maintenance hours per flight hour on Navy aircraft increased by about 61 percent between 1974 and 1980. Currently, an aircraft spends 30 hours in the shop for every hour that it flies.

Artificial Intelligence and Maintenance

We are here today because we all think that artificial intelligence (AI) holds some promise for alleviating the problems I have just discussed. The natural and perhaps dominant view of this promise was well expressed yesterday by Coppola (this volume), who suggested that a combination of AI and robotics could totally automate the maintenance process. That is not the view that I wish to convey today. Instead, I suggest that we seriously consider how artificial intelligence can alleviate some of the problems associated with the performance of maintainers.

Training of Maintainers

Basic skills. As I have mentioned, problems with maintenance in the services do not seem to arise at the workbench, but rather, in a sense, in the public schools. Our recruit pool is inadequately prepared to deal with both technical training and the demands of maintenance jobs. Although the application of artificial intelligence to this problem is difficult to see at first, it is worth pointing out that some of the most exciting work in education today uses AI techniques to model knowledge and processes normally associated with basic skills. Most of this work (e.g., Greeno, 1978, 1980; Lewis, 1981; Resnick, 1982; VanLehn, 1983) is concerned with the kinds of computational skills that are crucial to success in technical training.

Appropriate remediation of basic skill deficiencies can, at the least, increase success rates in technical training and thereby increase the supply of qualified maintainers (Baker & Hamovitch, 1983). AI offers a number of tools that may be helpful in the remediation of basic skills. Dealing with individuals who lack basic skills even after years of instruction is a much more complex

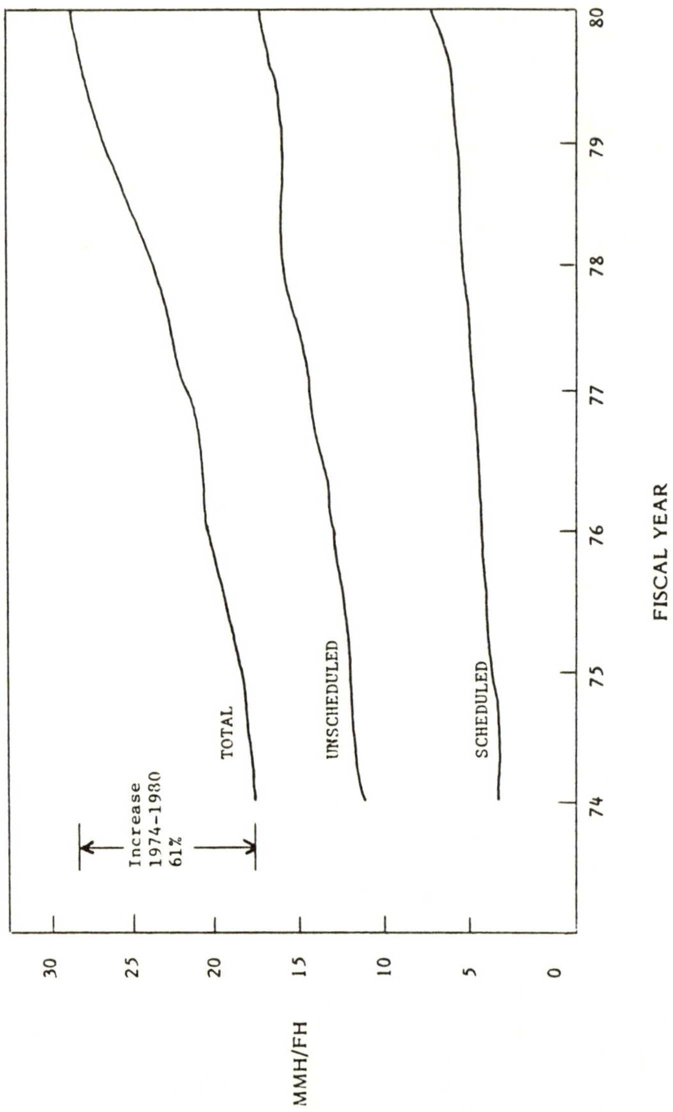

Figure 2. Maintenance Man-Hours Per Flight-Hour (MMH/FH).

Data Source:
Naval Aviation Plan

problem than that of initial acquisition. There are suggestions in current research that skill deficiencies are complex and subtle enough in origin that a computer will be required for successful diagnosis and remediation.

Simulation. The use of simulators for maintenance training is not a new idea and is one that ostensibly has nothing to do with AI. However, AI and associated developments in computer science are leading to a different view of the role and potential of simulation in technical training. To a large extent, this new view has developed as the consequence of STEAMER which Hollan will describe in more detail later. The general trend that I see in simulator design philosophy is one that leads us away from physical fidelity as a criterion towards designs based on the cognitive aspects of the skills to be mastered. Current research in cognitive science (Chi, Feltovich, & Glaser, 1981; Lesgold, Feltovich, Glaser & Wang, 1981) indicates that experts in technical fields view problems in their domains in terms of abstract entities and principles that are not immediately evident from the physical characteristics of the problem. This abstraction not only serves to encapsulate strategic problem solving knowledge (Greeno, 1978, 1980), but also provides the memory structures for expansion of the cognitive resources needed in successful problem solving (Chase & Ericsson, 1982). It follows that simulators might well function more effectively if they incorporated explicit representations of abstract entities and provided views of the domain that promoted the development of the knowledge structures needed for effective problem solving.

Within AI the research most relevant to conceptual simulators is that concerned with mental models and qualitative reasoning. Thus, I expect that theories of envisioning (de Kleer & Brown, 1981, 1983) will have a considerable impact on this field. In addition, simulators can be viewed as analogies of the target training domain so that theories such as structure mapping (Gentner, 1983) may also apply. There is some indication that schema theory may be a useful tool for describing system perception and device perception (Kieras, 1982). Simulators that make evident the schematic nature of the devices being simulated may, therefore, offer a singular advantage in training. Finally, the notion of qualitative interfaces (a term coined by Jim Hollan), in which abstract quantities (e.g., acceleration, current) are given concrete realizations via icons, may provide excellent ways of training students to think effectively about systems.

Intelligent computer-assisted instruction (ICAI). The use of computers to capture an instructor's expertise and thereby extend his or her instructional powers in both space and time is not new (Carbonnel, 1970). Artificial intelligence is involved in this enterprise because the subject matter in any significant domain requires intelligence and since teaching itself is an inherently intelligent activity. But years of research pursuing the dream of a fully automated tutor have taught us that computerizing expertise for instructional purposes is far more difficult than capturing expertise for, say, advisory purposes. This is so because successful ICAI must not only be grounded on a computational understanding of the subject matter, but also on a computational model of the student and of instructional methods. Good teachers teach to a mental model of their student, and the complexity and subtlety of this model continues to challenge researchers in this area (London & Clancey, 1982).

Although the idea of a fully automated tutor remains an elusive end-point in a continuum of computer-based training systems, it is possible to use artificial intelligence devices in a number of other ways in technical training. Wescourt (1977), for example, and more recently VanLehn (1983) have made suggestions relevant to the sequencing of exercises and examples. Brown (1983) has pointed out that the availability of advice when needed is as crucial as the quality of that advice. Following Burton and Brown (1982), he suggests a family of minimally intelligent computer coaches that operate in a carefully designed environment for exercising technical skills. In mimicking real world situations, these environments constitute simulators, but not ones that we normally associate with maintenance training.

Development of instructional materials. Finally, there is a prospect for the use of artificial intelligence in the development of instructional materials, particularly in view of the large literature on computational linguistics and machine models of learning. Much could be done to improve training documents and written materials, and a bit later I will discuss some of these possibilities in connection with technical documentation. For now, let me mention that other opportunities exist in the area of curriculum design. One possibility, for example, is to use computer models of learning to evaluate curricula. Another is for automation of the process of curriculum design or at least curriculum revision. Both of these technologies could involve an interesting combination of cognitive modeling and AI technology. I should note in passing that the average Navy course is revised on the order of once every 133 years, so that this area is also ripe for automation.

Design for Maintainability

There are other areas where artificial intelligence can help with a maintenance problem. We have heard quite a bit of evidence that systems are too complex to be effectively maintained. It is possible that AI could help us decrease the psychological complexity of devices and thereby make their maintenance more feasible.

Knowledge representation and structured design. Kieras (this volume) is going to tell us about research that I just alluded to in my mention of schema theory as a basis for system perception and comprehension. We may well be able to incorporate these schema theoretic accounts, which address the psychological or mental aspects of device representation, into the design process.

The software-engineering community has for some time now been concerned with the design of more maintainable software. In fact, the discipline of structured programming is rigidly applied in software development expressly for the purpose of enhancing its maintainability. Despite one's views on the effectiveness of this discipline it would be difficult to argue that its implementation has failed. Hardware design has been little affected by similar considerations, perhaps because software is inherently symbolic and, therefore, more amenable to cognitive analysis. Nonetheless, there may be important opportunities in the future for AI to guide the design of hardware for the specific purpose of improving its maintainability.

Cognitive models of maintenance performance. Apart from top-down approaches to design, I think cognitive modeling offers some promise in the area of design for maintainability. At least the topic gives me the excuse to talk about some research. Since ONR does not let me do any research on my own, I am forced, in situations like this, to talk about other people's research. Today I have chosen Towne (this volume) to misrepresent. He developed a simple but effective computer model of how people troubleshoot a microcomputer system down to the functional device level. The model, shown in Figure 3, is based on the kinds of widely known principles that have been discussed at this workshop. The technician modeled by Towne has available to him a collection of tests and a collection of replacement units. In selecting any action, either a test or a replacement action, the technician considers the information value of the particular tests and the certainty associated with any particular decision to replace. The model operates in an iterative fashion. Hence, it tends to first perform the most useful tests, and when it is reasonably certain that a unit is bad, it replaces that unit.

The model is a far cry from some of the more complex efforts at cognitive modeling of diagnostic behavior; nonetheless, it is surprisingly accurate, as Figure 4 shows. This figure is a scatterplot of test-and-replace times for nine different faults. The model's performance, averaged across reasonable minor variations in strategy, is plotted against the average peformance of real technicians. The times for individual test and replacement actions were precalibrated so that any points off the main diagonal indicate a discrepancy between the model and real technicians in their choice of tests and replacements. With no parameters to estimate, the fit of the model is virtually flawless. More importantly, it gives a clear indication of the faults that cause maintainability problems. Tools of this sort in the hands of designers could be a powerful means of ensuring that equipment is designed to be easily maintained.

Documentation

Print media. There is near universal agreement that technical documentation is, for the most part, grossly inadequate and often totally useless. AI's large concern with linguistic matters should provide considerable leverage on this problem. One immediate way to improve documentation might be to derive guidelines for authors using currently available knowledge in psycholinguistics and computational linguistics. I tend to doubt that this approach would have much of an effect since guidelines simple enough for a writer to apply consistently would probably be too weak and imprecise to have much of an effect.

Another more promising approach is to use automated authoring aids to help writers improve technical documentation. Systems such as the Writers' Workbench (Cherry, 1982; MacDonald, Frase, Gingrich, & Keenan, 1982), and the Navy's Computerized Readability Editing System (Braby & Kincaid, 1981-1982; Kincaid, Aagard, O'Hara, & Cottrell, 1981) are a good start in this direction, but these systems for the most part address mainly the surface aspects of text. That is, they provide critiques of vocabulary, sentence length, use of awkward phrases, etc. without really addressing the meaning or structure of the text. Later today Kieras (this volume) will discuss AI-based methods for examining more fundamental aspects of text. One notion that he will describe involves the use of

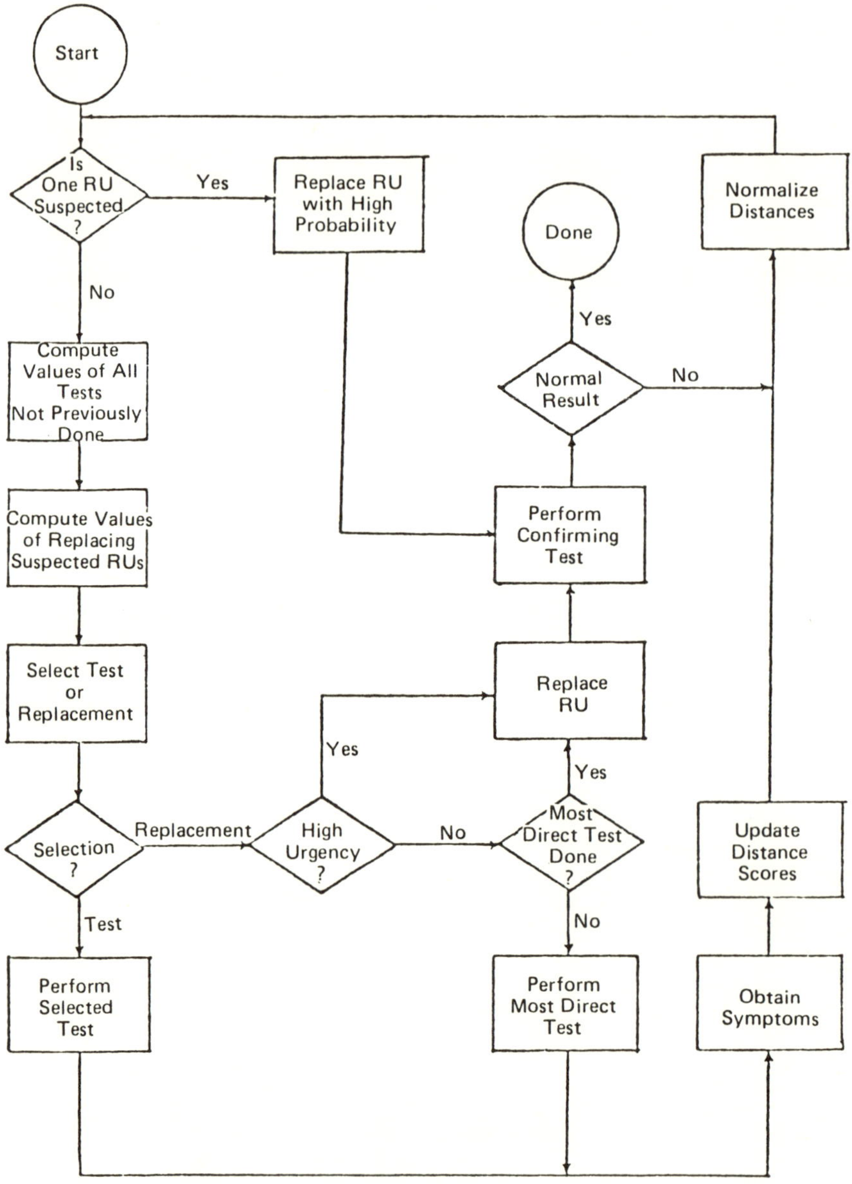
Start
Is One RU Suspected ?
Yes
Replace RU with High Probability
Normalize Distances
Done
No
Yes
Compute Values of All Tests Not Previously Done
Normal Result
No
Compute Values of Replacing Suspected RUs
Perform Confirming Test
Select Test or Replacement
Replace RU
Yes
Yes
Selection ?
Replacement
High Urgency ?
No
Most Direct Test Done ?
Update Distance Scores
Test
No
Perform Selected Test
Perform Most Direct Test
Obtain Symptoms

Figure 3.

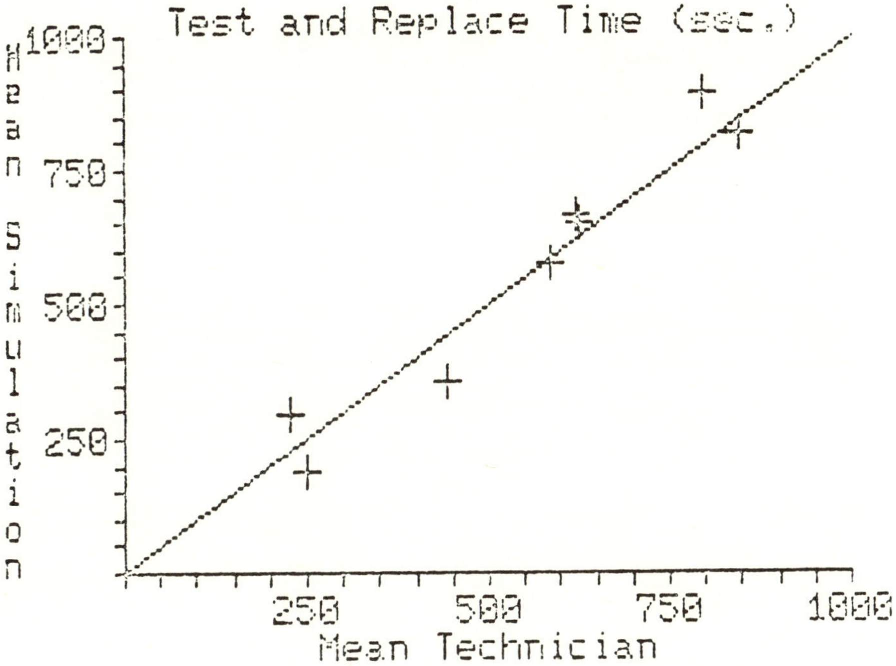
Test and Replace Time (sec.)
1000
750
500
250
Mean Simulation
250
500
750
1000
Mean Technician

Figure 4.

an AI-based parser that can provide a structural description of the text and rules that operate on that structure. Automated analysis of the semantic aspects of draft technical documentation is more challenging, but it might be possible to run certain checks for semantic completeness or to simulate readers and analyze what they might comprehend in the text.

Eventually, we should aim for top-down guidance at the discourse level. That is, we should be able to analyze the overall purpose of a document or set of documents and make recommendations about the discourse structures that should be used to convey the target material.

Interactive media. AI can also help in the design of computer-based performance aids. One possible role for such devices is simply to deliver technical data in a more convenient fashion than standard print media. Another role is to provide state information on the equipment being maintained. The use of automatic test equipment is particularly pertinent to this aspect of a performance aid's function. These aids could also serve to deliver procedural instructions interactively in a way that would lead to fewer errors in performance and the ability to incorporate more complex and sophisticated procedures into maintenance.

In all of these uses, AI could play a role. It could provide natural language interfaces, inference mechanisms for ATE, and knowledge representation methods for procedures. There is one other role that AI might have in a computer-based job aid, namely that of giving advice to a technician through an expert system. Strangely enough, it is this role, the use of expert systems in diagnostic maintenance, that seems to dominate this meeting. To understand the role of AI in maintenance, we must first recognize that diagnostic results are only one form of information useful to a technician repairing a system, and that delivery of information is only one aspect of the maintenance problem.

AI in the Real World of Maintenance

A narrow view of AI's role in maintenance is bound to lead to serious problems in the real world. I do not claim any real expertise about the real world, but my few reluctant sojourns there have given some cause for concern about the application of this technology.

Robustness. It is well known that typical, unstructured rule-based systems are not very robust. An expert system carefully designed for one application may be totally useless when applied to even a close cousin. Unfortunately, minor, and sometimes major, changes in configuration are the rule in the real world rather than the exception. One source of such problems is configuration failure. A technician who does not have the replacement parts necessary to properly repair a device uses a jerry-rig to make the unit work. A data processing technician on finding a bug in a ship's software, installs an unauthorized patch that, over the life span of the software, drives it ever further away from configuration. Who, if anyone, bothers to inform the expert system that troubleshoots these devices about these sub rosa changes? Even authorized changes, say, as the result of overhauls, may have difficulty finding their way into maintenance aiding systems.

Another aspect of the robustness problem was mentioned yesterday by Mr. McGrath. Faults, it appears, come in two sizes: the kind that are fixed almost immediately and the kind that can take from 10 to 100 hours to fix. Technicians' experience and expert knowledge are probably most effectively brought to bear on the former type of fault. The latter, more difficult faults may well require advanced reasoning and inference capabilities not found in the kinds of expert systems described yesterday.

Maintenance objectives. Multiple goals are characteristic of most of the people working in a maintenance environment. The primary goal of the typical technician is that of keeping himself or herself unhurt and alive. This kind of overriding contextual information is difficult to incorporate into an expert system decision aid; the tests and procedures that make sense in good weather, for example, might be completely unacceptable during a squall. Operational readiness is also a primary goal of maintainers. Keeping ships and other systems operational will often preclude maintenance actions deemed to be crucial from the narrow viewpoint of an expert system. Repair is often a goal that supercedes diagnosis, and maintenance systems must, therefore, be able to decide just how precise a diagnosis must be before a repair should be effected. Political and policy factors also figure heavily in the goals of a maintainer; the attitudes of managers may often determine false replacement rates and other properties of a maintenance operation. Thus, while troubleshooting and diagnosis remain an important problem in maintenance systems, they are far from primary goals and, in fact, lie at the tip of a very complex goal tree.

Other factors. Other noncerebral factors also work to limit the usefulness of expert systems and job aids. Many of the systems that are most difficult to troubleshoot are widely distributed. Radar systems and communications systems, for example, are distributed across the entire extent of a ship, and a single fault often requires three or four people to track it down. The idea that an expert system has to be a team player is not one that I see widely discussed in the literature.

Accessibility is another problem in the maintenance of many systems. Components that are accessible in some situations may not be in others. Hence, an expert system that demands access to these components may have to deal with ubiquitous and unpredictable physical constraints.

As Mr. McGrath mentioned yesterday, logistics is a large, complicating factor in maintenance systems. At one level, technicians are directed to repair systems on a modular basis, replacing a known bad module with a replacement module. When, however, these modules cost in the tens of thousands of dollars, it is often difficult to obtain replacement parts. Technicians more interested in readiness than in policy will often retain faulty modules as component caches. Designing maintenance aids that support or fail to support this kind of antipolicy behavior is an interesting problem.

Conclusions

The purpose of this workshop is to determine the course of research and development on AI in maintenance. Let me conclude, therefore, with recommendations oriented towards the planning of research and development.

Concerning the substance of research in the area, I think it essential that we be eclectic. I am disturbed that the typical view of AI applications to maintenance is one of an expert system that operates on the workbench to diagnose failures, aided or unaided by technicians. I hope that the considerations I have just discussed force us to consider a much broader attack on the problem and to consider applying AI at all levels from system design through documentation, training, and all aspects of performance aiding. Broadening our approach can only make it better integrated, more robust, and more successful in the long run.

Also worth recalling is DeJong's (this volume) point about the scientific status of expert systems. There remain serious unanswered scientific questions about this technology. I would not be at all surprised if the field of expert systems, like that of machine translation, became essentially dead in 5 or 10 years. Needed much more than the development of yet another expert system to troubleshoot a particular device is basic research on the hard scientific problems associated with expert systems.

One important barrier to the prosecution of essential research in AI is a shortage of expertise in the field. Industry does itself no favors by hiring individual graduates, each to start his or her own AI shop to build one more expert system. Companies that engage in this sort of practice usually do so with plans to expand their one-person shops as soon as experts become available. They seem to care little that they are withdrawing from the academic community the very resources needed to produce those experts or that they are fractionating the scientific community to the extent that serious and important research on AI may well become impossible.

In sum, if we cannot find the breadth of view to look for innovative approaches to solving maintenance problems at all levels, or if we cannot find the discipline to support the serious scientific work needed to create a proper foundation for AI, we will be rewarded with the attendant loss not only of resources but also of credibility to those who furnish those resources.

References

Baker, M., & Hamovitch, M. (1983). Job-oriented basic skills (JOBS) training program: An evaluation (NPRDC Tech. Rep. 83-5). San Diego, CA: Navy Personnel Research and Development Center.

Braby, R., & Kincaid, J. P. (1981-82). Computer aided authoring and editing. Journal of Eductional Technology Systems, 10(2).

Brown, J. S. (1983). Learning by doing revisited for electronic learning environments. In M. A. White (Ed.), The future of electronic learning. Hillsdale, NJ: Erlbaum.

Burton, R. R., & Brown, J. S. (1982). An investigation of computer coaching for informal learning activities. In Sleeman, D., & Brown, J. S. (Eds.), Intelligent tutoring systems. London: Academic Press.

Carbonnel, J. (1970). AI in CAI: An artificial intelligence approach to computer-assisted instruction. IEEE Transactions on Man-Machine Systems, MMS-11(4).

Chase, W. G., & Ericsson, K. A. (1982). Skill and working memory. In G. Bower (Ed.), The psychology of learning and motivation (Vol. 16). New York: Academic Press.

Cherry, L. (1982). Writing tools. IEEE Transactions on Communications, 30, 100-105.

Chi, M. T. H., Feltovich, P., & Glaser, R. (1981). Categorization and representation of physics problems by experts and novices. Cognitive Science, 5, 121-152.

de Kleer, J., & Brown, J. S. (1981). Mental models of physical mechanisms and their acquisition. In J. R. Anderson (Ed.), Cognitive skills and their acquisition. Hillsdale, NJ: Erlbaum.

de Kleer, J., & Brown, J. S. (1983). Assumptions and ambiguities in mechanistic mental models. In D. Gentner & A. L. Stevens (Eds.), Mental models. Hillsdale, NJ: Erlbaum.

Gentner, D. (1983). Structure mapping: A theoretical framework for analogy. Cognitive Science, 7, 155-170.

Greeno, J. G. (1978). A study of problem solving. In R. Glaser (Ed.), Advances in instructional psychology (Vol. 1). Hillsdale, NJ: Erlbaum.

Greeno, J. G. (1980). Some examples of cognitive task analysis with instructional implications. In R. E. Snow, P. A. Federico, & W. E. Montague (Eds.), Aptitude, learning and instruction: Vol. 2. Cognitive process analyses of learning and instruction. Hillsdale, NJ: Erlbaum.

Jeffries, R., Turner, A. A., Polson, P. G., & Atwood, M. E. (1981). The processes involved in designing software. In J. R. Anderson (Ed.), Cognitive skills and their acquisition. Hillsdale, NJ: Erlbaum.

Kieras, D. E. (1982). What people know about electronic devices: A descriptive study (Tech. Rep. 12). Tuscon, AZ: University of Arizona, Department of Psychology.

Kincaid, J. P., Aagard, J. A., O'Hara, J. W., & Cottrell, L. K. (1981). Computer readability editing system. IEEE Transactions on Professional Communications, 24, 38-41.

Lesgold, A. M., Feltovich, P. J., Glaser, R., & Wang, Y. (1981). The acquisition of perceptual diagnostic skill in radiology (Tech. Rep. PDS-1). Pittsburgh, PA: University of Pittsburgh, Learning Research and Development Center.

Lewis, C. (1981). Skill in algebra. In J. R. Anderson (Ed.), Cognitive skills and their acquisition. Hillsdale, NJ: Erlbaum.

London, B., & Clancey, W. J. (1982). Plan recognition strategies for student modeling: Prediction and description. Proceedings of AAAI-82, 335-338. Palo Alto: American Association for Artificial Intelligence.

Macdonald, N. H., Frase, L. T., Gingrich, P. S., & Kennan, S. A. (1982). The writer's workbench: Computer aids for text analysis. IEEE Transactions on Communications, 30, 105-110.

Resnick, L. B. (1982). Syntax and semantics in learning to subtract. In T. Carpenter, J. Moser, & T. Romberg (Eds.), Addition and subtraction: A cognitive perspective. Hillsdale, NJ: Erlbaum.

VanLehn, K. (1983). Felicity conditions for human skill acquisition: Validating an AI-based theory (Tech. Rep. CIS-21). Palo Alto: Xerox Palo Alto Research Centers.

Wescourt, K. T., Beard, M., Gould, L., & Barr, A. (1977). Knowledge-based CAI; CINS for individualized curriculum sequencing (Tech. Rep. No. 290). Stanford, CA: Stanford University, Institute for Mathematical Studies in the Social Sciences.

ABOUT THE AUTHOR

Dr. Henry Halff is a Scientific Officer in the Personnel and Training Research Group at the Office of Naval Research. He is involved with planning, implementation, and management of basic research programs in cognitive psychology, computer-assisted instruction and related areas. Prior to this, he was an Assistant Professor of psychology at the University of Illinois in Urbana-Champaign where his research interests were in mathematical models of learning, choice and decision theory, and applications of computers in psychology. He received a Ph.D. in experimental psychology from the University of Texas in 1969 and was a National Institute of Mental Health Postdoctoral Fellow at the University of Michigan.

Part II

The Science

AI APPROACHES TO TROUBLESHOOTING

Dr. Johan de Kleer

Xerox Palo Alto Research Center

I would like to point out that this talk represents work done with John Seely Brown. Like any good AI expert, I have an enormous pile of slides so I can dynamically adjust my talk depending on the necessity of the situation. I'm very tempted to give a talk today which I won't give, but it involves why AI is bad for you. It really is, but this is probably not the right forum for it.

Let me start with basics. Why are we here? The single common thread is that we have technological artifacts and they break faster than we can fix them. From that keen insight, one can make further observations about the two ways to fix broken machines--you get people to fix them or you get other machines to fix them. Right now, both of these approaches don't work very well. Is there a common theory of troubleshooting underlying these two approaches? To put the question another way: Is the theory of troubleshooting underlying human training and human aiding and doing maintenance any different from the theory underlying computer-based test equipment? The argument is often made that there is a fundamental difference because inference is cheap for computers. This, however, remains to be seen.

In this talk I'm going to take as an objective getting the best computer-based troubleshooter we can. What you'll see at the conclusion of my talk is that, although I never took it as a goal, the design that I come up with is something that is just right for the training problem.

We know that machines are hard to fix. However, we also notice that some people are good at fixing them, and we call those people experts. We talk to those experts for awhile and we discover that they use knowledge about circuits to diagnose. It takes intelligence to find faults. Now you will notice that any good data base indexing system would come up with a hit on those three key words I've just said. What is it? The hit is "artificial intelligence." (This, by the way, is the beginning of my 45 minute anti-AI talk.) The piece of reasoning I just went through about expert-knowledge-intelligence being equated with artificial intelligence is completely fallacious. If it were true, any problem in our society for which there exist a few experts and which seems to require intelligence would be placed in the arena of AI. And, by that definition, AI would include everything. Now I know lots of my friends in AI believe that, but it's completely false. You may be able to guess the other 44 minutes of what I would say about the dangers of AI.

Another story I'd like to tell you involves picking someone at random, say, a knowledge engineer. The knowledge engineer often uses a sledge hammer to crack a very small nut--a far too large sledge hammer. But perhaps it's a case of the nut cracking the sledge hammer. The point is that AI is hairy: it's hard, complicated, and usually doesn't work. Now the problem is that it is also sexy. I want to drive home a simple piece of engineering methodology that we should all be completely familiar with, but somehow is often forgotten--you don't want to do the intelligent thing, you want to do the simplest thing that works. If you don't do that, you're going to get into trouble. I am not in the business of building a troubleshooter that's going to work in the field in 2 years, so I have a different goal than some of you and have to make different kinds of decisions. If I had to build a troubleshooter to work in 2 years, I would do different things than I am doing now. The kinds of questions I'm interested in include: What is troubleshooting? What is the fundamental problem? What does it mean to understand a machine? Nevertheless, this little piece of methodology that I've described above applies to the science as well as to the engineering. If I propose a complex mechanism or artifact, I better have a reason for why I introduced the complexity. Whether it be engineering or science, do the simplest thing that works and have an explanation for any complications in the product.

In the rest of this talk, I'm going to get a little more technical and lay out my perspective on troubleshooting. I'm going to have to do that while I'm going through some examples. I won't go very deep, but I hate talking in completely high level terms.

Let's consider the regulated power supply circuit shown in Figure 1. I'm going to talk about six approaches to troubleshooting using this circuit. Some of them I have implemented; some of them are fictional. I'm presenting them to demonstrate the spectrum of possible AI approaches.

First of the six approaches to troubleshooting is the modern approach, which is, I gather from some of the other talks I've heard at this workshop, now the conservative approach. The second approach is the empirical association approach. The third approach examines organization of knowledge along structural and causal lines. Fourth, I'll describe the approach that I consider the most powerful--how to use deep knowledge about behavior to make troubleshooting inferences. Fifth, the use of deep knowledge about fault modes, and sixth, the use of causal models. Causal models is actually a separate talk so I won't go very deeply into that subject.

As we go through this list of six approaches to troubleshooting, we gain certain advantages with each successive approach. Thus, if we actually want to build something soon, we have to take a tradeoff someplace and choose a position along the spectrum. The way to view this framework is as a tradeoff of knowledge vs. inference. There's a disastrous slogan going around that states "knowledge is power." Actually, we want as little knowledge as possible and we want our inference to be as powerful as possible. The basic idea is that if we have a little knowledge it's easy to change, easy to debug, and takes less effort to make sure that it's right. So, as I go through these six approaches to troubleshooting, I'm going to lay out where the knowledge is, how it is used, and what it is good for.

Let's begin by discussing what a troubleshooter does. Superficially, the troubleshooter seems to do two things--makes a bunch of measurements, then replaces a component. It sounds very simple. But note that in the activity of measuring, the troubleshooter is presumably doing two things. He is making measurements from which he computes entailments about the components of the device and based on those entailments, he decides to make yet other

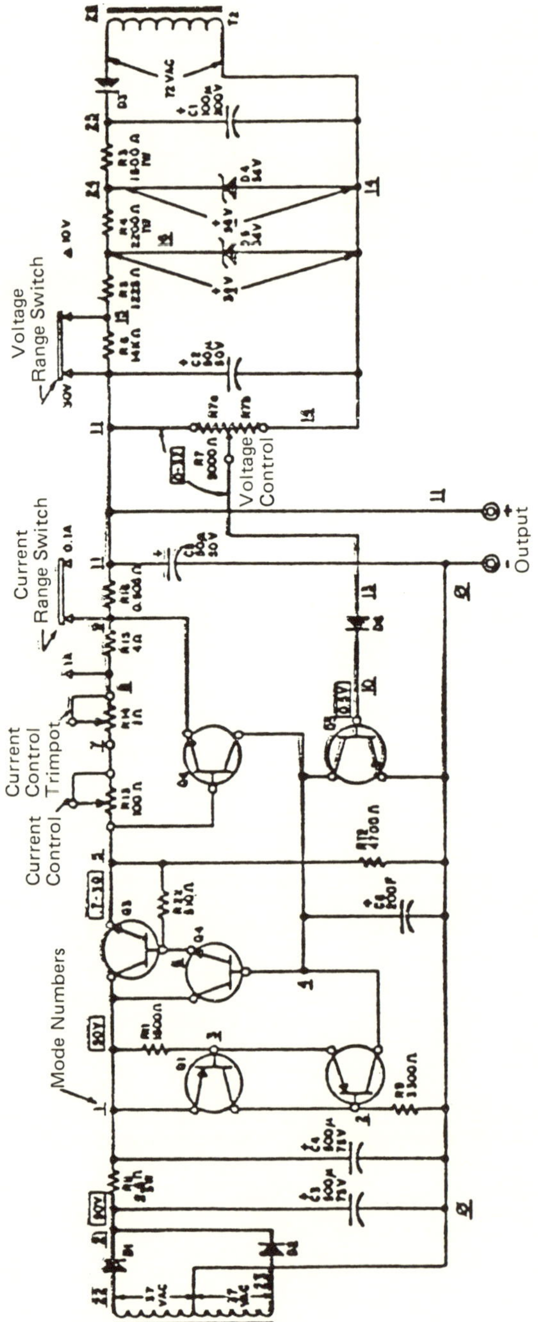

Figure 1. Schematic of the IP-28 Power Supply.

measurements. The point is, he wants to make the measurement that has maximum information gain.

What goals do we have for building a troubleshooter that has performance? There are four. The first one is robustness. We want the troubleshooter to succeed on faults that the designer of the system did not foresee. We do not want unexpected inputs or unexpected faults to blow the troubleshooting system out of the water. Second, we want it to be general and work on a wide number of cases. It should be able to apply to other circuits besides the one for which it was implemented. Third, we want it to be efficient. Anyone can build troubleshooters that make a measurement at every node and eventually figure out what is wrong. But measurements are expensive. Some are more expensive than others, so there is some metric within which a troubleshooter optimizes. The fourth goal is constructibility. It has t be easy to build the troubleshooter; if it takes 5 years, then something is wrong.

There is a fifth goal for building a troubleshooter that I have purposely not included on my list--explanation. Explanation is often oversold. The reason explanation is such an issue for expert systems is that the implementers of expert systems have to convince the other reseachers in this field, and their own managers, that these programs work when in actual fact they don't. An explanation facility provides a means for failing gracefully. It makes the system appear as if it might work and deflects questions from the real issue which is performance. If the conclusion of the expert system was always right, or mostly right, you wouldn't need an explanation, you'd just follow it. And the second point is, in many contexts, the technician that's using the expert system doesn't have the technical training to evaluate the explanation that the expert system would generate anyway. So explanation is oversold in this business.

Let me quickly outline the modern approach, although I'm sure many people at this workshop have given talks about it. As far as I can tell, the modern approach is to write 100,000 lines in Pascal code for your million dollar piece of diagnostic equipment which finds 30 percent of the faults in the device. Let's evaluate this approach using my four criteria. First of all, look at the knowledge in the system. The knowledge is all implicit in the code. There is no inference going on at all. The first problem is that presumably the writer of the Pascal program went in with a set of faults that had to be covered. How can you tell the Pascal program actually covered the faults? Secondly, how do you know that the original set of faults were the faults that were important? So the robustness of this 100,000 lines of Pascal program is pretty bad. It's also not general at all. There's no hope this Pascal program is going to work on another circuit. Regarding efficiency, it seems many of the programs I've heard about are very inefficient in the sense that they make the same set of measurements no matter what. I've heard of frustrated technicians who have to wait hours for the program to reach the test of that part of the modules they suspect is broken. But the Pascal code doesn't know when to start and when to stop. It just runs through all of the tests. Our fourth goal of constructibility is obviously poor for the modern approach.

So how can we do better? Well, we go observe and talk to real-life troubleshooters. The human expert says things to us that resemble "if-then" relationships. For example, "if the voltage is low, then the constant current source is open." Aha! These are called empirical associations abstracted from the expert. So we start writing these empirical associations and they work! So we collect a very large number of rules. Now, this is a little oversimplified, but I'd like to point out this simplified system actually works because empirical associations are useful for both of the troubleshooter's basic tasks: computing the entailments of measurements and proposing new ones.

Suppose the troubleshooter has a rule that says: "If V5 is low, then R9 is open." The troubleshooter then measures voltage at node 5. Suppose he discovers that this voltage is low. From that he can deduce by simple antecedent reasoning that R9 is open. So the rules allow the troubleshooter to compute the entailments of his measurements.

These rules can also be used to propose measurements. For example:

If V5 = low, then R9 is open.
If I3 = high, then [R1, R9, C6] is bad.
If I9 = low, then [R4, Q4, T1] is bad.
.
.
.

First, pull out all the rules whose consequences mention components still in the candidate set. From those choose an antecedent which is still unknown, but which if known, would provide maximum information about the remaining components in the candidate set. Maximum information gain is a function of the cost of measuring the antecedent and how well it works to split the candidate space in half. In the above example, we would measure I3.

What are some of the problems of using this approach to troubleshoot? The main problem is illustrated by the knowledge engineer trying to fit empirical associations into the knowledge base. I'd estimate that even a simple circuit like the IP-28 requires something like 10,000 rules. So, what happens when you have to add the 10,001st rule? Where do you put it? Well, you just don't know. The rules are flat and unstructured. How do you know the new rule doesn't contradict previous ones? How do you know that you haven't missed some set of faults? It's almost impossible to tell, and that's the intrinsic fatal flaw of any troubleshooting scheme based on empirical associations.

There are advantages to this approach, however. One is that the knowledge is now explicit in the program. It's also a bit easier to modify and we've got some inference, although it's very weak. However, its robustness is still suspect because there are 10,000 rules that had to be written down. The generality is low, but it's better because 10,000 rules are better than 100,000 lines of Pascal. Efficiency is actually good because the measurements that it proposes depend on previous measurements. In fact, it comes close to being optimal. Constructibility is still bad, however, because extracting 10,000 rules is a very painful task.

Before I move on to more complicated stuff, let's look at a very simple idea that gets around many of the problems associated with the empirical association method. Consider the pool of rules. We notice that the pool can be broken into subsets associated with circuit modules. That observation is based on the fact that the function of a circuit arises out of this structure. The device has a physical manifestation. This structure can be used to organize the rules.

Let's say the knowledge base contains rules which state that if V6 is low, this implies that Q6 is all right or "OK." If V6 is low, that implies that Q5 is OK; and if V6 is low, that implies that R6 is OK. If a troubleshooter incorporates an explicit notion of structure, these three rules can be collapsed into one rule: If V6 is low, this implies that V (ref) is OK. This idea is very simple, but it actually gives you a surprising amount of leverage. For example, if you see that the same antecedent says something about 3 of the 4 components of a module, maybe there's a rule missing for the fourth component.

Similarly, a causal model like that of Rieger and Grinberg can be used in the same way to organize the rules. In fact, it really doesn't matter much what is used to organize the rules. If there's only a little bit of truth in what you use to organize rules, the robustness is going to be improved as it is easier to notice missing rules.

The three approaches to troubleshooting we've discussed thus far have ignored the fact that the device operates as a consequence of the behavior of its parts. That's a radical observation for the people in the empirical association camp. The idea of the fourth approach to troubleshooting, the use of deep knowledge about behavior, is very simple. Consider the example in Figure 2:

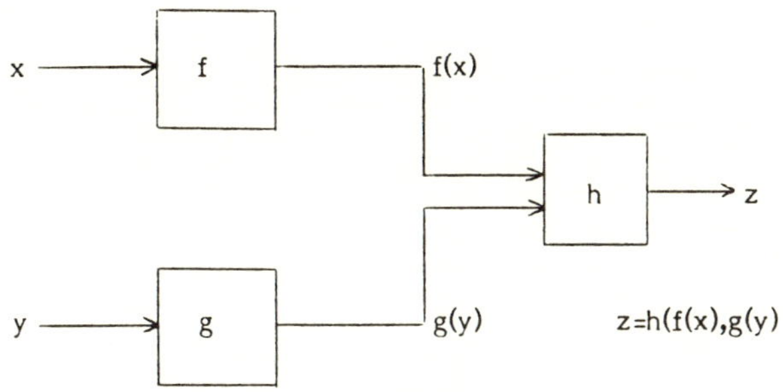

Figure 2.

There are two inputs to the device: x and y. X goes through module f causing f(x), y goes through module g causing g(y), and both are inputs to module h causing output (h(f(x),g(y)). This sort of reasoning allows us to compute an expectation of what the value at z must be if we know what are the inputs. Then we can make a measurement and see if it differs from expectations. Let's suppose that z measures differently than expected. One possibility is that h is faulted. Or, we can assume h is OK and g is correct and compute what the faulty f(x) is. Knowing x and the faulty f(x) we can compute the fault in f.

That's not a bad idea, but it won't quite work. It might work for simple cases like this one, but it won't work in general. Often this algorithm will impugn every component of the circuit. The reason is that if the circuit contains memory or feedback or is analog or if the wires are bidirectional or the functions are hard to invert, the method won't work. In other words, we are going to have to do something different, because I've just covered 99 percent of the circuits in the world.

What we should do is describe the behavior of every component by a constraint that can be used in any way--forward, backward, or sideways. There's no notion of forward and backward in constraints. An example of constraint is Ohm's Law E=IR. If you know the voltage and the current, then you can determine the resistance. It doesn't <u>cause</u> the resistance. If you know the resistance and the current, you can determine the voltage, but the resistance and the current don't <u>cause</u> the voltage.

We can use the constraint propagation, the idea of composing constraints with each other, to construct expectations. In Figure 3, suppose you measured the voltage between node 15 and node 14 and node 16 and node 14. Using Kirchhoff's Voltage Law, you can deduce the voltage across resistor R5. If you know the voltage across the resistor, you can deduce the current through it using Ohm's Law of constraint. This leads to an expected R5 current of 3 milliamperes (mA). However, that's only valid assuming that R5's resistance hasn't shifted from what it should be. If R5 has shifted in value, the predicted and measured currents are going to be different. Thus, R5 is an assumption of the propagated current of 3 mA.

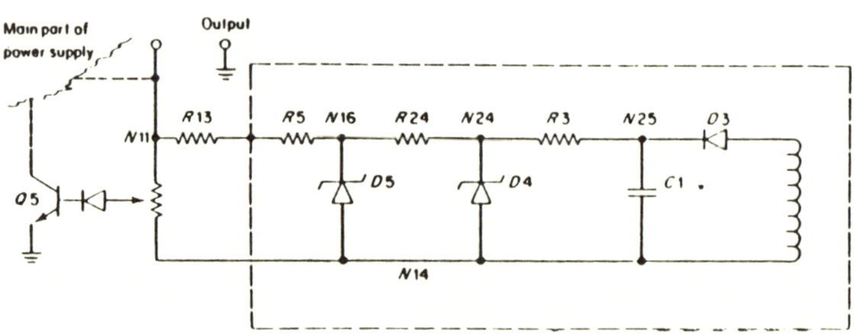

Figure 3. Constant voltage source

Moving on, the voltage across D5 was measured to be 34 volts which is less than the zener's breakdown voltage. Thus the current through D5 is zero. Notice that this propagation depends on two assumptions: (1) R5 is not faulted and (2) D5 is not faulted. Using Kirchhoff's Current Law we can propagate this current through R4. As I'm assuming there are no extra wires or open wires, this propagation step adds no new assumptions. Knowing the current through R4 allows us to propagate the voltage across it by Ohm's Law. Of course, this propagation is dependent on R4 still having its expected resistance. Thus, the voltage across R4 is 7.18 volts assuming that R5, D5, and R4 have not shifted in value.

Now, how do we use this information to troubleshoot? The basic idea of deep knowledge about behavior as an approach is that the propagations allow you to construct expectations of circuit behavior. If you construct an expectation and make measurements at a point of expectation, you get some information. There are two things that can happen. On the one hand, the measurement can corroborate the expectation. For example, we might measure the voltage across R4 and discover it actually is 7.18 volts. Thus, the fault does not lie in R5, D5, or R4. On the other hand, if we discover that the voltage across R4 is zero volts, the measurement disagrees with the propagation. We would then conclude that either R5, D5, or R4 is faulted. Furthermore, if we assume that the circuit contains only one fault, every other component in the circuit is unfaulted.

This troubleshooter proposes new measurements by choosing those expectations to corroborate or conflict. It examines the set of all expectations that have been constructed for which a measurement has not yet been made, picks the one which gives maximum information, and then makes that measurement. In other words, we have a troubleshooter that both computes entailments and proposes measurements.

Lest you think that I am completely out in a dream world with this simplistic scheme, let me illustrate a few of the things that have to be patched to make the propagation-based troubleshooter actually work. In the real world there are meter errors, manufacturing errors, and wide tolerances on transistor specifications. Therefore, the troubleshooter has to consider the variability, that's problem number one. Second, I know that component models aren't all constraints. The models are made up of inequalities on voltages and currents. So actual component models are fairly complex.

The second reason you might think that I'm wrong is that the corroborations and conflicts all go out the window when the values have tolerances. For example, it gets far more complicated when comparing expectations with measurements. In general, you have four cases. First, if the ranges of the expectation and the measured don't overlap, you've got a conflict unambiguously. Second, if they corroborate and they're roughly equal, you actually do not have the necessary evidence to rule out the assumptions underlying the expectations. This corroboration could be correct, yet the underlying components could still be faulted because there is so much variability in the values. Another more sophisticated mechanism is used to solve that problem.

Third, what happens if the measurement is very tight but the expectation has a very broad range, or the reverse? For each of these cases, information can be gathered about the candidate set.

So far we are constructing expectations that are not causal, we are merely using rules about how components behave in general. Now, one of the advantages of this new approach is that all of a sudden all the necessity for most of the empirical associations goes away. Most of the rules get automatically handled by the coincidence mechanism. The propagation-based mechanism directly obviates the need for most of the rules by instead making inferences about the faultedness of circuit components based on first principles.

Suppose, for example, we had a rule which said if the voltage across R5 was low, the CCS was open. Under the old system, another rule is needed which states that if the current through R5 was low, the CCS is open. In the propagation-based scheme, this second rule is now superfluous. If you discover the current through R5, the propagator will construct the expectation that the voltage across it is low, and that triggers "voltage low." (That expectation is based on R5, so that antecedent assumption must also be included in the consequent of the rule.) As a consequence, the rule set collapses dramatically. In fact, by this point, we have reduced the original set of 10,000 rules to about 100.

Since there are only 100 rules, robustness is dramatically improved. A fault in a component is now a violation of its own law, not a guess that some designer made beforehand. Generality is also much better. The approach can be applied to more circuits. Its efficiency is good, and its constructibility has become a lot better because now there are only 100 rules to discover. Look at what we've done--we've beaten on the knowledge until there's almost no knowledge in the system about the particular circuit. Instead, we've got a little bit of knowledge, deep knowledge, about the domain of circuits in general, and that deep knowledge applies to all circuits, not just this one.

Next, let's consider the fifth approach to troubleshooting deep knowledge about fault modes. So far we've only talked about a fault as being deviation from expected behavior, but devices also have fault modes, and those fault modes are very important. For example, consider this circuit:

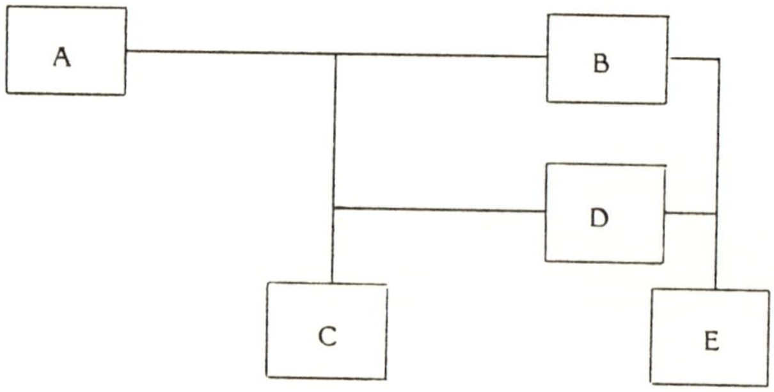

Suppose we measure a voltage at the input A, construct an expectation of what the voltage must be at the output of A using the model for A, and so on through B and E. Now we make a second measurement at the output of E and find it that conflicts. We can immediately deduce that one of A, B, or E is faulted. If there is only one fault in the circuit, D and C are definitely unfaulted. That's as far as we got by the old strategy, but we can actually get a lot further by asking the question: What caused it? Not what caused the fault, but what caused the expectations to go awry, and the only thing that can cause the expectation to go awry is something wrong with A, B, or E. I'm going to introduce a second propagator. The first propagator propagated behavior, the second one propagates errors or faults. You can only propagate causally back up through an expectation that you've constructed. The only thing that could cause the expectation to be wrong is A, B, or E. So this second propagator inverts expectations that have already been constructed by the first propagator. So, therefore, I need to have more rules about components and it gets rather complicated. In fact, there's quite a few rules one needs in order to run the propagator backwards, but I won't talk about these new rules in this talk.

This reduces the rule set from 100 to 25. Now why does it do that? We did not build this fault propagator for this purpose. We thought it would just give us better explanations, but it actually helped. In the old scheme, a component was either faulted or unfaulted. That means that the only information recorded was whether a component was faulted or not. But suppose I measure a voltage to be low, that might tell me that R6 can't be high. You know that, I know that, but the program with the candidate sets can't represent that fact. So if it makes a second measurement whose entailment is that R6 can't be low, all of a sudden you and I know that if R6 isn't high, and it isn't low, then it's OK. But the candidate set representation won't support that inference. By extending the representation to include fault modes, this information that the fault propagator collects is utilized. In the old scheme, there were many extra rules to handle situations like this. In the R6 example, the R6 rule could be deleted.

The game is--we want to get rid of knowledge. Knowledge isn't power. Knowledge is evil. So we're left with 25 rules for this device. And the first 16 are shown in Figure 4. In doing research, we spent a lot of time staring at these rules to identify what kinds of inferences lay behind them. What really stuck out from looking at those rules is that each depended on a very sophisticated inference on a causal model. So that pushed us into the research we're doing right now: How to use a causal model to troubleshoot a circuit.

Let me briefly illustrate this sixth and final approach to troubleshooting by showing an inference that the other propagation-based troubleshooters can't make but a causal model can. Let's look back at Figure 3. The rule is, "If Q5 is off, then this reference can't be too low." The only way the reference is connected to the rest of the power supply is through Q5. This is a topological inference. That doesn't tell you the rule, it's just an observation to help you understand the rule.

This rule is based on the fact that Q5 disconnects the voltage reference from the power supply. Suppose we have a causal model which identifies the two main control feedback paths of the IP-28. Thus, the way the supply works, is to compute the minimum of the two settings, and that's the output. This minimum is computed through a feedback path in which Q5 is a part. If this voltage reference were too low, it would turn on Q5 causing a symptom at the output. So there's no way that a low voltage on the voltage reference could be contributing to the power supply's faulty behavior if Q5 were disconnected. If Q5 were disconnected (i.e., Q5 off) the output could be high due to the reference being too high, but the output could not be too low due to the reference being too low. That's an example

```
Demon # 1  :
        (AND (STATE Q2 SATURATED-OFF))-->>
        (OK (BLK CURRENT/SOURCE)
            (BLK RECTIFIER/FILTER))
Demon # 2  :
        (AND (VOLTAGE (N11 GROUND)
                      VL-OVER))-->>
        (AND (LOCAL!/L REG OVER-V-LIM)
             (ASSERT (STATE IP-28 HIGH)))
Demon # 3  :
        (AND (VOLTAGE (N11 GROUND)
                      VL))-->>
        (LOCAL!/L REG OVER-I-LIM OK)
Demon # 4  :
        (AND (CURRENT N/OP CL-OVER))-->>
        (AND (LOCAL!/L REG OVER-I-LIM)
             (ASSERT (STATE IP-28 HIGH)))
Demon # 5  :
        (AND (VOLTAGE (N11 GROUND)
                      VL-UNDER)
             (CURRENT N/OP CL-UNDER))-->>
        (AND (LOCAL!/L IP-28 LOW)
             (ASSERT (STATE IP-28 LOW)))
Demon # 6  :
        (AND (VOLTAGE (N11 GROUND)
                      VERY-LOW)
             (CURRENT N/OP CL-UNDER))-->>
        (AND (LOCAL!/L IP-28 VERY-LOW)
             (ASSERT (STATE IP-28 LOW)))
Demon # 7  :
        (AND (CURRENT N/OP CL-UNDER))-->>
        (ELIM!/L REG OVER-I-LIM)
Demon # 8  :
        (AND (CURRENT N/OP CL))-->>
        (LOCAL!/L REG OVER-V-LIM OK)
Demon # 9
        (AND (STATE Q5 OFF))-->>
        (ELIM!/L V/DIF/CONT LIMIT-TOO-LOW ALWAYS-ON)
Demon # 10  :
        (AND (VOLTAGE (N11 GROUND)
                      VL-UNDER))-->>
        (ELIM!/L REG OVER-V-LIM)
Demon # 11  :
        (AND (VOLTAGE (N11 GROUND)
                      VERY-LOW))-->>
        (ELIM!/L REG OVER-V-LIM)
Demon # 12  :
        (AND (STATE Q6 OFF))-->>
        (AND (ELIM!/L I/VOL/CONT LIMIT-TOO-LOW ALWAYS-ON)
             (OK C5))
Demon # 13  :
        (AND (STATE Q5 ON))-->>
        (LOCAL-OR-FAULTED!/L (I/VOL/CONT ALWAYS-OFF LIMIT-TOO-HIGH)
                             (V/DIF/CONT ALWAYS-ON LIMIT-TOO-LOW
                                         LIMIT-TOO-HIGH))
Demon # 14  :
        (AND (CURRENT C/Q2 LOW))-->>
        (ELIM!/L CCS OK)
Demon # 15  :
        (AND (VOLTAGE (N4 GROUND)
                      NORMAL))-->>
        (ELIM!/L CCS HIGH-IMPEDENCE)
Demon # 16  :
        (AND (CURRENT C/Q2 NORMAL))-->>
```

Figure 4. Demon Rules

of an inference that cannot be captured in the other five troubleshooting approaches. The only reasonable way I've seen to do it is to construct a mechanistic model.

Here's my current game: You give me a schematic for a power supply, the program reads it in, parses it, constructs a causal model, then generates the 25 rules from the causal models. Then I have a complete troubleshooter. I have a troubleshooter that works if you give it a power supply, and it will troubleshoot it. You don't have to sit there and add more things to it. It works solely from the schematic like a human technician.

So look what I've done. I've used theory and inference to beat knowledge to almost nothing. The little bit of knowledge that I do have is about circuits in general. I have achieved robustness, generality, efficiency, and constructibility. But, there's a very high price: Why does it work and what did I have to do? It works because there was a deep theory of circuits, and it had to be made computational. The fundamental business of AI is getting deep theories of various domains and making them computational. But don't send away for my troubleshooter. I haven't got it completely working yet and there are still a few problems.

ABOUT THE AUTHOR

Dr. Johan de Kleer is a member of the Intelligent Systems Laboratory at XEROX Palo Alto Research Center. He is interested in understanding how machines work and how they can be repaired.

DIAGNOSIS BASED ON DESCRIPTION OF STRUCTURE AND FUNCTION

Randall Davis, Howard Shrobe, Walter Hamscher, Karen Wieckert, Mark Shirley

The Artificial Intelligence Laboratory
Massachusetts Institute of Technology

Steve Polit

Digital Equipment Corp.

Abstract

While expert systems have traditionally been built using large collections of rules based on empirical associations, interest has grown recently in the use of systems that reason from representations of structure and function. Our work explores the use of such models in troubleshooting digital electronics.

We describe our work to date on (*i*) a language for describing structure, (*ii*) a language for describing function, and (*iii*) a set of principles for troubleshooting that uses the two descriptions to guide its investigation.

In discussing troubleshooting we show why the traditional approach --- test generation --- solves a different problem and we discuss a number of its practical shortcomings. We consider next the style of debugging known as discrepancy detection and demonstrate why it is a fundamental advance over traditional test generation. Further exploration, however, demonstrates that in its standard form this approach is incapable of dealing with commonly known classes of faults. We explain the shortcoming as arising from a number of interesting assumptions made implicitly when using the techinque.

In discussing how to repair the problems uncovered, we argue for the primacy of *models of causal interaction*, rather than the traditional fault models. We point out the importance of making these models explicit, separated from the troubleshooting mechanism, and retractable in much the same sense that inferences are retracted in current systems. We report on progress to date in implementing this approach.

An earlier version of this report appeared in *Proc AAAI*, 1982.

This report describes research done at the Artificial Intelligence Laboratory of the Massachusetts Institute of Technology. Support for the laboratory's Artificial Intelligence research on electronic troubleshooting is provided in part by the Digital Equipment Corp.

Introduction

While expert systems have traditionally been built using large collections of rules based on empirical associations (e.g., [9]) interest has grown recently in the use of systems that reason from representations of structure and function (e.g., [8], [7], [5]). Our work explores the use of such models in troubleshooting digital electronics.

We view the task as a process of reasoning from behavior to structure, or more precisely, from misbehavior to structural defect. We are typically presented with a machine exhibiting some form of incorrect behavior and must infer the structural abberation that is producing it. The task is interesting and difficult because the devices we want to examine are complex and because there is no well developed theory of diagnosis for them.

Our ultimate goal is to provide a level of performance comparable to that of an experienced engineer, including reading and reasoning from schematics; selecting, running, and interpreting the results of diagnostics; selecting and interpreting the results of input test patterns, etc. The initial focus of our work has been to develop three elements that appear to be fundamental to all of these capabilities. We require (*i*) a language for describing structure, (*ii*) a language for describing function, and (*iii*) a set of principles for troubleshooting that uses the two descriptions to guide its investigation. This paper describes our progress to date on each of those elements.

In discussing troubleshooting we show why the traditional approach --- test generation --- solves a different problem and we discuss a number of its practical shortcomings. We consider next the style of debugging known as discrepancy detection and demonstrate why it is a fundamental advance over traditional test generation. Further exploration, however, demonstrates that in its standard form this approach is incapable of dealing with commonly known classes of faults. We explain the shortcoming as arising from a number of interesting assumptions made implicitly when using the techinque.

In discussing how to repair the problems uncovered, we argue for the primacy of *models of causal interaction*, rather than the traditional fault models. We point out the importance of making these models explicit, separated from the troubleshooting mechanism, and retractable in much the same sense that inferences are retracted in current systems. We report on progress to date in implementing this approach.

Structure Description

By structure description we mean simply the topology --- the connectivity of components. A number of structure description languages have been developed, but most, having originated in work on machine design, deal exclusively with *functional* components, rarely making any provision for describing *physical* organization.[1] In doing machine diagnosis, however, we are dealing with a collection of hardware whose functional and physical organizations are both important. The same gate may be both (*i*) functionally a part of a multiplexor, which is functionally a part of a datapath, etc., and (*ii*) physically a part of chip E67, which is physically part of board 5, etc. Both of these hierarchies are relevant at different times in the diagnosis and both are included in our language.

We use the functional hierarchy as the primary organizing principle because, as noted, our basic task involves reasoning from function to structure rather than the other way around.[2] The functional organization is also typically richer than the structural (more levels to the hierarchy, more terms in the vocabulary), and hence provides a useful organizing principle for the large number of individual physical components. Compare, for example, the functional organization of a board (e.g., a

---

1. This is curiously true even for languages billing themselves as *computer hardware description languages.* They rarely mention a piece of physical hardware.
2. We are typically confronted with a machine that misbehaves, not one that has visible structural damage.

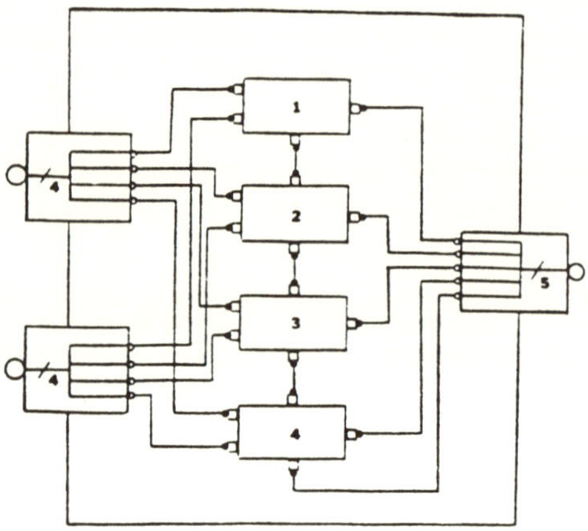

Figure 2 · Next level of structure of the adder.

The structural description of a module is expressed as a set of commands for building the module. Hence the adder of Fig. 2 is described by indicating how to "build" it (Fig. 3). These commands are then executed by the system, causing it to build data structures that model all the components and connections shown. The resulting data structures are organized around the individual components. Executing the first expression of Fig. 3, for example, produces 4 data structures that model the individual slices of the adder.

```
(definemodule  adder
    (repeat 4 i
        (part slice-i adder-slice)
        (run-wire (input-1 adder) (input-1 slice-i))
        (run-wire (input-2 adder) (input-2 slice-i))
        (run-wire (output slice-i)  (sum adder))

    (repeat 3 i  (run-wire (carry-out slice-i)  (carry-in slice-[i+1])))
    (run-wire (carry-out slice-4)  (sum adder)) )
```

Figure 3 · Parts are described by a pathname through the part hierarchy, e.g., (input-1 adder). This description can be abbreviated as a *bitslice* organization, but is expanded here for illustration.)

This approach to structure description offers two interesting properties: (a) a natural merging of procedural and object-oriented descriptions, and (b) the use of analogic representations.

To see the merging of descriptions, note that we have two different ways of thinking about structure. We describe a device by indicating how to build it (the procedural view), but then want to think about it as a collection of individual objects (the object-oriented view). The first view is memory controller with cache, address translation hardware, etc.) with the physical organization (1 pc board, 137 chips).

The most basic level of our description vocabulary is built on three concepts: *modules*, *ports*, and *terminals* (Fig. 1). A module can be thought of as a standard black box. A module has at least two ports; ports are the place where information flows into or out of a module. Every port has at least two terminals, one terminal on the outside of the port and one or more inside. Terminals are primitive elements; they store logic levels representing the information flowing into or out of a device through their port, but are otherwise devoid of substructure.

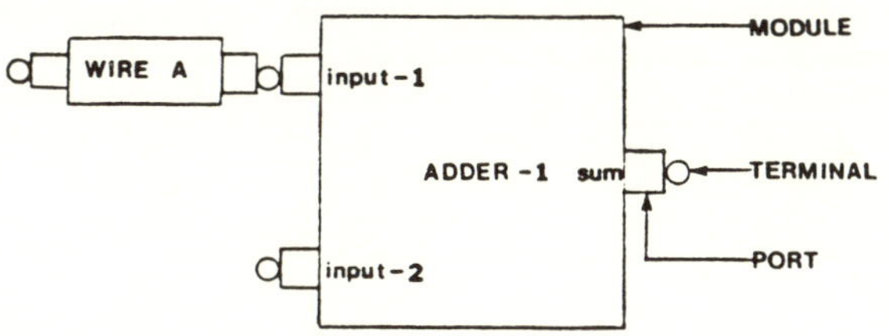

Figure 1 - The basic terms used in structure description.

Two modules are attached to one another by superimposing their terminals. In Fig. 1, for example, wire A is a module that has been attached to input-1 of the adder module in this fashion.

The language is hierarchical in the usual sense; modules at any level may have substructure. In practice, our descriptions terminate at the gate level in the functional hierarchy and the chip level in the physical hierarchy, since for our purposes these are black boxes --- only their behavior (or misbehavior) matters. Fig. 2 shows the next level of structure of the adder and illustrates why ports may have multiple terminals on their inside: ports provide the important function of shifting level of abstraction. It may be useful to think of the information flowing along wire A as an integer between 0 and 15, yet we need to be able to map those four bits into the four single-bit lines insider the adder. Ports are the place where such information is kept. They have machinery (described below) that allows them to map information arriving at their outer terminal onto their inner terminals. The default provided in the system accomplishes the simple map required in Fig. 2.

Since our ultimate intent is to deal with hardware on the scale of a mainframe computer, we need terms in the vocabulary capable of describing levels of organization more substantial than the terms used at the circuit level. We can, for example, refer to *horizontal*, *vertical*, and *bitslice* organizations, describing a memory, for instance, as "two rows of five 1K ram's". We use these specifications in two ways: as a description of the organization of the device and a specification for the pattern of interconnections among the components.

Our eventual aim is to provide an integrated set of descriptions that span the levels of hardware organization ranging from interconnection of individual modules, through higher level of organization of modules, and eventually on up through the register transfer and PMS level [2]. Some of this requires inventing vocabulary like that above, in other places (e.g., PMS) we may able to make use of existing terminology and concepts.

convenient for *describing* structure, the second makes it easy to *answer questions* about it, questions like connectivity, location, etc., that are important in signal tracing and other troubleshooting techniques. The two descriptions are unified because the system simply "runs" the procedural description to produce the data structures modeling the device. This gives us the benefit of both approaches with no additional effort and no chance that the two will get out of sync.

The representation is analogic because the data structures built are isomorphic to the structure being described. "Superimposing" two terminals, for instance, is implemented as a merging of the structure representing the terminals. The resulting data structures are thus connected in the LISP sense in the same ways that the objects are connected in Fig. 2. The benefit here is primarily conceptual, it simply makes the resulting structures somewhat easier to understand.

Our description language has been built on a foundation provided by a subset of DPL [1]. While DPL as originally implemented was specific to VLSI design, it proved relatively easy to "peel off" the top level of language (which dealt with chip layout) and rebuild on that base the new layers of language described above.

Since pictures are a fast, easy and natural way to describe structure, we have developed a simple circuit drawing system that permits interactive entry of pictures like those in Figs. 2 and 4. Circuits are entered with a combination of mouse movements and key strokes; the resulting structures are then "parsed" into the language shown in Fig. 3.

Behavior Description

A variety of techniques have been explored in describing behavior, including simple rules for mapping inputs to outputs, petri nets, and unrestricted chunks of code. Simple rules are useful where device behavior is uncomplicated, petri nets are useful where the focus is on modeling parallel events, and unrestricted code is often the last resort when more structured forms of expression prove too limited or awkward. Various combinations of these three have also been explored.

Our initial implementation is based on a constraint-like approach [10]. Conceptually a constraint is simply a relationship. The behavior of the adder of Fig. 1, for example, can be expressed by saying that the logic levels of the terminals on ports *input-1*, *input-2* and *sum* are related in the obvious fashion.

In practice, this is accomplished by defining a set of rules covering all different computations (the three for the adder are shown below) and setting them up as demons that watch the appropriate terminals. A complete description of a module, then, is composed of its structural description as outlined earlier and a behavior description in the form of rules that interrelate the logic levels at its terminals.

```
to get sum from (input-1 input-2) do (+ input-1 input-2)
to get input-1 from (sum input-2) do (- sum input-2)
to get input-2 from (sum input-1) do (- sum input-1)
```

A set of rules like these is in keeping with the original conception of constraints, which emphasized the non-directional, relationship character of the information. When we attempt to use it to model causality and function, however, we have to be careful. This approach is well suited to modeling causality and behavior of analog circuits, where devices are largely non-directional. But we can hardly say that the last two rules above are a good description of the *behavior* of an adder chip --- the device doesn't do subtraction; putting logic levels at its output and one input does not cause a logic level to appear on its other input.

The last two rules really model the *inferences we make about the device*. Hence we find it useful to distinguish between rules representing *flow of electricity* (digital behavior, the first rule above) and rules representing *flow of inference* (conclusions we can make about the device, the next two rules). This not only keeps the representation "clean", but as we will see, it provides part of the foundation for the troubleshooting mechanism.

A set of constraints is a relatively simple mechanism for specifying behavior, in that it offers no obvious support for expressing behavior that falls outside the "relation between terminals" view. The approach also has known limits. Propagating values, for example, works well when dealing with simple quantities like numbers or logic levels, but runs into difficulties if it becomes necessary to work with symbolic expressions.[3]

The approach has, nevertheless, provided a good starting point for our work and offers advantages like maintenance of dependency information: an indication of how the value at a terminal was obtained, expressed in terms of what rule computed the value and what other values the rule used in performing its computation. This is very useful in tracing backward to the source of misbehavior.

Our system design offers a number of features which, while not necessarily novel, do provide useful performance. For example, our approach offers a unity of device description and simulation, since the descriptions themselves are "runnable". That is, the behavior descriptions associated with a given module allow us to simulate the behavior of that module; the interconnection of modules specified in the structure description then causes results computed by one module to propagate to another. Thus we don't need a separate description or body of code as the basis for the simulation, we can simply "run" the description itself. This ensures that our description of a device and the machinery that simulates it can never disagree about what to do, as can be the case if the simulation is produced by a separately maintained body of code.

Our use of a hierarchic approach and the terminal, port, module vocabulary makes multi-level simulation very easy. In simulating any module we can either run the behavior associated with the terminals of that module (simulating the module in a single step), or "run the substructure" of that module, simulating the device according to its next level of structure. Since the abstraction shifting behavior of ports is also implemented with the constraint mechanism, we have a convenient uniformity and economy of machinery: we can enable either the behavior that spans the entire module or the behavior that spans the port.

Varying the level of simulation is useful for speed (no need to simulate verified substructure), and provides as well a simple check on structure and behavior specification: we can compare the results generated by the module's behavior specification with those generated by the next lower level of simulation. Mismatches typically mean a mistake in structure specification at the lower level.

We believe it is important in this undertaking to include descriptions of both design and implementation, and to distinguish carefully between them.[4] A wire, for example, is a device whose behavior is specified simply as the guarantee that a logic level imposed on one of its terminals will be propagated to the other terminal. Our structure description allows us to indicate the *intended* direction of information flow along a wire, but our simulation is not misled by this. This is, of course, important in troubleshooting, since some of the more difficult faults to locate are those that cause devices to behave not as we know they "should", but as they are in fact electrically capable of doing.

We encourage this separation by having a set of prototypical modules whose structure and behavior are defined first, independently of any particular circuit. Adders, wires, and-gates, etc., are defined "in vacuou", and then devices are constructed by assembling and interconnecting instances

---

3. What, for example, do we do if we know that the output of an or-gate is 1 but we don't know the value at either input? We can refrain from making any conclusion about the inputs, which makes the rules easy to write but misses some information. Or we can write a rule which express the value on one input in terms of the value on the other input. This captures the information but produces problems when trying to use the resulting symbolic expression elsewhere.

4. A related concept is described in [4], labelled the "no function in structure" principle.

of those prototypes. While this offers no formal guarantees that our behavior definitions are accurate, by distingushing clearly between behavior definition of an individual module and its intended use in a circuit, and by forcing every module of a particular type to share the same behavior specification, we provide an environment that strongly encourages attention to the issue.

Finally, the behavior description is also a convenient mechanism for fault insertion. A wire stuck at zero, for example, is modeled by giving the wire a behavior specification that maintains its terminals at logic level 0 despite any attempt to change them. Bridges, opens, etc., are similarly easily modeled.

Troubleshooting

The traditional approach to troubleshooting digital circuitry (e.g., [3]) has, for our purposes, a number of significant drawbacks. Perhaps most important, it is a theory of *test generation*, not a theory of *diagnosis*. Given a specified fault, it is capable of determining a set of input values that will detect the fault (ie, a set of values for which the output of the faulted circuit differs from the output of a good circuit). The theory tells us how to move from faults to sets of inputs; it provides little help in determining what fault to consider, or which component to suspect.

These questions are a central issue in our work for several reasons. First, the level of complexity we want to deal with precludes the use of diagnosis trees, which can require exhaustive consideration of possible faults. Second, our basic task is repair, rather than initial testing. Hence the problem confronting us is "Given the following piece of misbehavior, determine the fault." We are not asking whether a machine is free of faults, we know that it fails and know how it fails. Given the complexity of the device, it is important to be able to use this information as a focus for further exploration.

A second drawback of the existing theory is its use of a set of explicitly enumerated faults. Since the theory is based on boolean logic, it is strongly oriented toward faults whose behavior can be modeled as some form of permanent binary value, typically the result of stuck-ats and opens. One consequence of this is the paucity of useful results concerning bridging faults.

A response to these problems has been the use of what we may call the "discrepancy detection" approach ([6], [4], [7]). The basic insight of the technique is the substitution of violated expectations for specific fault models. That is, instead of postulating a possible fault and exploring its consequences, the technique simply looks for mismatches between the values it expected from correct operation and those actually obtained. This allows detection of a wide range of faults because misbehavior is now simply defined as anything that isn't correct, rather than only those things produced by a struck-at on a line.

This approach has a number of advantages. It is, first of all, fundamentally a diagnostic technique, since it allows systematic isolation of the possibly faulty devices, and does so without having to precompute fault dictionaries, diagnosis trees, or the like. Second, it appears to make it unnecessary to to specify a set of expected faults (we comment further on this below). As a result, it can detect a much wider range of faults, including any systematic misbehavior exhibited by a single component. The approach also allows natural use of hierarchical descriptions, a marked advantage for dealing with complex structures.

This approach is a good starting point, but has a number of important limitations built into it. We work through a simple example to show the basic idea and use the same example to comment on its shortcomings.

Consider the circuit in Fig. 4.[5] If we set the inputs as shown, the behavior descriptions will

5. As is common in the field, we make the usual assumptions that there is only a single source of error and the error is not transient. Both of these are important in the reasoning that follows.

indicate that we should expect 12 at F. If, upon measuring, we find the value at F to be 10, we have a conflict between observed results and our model of correct behavior. We employ the notion of dependency-directed backtracking [10] to enumerate the possible sources of the problem. We check the dependency record at F to find that the value expected there was determined using the behavior rule for the adder and the values emerging from the first and second multiplier. One of those three must be the source of the conflict, so we have three possibilities to pursue: either the adder behavior rule is inappropriate (ie, the first adder is broken), or one of the two inputs did not have the expected values (and the problem lies further back).

Consideration of the first possibility immediately generates hypothesis #1: adder-1 is broken.

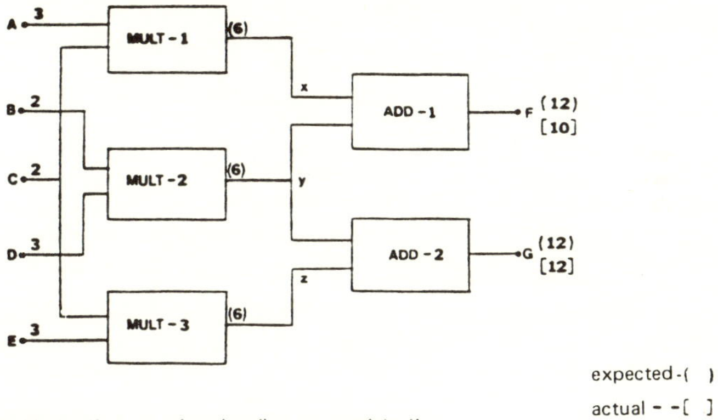

Figure 4 · Troubleshooting example using discrepancy detection.

To pursue the second possibility, we assume that the second input to adder-1 is good. In that case the first input must have been a 4 (reasoning from the result at F, valid behavior of the adder, and one of the inputs), but we expected a 6. Hence we now have a discrepancy at the input to adder-1; we have succeeded in pushing the discrepancy one step further back. The expected value there was based on the behavior rule for the multiplier and the expected value of its inputs. Since the inputs to the multiplier are primitive (supplied by the user), the only alternative along this line of reasoning is that the multiplier is broken. Hence hypothesis #2 is that adder-1 is good and multiplier-1 is faulty.

Pursuing the third possibility: if the first input to adder-1 is good, then the second input must have been a 4 (suggesting that the second multiplier might be bad). But if that were a 4, then the expected value at G would be 10 (reasoning forward through the second adder). We can check this and discover in this case that the output at G is 12. Hence the value on the output of the second multiplier can't be 4, it must be 6, hence the second multiplier can't be causing the current problem.

So we are left with the hypotheses that the malfunction lies in either the first multiplier or the first adder. The diagnosis proceeds in this style, dropping down levels of structural detail as we begin to isolate the source of the error.

This approach is a useful beginning. Note, for example, that it is diagnostic: it enumerates the devices that could have caused the symptoms noted. But the approach also has some clear shortcomings. Consider the slightly revised example shown in Fig. 5. Reasoning just as before,[6] the fault at F leads us to suspect adder-1. But if adder-1 is faulty, then everything else is good. This implies a 6 on lines y and z, and (reasoning forward) a 12 at G. But G has been measured to be 6, hence adder-1 can't be responsible for the current set of symptoms. If adder-1 is good, then the fault at F might result from bad inputs (lines x and y). If the fault is on x, then y has a 6. But (reasoning forward) this means a 12 at G. Once again we encounter a contradiction and eliminate line x as a candidate. We turn to line y, postulate that it is 0. This is consistent with the faults at both F and G, and is in fact the only hypothesis we can generate.

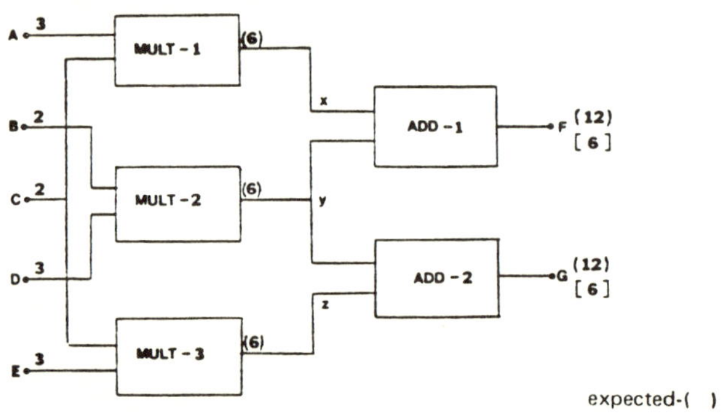

Figure 5 · Troublesome troubleshooting example.

The key phrase here is "the only hypothesis we can generate". In fact, there is another quite reasonable hypothesis: the third multiplier might be bad.[7] But how could this produce errors at both F and G? The key lies in being wary of our models. The thought that digital devices have input and output ports is a convenient abstraction, not an electrical reality. If, as sometimes happens (due to a bent pin, bad socket, etc.), a chip fails to get power, its inputs are no longer guaranteed to act unidirectionally as inputs. If the third multiplier were a chip that failed to get power, it might not only send out a 0 along wire z, but it might also pull down wire C to 0. Hence the symptoms result from a single point of failure (multiplier-3), but the error propagates along an "input" line common to two devices.

The problem with this straightforward use of discrepancy detection lies in its implicit acceptance of unidirectional ports and the reflection of that acceptance in the basic dependency-unwinding machinery. We implicitly assumed that wires get information only from output ports --- when checking the inputs to multiplier-1, we said the inputs were "primitive". We looked only at terminals A and C, never at the other end of the wire at multiplier-3.

Bridges are a second common fault that illustrates an interesting shortcoming in the

6 The eager reader has no doubt already chosen a likely hypothesis. We go through the reasoning in any case, to show that the method outlined generates the same hypothesis and is in fact simply a more formal way of doing what we often do intuitively.

7 Or the first.

approach: the reasoning style used above can *never* hypothesize a bridging fault, again because of implicit assumptions about the model and their subtle reflection in the method. Bridges can be viewed as wires that don't show up in the design. But the traditional approach makes an implicit closed world assumption --- the structure description is assumed to be complete and anything not shown there "doesn't exist". Clearly this is not always true. Bridges are only one manifestation; wiring errors during assembly are another possibility.

Let's review for a moment. One problem with the traditional test generation technology was its use of a very limited fault model. The discrepancy detection approach improves on this substantially by defining a fault as anything that produces behavior different from that expected. This seems to be perfectly general, but, as we illustrated, it is in fact limited in some important ways. We believe it is instructive to examine the source and nature of those limitations.

Models of Causal Interaction

One claim about the discrepancy detection approach is that it makes no assumptions about the character of the fault. Yet our counterexamples show this not to be the case. What is the source of the problem? We believe that the issue is not in fact the character of the fault models, it is assumptions about *models of causal interactions*. In the port problem, for example, the assumption was that there was only one possible *direction of causality* at an input port. For the bridge problem, the assumption was that the only possible *paths of interaction* were the wires shown in the diagram. These are assumptions about pathways of causality, not categories of faults.

There is, of course no problem in having assumptions about causal paths; candidate generation in fact can't function without them. Given a problem noticed at some point in the device, candidate generation attempts to determine which modules could have caused the problem. To answer the question we must know by what mechanisms and pathways modules can interact.

The obvious answer is "wires": modules interact because they're explicitly wired together. But that's clearly not the only possibility. Bridges, as we saw, are an exception; they are "wires" that aren't supposed to be there. But we also might consider thermal interactions, capacitive coupling, transmission line effects, etc., etc.[8]

Our task then, in generating possible candidates, is not to trace wires, it is to *trace paths of causality*. Wires are only the most obvious pathway, they are no means the only one. In fact, given the wide variety of faults we'd like to be able to deal with, we need many different models of interaction.

And that leaves us on the horns of a classic dilemma. If we omit any interaction model, there will be whole classes of faults we will never be able to diagnose. Yet if we include every model, our candidate generation becomes virtually indiscriminate.[9] What can we do?

The "Minimum Perturbation" Principle

We believe there is a way out of the problem, starting with the simple observation that some faults seem to be easier to think about than others. Stuck-ats are perhaps the simplest, failures of function (eg, a ROM cell malfunction) are slightly more difficult, bridges are more difficult yet, with errors of assembly and errors in design at the far end of the scale.

We believe this results from the amount of "behavior perturbation" each fault introduces: a measure of how "big" a change we get in the behavior of a device when we introduce each kind of

8. Notice that we can get behavioral interaction without explicit structural interconnection.

9. Another demonstration that the power lies not in the inference techniques -- in this case discrepancy detection and dependency-directed backtracking -- but in the knowledge that we supply those techniques, i.e., the models of interaction.

error.

Given such a metric, the suggestion is simply to start with the least complicated model and only introduce more the complex ones as the simpler ones fail. We thus come to view diagnosis as trying to find the "smallest" change that accounts for the behavior.

This seems to be a useful heuristic employed by human problem solvers, even in the face of physical absurdity: given a choice, data wires are often assumed to be the source of a problem before control wires. Since that makes no physical sense, the rationale must lie in the fact that it's much easier to envision (and track down) the effects of, say, a bridge fault on a pair of data wires than it is to deal with the same fault across a pair of control wires.

The difficult part, of course, is enumerating and ordering the models. As suggested above, we have made a small start. The system we have developed uses the candidate generation approach described above, and can handle both the original example in Fig. 4 and the "power loss" problem of Fig. 5. Exactly the same tracing through causes is used on both cases, the only change is in the model -- we modify how an input port can behave and the system then produces all three multipliers as candidates. But considerably more remains to be done. in testing and elaborating our list of causal models.

Summary

We have briefly described our work to date on developing languages and mechanisms for describing structure and function in digital circuitry. The techniques we have developed offer a number of useful advantages, including distinguishing clearly between design and implementation.

We traced briefly the evolution of automated troubleshooting. We noted that the traditional technology focuses on test generation, which is only a small part of the diagnostic task. We saw that the discrepancy detection approach offers a significant advance, but has a number of important shortcomings in its standard usage. We found that those limits arise from some subtle and important assumptions about the nature of the causal interactions between modules. Our response was to assert the primacy of models of causality rather than models of faults. We are building a system in which the complexity of the problem is handled by invoking the models explicitly, by layering them carefully, and by being able to retract one model and substitute another in the event of failure.

We have significant work yet to do in determining a more complete and correct list of models, and in determining the consequences of each assumption on the diagnostic process. But we feel this is a key to creating more interesting and powerful diagnostic reasoners.

References

[1] Batali J, Hartheimer A, The design procedure language manual, MIT AI Memo 598, Sept. 1980.

[2] Bell G, Newell A, *Computer Structures: Readings and Examples*, McGraw-Hill, 1971.

[3] Breuer M, Friedman A, *Diagnosis and Reliable Design of Digital Systems*, Computer Science Press, 1976.

[4] Brown J S, Burton R, deKleer J, Pedagogical and knowledge engineering techniques in the SOPHIE systems, Xerox Report CIS-14, 1981.

[5] Davis R, Expert systems: Where are we and where do we go from here? *AAAI Magazine*, summer 1982.

[6] deKleer J, Local methods for localizing faults in electronic circuits, MIT AI Memo 394, 1976.

[7] Genesereth M, The use of hierarchical models in the automated diagnosis of computer systems, Stanford HPP memo 81-20, December 1981.

[8] Patil R, Szolovits P, Schwartz W, Causal understanding of patient illness in medical diagnosis, *Proc. IJCAI-81*, August 1981, pp 893-899.

[9] Shortliffe E, *Computer-Based Medical Consultations: Mycin*, American Elsevier, 1976.

[10] Sussman G, Steele G, Constraints - a language for expressing almost-hierarchical descriptions, *AI Journal*, Vol 14, August 1980, pp 1-40.

DIAGNOSIS VIA CAUSAL REASONING: PATHS OF INTERACTION AND THE LOCALITY PRINCIPLE*

Randall Davis

The Artificial Intelligence Laboratory
Massachusetts Institute of Technology
545 Technology Square
Cambridge, MA 02139

Abstract

Interest has grown recently in developing expert systems that reason "from first principles", i.e., capable of the kind of problem solving exhibited by an engineer who can diagnose a malfunctioning device by reference to its schematics, even though he may never have seen that device before. In developing such a system for troubleshooting digital electronics, we have argued for the importance of pathways of causal interaction as a key concept. We have also suggested using a layered set of interaction paths as a way of constraining and guiding the diagnostic process.

We report here on the implementation and use of these ideas. We show how they make it possible for our system to generate a few sharply constrained hypotheses in diagnosing a bridge fault.

Abstracting from this example, we find a number of interesting general principles at work. We suggest that diagnosis can be viewed as *the interaction of simulation and inference* and we find that the concept of *locality* proves to be extremely useful in understanding why bridge faults are difficult to diagnose and why multiple representations are useful.

*This report describes research done at the Artificial Intelligence Laboratory of the Massachusetts Institute of Technology. Support for the laboratory's Artificial Intelligence research on electronic troubleshooting is provided in part by a grant from the Digital Equipment Corporation.

1. INTRODUCTION

Interest has grown recently in the development of expert systems that reason "from first principles", i.e., from an understanding of the structure and function of the devices they are examining. This approach has been explored in a number of domains, with the "devices" ranging from the gastro-intestinal tract [6], to transistors [1] and digital logic components like adders or multiplexors [3,5]. Our work has focused on the last of these, attempting to build a troubleshooter for digital electronic hardware.

By reasoning from first principles, we mean the kind of skill exhibited by an engineer who can troubleshoot a device by reference to its schematics, even though he may never have seen that particular device before. To do this we require something more than a collection of empirical associations specific to a given machine. We will see that the alternative mechanism has a degree of machine independence and is revealing for what it indicates about the nature of the diagnostic process.

We have previously proposed the use of a layered set of models as a mechanism for guiding diagnosis [2,3]. Here we describe the implementation of that idea and demonstrate its utility in diagnosing a bridge fault. We then abstract from this example to consider why bridge faults are difficult to diagnose and why multiple representations are useful. This results in a number of observations about the nature of diagnostic reasoning and the selection and design of representations.

2. CENTRAL CONCERNS

Four issues are of central concern in this paper. We describe them here briefly, enlarging on them in the remainder of the paper.

† *Diagnosis can be accomplished via the interaction of simulation and inference.*

Given knowledge of the inputs to a device and an understanding of how it is supposed to work, we can generate expectations about its intended behavior. Given observations about its outputs, we can generate conclusions about its actual behavior. Comparison of these two, in particular differences between them, provides the foundation for our troubleshooting.

† *Paths of causal interaction play a central role in diagnosis.*

An important part of the knowledge about a domain is understanding the mechanisms and pathways by which one component can affect another. We argue that such models of interaction are more fundamental than traditional fault models.

† *One technique for dealing with the complexity of diagnosis is layering the paths of interaction.*

To be good at hardware diagnosis, we need to handle many different kinds of paths of interaction. But this presents a problem: including all of them destroys our ability to discriminate among potential candidates, yet omitting any one of them makes it impossible to diagnose an entire class of faults. In response, we suggest the simple expedient of layering the models, using the most restrictive first and falling back on less restrictive models only in the face of contradictions.

† *The concept of* locality *proves to be a useful principle in both diagnosis and the selection of representations.*

We find that the concept of locality, or adjacency, helps to explain why bridge faults are difficult to diagnose: changes small and local in one representation are not necessarily small and local in another. We discover that locality can be defined by reference to the paths of interaction and find that the utility of multiple representations arises in part from the different definitions of locality they offer.

3. BACKGROUND

If we wish to reason from knowledge of structure and behavior, we need a way of describing both. We have developed representations for each of these, described in more detail elsewhere [3,4]. We limit our description here to reviewing only those characteristics of our representations important for understanding the example in Section 4.

The basic unit of description is a *module*, similar in spirit to the notion of a black box. Modules have *ports*, the places through which information enters and leaves the module.

3.1 Functional Organization, Physical Organization

By structure we mean information about the interconnection of modules. Roughly speaking, it is the information that would remain after removing all the textual annotation from a schematic.

Two different ways of organizing this information are particularly relevant to machine diagnosis: the *functional* view gives us the machine organized according to how the modules interact; the *physical* view tells us how it is packaged. We thus prefer to replace the somewhat vague term "structure" by the more precise terms *functional organization* and *physical organization*. In our system every device is described from both perspectives, producing two distinct (but interconnected) descriptions.

Both descriptions are hierarchical in the usual sense: modules at any level may have substructure. An adder, for example, can be described by a functional hierarchy (adder, individual bit slices, half adders, primitive gates) and a physical hierarchy (cabinet, board, chip). The two hierarchies are interconnected, since every primitive module appears in both: a single xor-gate for example, might be both functionally part of a half-adder, which is functionally part of a single bitslice of an adder, etc., and physically part of chip E67, which is physically part of board 5, etc. Cross-link information for primitive modules is supplied by the schematic; additional cross-links can be inferred by intersection (e.g., the adder can be said to be on board 3 because all of its primitive components are in chips on board 3).

3.2 Describing Behavior

We define behavior in terms of the relationship between the information entering and leaving a module, and describe it by writing a set of rules. A complete specification of a module, then, includes its structural description as outlined above and a behavior description in the form of rules interrelating the information at its ports.

As we have noted elsewhere [3,4], we use rules that capture two distinctly different forms of knowledge: *simulation rules* model the electrical behavior of a device, while *inference rules* capture the reasoning we can do about it.

As a simple example, consider the behavior of an OR gate. The device simulation rule is[1]

```
If either input is a 1, then the output is 1, else
the output is 0
```

1. This has been rendered in English to make it clear; for an example of the internal syntax see [3].

One of the device inference rules is

`If the output is 0, then both inputs must have been 0.`

Since the device is electrically unidirectional, it is clear that only the first rule can be modeling physical causality. The second rule, and the inference rules in general, capture conclusions we can make about the inputs of the device given its output.

This approach to describing behavior is very simple, but has nevertheless provided a good starting point for our work.

3.3 Troubleshooting

In previous papers [2,3] we outlined a progression of techniques that have been used in automated reasoning about circuits. We discussed test generation and argued that it handles only part of the problem, because it requires that we choose a part to test and specify how it might be failing. We then described discrepancy detection, showing how it offered important advantages.

But in examining cases involving a bridge fault or power failure, we discovered that straightforward use of discrepancy detection seemed unable to generate the appropriate candidates. We argued that the problem lay in distinguishing carefully between the machinery we use for solving problems and the knowledge that we give that machinery to work with.

3.3.1 Discrepancy Detection and Candidate Generation

Since understanding both the strengths and limitations of discrepancy detection is important in the remainder of this paper, we review the technique briefly. Consider the simple example shown in Figure 1.

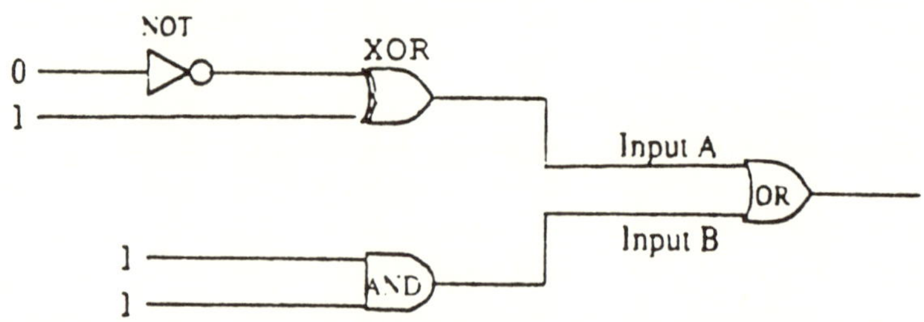

Figure 1 - Simple troubleshooting example

Assume that the actual device yields a 0, producing a discrepancy between what our simulation rules predicted and what the device produced.

We begin the process of generating plausible candidates --- devices whose misbehavior can explain the symptoms --- by asking why we expected a 1 at the output. There are three reasons: we expected that the OR gate was working, we expected `INPUT-A` to be 0, and `INPUT-B` to be 1. Assuming that there is a single point of failure, one of these expectations must be incorrect.

If the first expectation is incorrect, then the OR gate is failing, hence we can add that to our candidate list.

If one of the other expectations is incorrect, the OR gate is working and the problem lies further back. But if the OR gate is working, the inference rules about it are valid. In this case the inference rule shown earlier would indicate that both inputs must have been 0.

This matches our second expectation (`INPUT-A = 0`), so there is no discrepancy and thus no need to explore this expectation further. That is, the devices "upstream" of `INPUT-A` may or may not be completely free of faults, but under the current set of assumptions (made explicit below), none of them can be responsible for the observed misbehavior.

There is a discrepancy between our inference and the third expectation, since we expected a 1 from the AND gate. We proceed now with the AND gate just as we did with the OR gate, asking why we expected a 1, adding the gate to our list of candidates and pushing the inferred values yet further back in the circuit.

We describe this style of diagnostic reasoning as the *interaction of simulation and inference*. Simulation generates expectations about correct behavior based on inputs and knowing how devices work (the device simulation rules). Inference generates conclusions about actual behavior based on observed outputs and device inference rules. The comparison of these two, in particular differences between them, provides the foundation for our troubleshooting and has produced a system with a number of advantages.

It is, first of all, fundamentally a diagnostic technique, since it allows systematic isolation of possibly faulty devices. Second, since it defines failure functionally, i.e., as anything that doesn't match the expected behavior, it can deal with a wide range of faults, including any systematic misbehavior. Third, while we have illustrated it here at the gate level, the approach also allows natural use of hierarchical descriptions, a marked advantage for dealing with complex structures (see, e.g., [3]). Finally, the technique also yields symptom information about the malfunction. For example, if the OR gate is indeed the culprit, then we know a little about how it is misbehaving: it is receiving 0 and 1 and producing 0. This utility of this information is demonstrated below.

3.3.2 Mechanism and Knowledge

While this mechanism --- the interaction of simulation and inference --- is very useful, it is only as powerful as the knowledge we supply. Recall that in the example above, when exploring the cause of the discrepancy on INPUT-B, we looked only at the AND gate. Why didn't we think that some other module, like the inverter, could have produced the problem there? The answer of course is that there is no apparent connection between them, hence no reason to believe one might affect the other.

Note carefully the character of this assumption: it concerns the *existence of causal pathways, the applicability of a particular model of interaction*. We saw no way in which the inverter could affect INPUT-B, yet a pathway is clearly plausible --- a bridge fault, for example. We were implicitly assuming that there was no such pathway.

We believe that the important focus in this work is understanding such assumptions and the nature and character of the pathways. This understanding is crucial to candidate generation: given a discrepancy noticed at some point in the device, candidate generation attempts to determine which modules could have caused the problem. To answer the question we must know by what mechanisms and pathways modules can interact. Without some notion of how modules can affect one another, we can make no choice, we have no basis for selecting any one module over another.

In this domain the obvious answer is "wires": modules interact because they're explicitly wired together. But that's not the only possibility. As we saw, bridges are one exception; they are "wires" that aren't supposed to be there. But we also might consider thermal interactions, capacitive coupling, transmission line effects, etc.

Generating candidates, then, is not done by tracing wires, it is done by *tracing paths of causality*. Wires are only the most obvious pathway. In fact, given the wide variety of faults want to deal with, we need to consider many different pathways of interaction.

And that leaves us on the horns of a classic dilemma. If we include every interaction path, candidate generation becomes *indiscriminate* --- there will be some (possibly convoluted) pathway by which every module could conceivably be to blame. Yet if we omit any pathway, there will be whole classes of faults we will *never* be able to diagnose.

The key appears to lie in the models of interaction: we suggest that the difficult and important work is their enumeration and careful organization. We get a hint about organization from what a good engineer might do when faced with the dilemma above: make a number assumptions to simplify the problem, making it tractable, but be prepared to discover that some of those assumptions are incorrect. In that case, surrender them and solve the problem again with fewer simplifications.

This leads to the suggestion of layering the models. We start the diagnosis with the most restrictive model, the one that considers the fewest paths of interaction, and only use less restrictive models if this one fails. By "fail" we mean that we reach an intractable contradiction: given the current model and set of assumptions, there is no way to account for the observed behavior. This approach permits us to simplify the problem in order to get started, but does not prevent us from exploring more complex hypotheses.

A plausible guess at an ordering for the models might be[2]

- localized failure of function (e.g., stuck-at on a wire, failure of a RAM cell)
- bridges
- unexpected direction (inputs acting as outputs and driving lines)
- multiple point of failure
- timing errors
- assembly error
- design error

2. For the rationale behind this ordering see [2].

In terms of the dilemma noted above, the models serve as a set of *filters*. They restrict the categories of paths of interaction we are willing to consider, thereby preventing the candidate generation from becoming indiscriminate. But they are filters that we have carefully ordered and consciously put in place. If we cannot account for the observed behavior with the current filter in place, we remove it and replace it with one that is less restrictive, allowing us to consider additional categories of interaction paths.

4. LAYERS OF INTERACTION EXAMPLE: DIAGNOSING A BRIDGE FAULT

In this section we show how our system diagnoses a bridge fault, illustrating the utility of layering the interaction models.

There is, alas, a large amount of detail involved in working through this example. Where possible we have abstracted out much of it, but patience and a willingness to read closely will still be useful. A simple roadmap of the example will help make clear where we're going.

> The device is a 6-bit adder that displays an incorrect result in Test T1. The candidate generation mechanism outlined earlier produces a set S1 of three sub-components of the adder that can account for the misbehavior.
>
> A second test T2 is run to distinguish among the three possibilities in S1. Candidate generation produces a set S2 of two candidates capable of explaining the results of T2.
>
> Surprisingly, the intersection of S1 and S2 is null. We have reached a contradiction: no single component is capable of explaining all the data.
>
> Put slightly differently, we have a contradiction *under the current set of assumptions and interaction models*. We therefore have to surrender one of our assumptions and use a less restrictive model.
>
> The next model in the list --- bridge faults --- surrenders the assumption that the structure is as shown in the schematic

and considers one additional interaction path: wires between adjacent pins.

Surrendering the assumption that the schematic is correct only indicates that we know what the structure is *not*; the difficult problem is generating plausible hypotheses about what it *is*.

Knowledge of electronics offers insight into how the physical modification --- adding a wire --- manifests itself functionally. This provides us with a behavior pattern characteristic of bridges that can be used to hypothesize their location.

Physical adjacency then provides a strong additional constraint on the set of connections which might be plausible bridges. The combined requirement of functional and physical plausibility results in the generation of only a very few carefully chosen bridge hypotheses.

The first attempt to apply these ideas produces two hypotheses that are plausible functionally, but prove to be implausible physically.

Dropping down a level of detail in our description reveals additional bridge candidates, two of which prove to be physically plausible as well. Further tests determine that one of them is in fact the error.

4.1 The Example

Consider the six bit adder shown in Fig. 2. Assume that the attempt to add 21 and 19 produces 36 rather than the expected value of 40. Invoking the candidate generation process described above, we would find that there are three devices whose individual malfunction can explain the behavior (SLICE-1, A2 and SLICE-2).[3]

---

3. The example has been simplified slightly for presentation.

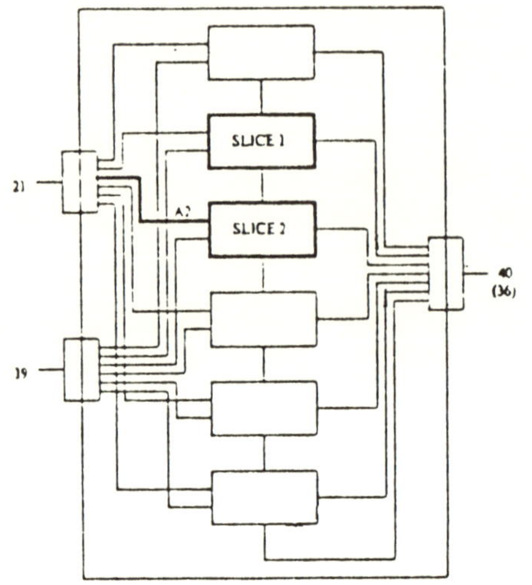

Figure 2 · Six bit adder constructed from single bit slices. Heavy lines indicate components implicated as possibly faulty.

A good strategy when faced with several candidates is to devise a test that can cut the space of possibilities in half. In this case changing the first input (21) to 1 will be informative: if the output of SLICE-2 does not change (to a 0) when we add 1 and 19, then the error must be in either A2 or SLICE-2.[4]

As it turns out, the result of adding 1 and 19 is 4 rather than 20. Since the output of SLICE-2 has not changed, it appears that the error must be in either A2 or SLICE-2.

But if we invoke the candidate generator, we discover an oddity: the only way to account for the behavior in which adding 1 and 19 produces a 4 is if one of the two candidates highlighted in Fig. 3 (B4 and SLICE-4) is at fault.

Therein lies our contradiction. The only candidates that account for the behavior of the first test are those in Fig. 2; the only candidates that account for the second test are those in Fig. 3. There is no overlap, so there is no single candidate that accounts for all the observed behavior.

4. The generation of tests in this paper is currently done by hand; everything else is implemented. Work on automating test generation is in progress [7].

The logic behind this test is as follows: if the malfunctioning component really were SLICE-1, then the both A2 and SLICE-2 would be fault-free (the single fault assumption). Hence the output of SLICE-2 would have to change when we changed one of its inputs. (Notice, however, if the output actually does change, we don't have any clear indication about the error location: SLICE-2, for example, might still be faulty.)

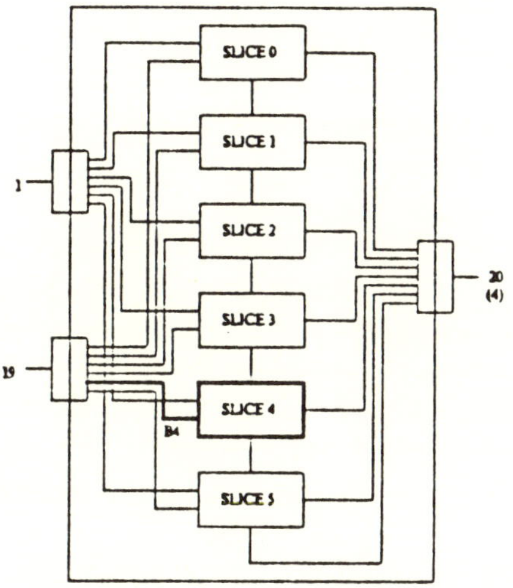

Figure 3 · Components indicated as possibly faulty by the second test.

Our current model --- the localized failure of function --- has thus led us to a contradiction.[5] We therefore surrender it and consider the next model, one that allows us to consider an *additional kind of interaction path* --- bridging faults. The problem now is to see if there is some way to unify the test results, some way to generate a single bridge fault candidate that accounts for all the observations.

Much of the difficulty in dealing with bridges arises because they violate the rather basic assumption that the structure of the device is in fact as shown in the schematic. But admitting that the structure may not be as pictured says only that we know what the structure *isn't*. Saying that we may have a bridge fault narrows it to a particular class of modifications to consider, but the real problem here remains one of *making a few plausible conjectures about modifications to the structure*. Between which two points can we insert a wire and produce the behavior observed?

5. Note that dropping down another level of detail in the functional description cannot help resolve the contradiction, because our functional description is a tree rather than a graph: in our work to date, at least, no component is used in more than one way.

To understand how we answer that question, consider what we have and what we need. We have test results, i.e., *behavior*, and we want conjectures about modification to *structure*. The link from behavior to structure is provided by knowledge of electronics: in TTL, a bridge fault acts like an and-gate, with ground dominating.[6]

From this fact we can derive a simple pattern of behavior indicative of bridges. Consider the simple example of Fig. 4 and assume that we ran two tests. Test 1 produced one candidate, module A, which should have produced a 1 but yielded a 0 (the zero is underlined to show that it is an incorrect output). Module B was working correctly and produced a 0 as expected. In Test 2 this situation is exactly reversed, A was performing as expected and B failed.

The pattern displayed in these two tests makes it plausible that there is a bridge linking the outputs of A and B: in the first test the output of A was dragged low by B, in the second test the output of B was dragged low by A.

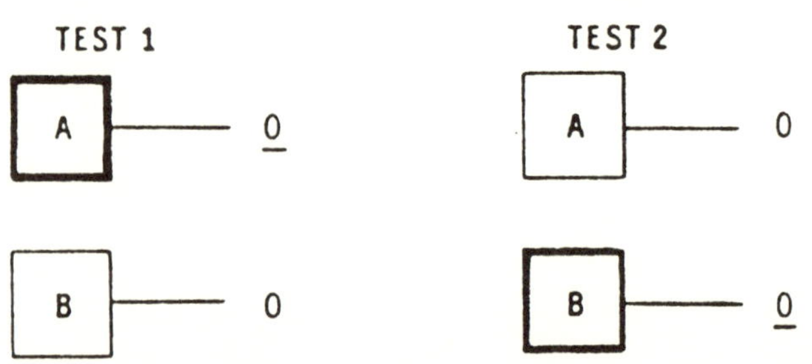

Figure 4 · Pattern of values indicative of a bridge. Heavy lines indicate candidates.

We have thus turned the insight from electronics into a pattern of values on the candidates. It is plausible to hypothesize a bridge fault between two modules A and B from two different tests if: in test 1, A produced an erroneous 0 and B produced a valid 0, and in test 2, A produced a valid 0 while B produced an erroneous 0. Note that this can resolve the contradiction of

6. This is in fact an oversimplification, but accurate enough to be useful. In any case, the point here is how the information is used; a more complex model could be substituted and carried through the rest of the problem.

non-overlapping candidate sets: it hypothesizes one fault that involves a member of each set and accounts for all the test data.

Thus, if we want to account for all of the test data in the original problem with a single bridge fault, we need a bridge that links one of the candidates from the first test (SLICE-1, A2, SLICE-2) with one of the candidates from the second test (B4, SLICE-4), and that mimics the pattern shown in Fig. 4.

Fig. 5 shows the candidate generation results from both tests in somewhat more detail.[7] In that data there are two pairs of devices that match the desired pattern, yielding two functionally plausible bridge hypotheses:

Dotted line X, bridging wire A2 to the sum output of SLICE-4;

Dotted line Y, bridging the carry output of SLICE-2 to the sum output of SLICE-4.

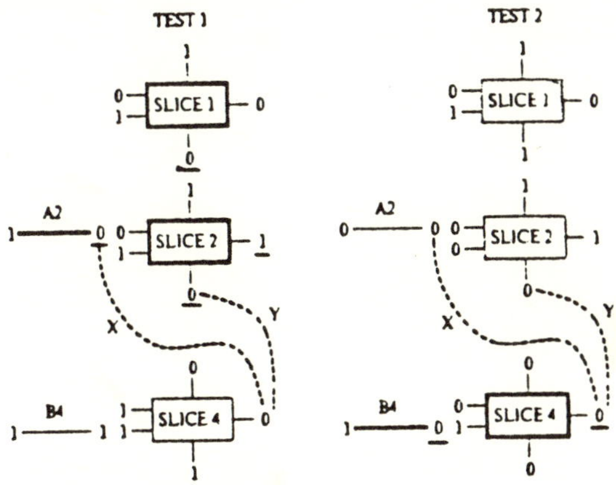

Figure 5 - Candidates and values at their ports.

But the faults have to be physically plausible as well. For the sake of simplicity, we assume that bridge faults result only from solder splashes at the pins of chips.[8] To check physical

7. As indicated earlier, the candidate generation procedure can indicate for each candidate the values that would have to exist at its ports for that candidate to be the broken one. For example, for SLICE-1 to be at fault in test 1, it would have to have the three inputs shown, with its sum output a zero (as expected) and its carry output also a zero (the manifestation of the error, underlined).

8. Again this is correct but oversimplified (e.g., backplane pins can be bent or bridged), but as above we can introduce a more complex model if necessary.

plausibility, we switch to our physical representation, Fig. 6. Wire A2 is connected to chip E1 at pin 4 and chip E3 at pin 4; the sum output of SLICE-4 emerges at chip E2, pin 13. Since they are not adjacent, the first hypothesis is not physically reasonable. Similar reasoning rules out Y, the hypothesized bridge between the carry-out of SLICE-2 and the sum output of SLICE-4.

I - end of A2
II - sum output of SLICE-4
III- carry out of SLICE-2

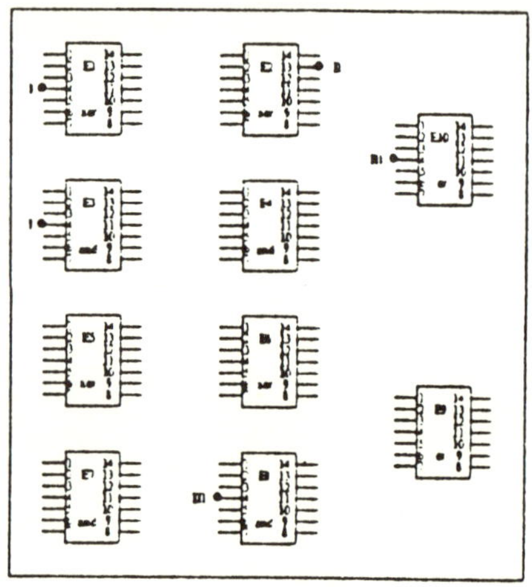

Figure 6 · Physical layout of the board with first bridge hypotheses indicated. (Slices 0, 2, and 4 are in the upper 5 chips, slices 1, 3, and 5 are in the lower 5.)

So far we have considered only the top level of functional organization. We can run the candidate generator at the next lower level of detail in each of the non-primitive components in Fig. 5. (Dropping down a level of detail proves useful here because additional substructure becomes visible, effectively revealing new places that might be bridged.)

We obtain the components and values shown in Fig. 7. Checking here for the desired pattern, we find that either of the two wires labeled A2 and S2 could be bridged to either of the two wires labeled S4 and C4, generating four functionally plausible bridge faults.

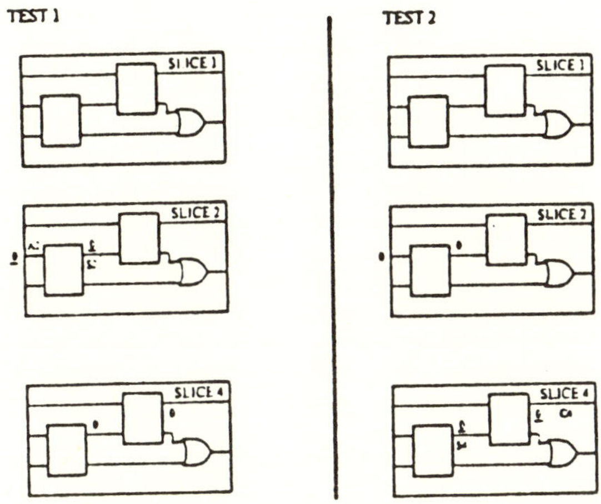

Figure 7 · Candidates at the next level of functional description. Each single bit adder is built from two "half-adders" and an OR gate. (To simplify the figure, only the relevant values are shown.)

Once again we check physical plausibility by examining the actual locations of A2, S2, S4, and C4, Fig. 8.[9] As illustrated there, two of the possibilities are physically plausible as well: A2-S4 on chip E1 and S2-S4 on chip E2.

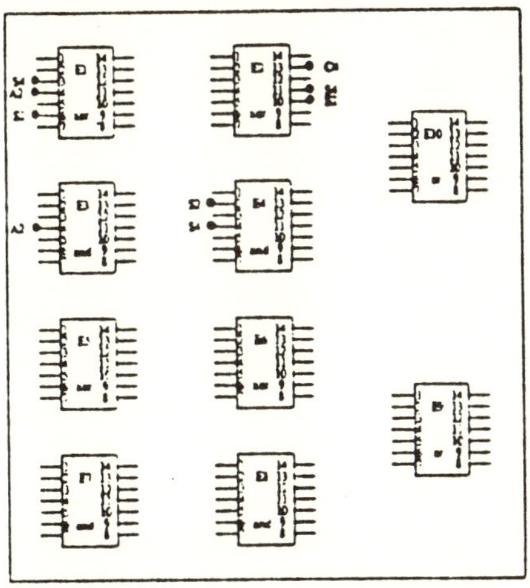

Figure 8 · Second set of bridge hypotheses located on physical layout.

9. Note that the erroneous 0 on wire S2 can be in any of three physical locations, because S2 fans out (inside the module it enters on its right).

Switching back to our functional organization once more, Fig. 9, we see that the two possibilities correspond to (X) an output-to-input bridge between the xor gates in the rear half-adders of SLICE-2 and SLICE-4, and (Y) a bridge between two inputs of the xor in the forward half-adders of slices 2 and 4.

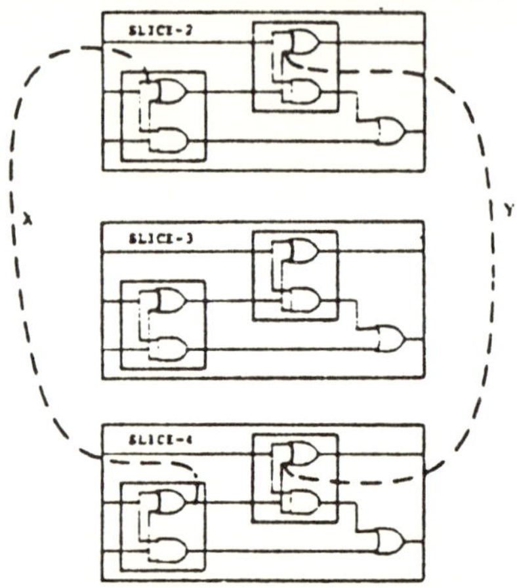

Figure 9 · Functional representation with bridge fault hypotheses illustrated.

It is easy to find a test that distinguishes between these two possibilities[10] : adding 0 and 4 means that the inputs of SLICE-2 will be 1 and 0, with a carry-in of 0, while the inputs of SLICE-4 will both be 0, with a carry-in of 0. This set of values will show the effects of bridge Y, if it in fact exists: the sum output of SLICE-2 will be 0 if it does exist and a 1 otherwise. When we perform this test the result is 1, hence bridge Y is not in fact the problem.

Bridge X becomes the likely answer, but we should still test for it directly. Adding 4 and 0 (i.e., just switching the order of the inputs), is informative: if bridge X exists the result will be 0 and 1 otherwise. In this case the result is 0, hence the bridge labeled X is in fact the problem.[11]

5. PATHS OF INTERACTION; THE LOCALITY PRINCIPLE

Two interesting questions are raised by the problem solving used just above.

10. As above, tests are generated by hand.

11. Had both been ruled out by direct test, then we would once again have had a contradiction on our hands and would have had to drop back to consider yet a more elaborate model with additional paths of interaction.

Why are bridge faults difficult to diagnose?

Why does the physical representation prove to be so useful?

To see the answer, we start with the trivial observation that all faults are the result of some difference between the device as it is and as it should be. With bridge faults the difference is the addition of a wire between two physically adjacent points.

Now recall the nature of our task: we are presented with a device that misbehaves, not one with obvious structural damage. Hence we reason from behavior, i.e., from the functional representation. And the important point is that for a bridge fault, the difference in question --- the addition of a single wire --- is not *local* in that representation. As the comparison of Figs. 8 and 9 makes clear, the new wire connects two points that are adjacent in the physical representation but widely separated in the functional representation.

The difference is also not as *simple* in that representation: if we include in our functional diagram the AND gate implicitly produced by bridge X, we see that a single added wire in the physical representation maps into an AND gate and a fanout in the functional representation (Fig. 10).

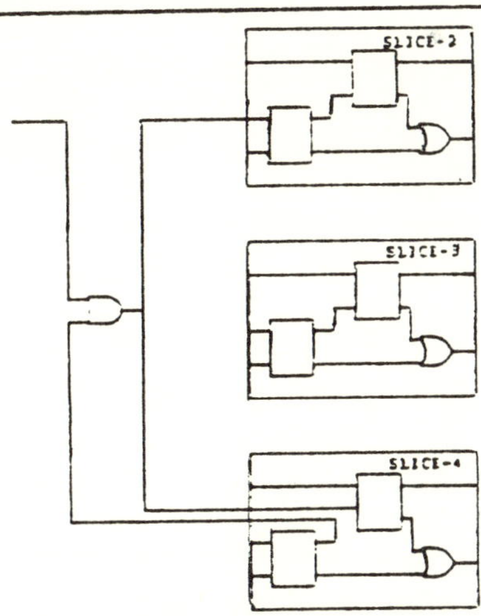

Figure 10 · Full functional representation of bridge fault X.

This view helps to explain why bridge faults produce behavior that is difficult to envision and diagnose. Bridge faults are modifications that are simple and local in the physical description, but our diagnosis is done using the functional description. Hence the dilemma: *The desire to reason from behavior requires us to use a representation that does not necessarily provide a compact description of the fault.*

This non-locality and complexity should not be surprising, since devices physically adjacent are not necessarily functionally related. Hence there is no guarantee that a change that is small and local in one will produce a change that is small and local in the other. More generally, *changes local in one representation are not necessarily local in another.*

We can turn this around to put it to work for us:

> *Part of the art of choosing the right representation(s) for diagnostic reasoning is finding one in which the change in question* is *local.*

This explains the utility of the physical representation: it's the "right" one because it's the one in which the change is local.

But why is locality the relevant organizing principle? We believe the answer follows from two facts: (a) devices interact through physical processes (voltage on a wire, thermal radiation, etc.) and (b) physical processes occur locally, or more generally, causality proceeds locally: there is no action at a distance. To make this useful, we turn it around:

> *The mechanisms (paths) of interaction define locality for us. That is, each kind of interaction path can define a representation.*

Bridge faults arise from *physical adjacency* and hence are local in the physical representation. The notion of *thermal adjacency* would be useful in dealing with faults resulting from heat conduction or radiation, *electromagnetic adjacency* would help with faults dealing with transmission line effects, etc.

> *Each of these produces a different representation, different in its definition of locality. And each will be useful for understanding and diagnosing a category of fault.*

There is still substantial work to do in enumerating the pathways of interaction, but we seem at least to be asking the right question. It seems to make sense for a wide range of faults and appears to be applicable to other domains as well. When debugging software, for example, the pathways of interaction differ (e.g., procedure call, mutation of data structures), but the resulting perspectives appear to make sense and there are some interesting analogies (e.g., unintended side effects in software are in some ways like bridge faults; there are even faults where the notion of "physical adjacency" is useful in understanding the bug, as in out of bounds array addressing).

6. SUMMARY

We seek to build a system that reasons from first principles in diagnosing hardware failures. We view diagnosis as the interaction of simulation and inference, with discrepancies between them driving the generation of candidates. In exploring this interaction, we find that the concept of paths of causal interaction plays a key role, supplying the knowledge that makes the diagnostic machinery work. But the desire to deal with a wide range of faults seems to force us to choose between an inability to discriminate among candidates and the inability to deal with some classes of faults.

In response, we suggest layering the interaction models, using the most restrictive first and hence considering the fewest paths of interaction initially. If this fails to generate a consistent hypothesis, we use the next model in the sequence, one which allows consideration of an additional pathway.

We illustrated this approach by diagnosing a bridge fault, sharply constraining the generation of hypotheses by using the physical representation as well as the functional. Finally, we found this to be one example of an important general principle --- locality --- and discovered that one useful definition of locality is given by the pathways of interaction.

Acknowledgments

Contributions to this work we made by all of the members of the Hardware Troubleshooting project at MIT, including: Howie Shrobe, Walter Hamscher, Karen Wieckert, Mark Shirley, Harold Haig, Art Mellor, John Pitrelli, and Steve Polit.

Bruce Buchanan and Patrick Winston offered a number of very useful comments on earlier drafts.

REFERENCES

[1] Brown J S, Burton R, deKleer J, Pedagogical and knowledge engineering techniques in the SOPHIE systems, Xerox Report CIS-14, 1981.

[2] Davis R, Reasoning from first principles in hardware troubleshooting, *Intl Journal of Man-machine Studies*, to appear, 1983.

[3] Davis R, et al., Diagnosis based on structure and function. *Proc AAAI 1982*, pp 137-142, August 1982.

[4] Davis R, Shrobe H E, Representing structure and function, *IEEE Computer*, to appear Sept 1983.

[5] Genesereth M, The use of hierarchical models in the automated diagnosis of computer systems, Stanford HPP memo 81-20, December 1981.

[6] Patil R, Szolovits P, Schwartz W, Causal understanding of patient illness in medical diagnosis, *Proc IJCAI-81*, August 1981, pp 893-899.

[7] Shirley W, Davis R, Digital test generation from symptom information, *IEEE 1983 VLSI Workshop*, to appear.

A REPRESENTATION FOR THE FUNCTIONING OF DEVICES THAT SUPPORTS COMPILATION OF EXPERT PROBLEM SOLVING STRUCTURES

An Extended Summary

V.S. Moorthy and B. Chandrasekaran

Department of Computer and Information Science
The Ohio State University
Columbus, OH 43210

(September 1983)

ABSTRACT

Most of the diagnostic systems that have been developed in medicine as well as other domains can properly be called "compiled" knowledge systems in the sense that the knowledge base contains the relationships between symptoms and malfunction hypotheses in some form. However, often in human reasoning, an expert's knowledge of how the device "functions" is used to generate new relationships during the reasoning process. This deeper level representation which can be processed to yield more compiled diagnostic structures is the concern of this paper. Using the example of an household buzzer, we show in this paper what a functional representation of a device looks like. We also indicate the nature of the compilation process that can produce the diagnostic expert from this deeper representation.

1. Introduction

Recently the domain of devices has attracted theoretical as well as applied AI researchers [1, 2, 3, 4, 13, 14,16]. To troubleshoot, modify and monitor devices (eg. nuclear power plant, physiological organs, electronic circuits, computer software, etc.), it is necessary for an agent to represent and use the knowledge about the functioning of the devices. Moreover, an agent needs to know the functioning of similar devices in order to become an expert in designing a new device.

Referring to the "depth" of knowledge in expert systems, Hart [5] and Michie [6] have suggested that systems with deep knowledge will be able to solve problems of significantly greater complexity than the so called surface systems. Their remarks on deep vs. surface systems seem to capture a fairly widespread feeling about the inadequacy of the first generation expert systems. However, in Chandrasekaran and Mittal [7], it is argued that, in principle, given any deep model of a domain, it is possible to compile an expert diagnostic system (more specifically an MDX-like diagnostic system [8, 9, 17]) which is as powerful as the deeper model, but more efficient than the deeper model for diagnostic purposes.

Also, there is no general agreement on the form and content of these deep knowledge structures. Hart [5] suggests that they should model causality by multi-level systems, while Michie, following Rouse [10], proposes that they should represent knowledge of the form "situation x action -> situation". The work of Patil [11] and Pople [12] is based on the idea that the appropriate form for the representation of deep knowledge is a causal net. We propose that with respect to the "surface causality" modeled in systems like MYCIN, the next deeper level to model causality is the functional representation of devices. An agent becomes an expert in various tasks such as diagnosis, design, explanation, etc., by compiling appropriate problem solving structures from the functional representation.

In this paper we describe a representational scheme for the functioning of devices and its utility for compiling an MDX-like [8,9, 17] diagnostic expert system. Our focus here is on the representation; we discuss the compilation in more detail in [15].

2. Comparison with Related Research

De kleer and Brown [1, 2, 3] have been working on the representation of an agent's knowledge about how a device actually functions. This representation, which they call "functional", is actually a causally related sequence of behavioral states, some of which either belong to the components or refer to the attributes of the interconnections between the components. They then proceed to discuss the process of acquiring the above "functional" representation from the structural knowledge of the device. They impose three interesting criteria that such a process, as well as the "functional" representation, should satisfy — namely, "no-function-in-structure", "weak causality" and "strong causality."

Our work differs from that of De kleer and Brown in two aspects: Firstly,our definition of what constitutes a functional representation is different from theirs. Secondly, while they are concentrating on the acquisition of function from structure, we wish to understand the process by which an agent uses the functional representation for various problem solving activities, i.e., transforms the functional representation into "expert" problem solving structures. However, these apparently different objectives are not as disjoint as they might appear. In fact, we strongly believe that our functional representation will ultimately satisfy the twin requirements of acquirability and transformability into expert problem solving structures.

The functional representation of Davis et al [13] has "functional" as well as "physical" hierarchies. Their "inference rules" and "simulation rules" enable their "violated expectation" approach to troubleshooting. However, their "functional" and "physical" hierarchies neither differentiate nor relate "function","structure","behavior", "assumptions" and "deeper causal Knowledge " as ours.

3. A Representational Scheme for the Functioning of Devices

3.1. The Representational Scheme

Our scheme allows multiplicity of levels in functional representation. The topmost level describes the functioning of a device in terms of the abstractions of its components. The next level describes the functioning of these components using the abstractions of their subcomponents, and so on. As we shall see later, the hierarchy is not just functional. The abstractions from the lower level include, in addition, the states of components as well as other entities.

At each level of our functional representation we propose that there are five significant aspects to an agent's knowledge of functioning of devices:

- STRUCTURE: that specifies the components (subcomponents) of a device (a component) and the interconnections between them.

- FUNCTION: that specifies WHAT is the response of a device or a component to an external or internal stimulus.

- BEHAVIOR: that specifies HOW, given a stimulus, the response is accomplished.

- GENERIC KNOWLEDGE: chunks of deeper causal knowledge that have been compiled from various domains to enable the specification of behavior of devices and their components. For example, a specialized version of Kirchoff's law from the domain of electrical circuits.

- ASSUMPTIONS: under which a behavior is accomplished.

Next we describe the roles of these five aspects in representing the functioning of devices and their notations. Following De kleer and Brown [1, 2], we shall use the household buzzer shown in fig. 3-1 to illustrate our ideas.

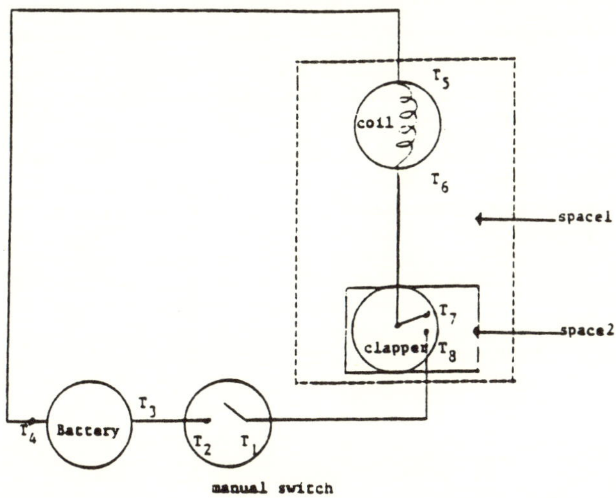

Figure 3-1: A Schematic Diagram of a Household Buzzer

FUNCTION

The functional specification of a device is illustrated below by describing one of the functions of the buzzer.

```
FUNCTION:
 Buzz: TOMAKE buzzing(buzzer)
       IF pressed(manual-switch)*
        PROVIDED assumption2  BY behavior1
```

"buzz" is the name of the function; "buzzing(buzzer)" denotes the buzzing state of the buzzer. "t7" and "t8" are distinguished elements of a component of buzzer (we discuss this below). "assumption2" will specify the initial state i.e., "t7","t8" are electrically connected (more about assumptions later). The "BY" clause relates the function with its behavior i.e., the manner in which the function is accomplished (behavioral specification is described below). As we shall see in section 4.2, this association between function and behavior is important at the compilation stage.

STRUCTURE

The structure of a device (component) is represented using the abstractions of its components (subcomponents) and generic relations between them (such as "serially-connected"). As an illustration consider the structure of the buzzer given below:

```
STRUCTURE:
   COMPONENTS:
        manual-switch (t1,t2), battery (t3,t4),
        coil (t5,t6,space1), clapper (t7,t8,space2)
   RELATIONS:  serially-connected (manual-switch,
                           battery,coil,clapper)
              AND includes(space1,space2)

   ABSTRACTIONS-OF-COMPONENTS:
       COMPONENT  clapper (T1,T2,SPACE)
           FUNCTIONS: mechanical,acoustic,magnetic
           STATES: elect-connected (T1,T2),
                   repeated-hit(clapper)
       END COMPONENT

       COMPONENT  coil (T1,T2,SPACE)
              .
              .
              .
       END COMPONENT
   END ABSTRACTIONS-OF-COMPONENTS
END STRUCTURE
```

"t1",t2"...., "space" are distinguished elements (terminals) of components ; only between distinguished elements can relations be defined. "mechanical","acoustic", etc., are the names of functions of clapper. These functions (as well as the structure, behavior, generic knowledge and assumptions relating to the clapper as well as other of the components) are represented at the next level of our representation in the same manner as the buzzer. The capitalized parameters such as T1,T2,etc., are local to the associated component.

It is important to note the following:

a) A component (subcomponent) is specified independent of the representation of the device (component) which contains it. More specifically, the specification of a component does not refer to the role of the component in the composite. Thus our representation obeys the "no-function-in-structure" principle of De kleer and Brown [1, 2].

b) Not the behavioral specifications of components but only the names of the functions are carried over to the higher level. This property is important when an agent needs to replace a malfunctioning component by a functionally equivalent but behaviorally different one. Note that neither the "intrinsic mechanism" nor the "causal model" of De kleer and Brown [1] distinguishes between function and behavior as we do. The "behavioral description" of Davis et al [13] and Davis [14] is similar to our functional specification. They do not have any construct equivalent to our behavioral specification. (The significance of having a behavioral specification will become clear when we discuss it below.)

c) We model interconnections between components by relations such as ´serially-connected´, ´includes´, etc.

BEHAVIOR

The behavioral specification of a device

describes the manner in which a function is accomplished by "gluing" together the functions of components, generic knowledge, assumptions relating to behavioral alternatives, and sub-behaviors. For example, the specification of of 'behavior1' in fig. 3-2 illustrates how the 'buzz' function discussed above is realized.

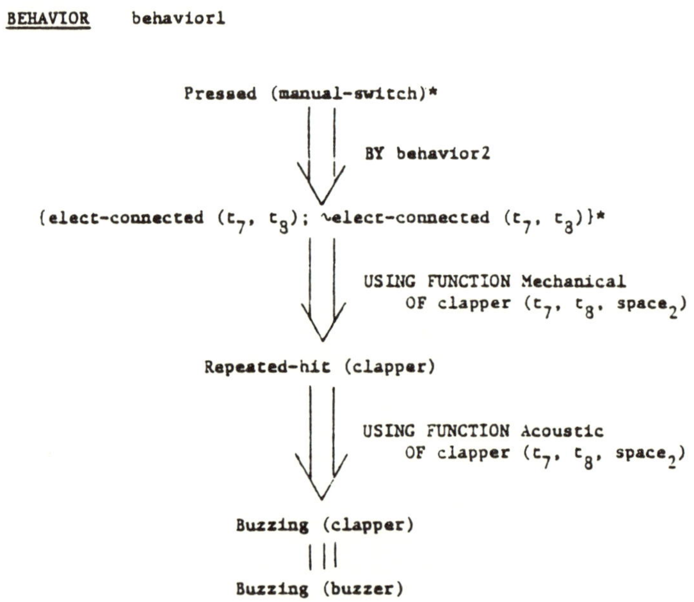

Figure 3-2: An Illustration of Behavioral Specification

We have made use of five conceptually important notations in behavioral specification. They are described below:

```
1:          s1
            ||
            ||  BY <name-of-a-behavior>
            \/
            s2
```

For example,

```
        Pressed (manual-switch)*
                ||
                ||  BY behavior2
                \/
      { elect-connected (t7,t8);   } *
      { ~ elect-connected (t7,t8)  }
```

This means that the state s1 causes the state s2 and the details are in another behavioral specification ("behavior2"). This relation enables the the specification of behavior of a component (or a device) at many levels of detail but still at the level of the component (or device).

```
2:    s1
      ||
      ||  USING FUNCTION  <name-of-a-function>
      ||          OF <component>
      \/
      s2
```

For example,

```
repeated-hit (clapper)
      ||  USING FUNCTION acoustic
      ||  OF clapper(t7,t8,space2)
      \/
buzzing (buzzer)
```

The above notation means that the state s2 is caused from s1 by making use of a function ("acoustic") of the component (clapper). This relation makes it possible to glue the functions of the components together to obtain a behavior.

3:

$$S1 \equiv S2$$

The above notation means that the agent will "equivalence" the state s1 of a component (or subcomponent) with s2, the state of a device (or a component). For example, as in the specification of "behavior1" (ref. to fig. 3-1 "buzzing(clapper)" is "equivalenced" with "buzzing(buzzer)". Note that without this relation, it is impossible to connect the result of a function of a component (the buzzing of the clapper) with the result of a function of the device (the buzzing of the buzzer which is the result of its function "buzz"). Without this connection, "behavior1" cannot be claimed to implement the function "buzz" of the buzzer.

```
4:      s1
        ||
        ||  AS-PER <name-of-a-knowledge-chunk>
        ||    IN-THE-CONTEXT-OF  < one or more
        \/       of a "relation", "state" or a
        s2       "function of a component" >
```

For example,

```
elect-connected(t7,t8)
        ||
        ||  AS-PER knowledge1 IN-THE-CONTEXT-OF
        ||   FUNCTION  voltage OF battery(t1,t2),
        ||    serially-connected(battery,coil,
        \/    clapper,manual-switch)
voltage-applied(t5,t6)
```

This means that if the terminals t7 and t8 are electrically connected, then voltage will be applied between t5 and t6. This is true as per the knowledge chunk called 'knowledge1' when it is applied in the context of battery, coil, clapper and manual switch being serially connected, and the battery makes voltage available at its terminal. (The representation of 'knowledge1' is discussed below.) It is through this primitive that the role of generic knowledge in describing a behavior is represented.

```
5:     magnetized(space2)
           ||
           ||  USING FUNCTION magnetic
           ||     OF clapper(t7,t8,space2)
           ||     WITH assumption3
           \/

       ~elect-connected(t7,t8)
```

"assumption3" will specify that there exists a force F such that if space2 is magnetized, then the resulting magnetic force will be greater than F. Note that "assumption3" does not specify what is F, how it is to be realized and so on. The "WITH" clause, like "PROVIDED", relates an assumption with the state transition. However, "WITH" is different from "PROVIDED" since it relates an assumption that is passed from a device (component) to a component (sub-component) while "PROVIDED" relates the one from a component (sub-component) to the device (component). Also, assumptions related by "WITH" clause can be used to make a state transition deterministic.

GENERIC KNOWLEDGE

The generic knowledge specification of a device (component) describes all chunks of deeper knowledge used in its behavioral specification.

The following is a specification of ´knowledge1´.

```
GENERIC KNOWLEDGE:
    knowledge1:

      voltage-applied (t1,t2)
             ||
             || AS-PER kirchoff´s-law
             ||   IN-THE-CONTEXT-OF
             ||   elect-connected(t1,t3)
             ||     ^ elect-connected(t2,t4)
             \/
      voltage-applied (t3,t4)
```

It is worth noting that the specification of generic knowledge is context-free. The context in which it is applied is specified in the behavioral specification (as illustrated above). As we shall see soon, there is a mechanism ("REFERENCES") by which a user task of the functional representation knows where to look for the definition of Kirchoff´s law.

We would like to draw particular attention to the notion of GENERIC KNOWLEDGE in our representation. This enables us to capture the relation between functional representation and deeper causal knowledge. Moreover, without an explicit link with such generic knowledge it is not possible to support the recognition of incorrect application of such knowledge during "envisioning" [1,2,3]. Also it cannot support queries relating to the role of such knowledge in understanding,describing,explaining,etc., of the behavior of devices.

ASSUMPTIONS

All assumptions made use of in the behavioral specification of a device (component) are described in ASSUMPTIONS as illustrated below with reference to the clapper.

```
ASSUMPTIONS:
  DEFINITIONS:

   f1 = magnetic-force DUE-TO magnetized(space) AND
   f2 = spring-force DUE-TO loaded (spring)

  ASSUMPTION1:
   IF magnetized(space)  THEN  f1 > f2

  ASSUMPTION2:
   IF ~ magnetized(space)  THEN  f1 < f2

END ASSUMPTIONS
```

"spring-force" and "magnetic-force" are concepts; we discuss below about their definition. The primitive "DUE-TO" relates a concept with a state of a component.

Note that though De kleer and Brown [2] state that a difference between a novice and an expert is that the latter has made explicit all the assumptions underlying behavior of devices, their causal model, unlike our functional representation , does not represent explicitly the role of assumptions in behavior.

REFERENCES

Clearly an agent's knowledge of the functioning of devices will have references to elements of different domains ,e.g., electrical circuits,electro-magnetism ,etc. These references are specified in the "REFERENCES" part of our representational scheme as illustrated below:

```
REFERENCES:

   FOR kirchoff's-law, elect-connected
        REFER-TO elect-circuits
   FOR magnetic-force  REFER-TO electro-magnetism

END REFERENCES
```

Note that we do not yet know how to represent domains such as "elect-circuits", "electro-magnetism",etc.

4. Compilation of a Diagnostic Expert

The principal function of the compiler that we shall discuss here is to generate a diagnostic expert from the functional representation. Checking the correctness/ consistency of a functional representation, optimization of the generated expert systems are also significant aspects of the compilation process. However, for want of space , we discuss here only the generation of an MDX-like diagnostic expert. Other aspects of compilation are discussed in [15].

4.1. The Structure of the Generated Diagnostic Expert System

As shown in fig. 4-1, the generated expert is a hierarchy of specialists. Each specialist corresponds to a malfunction in the device at a certain level of abstraction. For example, a bad clapper, bad serial connection, etc. Specialists corresponding to more general or abstract malfunctioning are higher in the hierarchy. For

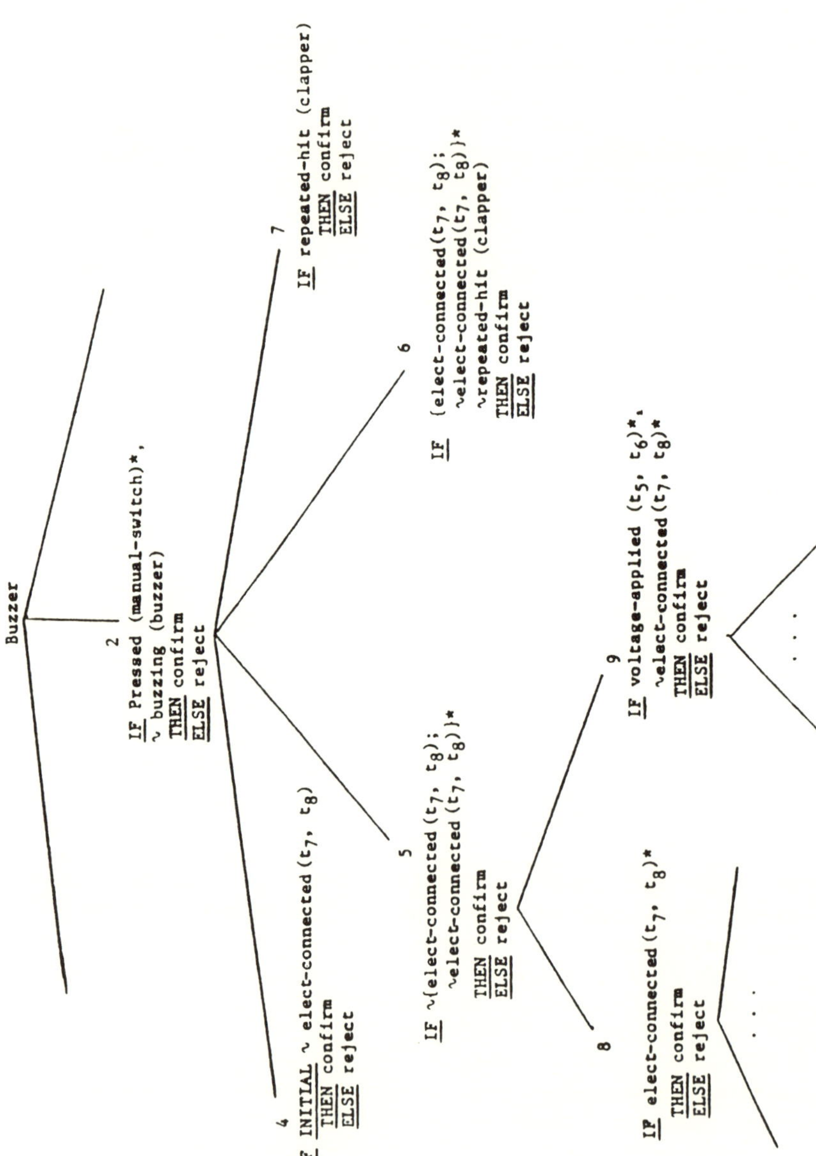

Figure 4–1: An Example of a Generated Diagnostic Expert

example, the root specialist in fig. 4-1 corresponds to a "malfunctioning buzzer". Its three sub-specialists correspond to the following three malfunctions (only the first one is shown in fig. 4-1):

1. The buzzer does not buzz when the manual switch is pressed.

2. A buzzing buzzer does not stop buzzing when the manual switch is released.

3. The buzzer keeps buzzing independent of the state of the manual switch.

•Every specialist has knowledge to establish the associated malfunctioning and to refine it by calling its sub-specialists. The knowledge of a specialist is in the form of three types of rules: confirmatory rules, exclusionary rules and recommendations. (We will not discuss "recommendations" here since it is concerned with optimization of the generated expert.) For example,

```
IF elect-connected (t1,t2) ^
  ~ voltage-applied (t5,t6)
    THEN  confirm
IF voltage-applied (t5,t6) THEN reject
```

A malfunction is diagnosed top-down by establishing a specialist and refining the malfunction represented by it by calling its sub-specialists. This discussion of the structuring and functioning of the diagnostic expert is grossly simplified. More detailed information can be obtained from [8, 9].

There are three types of malfunctioning and hence three types of specialists:

1. An assumption might have been violated. The specialist associated with it is called an <u>assumption</u> <u>checker</u>.

2. A function may not be functioning correctly. The associated specialist is called a function checker.

3. A relation between components may not hold. For example, the battery, coil and clapper may not be connected serially. Let us call the specialist the relation checker.

4.2. The Compilation Process

At the start, the compiler generates the root specialist. The root specialist needs no knowledge to establish itself. The fact that the expert is invoked leads automatically to the establishment of the root specialist. The compiler then processes the various functions of the device and generates a function checker corresponding to each function. For example, given

```
FUNCTION:
  buzz: TOMAKE  buzzing(buzzer)
          IF pressed(manual-switch)* BY behavior1
```

the compiler will generate a function checker with the following rule:

```
     IF  pressed(manual-switch)* ^ ¬buzzing(buzzer)
         THEN confirm
         ELSE reject
```

Then the function checkers generated as above will be attached to the root specialist. Afterwards the compiler, using the "BY" clause, obtains the behavior associated with each function and compiles it. For example, if the behavior is specified in the form:

```
s1 ====> s2 ====> .......... ====> sn
```

then the compiler will generate a set of n-1 specialists for the function checkers associated with the behavior. The rules for them will be:

```
IF s1 ^~ s2       THEN confirm
                  ELSE reject
             .
             .
             .
IF sn-1 ^~ sn     THEN confirm
                  ELSE reject
```

For the "buzz" function example given above, nodes 5, 6 and 7 in fig. 4-1 will be generated using "behavior1" in fig.3-2. Note that the rule associated with node 5 should be:

```
IF pressed(manual-switch)*
 ^{elect-connected(t7,t8);~elect-connected(t7,t8)}*
     THEN confirm
     ELSE reject.
```

However, the condition "pressed(manual-switch)*" is not checked since it is done at node 2, i.e., the parent of the node 5.

Further processing of a behavioral specification depends on the kind of composition of behavior.

CASE 1:

Assume that node 5 is generated corresponding to the following state transition in fig. 3-2.

```
    Pressed(manual-switch)*
        ||
        ||          BY  behavior2
        \/
{elect-connected(t7,t8) ; ~elect-connected(t7,t8)}*
```

The above state transition will also result in compiling 'Behavior2' as described above, and attaching the generated specialists to node 5.

CASE: 2

Let the state transition in fig.3-2corresponding to node 6 in fig.4-1 be:

```
{elect-connected(t7,t8); ~elect-connected(t7,t8)}*
       ||
       ||   USING FUNCTION mechanical
       \/        OF clapper(t7,t8,space2)
  repeated-hit(clapper)
```

After generating the node 6 for the above state transition, the compiler will look at the function ´mechanical´ in the functional representation of the component ´clapper´ and compile the behavior associated with the function. If there is no behavioral specification for the function, node 6 will be a tip specialist. If there is one for the function, then it will be compiled, and the generated specialists will be attached to node 6. If the function of the component is implemented under, say, "assumption1" and the specification of "assumption1" is of the form:

```
IF s3 THEN s4
```

then the additional specialist with the rule

```
IF s3 ^ ~s4 THEN confirm
             ELSE reject
```

will be generated and attached to the node corresponding to the above transition. An example of an assumption checker is node 4 in fig.4-1.

CASE 3:

The state transition

```
s1
||  AS-PER knowledge1
||   IN-THE-CONTEXT-OF s3^s4...sn
\/
s2
```

will result in a set of sub-specialists with the rules:

```
IF ~s3 THEN confirm
       ELSE reject
```

```
IF ~s4 THEN confirm
       ELSE reject
    .
    .
    .
IF ~sn THEN confirm
       ELSE reject
```

REFERENCES

1: De Kleer, J., Brown, J.S., "Mental Models of Physical Mechanisms and Their Acquisition," in Cognitive Skills and Their Acquisition, (ed) J.R. Anderson., Erlbaum, 1981.

2: De Kleer, J., Brown, J.S., "Assumptions and Ambiguities in Mechanistic Mental Models," tech rept. CIS 9, Xerox Palo Alto Research Centers, 1982.

3: De Kleer, J., Brown, J.S., "Foundations of envisioning," Proceed. of AAAI, 1982.

4: Kuipers, B., De Kleer and Brown 'Mental Models', A Critique," TUWPICS No. 17, Working Papers in Cognitive Science, Tufts Univ., 1981.

5: Hart, P.E., "Directions for AI in the Eighties," SIGART newsletter, no. 79, Jan. 1982.

6: Michie D., "High-road and Low-road Programs," AI magazine, 3:1, 1982.

7: Chandrasekaran, B., and Mittal S., "Deep vs. Compiled Knowledge Approaches to Diagnostic Problem Solving," Proc. Second National AI Conf., AAAI, Pittsburgh, PA., 1982., revised version to appear in International Journal of Man Machine Studies, 1983.

8: Gomez, F. and Chandrasekaran, B., "Knowledge Organization and Distribution for Medical Diagnosis," IEEE Trans. System, Man and Cybernetics, SMC-11:1, 1981.

9: Chandrasekaran, B., "Decomposition of Domain Knowledge into Knowledge Sources: The MDX Approach," Proc. of Fourth National Conf. of Canadian Society for the Computational Studies Of Intelligence (CSCSI/SCEIO), 1982., Revised in "Towards a Taxonomy of Problem Solving Types," AI magazine, Winter/Spring , 1983.

10: Rouse, W.B., and Hunt, R.M., "A Fuzzy Rule-Based Model Of Human Problem Solving in Fault Diagnosis Task," Working Paper, Coord. Science Lab, Univ. Illinois, Urbana, 1980.

11: Patil, R.S., "Causal Representation of Patient Illness for Electrolyte and Acid Base Diagnosis," Ph.D. Dissert., TR-267, MIT Lab for Computer Science, Cambridge, Mass., 1981.

12: Pople H.E., "Heuristic Methods For Imposing Structures On Ill-Structured Problems," Artificial Intelligence In Medicine, ed. by Szolovits, Westview, 1982.

13: Davis R., Shrobe H., Hamscher W., Wieckert, K., Shirly M., Polit S., "Diagnosis Based on Description of Structure and Function ," Natnl conf. on AI, 1982.

14: Davis R., "Diagnosis via Causal Reasoning: Paths of Interaction and the Locality Principle," Natnl. conf. on AI , 1983.

15: Moorthy V.S., and Chandrasekaran B., "A Functional Representation of Devices and Compilation of Expert Problem Solving Systems", Tech. report, AI group, Dept of Comp and Info Science, Ohio State University, Sept.,1983.

16: Chandrasekaran B., "Expert System: Matching Techniques to Tasks", Invited Presentation at the Newyork Univ. Symposium on "Artificial Intelligence Applications for Business", May 1983.

17: Chandrasekaran B., Mittal S., "Conceptual Representation of Medical Knowledge for Diagnosis by Computer: MDX and related Systems", in Advances in Computers Vol.,22, Academic Press,Inc. 1983.

ACKNOWLEDGEMENTS

Research was supported in part by AFOSR Grant 82-0255 and NSF Grant MCS 8103480.

APPENDIX

Details of the functional representation of FUNCTION: buzz of the buzzer

NOTE: We have represented below only the buzzer;
Battery,coil,clapper and manual switch have NOT been represented.

```
DEVICE   buzzer
   FUNCTION:
        buzz: TOMAKE buzzing (buzzer)
              IF pressed (manual-switch)*
              PROVIDED  INITIAL elect-connected (t7,t8)
              BY behavior1

        stop-buzz:TOMAKE  ~buzzing (buzzer)
                  IF  ~pressed (manual-switch)
                  PROVIDED INITIAL buzzing (buzzer)
                  BY behavior5



   STRUCTURE:
        COMPONENTS:
            manual-switch (t1,t2), battery (t3,t4),
            coil (t5,t6,space1), clapper (t7,t8,space2)

        RELATIONS:
            serially-connected (manual-switch,battery,coil,clapper),
            includes (space1,space2)

        ABSTRACTIONS-OF-COMPONENTS:
            COMPONENT clapper (T1,T2,SPACE)
                FUNCTIONS: mechanical,acoustic,magnetic
                STATES: elect-connected (T1,T2),
                        repeated-hit (clapper)
            COMPONENT coil (T1,T2,SPACE)
                FUNCTIONS: magnetic
                STATES: magnetized (SPACE), voltage-applied(T1,T2)

            COMPONENT  manual-switch(T1,T2)
                FUNCTIONS: connect
                STATES: elect-connected (T1,T2),
                        pressed (manual-switch)

            COMPONENT  battery (T1,T2)
                FUNCTIONS: voltage
```

```
BEHAVIOR:

     behavior1:

               pressed (manual-switch)*
                        ||
                        ||  BY behavior2
                        ||
                        \/
   { elect-connected (t7,t8);  elect-connected (t7,t8)} *
                        ||
                        ||  USING FUNCTION mechanical OF
                        ||      clapper(t7,t8,space1)
                        ||
                        \/
               repeated-hit (clapper)
                        ||
                        ||  USING FUNCTION acoustic OF
                        ||      clapper (t7,t8,space2)
                        ||
                        \/
               buzzing ( clapper)
                        |||
                        |||
               buzzing (buzzer)


     behavior2:

          {    pressed (manual-switch)
                        ||
                        ||  BY behavior3
                        ||
                        \/
               ~elect-connected (t7,t8)
                        ||
                        ||  AS-PER knowledge1 IN-THE-CONTEXT-OF
                        ||      serially-connected (battery,coil,
                        ||               clapper,manual-switch) ^
                        ||      FUNCTION voltage OF battery
                        \/
               ~voltage-applied (t5,t6)
                        ||
                        ||  BY behavior4
                        ||
                        \/
               elect-connected (t7,t8) } *
```

```
behavior3:

        pressed (manual-switch)
                ||
                ||  USING FUNCTION connect OF
                ||    manual-switch (t1,t2)
                ||
                \/
        elect-connected (t1,t2)
                ||
                ||  AS-PER  knowledge1 IN-THE-CONTEXT-OF
                ||    FUNCTION voltage OF battery ,
                ||    serially-connected (battery,coil,
                ||        clapper,manual-switch)
                ||
                \/
        voltage-applied (t5,t6)
                ||
                ||  BY  behavior4
                ||
                \/
        ~elect-connected (t7,t8)




behavior4: IFF

        voltage-applied (t5,t6)
                ||
                ||  USING FUNCTION magnetic OF
                ||     coil (t5,t6,space1)
                ||
                \/
        magnetized (space1)
                ||
                ||  AS-PER knowledge2 IN-THE-CONTEXT-OF
                ||    includes (space1,space2)
                ||
                \/
        magnetized (space2)
                ||
                ||  USING FUNCTION magnetic OF
                ||     clapper (t7,t8,space2)
                ||
                \/
        ~elect-connected (t7,t8)
```

```
GENERIC KNOWLEDGE:
   knowledgel:

               Voltage-applied (tl,t2)
                       ||
                       ||  AS-PER kirchoff's-law
                       ||    IN-THE-CONTEXT-OF
                       ||    elect-connected (tl,t3),
                       ||    elect-connected (t2,t4)
                       ||
                       \/
               voltage-applied (t3,t4)


   knowledge2:

               magnetized (spacel)
                       ||
                       ||  AS-PER laws-of-space
                       ||   IN-THE-CONTEXT-OF
                       ||      includes (spacel,space2)
                       ||
                       \/
               magnetized (space2)




 ASSUMPTIONS:
   DEFINITIONS:
        fl= magnetic-force DUE-TO magnetized (space)
        f2= spring-force  DUE-TO  loaded (spring)

     assumptionl:
        IF magnetized (space) THEN fl > f2

     assumption2:
        IF ~magnetized (space) THEN fl < f2


END-DEVICE buzzer
```

ABOUT THE AUTHORS

V.S. Moorthy received his Bachelor of Engineering from Madras University in 1967; Master of Technology from Indian Institute of Technology, Bombay in 1970; and Ph.D. from Indian Institute of Technology, Bombay in 1978. He is currently visiting assistant professor at the Department of Information and Computer Science, OSU. His current interests include expert systems, natural language processing, and programming languages. He is a member of ACM, SIGART, and American Association for Artificial Intelligence.

Dr. B. Chandrasekaran is a professor of computer and information science at Ohio State University where he heads a group of faculty and graduate students in knowledge-based systems research. He is supported by grants and contracts from the National Science Foundation, Air Force Office of Scientific Research, Department of Defense, Wright-Patterson Air Force Base, and Battelle Labs. He has developed a collection of new ideas for the design of diagnostic systems and designed a medical diagnosis system called MDX. His group has also developed CSRL, a family of special knowledge engineering languages. He is author of over 50 papers and chair of the IEEE Systems, Man and Cybernetics Society Technology Communications on AI, as well as associate editor of the SMC Transactions.

APPLICATION OF THE CSRL LANGUAGE TO THE DESIGN OF EXPERT DIAGNOSIS SYSTEMS: THE AUTO-MECH EXPERIENCE

Michael C. Tanner and Tom Bylander

Department of Computer and Information Science
The Ohio State University
Columbus, OH 43210

Abstract

Auto-Mech is an expert system which diagnoses automobile fuel systems. Its organization and strategies are patterned after MDX, an expert diagnosis system developed in our AI laboratory. The problems that these systems are able to diagnose are represented as nodes within a hierarchy. Each node has knowledge about how to confirm or reject the problem hypothesis, as well as knowledge about what nodes to consider next. This approach is intended to be a domain-independent methodology for providing focused problem solving and for localizing knowledge in a conceptually relevant manner. Auto-Mech is implemented in a recently developed language called CSRL, which is specifically intended for building diagnostic expert systems. This paper describes Auto-Mech and discusses why the MDX approach and CSRL were useful in developing Auto-Mech, and where some difficulties were encountered.

1. Introduction

Over the past few years, our AI laboratory has developed an approach to the design of expert diagnosis systems based on the paradigm of "cooperating specialists." This approach is exemplified in an expert system called MDX [3, 6], whose expertise is in cholestatic liver disease. In order to demonstrate the viability of this approach to non-medical domains, we have developed a system called Auto-Mech which diagnoses problems in automobile fuel systems. We show that an organization of diagnostic knowledge which is similar to MDX can be used in this domain to provide focused problem solving, and to localize knowledge in a conceptually relevant manner.

Auto-Mech is implemented in a recently developed language called CSRL [2], which was designed specifically for building MDX-like diagnostic expert systems. Thus another goal of this work was to determine the strengths and weaknesses of CSRL and to make recommendations for future versions of CSRL.

Briefly, Auto-Mech works as follows. When Auto-Mech begins diagnosis, it obtains a specific complaint about the way the car operates. Then general hypotheses about the nature of the problem are evaluated. When a hypothesis is confirmed, any hypotheses which are immediately more specific are considered. The user is queried for additional information as needed during this process. Auto-Mech is not intended to be a complete model of an automobile mechanic, but is intended to reflect the information processing capability of a mechanic when she attempts to determine the specific cause of a fuel problem from an initial complaint and from things that a typical mechanic can observe when she looks under the hood.

Before we present a more detailed description of Auto-Mech, we give an overview of our approach to diagnostic problem solving. We then describe the program, explaining the assumptions that we have made, and outlining its organization. An annotated session of Auto-Mech and a sample of its CSRL code is included. Finally, we discuss why our approach and CSRL were useful in developing Auto-Mech, and where some difficulties were encountered.

2. Introduction to Diagnostic Problem Solving

The central problem solving of diagnosis, in our view, is classificatory activity. This is a specific type of problem solving in our approach, meaning that a special kind of organization and special strategies are strongly associated with performing expert diagnosis. We will not examine here how classificatory diagnosis fits in with our overall theory of problem solving (see Chandrasekaran [4]). Instead, we will briefly overview the structure and the strategies of classificatory diagnosis. For the purposes of this discussion, we will use "diagnosis" in place of "classificatory diagnosis" with the understanding that the complete diagnostic process includes other elements as well.

The diagnostic task is the identification of a case description with a specific node in a pre-determined diagnostic hierarchy. Each node in the hierarchy corresponds to a hypothesis about the state of the "patient" (a car in the Auto-Mech program). Nodes higher in the hierarchy represent more general hypothesis, while lower nodes are more specific. In medicine, a case description is the manifestations and the history of a patient, and a diagnostic hierarchy is a classification of diseases and disease classes. For example, MDX [3, 6] attempts to classify a medical case into a diagnostic hierarchy of cholestatic diseases. Figure 1 illustrates a fragment of MDX's hierarchy. The most general disease, cholestasis in this example, is the head node of the hierarchy. More specific cholestatic diseases such as extra-hepatic cholestasis are classified within the hierarchy. In the following discussion, we will use the generic term "problem" rather than "disease".

```
                      Cholestasis
                  _______/    \_______
                 /                    \
          Extra-hepatic           Intra-hepatic
           Cholestasis             Cholestasis
            /        \
           /          \
   EHC Due to        EHC Due to
 Bile Duct Stone   Bile Duct Tumor
```

Figure 1: Fragment of MDX's diagnostic hierarchy

Each problem in the hierarchy is associated with a *specialist* which contains the diagnostic knowledge to evaluate the presence or absence of the problem from the case description. From this knowledge, the specialist determines a confidence value representing the amount of belief that the problem exists. If this value is high enough, the specialist is said to be *established*. Note that each specialist is a problem solver with its own knowledge base.

The basic strategy of the diagnostic task is a process of hypothesis refinement, which we call *establish-refine*. In this strategy, if a specialist establishes itself, then it *refines* the problem hypothesis by invoking its subspecialists, which also perform the establish-refine strategy. If the confidence value is low, the specialist *rejects* the problem hypothesis, and performs no further actions. Note that when this happens, the whole hierarchy below the specialist is eliminated from consideration. Otherwise the specialist *suspends* itself, and may later refine itself if its superior requests it. The processing ends (if we assume that only one problem is present) when a tip node specialist, a specialist with no subspecialists, has been established.

With regard to Figure 1, the following scenario might occur. First, the cholestasis specialist is invoked, since it is the top specialist in the hierarchy. Cholestasis is then established, and the two specialists below it are invoked. Extra-hepatic cholestasis is rejected, also eliminating EHC due to stone and bile duct cancer from further consideration. Finally, intrahepatic cholestasis establishes itself, and invokes its subspecialists.

Due to space and time limitations, we have not addressed several issues relevant to diagnostic problem solving (such as handling multiple problems). For a more detailed analysis, see Gomez and Chandrasekaran [5]. Test ordering, causal explanation of findings, and therapeutic action do not directly fall within the auspices of classificatory diagnosis, but expertise in any of these areas would certainly enhance a diagnostic system. Fully resolving these issues and integrating their solutions into the diagnostic framework are problems for future research.

3. The Automobile Diagnosis Program

3.1. Description of Auto-Mech

Auto-Mech is a program which diagnoses fuel problems in automobile engines. It was developed using CSRL (which will be described in Section 3.3) and the establish-refine problem-solving methodology described in Section 2.

One reason the domain of automobile diagnosis was chosen is that most people feel comfortable discussing car problems thus making such a program easy to demonstrate. We also had two good amateur mechanics available to serve as experts. We decided to concentrate on fuel problems because the fuel system is sufficiently complex to be interesting and simple enough to do in a short time.

Before discussing the program further a brief discussion of automobile fuel systems is in order. The purpose of the fuel system is to deliver a mixture of fuel and air to the cylinders of the engine. It can be divided into four major subsystems:

1. the fuel delivery subsystem which brings fuel from the tank to the carburetor,

2. the air intake which brings air into the carburetor,

3. the carburetor which mixes the air and fuel in the proper ratio, and

4. the vacuum manifold which brings the mixture to the cylinders.

These subsystems correspond to initial hypotheses about fuel system faults and each can be further refined by more detailed descriptions.

Just as hospitals have a routine series of data to collect about every patient admitted, Auto-Mech collects a set of initial data to get the diagnosis running. We refer to the initial data as defining the user's <u>complaint</u>. The complaint is a problem-condition pair where the problem is the symptom the user notices (such as stalling or running rough) and the conditions include the kind of driving in which the problem occurs (accelerating, idling, etc.) and the approximate engine temperature (hot, cold, or both). Note that the complaint is highly symptomatic.

We chose to implement a program around a generic automobile fuel system rather than the fuel system of a particular car. Reasoning about the fuel system depends on its design, which can vary in many ways. Within the CSRL framework each design requires its own diagnostic hierarchy so we had to make a few assumptions about the system. The major assumptions are:

- carbureted engine
- single barrel, single stage, downdraft carburetor
- mechanical fuel pump
- automatic transmission
- non-computer ignition
- automatic choke
- minimal pollution control systems

Each of these assumptions has diagnostic consequences. A carbureted engine, for example, will have a different set of problems than a fuel injected engine (the former can have a broken carburetor). Many of these assumptions would be valid for most cars built before 1980 or so. Those that are not would either add complexity without making the problem more interesting (such as a two-stage carburetor) or vary so widely that no single generic arrangement can be imagined (such as pollution controls).

We also made a few simplifying assumptions about the problem solving required of the program. The most important of these is our single complaint assumption.* This means that for any session with the program the user can specify only one major complaint (a problem-condition pair as described above). One difficulty with multiple complaints is the need to keep the problem-condition pairs together. If the complaints were "stalls while idling" and "hesitates on acceleration" it would be necessary to know "stalls", "hesitates", "idling", "acceleration", and that the complaints are not "stalls on acceleration" and "hesitates while idling". The simple data base provided with CSRL does not provide for this kind of reasoning. This could be rectified by implementing a special data base. Another difficulty with allowing many complaints is keeping the line of questioning focused on one complaint. Given many complaints, large portions of the hierarchy will be relevant and the questioning may appear random to a user unless some mechanism is used for focusing the questioning. Such a mechanism was not readily available. Solving these problems would have either added to the time taken for the project as a whole or subtracted from the time devoted to the main purpose of developing Auto-Mech — to test CSRL and establish-refine problem-solving. So we chose to restrict the problem-solving to a single complaint at a time.

Another simplifying assumption we made is that the data to be used by the system be from commonly available sources. Mechanics now have an array of computer analysis information available which our experts were unfamiliar with. So we limited ourselves to such data as whether a component is working and how the car behaves in certain situations.

Figure 2 shows part of the diagnostic hierarchy for Auto-Mech. Each node in the hierarchy is a specialist representing a hypothesis together with knowledge about how to confirm or reject the hypothesis. For example, the specialist named Delivery represents the hypothesis "Fuel delivery subsystem is causing the problem." Delivery also contains knowledge about the types of

---

*This is most emphatically <u>not</u> a single fault assumption. If there is more than one fault causing the complaint, Auto-Mech can find it.

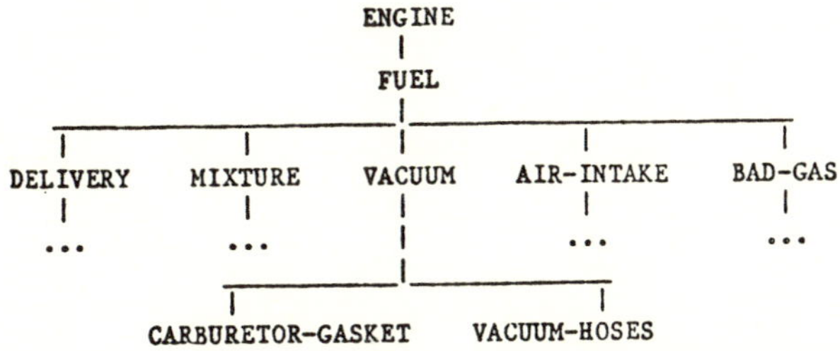

Figure 2: Partial Diagnostic Hierarchy for Auto-Mech

complaints for which fuel delivery problems should be considered and how to infer that fuel is not being delivered to the carburetor. The purpose of the top-level specialist, Engine, is to collect the initial complaint information and begin diagnosis. The ellipsis in the diagram represent points where the hierarchy continues down.

3.2. Annotated Transcript of a Session with Auto-Mech

In the following transcript of a session with Auto-Mech the user's responses follow the ">" prompt, comments are underlined, and everything else comes from the program.

> The user first tells the top level specialist, Engine, to establish and then refine itself. The program then prints a brief statement of the diagnostic system's scope and begins collecting information about the problem.

```
>DoCSRL Engine Establish-Refine

This is a program to diagnose automobile problems.  At the present
time the the program only knows about fuel problems.  The first series
of questions is an attempt to determine what the problem is (starting
problem, rough running, stalling, hesitation, slow response,
knocking), and the conditions under which it occurs (idling, loading,
accelerating, cruising, turning, decelerating, engine temperature).
After this the rest of the questions are attempts to confirm or reject
hypotheses.

Do you have problems starting your car?>?

  Answers:
     Y = Yes
     N = No
```

U = Unknown

If the user doesn't know how to respond, "?" will provide a description of acceptable answers. All of the questions in this program are answered "yes", "no", or "unknown" for simplicity. CSRL does provide facilities for using any answers which are appropriate including such things as numerical values and multiple choice.

Do you have problems starting your car?>N

Does the car stall?>N

Does the car run rough?>Y

Does the problem occur while idling?>N

Does the problem occur on loading?>Y

Does the problem occur while the engine is both hot and cold?>Y

The problem the user has specified is "the engine runs rough" and the conditions are "on loading and independent of engine temperature". The only purpose of the Engine specialist is to determine the complaint. Certain terms require specific definitions in order to clearly separate some problems and conditions. For example, loading means putting some strain on the engine without accelerating, idling means the engine is running but there is no load on it.

```
>>> Message Trace <<<
From: ENGINE To: FUEL
Message: ((ESTABLISH FUEL))
```

Engine now refines by first telling its subspecialist, Fuel, to establish.

Have you eliminated ignition as a possible cause of the problem?>Y

This question shows the need to know what other specialists have done. Auto experts have determined that many problems which might be fuel problems are more likely to be ignition problems. This user's auto complaint is one of those cases so Fuel wants to make sure Ignition has rejected itself. However, Ignition has not been implemented so the user is asked if the ignition system has been considered and rejected.

```
>>> Message Trace <<<
From: FUEL To: ENGINE
Message: ((ESTABLISHED FUEL 2))
```

```
>>> Message Trace <<<
From: ENGINE To: FUEL
Message: ((REFINE FUEL))
```

Once its subspecialist, Fuel, establishes, Engine continues to refine by telling Fuel to refine itself. The next series of messages and questions show the program considering Delivery, Mixture, Vacuum, Air-Intake, and Bad-Gas as hypotheses about the cause of the problem. The data base provided with CSRL records each question asked and the user's answers to avoid asking them again. So the decisions the specialists make are not based entirely on the answers to questions shown under each specialist, but on combinations of the answers to those and previous answers.

```
>>> Message Trace <<<
From: FUEL To: DELIVERY
Message: ((ESTABLISH DELIVERY))

Is any fuel delivered to the carburetor?>U

>>> Message Trace <<<
From: DELIVERY To: FUEL
Message: ((REJECTED DELIVERY -2))

>>> Message Trace <<<
From: FUEL To: MIXTURE
Message: ((ESTABLISH MIXTURE))

Have you been getting bad gas mileage?>N

>>> Message Trace <<<
From: MIXTURE To: FUEL
Message: ((REJECTED MIXTURE -3))

>>> Message Trace <<<
From: FUEL To: VACUUM
Message: ((ESTABLISH VACUUM))

>>> Message Trace <<<
From: VACUUM To: FUEL
Message: ((ESTABLISHED VACUUM 3))

>>> Message Trace <<<
From: FUEL To: AIR-INTAKE
Message: ((ESTABLISH AIR-INTAKE))

Is the air filter old?>N

>>> Message Trace <<<
From: AIR-INTAKE To: FUEL
Message: ((REJECTED AIR-INTAKE -2))
```

```
>>> Message Trace <<<
From: FUEL To: BAD-GAS
Message: ((ESTABLISH BAD-GAS))

Have you tried a higher grade of gas?>Y

>>> Message Trace <<<
From: BAD-GAS To: FUEL
Message: ((REJECTED BAD-GAS -3))

>>> Message Trace <<<
From: FUEL To: VACUUM
Message: ((REFINE VACUUM))
```

Fuel now asks its established subspecialists to refine. In this case only Vacuum has established.

```
>>> Message Trace <<<
From: VACUUM To: VACUUM-HOSES
Message: ((ESTABLISH VACUUM-HOSES))

Are there any cracked, punctured or loose vacuum hoses?>U
```

This question seems strange because it appears to be equivalent to asking whether the hypothesis should be confirmed. But when Auto-Mech gets to a very specific hypothesis usually the only data for confirming or rejecting it comes from direct observation of a part.

```
Can you hear hissing while the engine is running?>N

Are the vacuum hoses old?>Y

>>> Message Trace <<<
From: VACUUM-HOSES To: VACUUM
Message: ((UNKNOWN VACUUM-HOSES 1))
```

The information that Vacuum-Hoses has is not certain, some indicates trouble and some doesn't. So the answer is "unknown", but the value "1" indicates that it leans toward establishing.

```
>>> Message Trace <<<
From: VACUUM To: CARBURETOR-GASKET
Message: ((ESTABLISH CARBURETOR-GASKET))

Can you see cracks in the carburetor gasket?>Y

>>> Message Trace <<<
From: CARBURETOR-GASKET To: VACUUM
Message: ((ESTABLISHED CARBURETOR-GASKET 3))
```

Here is an example of how the hierarchy sets context for lower level specialists. The carburetor gasket often appears cracked or split but does not cause problems. Cracks in it are thus indicative of trouble only in a context in which a vacuum leak is suspected.

```
Is the diagnosis of VACUUM finished?>Y
```

CSRL and Auto-Mech are unable to determine when diagnosis is finished. The mechanism we use asks the user as control passes up through the hierarchy from the lowest point reached. If the user answers "Yes", as in this case, then control passes on up the hierarchy. Another of the user's options here is to answer "No". In that case CSRL would refine those subspecialists of Vacuum which were "unknown", such as Vacuum-Hoses. Unless the program is told to do this only "established" subspecialists will get refined. In this particular case the question indicates a bug in the Auto-Mech program itself since Vacuum's subspecialists are all tip specialists.

```
>>> Message Trace <<<
From: VACUUM To: FUEL
Message: ((ESTABLISHED CARBURETOR-GASKET 3) (UNKNOWN  VACUUM-HOSES 1))

Is the diagnosis of FUEL finished?>Tree

FUEL -- 2
   DELIVERY -- -2
   MIXTURE -- -3
   VACUUM -- 3
       VACUUM-HOSES -- 1
       CARBURETOR-GASKET -- 3
   AIR-INTAKE -- -2
   BAD-GAS -- -3
```

The user also has the option of printing out the diagnostic hierarchy with the values displayed for each specialist.

```
Is the diagnosis of FUEL finished?>Y

>>> Message Trace <<<
From: FUEL To: ENGINE
Message: ((UNKNOWN VACUUM-HOSES 1) (ESTABLISHED  CARBURETOR-GASKET 3)
(REJECTED BAD-GAS -3) (REJECTED  AIR-INTAKE -2) (ESTABLISHED VACUUM 3)
(REJECTED MIXTURE -3) (REJECTED DELIVERY -2))

Is the diagnosis of ENGINE finished?>Y

(ANSWER (REJECTED DELIVERY -2)
        (REJECTED MIXTURE -3)
```

```
(ESTABLISHED VACUUM 3)
(REJECTED AIR-INTAKE -2)
(REJECTED BAD-GAS -3)
(ESTABLISHED CARBURETOR-GASKET 3)
(UNKNOWN VACUUM-HOSES 1)
(ESTABLISHED FUEL 2)
(ESTABLISHED ENGINE 3))
```

The answer is simply a list of the specialists which ran and their values. The diagnosis is the established tip specialists, Carburetor-Gasket in this case.

3.3. How One of Auto-Mech's Specialists Reasons

Figure 3 shows the CSRL code for implementing the Bad-Gas specialist which considers the hypothesis "Something wrong with the fuel is causing the problem." The specialist is defined by the Define-Concept statement. Like all CSRL specialists it is made of three parts:

- Declarations, containing information about where the specialist fits in the hierarchy.
- Knowledge-Groups, showing the major categories of decisions to be made.
- Body, which controls the way in which the specialist responds to various messages.

The boldface represents built-in CSRL primitives, everything else is determined by the system builder. And-YNU is a three-valued logical AND which is defined for Y, N, and U. Use-Declaration and Use-Statement invoke CSRL macro-instructions that expand into longer sequences of statements which do not vary from specialist to specialist. The Use-Declaration's here set up standard variables and constants for the CSRL interpreter to use. The Use-Statement's implement the establish-refine problem-solving process. Since the interesting thing is how Bad-Gas establishes or rejects itself, we will not discuss these other processes here.

The general description of how Bad-Gas reasons is:

> First make sure Bad-Gas is a relevant hypothesis to hold. If it is not then reject. If it is relevant find out if there is any reason to believe something has happened to the fuel recently. If there is none then reject. But if there is some reason to believe this then establish with value depending on how relevant the hypothesis is.

```
(Define-Concept Bad-Gas
  (Declarations (Subconcept-Of Fuel)
                (Subconcepts Low-Octane
                             Water-In-Fuel
                             Dirt-In-Fuel)
                (Use-Declaration Usual-Variables)
                (Use-Declaration Usual-Constants))
  (Knowledge-Groups
    (Relevant
       (Options (End-After (Match 1)))
       (Table (Conditions
                (Ask-YNU? "Is the car slow to respond")
                (Ask-YNU? "Does the car start hard")
                (And-YNU
                 (Ask-YNU? "Do you hear knocking or pinging sounds")
                 (Ask-YNU? "Does the problem occur while accelerating")))
               (Match (If ( Y  ?  ? ) Then -3)
                      (If ( ?  Y  ? ) Then -3)
                      (If ( ?  ?  Y ) Then  3)
                      (If ( ?  ?  ? ) Then  1))))
    (Gas
       (Options (End-After (Match 1)))
       (Table (Conditions
                (Ask-YNU? "Have you tried a higher grade of gas")
                (Ask-YNU? "Did the problem start after the last fillup")
                (Ask-YNU? "Has the problem gotten worse since the last
                           fillup"))
               (Match (If ( Y  ?  ? ) Then -3)
                      (If ( ?  Y  ? ) Then  3)
                      (If ( ?  N  Y ) Then  2)
                      (If ( ?  ?  ? ) Then -3))))
    (Summary
       (Options (End-After (Match 1)))
       (Table (Conditions Relevant  Gas)
              (Match (If (   3     (Ge 0) ) Then  3)
                     (If (   1     (Ge 0) ) Then  2)
                     (If (   ?     (Lt 0) ) Then -3)))))
  (Body
    (Use-Statement Usual-Establish-Refine)
    (Message-Block (Establish Self)
        (Execute Relevant)
        (Case Relevant
          ((Ge 0)(Execute Gas Summary)
                 (Establish-Reply Summary))
          (Otherwise (Establish-Reply Relevant))))
    (Use-Statement Simple-Refine)
    (Use-Statement Pass-Messages)))
```

Figure 3: CSRL code for a specialist

To implement this Bad-Gas has a group of statements in the Body which begin

```
(Message-Block (Establish Self) ... )
```

and which will be activated when a message to establish is received from the Fuel specialist.* The Message-Block controls the order in which the Knowledge-Groups (Relevant, Gas, and Summary) are evaluated. Summary combines the results of Relevant and Gas. The

```
(Execute Relevant)
```

statement causes the Relevant knowledge-group to run. If Relevant returns a non-negative value the Gas and Summary groups run with the establish-value of Bad-Gas set by Summary. If Relevant returns a negative value the establish-value of Bad-Gas is set by Relevant and the other two groups are not run. This choice is implemented by the construct:

```
(Case Relevant
  ((Ge 0)    ... )
  (Otherwise ... ))
```

Very detailed descriptions of how all of the knowledge groups work is not necessary. In general, running a knowledge-group consists of testing its Conditions and trying to match their results to one of the rows in the Match table. A condition which begins with Ask-YNU? causes CSRL to look in its string-value data base for the given string. If found then the value stored there becomes the value of the condition. If not found, the string is displayed as a question to the user. The user's response is stored in the string-value data base and is used as the value of the condition. If the condition is the name of a knowledge-group its value is the value of the knowledge-group. The rows (or "rules") of the Match table are tried one at a time, from the top down. As soon as a row is found which matches the value of the conditions, the Then-part gives the value of the knowledge-group and the evaluation of the knowledge-group stops. The "?" in the tables is a wild-

---

*CSRL can be viewed as a restricted object oriented language in which the objects are the specialists and the messages are instructions to the specialists.

card, it matches any value.

In the transcript given earlier the value of the conditions in the Relevant knowledge-group are (N N N) so the row

If (? ? ?) Then 1

matches and the value of Relevant is 1. This is a result of the previously supplied information that the complaint is "runs rough on loading" combined with the single complaint assumption. As a result Gas and Summary are run. The value of the conditions in Gas are (Y - -), where "-" signifies "did not ask", and the row

If (Y ? ?) Then -3

matches. This is the result of asking a question of the user. So now the values of the conditions for Summary are (1 -3) which matches

If (? (Lt 0)) Then -3

and the value of Summary is -3, causing Bad-Gas to reject.

For more detail about CSRL see [2] and [1].

3.4. Usefulness of CSRL in Developing Auto-Mech

One of the first things we noticed in using CSRL is that the internal workings of a specialist and the overall problem-solving method is easy to explain to a computer-naive expert.* Establish-refine seemed to be a natural way for the experts to solve the problems and was not in any way imposed upon them. The specialists in the diagnostic hierarchy of Auto-Mech represent the hypotheses considered by the experts during the solution of practice problems. The experts quickly understood the CSRL specialists and could point out flaws in their reasoning during debugging sessions.

---

*Our experts were Ph.D. students in Nuclear Engineering, they were not computer specialists and knew very little about AI.

Another helpful feature of CSRL is that it makes it easy to get something running quickly. This gives the experts a chance to actually run the program to see the results of their suggestions. It is much easier for experts to help debug a running program than to debug a paper construct. CSRL makes possible the development of partial systems, the obvious evidence for which is that we can develop a fuel system program without being concerned with the rest of the car. Much of this is due to our approach to diagnosis in which knowledge is localized within specialists and the interaction among specialists is simple and well-defined. Concerns about global interaction of knowledge are minimized. Changes in the Delivery specialist will not affect any other specialists in the hierarchy (except for the context assumed by its subspecialists, an easy thing to check). So if Vacuum works right but Delivery has bugs in it, fixing Delivery will not affect Vacuum. This greatly simplifies building and debugging a system over the traditional knowledge-base/inference-engine approach.

Auto-Mech consists of 34 specialists in a hierarchy which varies from four to six levels deep. Four people were actively involved with its development, two computer specialists and two domain experts. The total labor was approximately five man-months of which about 30% was domain expert time. The project extended over nine calendar months.

3.5. Some Difficulties

CSRL was built to embody a theory of diagnosis which was developed in the medical domain. The diagnostic reasoning of an automobile mechanic, however, is slightly different from that of a doctor. Once a hypothesis is confirmed a doctor will carefully consider the competing refinement hypotheses and follow up on the best. This is the behavior modeled by the establish-refine theory. But an auto mechanic seems to follow up the first reasonable refinement. Auto-Mech does not capture this latter behavior. It could be done in CSRL, though it would be a little more difficult to do than using the standard establish-refine routines. The end result of diagnosis in both cases is the same, but presently Auto-Mech seems dumb to an expert since it is being more careful than necessary.

Mechanics usually do not go straight into the kind of diagnostic reasoning which requires a diagnostic hierarchy. The complaints are associated with typical maintenance or repair procedures as a result of the training or experience of the mechanic. An example of this is:

> Temperature dependent problems (those that happen only when the engine is cold or only when it is hot) are usually caused by a malfunction of the choke. So for those problems first check to see that the choke works correctly and if it does not then fix it. Also, since you have to go past the air filter to get to the choke, make sure the air filter is good.

Only after all the applicable procedures like this get tried does the mechanic do the more serious diagnosis done by Auto-Mech. This process is outside the scope of both CSRL and the establish-refine theory but it is actually only an efficiency measure. The final diagnoses using the mechanic's method and using establish-refine are the same, with establish-refine possibly doing more work.

One of the problems we had in developing Auto-Mech is that we could not treat establishing a specialist, or confirming a hypothesis, as indicating a high degree of belief in the hypothesis. Sometimes in Auto-Mech a specialist establishes because it is not possible to reject it and one of its subspecialists may be able to establish. So during diagnosis, when a specialist establishes it really means "this hypothesis is worth pursuing." This is mainly due to the type of domain that we were working with. Most of the data used by Auto-Mech are very weak at indicating specific problems. Data that are direct are usually about tip hypotheses and of the form "is xxx working correctly." Thus the specialists which rely on indirect data are unable to produce high confidence in their associated hypotheses, although they can still determine a "pursuit value." The theory of establish-refine problem solving, which CSRL is based on, needs to be modified to take this into account.

The question of when to stop is a difficult one for diagnosis in general. Human experts have the concept of a diagnosis "explaining" the data and that certain data must be explained while other data need not be. Automating this decision has proven to be difficult, though it seems clear that it is not a decision appropriately made by the diagnostic expert itself but rather by some outside entity having additional knowledge and skills. This is why CSRL currently asks if the user is satisfied as control passes back up through the hierarchy. However, in the automobile domain the system should recommend fixing the problems represented by established tip specialists and then ask if the problem persists after the repairs are made. The answer to that question could be data for another round of diagnosis. Once again, this could be fixed within CSRL (the problem arises from the built-in Simple-Refine macro which was designed to be very general and would need to be customized for Auto-Mech).

In the establish-refine theory of diagnostic problem-solving, diagnosis is seen as an inherently parallel process [5]. All specialists at a given level in the hierarchy may be active simultaneously. These specialists communicate their status (established or rejected) to each other via a blackboard. This makes it possible for a specialist to know what another specialist has done. Sometimes this knowledge is necessary, as can be seen in the example session given earlier where the Fuel specialist wanted to know the status of the Ignition specialist. CSRL is presently implemented as a serial language without a blackboard. This leads to some occasional awkwardness as the Fuel specialist's question to the user shows.

Another feature of establish-refine theory is that it is strictly a theory of classificatory reasoning and that other kinds of reasoning are needed to do diagnosis. In particular inferential reasoning about data is needed. For example, if the user's problem is one which involves the engine running then the system should know that there is fuel in the tank even if that piece of data is not explicitly given to it. This is reasoning about relationships between pieces of data and is not classificatory in nature. In MDX there is an intelligent data base component, called PATREC [6, 7], for doing such reasoning about medical data. CSRL is intended to be used for the diagnostic component and so it does not contain an intelligent data base. Since this component is absent in Auto-Mech, we have had to clutter our diagnostic specialists with data base reasoning.

4. Summary and Recommendations

The relative length of the "difficulties" section compared to the "usefulness" section is due to the need for additional programming and the CSRL language rather than deficiencies in the theory of diagnostic problem-solving. The difficulties point to some recommendations for improvements in CSRL:

1. Changes from the standard control flow should be easier to make. Presently all hypotheses at one level are tried before going down to the next level. The control needed by Auto-Mech is a natural complement to this -- pursue the first reasonable hypothesis.

2. CSRL needs a more flexible facility for determining when to stop than simply asking the user. System builders may have ideas on how to do it for specific problems without necessarily being able to solve the general problem of deciding when diagnosis is complete.

3. Since CSRL is to be used for building diagnostic experts it should provide a facility for limited communication between specialists across the hierarchy, such as a blackboard. Such a facility would be useful even if CSRL remains a serial language.

Our other problems were the result of things which it would not be appropriate for CSRL to address since they are outside the scope of classificatory diagnosis. These include the intelligent data base and the execution of typical maintenance procedures prior to diagnosis.

Overall CSRL was a very useful tool for developing a diagnostic expert system. It was easy to explain to an expert, the specialists were fairly easy to write based on protocols, and a partial system could be running quickly for debugging purposes. CSRL was also easy to use from a programmer's point of view.

Auto-Mech does not verify the validity of establish-refine problem-solving but it does demonstrate that establish-refine is a viable method for doing diagnosis. It is a natural way for experts to solve problems. The hypotheses they consider can be used as specialists within the diagnostic system. The localization of knowledge proved to be useful for development purposes.

Acknowledgments

We thank B. Chandrasekaran for his guidance and support during the course of this project. We also wish to thank Jiten Ruparel and Siavash Hashemi who served as our domain experts and Sriram Mahalingam who helped think out the problems associated with building Auto-Mech. Research on diagnostic expert systems for the domain of mechanical systems is supported by the Air Force Office of Scientific Research grant 82-0255.

References

1. T. Bylander. The CSRL Manual. in prep.

2. T. Bylander, S. Mittal, and B. Chandrasekaran. CSRL: A Language for Expert Systems for Diagnosis. IJCAI-83, 1983.

3. B. Chandrasekaran, F. Gomez, S. Mittal, and J. W. Smith. An Approach to Medical Diagnosis Based on Conceptual Structures. IJCAI-79, 1979.

4. B. Chandrasekaran. "Towards a Taxonomy of Problem Solving Types." AI Magazine 4, 1 (Winter/Spring 1983), 9-17.

5. F. Gomez and B. Chandrasekaran. "Knowledge Organization and Distribution for Medical Diagnosis." IEEE Trans. SM&C SMC-11, 1 (January 1981), 34-42.

6. S. Mittal. Design of a Distributed Medical Diagnosis and Database System. Ph.D. Th., Dept. of Comp. and Info. Sci., The Ohio State University, 1980.

7. S. Mittal and B. Chandrasekaran. "Conceptual Representation of Patient Data Bases." J. of Medical Systems (1981).

ABOUT THE AUTHORS

Michael C. Tanner is a doctoral student at Ohio State University. He received a B.S. in mathematics education and his M.S. in computer science from OSU. In addition to expert systems, his interests include learning, psychology, and computer graphics. He is an advisee of Dr. Chandrasekaran and has been working for him as a graduate research assistant for a year.

Tom Bylander is a doctoral graduate student in the Computer and Information Science Department at Ohio State University. He received his B.S. at the University of South Dakota and his M.S. at OSU. His dissertation research is concerned with commonsense reasoning about physical systems. Other interests include expert systems and linguistics. He is currently an advisee of Dr. Chandrasekaran and has been working for him as a graduate research assistant for the past 2 years.

AN EXPERT SYSTEM FOR REPRESENTING PROCEDURAL KNOWLEDGE

Michael Georgeff

Artificial Intelligence Center
SRI International
333 Ravenswood Avenue
Menlo Park, CA 94025

Abstract

Development of effective automatic systems for fault isolation and diagnosis requires reasoning about *sequences* of tests and actions. Unfortunately, traditional expert systems are not well suited to representing such procedural knowledge. In this paper, a scheme is presented that allows the explicit representation of both declarative and procedural knowledge within a unified framework, yet retains all the desirable properties of expert systems such as flexibility, explanatory capability and extendibility. In particular, the scheme allows any heuristic declarative knowledge that maintenance engineers may possess to be integrated easily and uniformly with the strong procedural methods of maintenance plans. Domain-specific metalevel knowledge can also be represented within the same formalism. A simple version of the scheme has been fully implemented and applied to the domain of automobile-engine fault diagnosis.

§1 Introduction

Maintenance teams play a very important role in military operations. However, maintenance technicians often lack the engineering knowledge necessary for effective fault diagnosis of technologically-advanced equipment. Sometimes, operational conditions may be such that it is simply not possible to provide sufficient maintenance support. It is therefore essential to automate as much of the fault-diagnosis process as possible.

The current approach is to provide automatic test equipment to guide technicians through a prespecified sequence of tasks, with the system making predefined decisions on the basis of the incoming data. This reduces the number of errors made in executing the maintenance procedures and frees the technicians from performing complex arithmetic and algebraic calculations.

However, the use of automatic test equipment as currently implemented is limited. The equipment is inflexible and insensitive to the skill level of the engineers using it. Such systems cannot modify their diagnostic procedures to match the requirements of the current situation nor can they accept potentially useful advice from technicians. Because these systems perform a prespecified sequence of tests, they cannot use knowledge of the particular situation to focus attention on more likely trouble spots. Consequently, turn-around time is high, and this is of critical importance under battle conditions. Further, the development cost of test software is large and time to maturation is lengthy.

These difficulties are unlikely to decrease with time. Advances in technology tend to make equipment more complex, rather than less. Operational scenarios are becoming more demanding, with the need for high sortie rates, very mobile units, and dispersed operations. Neither is the recruiting base likely to increase, and so far there is little evidence to suggest that the aptitudes or educational level of trainees are increasing. Even if they were, none but the most experienced and highly-educated engineer could be expected to understand adequately the functioning of advanced military equipment.

The design of current automatic test equipment is inadequate to meet these problems. What one really requires is a fault-diagnosis system that can effectively increase the expertise of the maintenance team, thereby minimizing referrals to senior engineering personnel and reducing the time taken in diagnosis. The system needs to be flexible and responsive to changes in conditions. It must focus on the problem at hand by opportunistically using knowledge and must interact with technicians in a way that uses their skills to maximum effect.

Such systems would enable effective fault isolation in conditions where it is not possible to refer problems to senior engineers (as in submarine operation, small in-field air support, and satellite applications), or where, because of mobility requirements, it is not possible to provide sufficient maintenance personnel. They have the potential for greatly reducing the time taken in fault diagnosis, and thus can provide a significant military advantage. Furthermore, the provision of additional expertise at a high level of competence enables problems to be correctly identified in the field rather than at a service depot, thus reducing logistics problems.

Recently, significant advances have been made in providing systems with just this sort of reasoning ability. Such systems are known as *expert systems* or *knowledge-based systems*. These systems utilize the knowledge of experts to reason about problems in the domain of interest in much the same way as the experts themselves. They have the ability to explain their reasoning to the expert or user, and can incrementally acquire new knowledge. They are flexible, can respond opportunistically to incoming data, and can modify their behaviour under variant conditions.

However, most of these systems are not well suited to problem domains where much of the expert knowledge is procedural and where tests and actions need to be carried out in a particular time order. Yet, this is exactly the type of knowledge that is common to the problem of fault diagnosis in complex military machinery.

In this paper we describe a scheme for *explicitly* representing procedural knowledge while still retaining the benefits of traditional expert systems. The basis of the scheme is to use a representation that is sufficiently rich to describe arbitrary sequences of actions in a simple and natural way, while at the same time avoiding explicit procedure "calling". The scheme also provides a mechanism for reasoning about the use of this knowledge, thus enabling fault isolation to proceed in an effective way. Systems that are based on this scheme are called *procedural expert systems* [Georgeff 83].

§2 Knowledge of the Domain

The major consideration in choosing a system architecture suitable for interactive fault diagnosis of military equipment is that much of the domain knowledge is represented procedurally. These procedures reflect knowledge about operational conditions, usage and experience with similar equipment, best engineering judgment, technical edicts, and economic considerations. The procedural nature of this knowledge is critical both to the conclusions made and to the efficiency of fault isolation.

Some of this knowledge is set down in the maintenance plans for the equipment under test. Some, also, is part of the general technical expertise of experienced maintenance engineers. It is clearly desirable that a maintenance system utilize both these sources of knowledge.

2.1 The Knowledge Represented in the Maintenance Plan

The maintenance plans for most military equipment include extensive instructions describing tests to perform and actions to carry out dependent on the outcome of the tests. Most are written as a sequence of steps in English, including conditional statements, "go to" statements, and transfers to specialized procedures. For example, a sample portion of the maintenance procedure used for testing the proper functioning of the F404 engine on the FA-18 aircraft is given in Table 1.

Some of the procedures are necessary to establish certain conclusions (i.e., the conclusions are *context dependent* or *time dependent*), and would be invalid if the procedures were not carried out in the order specified. For example, in Table 1, confirmation that all vibrations are less than 0.5 in/sec. (step B-9b) must be done *after* engine speed is stabilized if any conclusions based on this information are to be valid. Similarly, the time at which unusual noises are observed (e.g., step B-10b) is critical in determining the cause of any fault.

Other procedures reflect ease of maintenance, or tradeoffs between the likelihood of a particular component being faulty and the ease with which it can be examined or replaced. For example, it might not be *necessary* to check the setting of the fuel bypass button at the same time as checking the lube bypass button, but, as both buttons are adjacent to each other, it is *sensible* to do so. Similarly, checking the absence of fluid leaks (step B-10a) is done after deactivating the starter because it is both easiest and sufficient to do so then.

On the other hand, some information, particularly cautionary advice, needs to be made known at any time a particular condition is observed. For example, the cautions on reactivating the starter need to be advised at any time the engine is running and there is a possibility that the engineer will attempt a restart (step B-10). Also, some steps need not be done in the exact order specified in the maintenance plan (e.g., steps a, b and c of step B-9).

2.2 The Knowledge of Expert Maintenance Engineers

Much of the knowledge of expert maintenance engineers is declarative in nature, and, indeed, it is this component of expertise that most expert systems seek to utilize. For example, a typical piece of such knowledge might be:

"If there is oil on top of the engine housing, then it is likely that the seal on the oil-pressure sensor has failed."

However, a considerable part of maintenance expertise is also procedural in nature. Much of this is reflected in the procedures described in maintenance plans. However, an engineer's knowledge is usually more flexible than the strict algorithmic form of maintenance procedures. Also, it is often based on functional considerations rather than being specific to a particular engine. For example, in attempting to isolate a fault in an electrical system, a typical procedure is the feed-device-ground strategy [Feurzeig 83]: the expert focuses on the device, considers its input and output behavior, tests it using alternate feeds and grounds, and, depending on the outcome, moves along the feed or ground chain to another device.

Skilled maintenance engineers also know when to apply a piece of knowledge, such as when to terminate a diagnostic test if some particularly unusual fact suggests an alternative hypothesis. Such utilitarian knowledge, often called *metalevel* knowledge [Davis 76], is very important in enabling faults to be isolated in a reasonable amount of time.

2.3 The Representation of Maintenance Knowledge

The procedural knowledge typical of the maintenance domain is often difficult and cumbersome to describe using traditional expert systems, which encode most of their knowledge in declarative form. Even though some procedural knowledge can be incorporated in these systems, it is there only because the interpreter executes the rules procedurally in some specified order. This means that procedural knowledge and the establishment of contexts in which a particular inference is valid can only be represented implicitly in the system (e.g., by ordering the clauses of a premise and thus ensuring a particular sequence of evaluation).

This can create dependencies and interrelationships that tend to make the knowledge base not quite as modular or flexible as perhaps was originally intended. Because of the homogeneity of the rule representation, it is not possible to distinguish between those rules for which the order of invocation is important and those for which it is not. This is not only bad methodology, but it impairs the explanatory capability of the system and reduces the possibilities for efficient implementation on multiprocessor machines.

Note that we are not saying that such knowledge *cannot* be represented declaratively — all we are saying is that, in some domains, it cannot *easily* or *naturally* be so represented, which complicates the construction of the expert system and reduces its explanatory capability.

These problems have encouraged some researchers to investigate ways of representing procedural knowledge explicitly [Genesereth 82, Georgeff 82]. In the simplest cases, special mechanisms are introduced, such as heterogeneous sets of rules that are dissimilar in nature from the rest of the knowledge base (e.g., the therapy rules in MYCIN [Shortliffe 1976]), or precedence relations, which require that certain rules be invoked before others (e.g., "contexts" in Prospector [Reboh 1981]). Alternatively, specialist procedures may be used for certain sections of the problem-solving process. Some more general schemes have also been attempted [Reinstein 81, Aikins 83]. However, these approaches are either not sufficiently general to express procedural knowledge of any complexity, or tend to destroy many of the desirable properties of the system, such as flexibility, explanatory capability, and the ease with which new knowledge can be integrated incrementally into the existing knowledge base.

This suggests that a new form of expert system is required that allows for a more direct and explicit representation of procedural knowledge than provided by previous expert systems. Procedural expert systems [Georgeff 83, Bonollo 83] are one such approach.

§3 Procedural Expert Systems

The basic structure of a procedural expert system (PES) is similar to that of most rule-based expert systems. That is, it consists of (1) a knowledge base for storing information about both the problem domain and the specific problem being examined and (2) an inference mechanism for manipulating this knowledge [Buchanan 82]. The knowledge base itself comprises a data base containing *facts* about the problem and a set of specialized inference procedures called *knowledge areas* (KA).

A knowledge area consists of an *invocation part* and a *body*. The invocation part provides information on the utility of the KA, and may include cost estimates and conditions on both currently known facts and currently active goals. The invocation parts of the KAs can thus be used to reason about which KAs are potentially useful in solving the problem at hand.

The body of a KA can be viewed as a specialized inference procedure. In essence, it is simply a procedure that establishes sequences of subgoals to be achieved (facts to be discovered) and draws conclusions (establishes other facts) on the basis of achieving (or not achieving) these subgoals.

In order to aid in the construction of procedural expert systems, a system called Peritus has been implemented [Bonollo 83]. Although we will not discuss this system in any detail, for most of the examples we will use an actual example from an automobile engine fault-diagnosis system constructed using Peritus.

3.1 Representing Procedural Knowledge

In a procedural expert system, procedural knowledge is specified by using a recursive transition network (RTN). The arcs of the RTN are labeled with predicates (tests) and functions (actions), in much the same way as for an augmented transition network (ATN) [Woods 1970].

A given arc of the network can be traversed only if the predicate labeling that arc evaluates to "true". All traversable paths in the RTN are explored, beginning at a specified start state and ending at a specified final state. (This is unlike the procedure adopted for ATNs, which exit as soon as one path has been traversed to the final state.) The order in which the paths are explored should be considered as undefined (i.e., the validity of the inference procedure should not depend on this ordering). However, in the implementation described in this paper, paths are explored in a depth-first manner.

A typical KA body is shown in Figure 1. "*Start*" is the start state and "*end*" the final state of the network; the tests on arcs are indicated by a "?". Now if, for example, all the arc tests evaluated to "true," the transitions tr_1, tr_2, tr_3, tr_4, and tr_5 would all be made, and the actions a_2, a_3, a_4 and a_5 all executed, in that order, before the KA exited. If, on the other hand, test t_2 fails, then only the transitions tr_1 and tr_5 would be effected, and only action a_5 would be executed.

The functions and predicates labeling the arcs of the RTN can be any computable functions or predicates. In the Peritus system, these are specified in LISP and can make use of variables local to the KA. Free variables are not allowed.

There is also a special class of functions and predicates that access the data base and add new facts to it. Some of these predicates ask whether certain facts are true or not, and will set up subgoals to ascertain these facts if they are not currently known (i.e., not currently in the data base). Similarly, some of the functions labeling the arcs may draw conclusions that add facts to the data base, thus making it possible for previously requested subgoals to be achieved.

For example, consider the following procedure for isolating an electrical-system fault in an automobile engine that will not start [Gregory 1980]:

Spark-plug test: Disconnect a spark plug lead and see if a spark jumps to the cylinder head on attempted engine start. If the spark is satisfactory or blue, then the spark plug may be faulty. If the spark is absent, weak, or yellow, proceed to the next test.

Coil-lead test: (Instructions on how to test the spark from the coil) If the spark is satisfactory or blue, proceed to the next test. If the spark is absent, weak, or yellow, then the low-tension circuit is suspect; proceed to the low-tension test.

Distributor test: If there is evidence to suggest that the high-tension leads from the distributor are not operating properly, conclude that they may be faulty. If the high-tension leads appear to be in order, conclude that the distributor may be at fault.

Low-tension test:(Instructions about how to perform this test) If a test lamp lights on the ignition side of the coil but not on the distributor side, conclude that the coil and/or the coil lead may be faulty. If the test lamp doesn't light on the ignition side of the coil, conclude that the low-tension circuit may be faulty.

A KA corresponding to this procedure is shown in diagrammatic form in Figure 2. There are a number of things to note about the body of this KA (we shall consider the invocation part later). First, when facts are required to be established (e.g., as in "spark is satisfactory or blue") other KAs may be invoked to ascertain this information. In this case, an "ask-user"

KA might be invoked, but, in general, many KAs might respond before the fact is established (as might be the case, for instance, in checking the status of the high-tension leads).

Second, although this KA uses a simple tree structure, the RTN formalism can also represent other control constructs, including iteration and recursion. Such control constructs are needed when it is desired to examine different instances of a given object type. For example, we might have a KA (or KA "schema") for determining whether or not a single spark plug is faulty. This KA would be invoked whenever a goal was set up to determine the status of some *particular* spark plug. However, by using iteration (represented as a loop in an RTN), we can also set up this goal for any arbitrary number of spark plugs in the engine, thus creating multiple instances of the spark plug KA. The ability to explicitly establish goals in this way can be very useful when one wishes to examine different instances of a given object type in a specified order (e.g., such as testing the spark plugs in firing order) or when a certain conclusion depends on interactions among instances.

Third, note that the KA given in Figure 2 is applicable to a wide class of engines, and not just one particular configuration. In general, the system can base its reasoning on structural models of the device, and use "generic" KAs rather than specific ones. For example, the feed-device-ground strategy mentioned in Section 2.2 can easily be represented as a KA.

3.2 Representing Utilitarian Knowledge

The invocation part of a KA provides domain-specific knowledge on the utility of the KA and can be used by the system in deciding which KA to invoke next. Such knowledge can be utilized directly by the interpreter, or, in a more general system, by *metalevel* KAs to constrain and order the application of object-level KAs.

In the current implementation, the only knowledge provided in the invocation part is a statement describing what *goals* (hypotheses) the KA is useful for investigating or what *facts* (new data) the KA is useful for explaining. An invocation part consisting solely of a goal statement results in standard goal-directed invocation, whereas a fact statement results in standard data-driven invocation. For example, two simple KAs from the automotive domain are shown in Figure 3. In Figure 3(a), the KA is goal-directed and corresponds to a standard MYCIN-like rule. This KA will be invoked only if *some* current goal is to identify a fuel-system problem, and the required information is not currently known (i.e., in the data base). Invocation of the KA will then test whether there is reduced fuel flow in the fuel pump, possibly invoking other KAs to ascertain this. If reduced fuel flow is concluded, the [single] arc of the network can be traversed and the fuel system problem identified (with some degree of certainty) as being a choked suction line.

An example of a data-driven KA is given in Figure 3(b). Note that the test in the body of the KA seems redundant in this case, as the KA would not have been invoked if it had not already been known that the oil was contaminated with water. However, it is important from a methodological point of view to require that the body of a KA be valid irrespective of the invocation criteria. Under these conditions, if the inference procedures forming the bodies of all the KAs in the knowledge base are consistent, the system will be consistent. The apparent inefficiency of having to check the data base twice for (in this case) the condition of the oil can be eliminated during a compilation stage.

KAs can also be partly goal-directed and partly data-driven, as is the case for the KA shown in Figure 2. It will be invoked if one of the current goals is to identify an ignition fault, and it is noticed that one of the trouble symptoms is that the engine does not start. The system can thus be opportunistic in the sense that KAs might be invoked because certain facts are noticed during an attempt to establish particular goals.

In a more general version of the system, any utilitarian knowledge could be incorporated in the invocation part. This could include information on the costs and benefits of using the KA, the worst case or average time to diagnosis, probability of success, etc.

3.3 The Inference Mechanism

The system's main task, at a particular point in time, is to discover all it can about the current goals by executing relevant KAs. To do this, an invocation mechanism is called implicitly by the currently executing KA when some currently unknown fact is requested or when some new conclusion is drawn. The mechanism examines the invocation part of all *instances* of the KAs occurring in the knowledge base to decide which ones are potentially useful. These KAs are then executed or invoked in turn until either they have all been executed or a definite conclusion has been reached about one of the current goals on the goal stack.[1]

The invocation mechanism is outlined in Figure 4. The set S is initialized to contain all relevant instances of the KAs occurring in the knowledge base. The function *select*(S) [destructively] selects an element p from the set of applicable instances of KAs S. and *execute*(p) executes the body of p.

Execution of a KA body consists simply of traversing the body of the KA, as described in Section 3.1. In fact, Peritus actually compiles the networks into LISP code, in a manner similar to ATN compilers (see [Bonollo 83]). This makes the system much more efficient than if KAs were evaluated interpretively.

It is important to note that, although the body of a KA sets up sequences of goals to be achieved, it may be that, during its execution, some data-invoked KA suggests an alternative hypothesis and thus changes the course of events. Progress through the original KA is then suspended and will only be resumed when the alternative hypothesis has been investigated. If we had more control over the selection of tasks (say, by using metalevel KAs), the currently executing KA could also be suspended simply because other goals (hypotheses) became more interesting. Thus, it is preferable to view KA bodies as placing *constraints* on the sequencing of goals, while not precluding the possibility that certain observations may (at least temporarily) interrupt this sequencing.

§4 Time-Dependent Domains and the Frame Problem

In many maintenance domains, tests and actions may dynamically alter the state of the world. This means that conclusions reached at one stage of the diagnosis (e.g., when the engine is running) may not hold at another stage (e.g., when the engine is stopped). How to decide what is true in one situation, given what was true in a previous situation, is an old problem in artificial intelligence and is known as the *frame problem* (e.g., see [Doyle 80]).

[1] In the current implementation, the invocation part only contains information regarding the goal and fact contexts in which the KA is likely to be useful. This information is used solely to determine the set of useful KAs, not to order them. However, as mentioned above, the invocation part can readily be generalized to include additional information, which could then be used either by the interpreter or by metalevel KAs to guide and control invocation more effectively.

The KAs of procedural expert systems provide a means for directly representing the effects of events and actions in a time-dependent domain. Each node in the body of a KA can be considered to represent a particular "situation" or state of the world at a given time instant. Arcs represent transitions from one situation to another. Because arbitrary tests can be included on the arcs, which new situations are reached can be conditional on quite complex events (e.g., upon how long the engine has been running, or whether the vibrations have been steadily decreasing over the last 10 minutes).

The inference mechanism used in procedural expert systems solves a number of problems in a relatively straightforward way. The bodies of KAs and their history of invocation provide an explicit record of the inferences and computations made, and thus explicitly represent the data dependencies. This enables the basis of beliefs to be examined and, if necessary, to be updated in a way that maintains the consistency of the entire system (e.g., see [Doyle 79]). It also provides a foundation for a rich explanation system.

Default knowledge can be explicitly represented as "default" KAs that allow inferences to be drawn in the absence of counter-evidence. For example, assume that some KA needs to know the quantity of oil in the engine. Assume, further, that this information is not known in the current situation, but the knowledge base contains a KA that allows the system to infer the likely value from knowledge of previous situations:

"If, in some previous situation s_1, the oil quantity was q and in situation s_2 the oil consumption rate was r, then it is likely that, in the current situation, the oil quantity is $q-(r \times t)$, where t is the time interval between the occurrence of situation s_1 and the current time."

If the oil quantity and its rate of consumption have been previously determined, the above rule enables the system to infer the likely quantity of oil at the present time without having to ask the engineer. If subsequent predictions do not match with the available data, then the data dependencies can be examined and the possible invalidity of this inference detected. If necessary, the engineer can then update the data base by actually measuring this value.

Thus, depending on the likelihood of such default rules being valid, the user is, to a greater or lesser extent, relieved of the task of having to continually update the database as events modify values of quantities and the truth of propositions. This is very important, as the number of measurements a technician must make is a strong determinant of the time taken in fault isolation.

§5 Conclusions

Fault isolation and diagnosis require a high degree of procedural knowledge, as well as knowledge of a more declarative kind. Procedural expert systems appear to provide a means for representing both these forms of knowledge without sacrificing any of the desirable properties of traditional expert systems.

There are a number of important features of procedural expert systems that are critical to achieving this. First, KAs are not directly "called", but are invoked only when they can contribute to finding some current goal or when some particularly relevant fact is observed. As KAs cannot be directly called, neither can they directly call any other KA. They thus serve only to specify what goals are to be achieved and in what order. Second, the system is, in general, nondeterministic, and any number of KAs may be relevant at any one time. These properties enable the knowledge base of the system to be modified and augmented without forcing substantial revision.

Furthermore, the representation of inference procedures in the form of augmented RTNs is simple and homogeneous, which aids both in the acquisition of knowledge and in verifying correctness. This simplicity also aids the system in explaining its reasoning. In the simplest case, the goal stack can be traversed to answer "how" and "why" questions (as in MYCIN-like systems). But, by tracing the bodies of the KAs as well, the system can also describe the context in which hypotheses are being explored. This kind of explanation is not deep, but the formalism itself does not preclude the development of a richer explanation system.

The procedural control component is also very general, allowing, at one extreme, the construction of purely declarative programs, while, at the other extreme, it allows purely deterministic procedural programs. In particular, the scheme allows any heuristic declarative knowledge that maintenance engineers may possess to be easily and uniformly integrated with the strong procedural methods of maintenance plans.

The fact that the knowledge representation allows the specification of procedures means that the inference mechanism of the system can itself be written by using the same representation. For example, the description of the current invocation mechanism given in Figure 4 is already in this form. In this way, knowledge about how best to use object-level KAs can readily be encoded as metalevel KAs, thus allowing utilitarian expertise to be explicitly represented.

The generality of the invocation scheme makes it possible for the system to pursue a diagnosis in a goal-directed way, yet react opportunistically and change the direction of the consultation if an event occurs that suggests an alternative diagnosis. In fact, after using primarily goal-directed systems like MYCIN, the way in which data-invoked KAs suddenly wake up and begin exploring alternative diagnoses was a constant surprise (not always pleasant!).

The representation is also suited to dynamic domains where the state of the world is influenced by events and actions. The body of a KA can then be viewed as specifying how and under what conditions one situation changes into another. This capability is not only important in the maintenance domain — it is also critical in areas such as battlefield assessment and pilot assistance, where choice of action is strongly dependent on external events.

There are a number of questions that still remain to be answered, and this will require further experimentation with the system. For example, the representation of temporal domains needs to be properly formalized, and suitable techniques for truth maintenance developed. Further, the implemented system, Peritus, contains limited information in the invocation part, and this could usefully be extended. The incorporation of metalevel KAs also needs to be explored.

Acknowledgment

The author wishes to acknowledge the contribution of Umberto Bonollo in helping clarify the ideas presented in this paper.

References

[Aikins 83] Aikins, J.S., "Prototypical Knowledge for Expert Systems," *Artificial Intelligence*, Vol. 20, pp 163 - 210, 1983.

[Allen 81] Allen, J.F., "A General Model of Action and Time," Comp. Sci. Report TR 97, University of Rochester, N.Y., 1981.

[Bonollo 83] Bonollo, U. and Georgeff, M.P. "Peritus: A Knowledge Engineering Tool for the Development of Procedural Expert Systems," Comp. Sci. Tech Report 39, Monash University, Melbourne, Australia, 1983.

[Buchanan 82] Buchanan, B.G., and Duda, R.O., "Principles of Rule-Based Expert Systems," Report HPP-82-14, Heuristic Programming Project, Stanford University, Stanford, Ca., 1982.

[Davis 76] Davis, R., "Applications of Metalevel Knowledge to the Construction, Maintenance, and Use of Large Knowledge Bases," STAN-CS-76-552, HPP-76-7, Stanford University, Stanford, Ca., 1976.

[Doyle 79] Doyle, J., "A Truth Maintenance System," *Artificial Intelligence*, Vol 12, 1979.

[Doyle 80] Doyle, J. and London, P. "A Selected Descriptor-Indexed Bibliography to the Literature on Belief Revision," AI Memo 568, MIT-AI Lab, Mass., 1980.

[Feurzeig 83] Feurzeig, W. "An Expert System for Training Automotive Ignition Troubleshooting", this volume.

[Genesereth 82] Genesereth, M.R., and Smith, D.E., "Metalevel Architecture," Memo HPP-81-6, Stanford University, Stanford, Ca., 1982.

[Georgeff 82] Georgeff, M.P., "Procedural Control in Production Systems," *Artificial Intelligence*, Vol 18, pp 175-201, 1982.

[Georgeff 83] Georgeff, M.P. and Bonollo, U. "Procedural Expert Systems," *Proc. 8th Int'l. Joint Conf. on Artificial Intelligence*, Karlsruhe, Germany, pp 151-157, 1983.

[Gregory 80] *Gregory's SP Manual No. 165: Falcon - Fairmont XD Series 6 Cylinder Service and Repair Manual*, Gregory's Pub. Co., Sydney, 1980.

[Reboh 81] Reboh, R. "Knowledge Engineering Techniques and Tools in the Prospector Environment," Tech Note 243, Artificial Intelligence Center, SRI Int'l., Menlo Park, Ca., 1981.

[Reinstein 81] Reinstein, H.C. and Aikins, J.S., "Application Design: Issues in Expert System Architecture," *Proc. 7th Int'l. Joint Conf. on Artificial Intelligence*, Vancouver, Canada, pp 888 - 892, 1981.

[Shortliffe 76] Shortliffe, E.H., *Computer Based Medical Consultations: MYCIN*, American Elsevier, New York, 1976.

[Woods 70] Woods, W. A., "Transition Network Grammars for Natural Language Analysis," *Comm. ACM.*, Vol. 13, 1970.

B. Initial Rollover

1. Starter air pressure at 0 PSI.

2. Shafting oil mist system in operation

3. PLA at 0 degrees (stopcocked)
   a. Set E-put multiplier to 1.4286 for NL and 4.1910 for NH

4. Fuel pressure at 5-50 PSIG

5. Ignition in "OFF" position

6. a. FVG actuator fully retracted at 0 degrees
   b. CVG actuator fully retracted at -3.5 degrees

7. Activate the rollover switch and slowly increase starter air pressure

   NOTE: Record time from speed indication to positive EOP indication (30 seconds max.)

8. Increase starter air pressure to obtain 5360 +- 60 RPM NH

   CAUTION: Do not rollover for more than 30 seconds without the fan rotation to avoid number 4 bearing over-heating

9. When speed is stabilized:
   a. Confirm EOP is 10 PSID min.
   b. Confirm all vibs are less than 0.5 in/sec
   c. Confirm 0 fuel flow
   d. Record: NL, NH, WFT1, FVG, CVG, EOP, starter pressure, all vibs

10. De-activate the starter

    CAUTION: Do not re-activate the starter before engine has come to a complete stop

    a. Enter the cell: Confirm no leaks (fuel, lube, VEN hydraulic)
    b. Check the coastdown and listen for unusual noise
    c. VG angles must be full closed
    d. Check oil tank sight gauge. Record results on Log Sheets

11. Top off the engine oil system per Section II. Record net amount added. If the amount exceeds 4 quarts, repeat the rollover and top off. If more than 1 pint is required, notify Engineering

Table 1. Section of the Maintenance Plan for the F404 Engine.

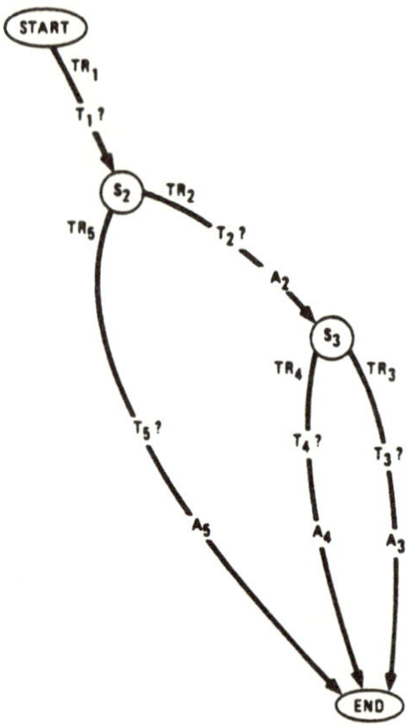

FIGURE 1 A TYPICAL KA BODY

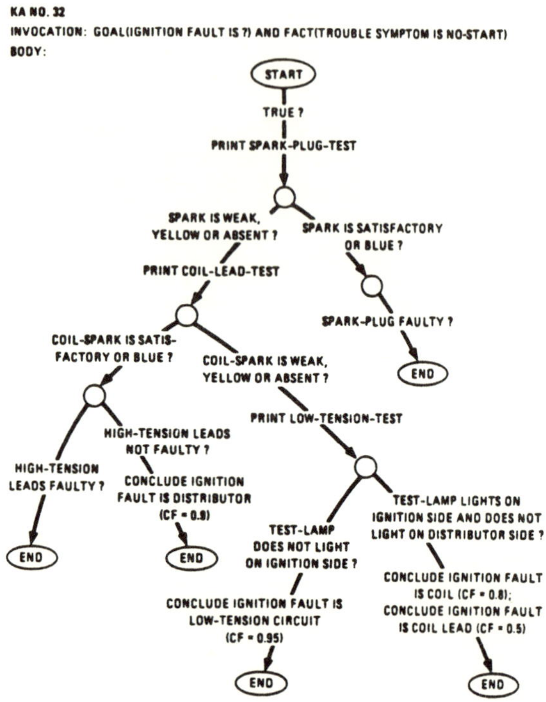

FIGURE 2 A SAMPLE KA FROM THE AUTOMOTIVE DOMAIN

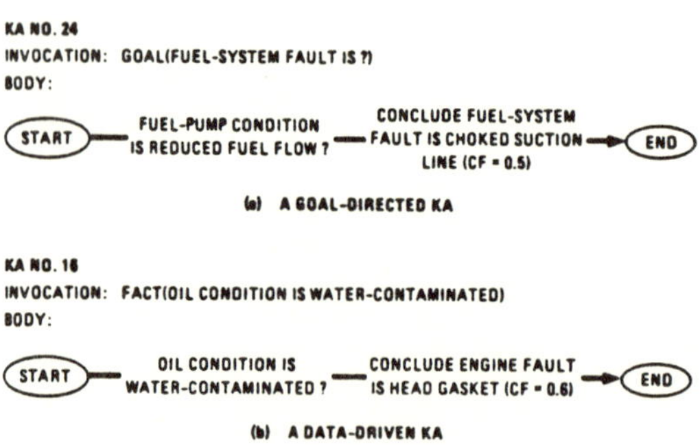

FIGURE 3 SOME SIMPLE KAs FROM THE AUTOMOTIVE DOMAIN

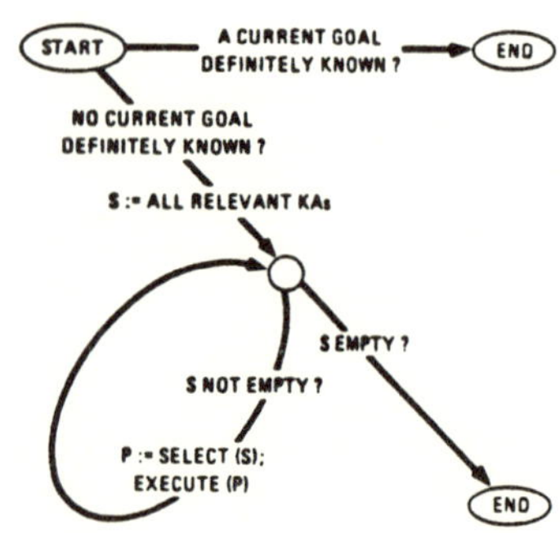

FIGURE 4 THE INVOCATION MECHANISM

ABOUT THE AUTHOR

Dr. Michael Georgeff is a Research Computer Scientist in the Artificial Intelligence Center at Stanford Research Institute (SRI) International. Currently, his research interests include multi-agent planning, expert systems, search techniques, and programming languages. Previously, he held a position at Monash University (Australia) as Head of the Department of Computer Science. Dr. Georgeff received a Ph.D. in aeronautical engineering from Imperial College, London.

FAILURE DETECTION PROCESSES BY PATTERN RECOGNITION AND EXPERT SYSTEMS

L.F. Pau

Battelle Memorial Institute
7, route de Drize, CH - 1227 Carouge, Switzerland

SUMMARY

This paper analyses the failure diagnostic processes involved in automatic testing, automatic imaging inspection and more general technical diagnostic systems. It is shown how properly selected pattern recognition methods, artificial intelligence procedures, and relational data base search schemes, must be assembled to achieve operational requirements which these diagnostic systems must meet. This paper will indicate some basic design and selection criteria, and outline how it can be simplified in a number of practical cases. It will also describe the corresponding failure diagnostic system architecture.

1. INTRODUCTION

The basic troubleshooting process includes failure detection, localization, diagnostic, analysis and monitoring [1]. The key element is failure diagnosis which carries out a breakdown of the observations $y \in Y$ (signals, images, text, alltogether) into individual failure modes $E_0, E_1, \ldots, E_N$, where E_0 is the no-failure operating mode. Each diagnostic strategy S, is a sequential search decision process:

$$D \times I \times Y \xrightarrow{S} (\hat{E}, T(\hat{E})) \quad \hat{E} \in \{E_0, \ldots, E_N\}$$

where the diagnosed failure mode $\hat{E}$ must minimize either of the average risks, error probability, and/or failure diagnosis delay, and:

$D \triangleq$ functional decomposition of the system under test (modules, logic states, etc.).

$I \triangleq$ learning information data base (operational environment, failure events, maintenance actions, etc.).

$Y \triangleq (Y^a, Y^p)$ diagnostic observations derived from passive sensors (Y^p) and active sensors (Y^a) interacting with the system under test. These observations include signals, images, logic variables, and text.

$T \triangleq$ action required on the system under test, owing to the diagnosis $\hat{E}$ (repair, reconfiguration, test generation).

2. ASSUMPTIONS

This paper essentially assumes the intrinsic weakness of the defect or process modelling approach of the various failure modes. It also accepts the inaccuracy of most physical device models in failed conditions, and even in nominal conditions.

The case where failed or nominal conditions are known with good confidence will be accounted for by a simplifying truth maintenance procedure on the limited subset of such conditions.

In this paper, we claim that there is robustness to be expected from the combined use of a learning information data base I (domain dependent), and of a set of diagnostic meta-rules S (domain independent). This robustness is in terms of failure diagnosis correctness, and also of efficient automatic test generation (Y^a). At the same time, we here claim that one cannot separate the diagnostic inference and failure recognition into two separate expert systems, with one for test generation and the other for failure detection. The diagnostic inference unit described below carries out both in an intertwinned fashion.

3. DIAGNOSTIC SYSTEM ARCHITECTURE

The overall diagnostic system architecture (see Figure 4) includes knowledge representation, inference, decision and action steps.

3.1 KNOWLEDGE REPRESENTATION F

This includes a list frame data structure F, with an associated vector of attributes A(F), building together a script (F, A(F)).

3.1.1 LIST FRAME DATA STRUCTURE F

The system under test is represented by a nested set of decision tables $\{C_i\}$, constructed starting with the basic modules and linked in a hierarchical tree structure.

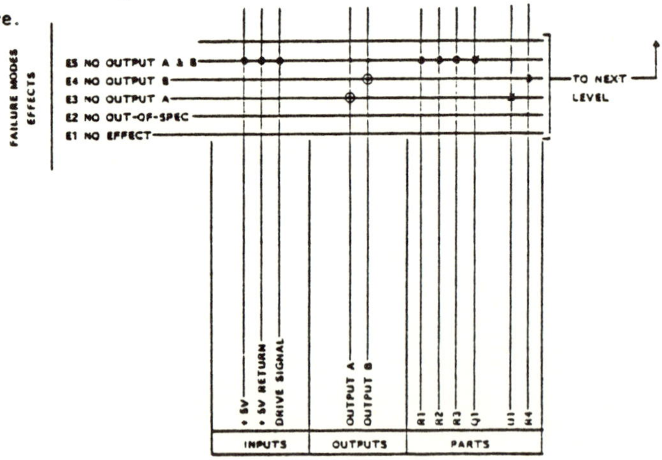

FIGURE 1 - DECISION TABLE C_i FOR ITEM i

These decision tables represent jointly the effects of inputs, outputs, and structure, and are nested together as indicated in Figure 2.

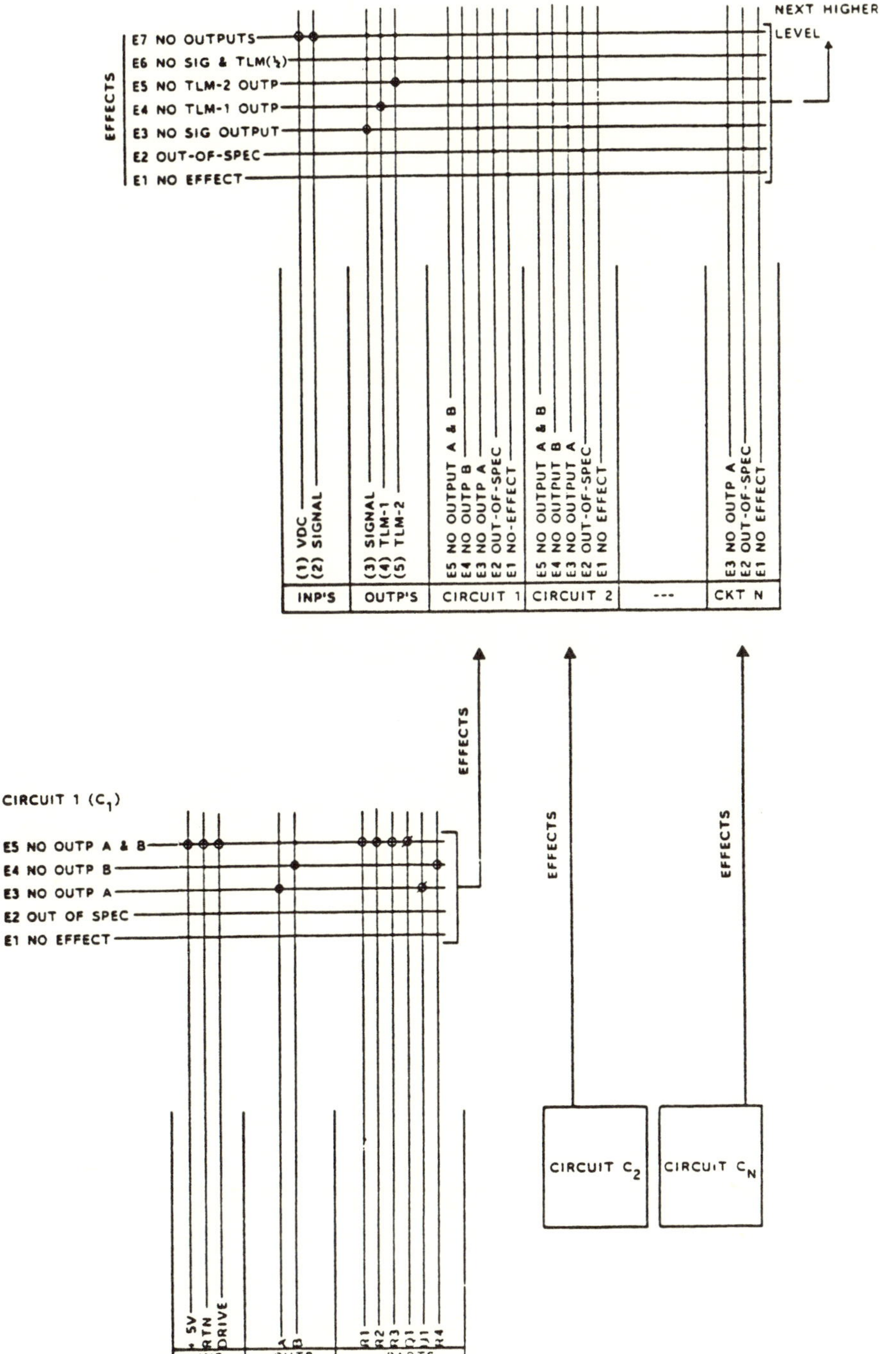

FIGURE 2 - NESTING LIST STRUCTURES

The result is a nested list structure L $(C_1, \ldots, C_N)$ amenable to efficient list processing and predicate verification, made of the all horizontal and vertical labels in said decision tables, organized into inputs, outputs, structure: L_i, L_0, L_s. As some inputs are test stimuli, while other outputs are only measurements, the diagnostic measurements Y^a, Y^p are merged into these lists, regarless of observability or not.

This list frame structure obviously encompasses both signals, images, text and logic variables in the diagnostic observations Y.

3.1.2 ATTRIBUTES A(F)

These attributes are made of:

i Attribute labels in the decision matrix, expressing labelled values for each (row, column) pair element in the list structure; this accounts for structural attributes, e.g.:

- Open mode
- Open/Short mode
- Short mode
- Output Intersection
- Intersection and open mode
- Failure at one or the other intersections, not both at the same time

FIGURE 3 - STRUCTURAL ATTRIBUTES IN L_s

ii Measurement attributes, which are the values of all measurement

$Y = (Y^a, Y^p)$,

whether signals, text, images or logic relations.

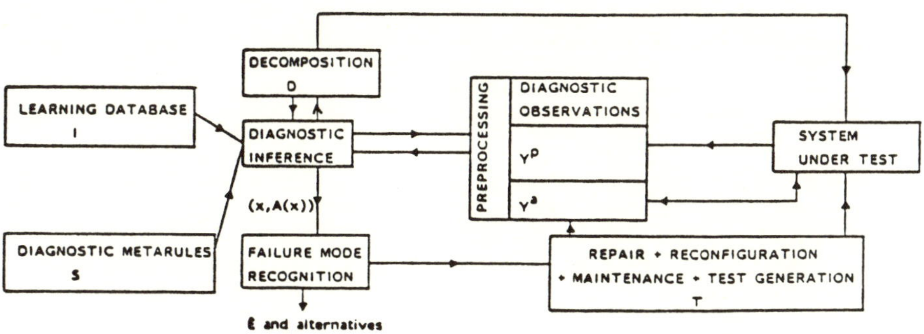

FIGURE 4 - DIAGNOSTIC SYSTEM ARCHITECTURE

3.2 LEARNING DATABASE I

This database specifies the operating environment, component characteristics, operating modes, normal reference images, and required actions. It is organized in declarative form, and decomposed into open worlds. A natural language interface is possible to outside users.

3.3 DIAGNOSTIC META-RULES S

This unit specifies in predicate form the three basic diagnostic and test generation strategies identified in earlier research: failure mode removal by analysis, validation, and exploration of the operational envelope. It also carries out an arbitrage between these strategies. This unit is domain independent,and has been developed as such.

3.4 TEST GENERATION T

The estimated failure mode $\hat{E}$ triggers the specific types of probing energy applied to the system under test (sensitizing probing, deterministic, random). Thus the meta-rules S must include test generation.

3.5 FAILURE DIAGNOSTIC PROCESS

This process is here decomposed into:

i diagnostic inference,

ii failure mode recognition,

as described below.

4. DIAGNOSTIC INFERENCE EXPERT SYSTEM

This domain independent expert system, geared towards analysis, assembles scripts (F, A(F)), where F is a frame data structure with all knowledge stored together, and A(F) the vector of attributes of this frame. It produces from there attributed features (X, A(X)), while excluding contradictory information by proof of hypothesis, and obtaining a pre-diagnosis by using S and I. This expert system must operate efficiently (time, memory size) with domain dependent knowledge in F, and is activated by a control structure D with propagating constraints. As a consequence of these requirements, semantic networks and simple frames cannot be used.

When the inference unit questions I, D and Y, one faces all the problems of a non-monotonous logic, with new axioms added through Y which may be inconsistent with the current theory as inferred. Frame axioms to describe transitions from one situation to another cannot be used, because the failure modes which may occur are unknown. Therefore, the best approach, as we have chosen it, is a truth maintenance system (mode E_0), where the truth values are scalar functions of the attribute values A(F), with backtracking to rules explaining the contradictions, and inclusion of these rules among the features X.

The diagnostic inference thus includes the following steps:

1) restrict modules M $\in$ (IxDxS) candidates for confrontation;
2) confront these modules as selected to the current situation Y, by checking on preconditions in IxD: this involves checking a predicate formula in the first order logic by a saturation procedure;
3) select the features X from the modules as selected by the diagnostic meta-rules S, which further eliminates some modules according to their hierarchy. This hierarchy expresses causality relations, failure mode propagation, and time constants.

5. FAILURE MODE RECOGNITION

This is carried out by a domain dependent combined syntactic-semantic approach [2] based upon an attribute grammar with semantic decision rules. The grammar is $G = (V_N, V_T, P, S)$, where the production rules are of the type $N \rightarrow a$, $N \in V_N$, $a \in (V_T \cup V_N)^*$, with attribute vector A(a). These attributes are those derived in the diagnostic inference from the feature vectors X. The feature X representing the frame F, is applied to the semantic discriminant functions $C_i(.)$ and $F \in \hat{E} = E_i$ such that $C_i(X) = \text{Max } C_j(X)$, $0 \leq j \leq N$. Alternative decision rules, and examples of attribute features A(a) are given in [1]. The alternative diagnoses to $\hat{E}$ are those failure modes whose attributes yield similar values of $C_j(X)$ close to $C_i(X)$.

The attribute grammar G allows to combine data in the frame F processed by the expert system, coming from signals, images, text, and logical predicates (e.g. lengths, angles, texture features, amplitudes, boundary shapes, auto-regressible features). By using here attributes features A(a) with continuous values, we avoid the need to quantify the attributes A(F) in Section 4. The semantic discriminants also assist in the sensor fusion, by allowing for statistical vs. syntactic tradeoffs in terms of combining the attribute values.

The list structure of Section 3.1 gives a simple grammar G, which is of a regular type, for which inference should not be a major obstacle for a known list structure F.

6. CONCLUSION

The above framework serves as a unification for a number of past or on-going projects in failure diagnosis and automatic imaging inspection. By unloading the domain dependent aspects into a few units, this approach has helped substantially in reducing the time required for the design of solutions to a number of practical problems.

REFERENCES

[1] L.F. PAU, "Failure diagnosis and performance monitoring", Marcel Dekker, New York, 1981.

[2] K.S. FU, "A step towards unification of syntactic and statistical recognition", IEEE Trans., Vol. PAMI-5, No. 2, 200-, March 1983.

[3] R. DAVIS, "Diagnosis based on description of structure and function", Proc. National Conf. on AI, Pittsburgh, Pa, 1982, 137-142.

[4] D. Mc DERMOTT, R. BROOKS, "Arby: diagnosis with shallow causal models", same as [3], 278-283.

DESIGNING AN EXPERT SYSTEM FOR TRAINING AUTOMOTIVE ELECTRICAL TROUBLESHOOTING

Wallace Feurzeig, John Frederiksen, Barbara White and Paul Horwitz

Two key issues in the design and development of expert systems for maintenance training are the choice of an appropriate expert model and the function of the expert in instruction. We are confronting these issues in instructional research involving the design of an expert instructional system for automotive electrical troubleshooting. In studying expert troubleshooters and in examining troubleshooting procedures used in the military, we have encountered three distinctly different types of expertise. Each of these requires different forms of knowledge and produces qualitatively different troubleshooting behaviors. One kind of expert has established a large repertoire of symptom-fault associations through extensive experience in troubleshooting. Another kind of mechanic utilizes fixed troubleshooting procedures from shop manuals and various maintenance aids. A third kind of expert does extensive inferencing in attempting to diagnose faults.

Each of these approaches can, in principle, be modeled and form the basis for an expert aiding or training system. The first mode requires experience gathered over many years and thus cannot be learned in the training time usually available. The third is usually rejected because of the presumed difficulty that typical trainees would have in learning the inferencing methods. Probably for these reasons, the military has opted for teaching fixed procedures and relies on the availability of manuals and job aids. However, there are drawbacks to the use of fixed procedures. Sets of fixed procedures are seldom complete, thus, some faults remain undiagnosed. Furthermore, following fixed procedures does not develop transferable skills which would enable a mechanic to troubleshoot systems not covered by the manual. We believe that an appropriate choice of a knowledge-based inferencing model makes possible the teaching of the basic principles and skills of troubleshooting electrical circuits and provides a strong foundation for practical work in the field.

Our belief is empirically based. It derives from working closely with expert mechanics. One of these experts, an instructor in a technical school who is exceptionally analytic and articulate, employs such an inferential approach to troubleshooting in both his instruction and his actual diagnostic work. We have observed his troubleshooting instruction in formal courses and with individual students. Also, we have studied, video taped, and analyzed his troubleshooting practices while locating faults that we introduced into an automotive system.

His approach to troubleshooting involves focusing on a particular device and concatenating the rest of the circuit into a feed system and a ground system. This approach requires knowledge about the device specifying (1) the conditions that must be met in the feed and ground systems and (2) the operation of the device when those conditions are met. The Feed-Device-Ground (FDG) strategy for troubleshooting enables one to make inferences about the states of the three components. The key measurement used is voltage drop from a test point to ground. The test point can be either the input or output to the device. For example, presence of a correct voltage at the output indicates that the feed and device are providing continuous electrical paths, and that the ground system (which is in parallel with the voltmeter) is not shorted (although it may be open). On the other hand, lack of voltage is a more ambiguous result leaving multiple possibilities for the location of the fault. The FDG strategy employs operations as well as measurements as steps for reducing these ambiguities: for example, disconnecting a ground system, or providing an alternative path to bypass the normal feed system.

The FDG strategy is knowledge-based. It requires extensive knowledge of device functions and interactions, knowledge of electrical circuits including the fundamental voltage and current relationships, and knowledge of the characteristics of automotive devices such as coils, spark plugs, and condensers. Thus, teaching troubleshooting with the FDG strategy requires instruction in electrical theory and system operation, as well as instruction in the strategy itself. These components of understanding are the foci of our instructional research.

The goal of our instruction in electrical theory is to help students gain a clear, qualitative understanding of the concepts of voltage and current flow in series and parallel circuits. Traditionally, in dealing with these difficult concepts, analogies to fluid flow are employed. In troubleshooting work, including the FDG strategy, an understanding of voltage drop is essential. The representation of this concept in the fluid flow model is by analogy to differential pressure. Unfortunately, pressure is poorly understood by most people, and a reference to it may be self-defeating. To improve students' understanding, we are devising a computer system for graphically and dynamically representing current and voltage relationships in circuits.

In this system, voltage is concretely represented by different colors, ranging in hue continuously from red to blue. Current appears as simulated motion along wires. This representation offers two major advantages over the fluid flow model. Color is more easily visualized as a local variable than pressure, and our system avoids a major failing of the fluid flow analogy, namely the fact that fluids can flow even in the absence of a completed circuit. In our system, because the behavior of the graphical icons is constrained by a realistic model of the circuit, there can be no flow of current unless a closed path exists between the terminals of a voltage source.

The graphical representation we are implementing is multilevel. One can either see the entire electrical system or a more detailed (full screen) graphic representation of any device showing its components and their electrical circuitry. This enables one to study circuit behavior and to troubleshoot circuits either at the functional module level or at the component level.

Using this system, we will teach both circuit theory (including the behavior of normal and faulted circuits) and troubleshooting, using the FDG strategy. The system can provide a general framework for instructional activities of many kinds. It can be used to support open-ended student exploration, permitting students to study the operation of both unfaulted circuits and circuits embedding faults of their choice. The system can also be used in a more directed fashion to present students with problems and tasks of various kinds. For example, they can be asked to predict the consequences of specified circuit operations such as closing a switch or faulting a device. Also, they can be assigned the task of isolating an unknown fault.

Artificial intelligence methods will play a fundamental role in the instruction. We are implementing two AI-based instructional systems. The first is an articulate expert to demonstrate the application of the FDG strategy on a variety of problems including those set up by the student. The system is capable of generating explanations for its decisions and actions along the way. The system will be able to respond to certain kinds of "why" questions posed by the student. The second type of AI facility will monitor and evaluate student performance on troubleshooting problems posed by the system. The student's task will be the application of the FDG strategy. In evaluating student performance, the system will permit a variety of troubleshooting paths: the FDG strategy does not require a fixed or an optimal path. It will, however, look for measurements or operations that are redundant or contraindicated by the student's knowledge of the state of the circuit thus far. These AI facilities will employ extensive use of interactive graphics involving the use of pointing devices and menus as well as dynamic displays. Also, they will employ models of expert performance expressly chosen to mirror the kind of human expertise that we believe to be most effective.

To test the effectiveness of these models in promoting the development of students' troubleshooting skills, we plan a number of instructional experiments. These are designed to address the following issues: the effect of different circuit representations on helping students understand circuit operations; the effectiveness of the AI-based instructional facilities in helping students acquire troubleshooting skills; and the transfer of troubleshooting skills to problems significantly different from those previously studied. We expect that the integration of models of human expert performance and AI instructional methods will have valuable learning benefits. This type of intelligent CAI system, based on such integration, will, we believe, have applications to many areas of maintenance training.

ABOUT THE AUTHORS

Mr. Wallace Feurzeig is Division Scientist of the Bolt, Beranek and Newman, Inc. Information Sciences Division. His major research interest is in the development of more powerful systems to improve learning. He is currently working on two AI-based training systems: a real-time tactical trainer for F-14 radar intercept officers and the automotive electrical troubleshooting training system. From 1965 to 1983 he headed the Educational Technology Department at Bolt, Beranek and Newman, Inc. Mr. Feurzeig is co-developer of the LOGO programming language and has implemented training systems in a number of domains, including mathematics, clinical medicine, electronics, ship navigation, and air intercept tactics.

Dr. John Frederiksen joined the Bolt, Beranek and Newman, Inc., Information Sciences Division in 1975. Under the auspices of the Office of Naval Research and the Navy Personnel Research and Development Center, he is currently developing a second generation of training systems for remediating reading skill deficiencies of name recruits. He is also Co-director of a cognitive sciences project supported by the Army Research Institute and the Office of Naval Research which integrates AI methods in developing a system for teaching inferential troubleshooting. Dr. Frederiksen received his Ph.D. in psychology and psychometrics from Princeton in 1966.

MODELS OF NATURAL INTELLIGENCE IN FAULT DIAGNOSIS TASKS: IMPLICATIONS FOR TRAINING AND AIDING OF MAINTENANCE PERSONNEL

Dr. William B. Rouse

Georgia Institute of Technology

I have decided to orient my remarks today around natural intelligence as opposed to artificial intelligence. That is, I'll look at human behavior and try to present a summary of some work we've done attempting to understand human intelligence and abilities in problem solving. Particularly, I'd like to look at human problem solving in diagnostic situations in both maintenance and operational environments.

Before I give you an overview of the talk, I'd like to emphasize something about the models that I'm going to talk about. You'll see that some of the models have an AI flavor. In a sense, the models are not an end product in themselves, they are a process. We are just trying to understand how people approach problem solving and diagnostic tasks. I think a lot of what AI has to offer is a process for thinking about things rather than a product. I'll elaborate on the application of these models in training and aiding later.

There are three topics I'm going to talk about. First, I'm going to give you a quick background on some experimental studies we've done over several years so you can see where our knowledge base is as experimenters. As each experiment represents a paper itself, I certainly won't go into them in great detail. Second, I'll talk about a series of models that we try to use to describe human behavior in diagnostic tasks. Finally, I'll talk about the results and implications for the topic for this meeting.

As background, we've done a series of efforts over the last 8 years funded by many agencies. At this point, they've resulted in 18 experimental studies and three training programs that we've devised and implemented. One thing I want to empahsize is that of these 18 experiments, 16 of them were performed with professional operational and maintenance personnel as opposed to students. Two were performed with students, and in one case the use of engineering students was actually a high-fidelity choice of subjects.

To give you a feeling of the range of the topics we looked at, I'll go through some of these experiments briefly. Some early experiments looked at logic networks, but we fairly quickly got on to more operational types of systems, such as aircraft, automobile, power plants, and avionics. We looked at a lot of people and had a tremendous data base of results. This communications network is current work funded by ARI and is an interesting problem of people troubleshooting large-scale systems. I'll talk a little later about how a very smart system can help you for 99 percent of your problems and then for 1 percent it succeeds in burying the problem until it's absolutely impossible to solve it.

Figure 1 gives you a feeling for some of the experiments we looked at with real equipment, simulators, and ship environments. Again, all subjects were

EXPERIMENTS WITH

HIGH FIDELITY SIMULATORS AND REAL EQUIPMENT

NO. OF EXPERIMENTS	NATURE OF TASK	NO. OF SUBJECTS	NATURE OF SUBJECTS
2	AIRCRAFT POWERPLANTS	62	AIRCRAFT MECHANICS
3	AIRCRAFT SIMULATORS	14	AIRCRAFT PILOTS
1	SHIP SIMULATOR	36	MARINE ENGINEERS

Figure 1.

professional personnel. Figure 2 shows you some of the training programs we've been involved in. One of our concerns was taking some of the ideas that we devised and actually getting them used rather than just published. So, for example, we became involved in the nuclear power industry and developed a problem solving training program for diagnostic performance of maintenance and operations personnel. These two programs are in place, about 100 students have been through so far, and that's the through-put we expect. A lot of my comments reflect the fact that we were trying to get it into place, trying to get it into schools, and have it reside there. There are a lot of problems that I won't have time to elaborate on here, but they deal with interpersonal relationships of instructors and reseachers as much as they deal with problem solving abilities of trainees.

Question: Why would nuclear operators be interested in diesel generator diagnostics?

Rouse: Because the backup diesel generator system is essential if they're going to keep the plant up and they have no simulator for it. There are some systems like GE's DELTA system for doing some maintenance, but it's a particular maintenance problem. There is a tremendous number of Licensee Event Reports (LERs) in diesel generator problems. In fact, there's a special symposium a couple weeks from now where several utilities are getting together to bemoan their difficulties with their diesel generators. So, it turns out it's an interesting application for computer-based simulators as opposed to full scope simulation because they don't have the full scope simulator yet. One of the things that is crucial in implementing a training program is that it be complementary to the technology they're already committed to. If they're already committed to a full scope simulator, often you'll have a hard time suggesting alternatives.

In the process of these studies, besides our empirical results, to organize our thinking we developed models of how we thought people were doing problem solving. Each of these models was part of a series because as we got to more robust domains and into operational situations, we found that there were a lot of things we didn't think about. For example, we really haven't thought too much about context and context is absolutely overwhelming in terms of its impact both for good and for bad. Also, we didn't think too much about dynamic environments where the problem is changing in time and you're trying to operate the system at the same time you're trying to maintain it.

Let me go through each of these five models very briefly. The first model, shown in Figure 3, arrived out of the question "Why do some problems take a long time while other problems do not?" One notion is that some problems are complex and there's a scale of complexity. This Information Theoretic Model turned out to correlate very well with people's diagnostic performance, or the time it took them to find faults. It may not be obvious in the model, but it turns out that this measure has embedded in it the particular individual strategy. One of the conclusions we came to was that the complexity of a problem is as much related to the problem solver as it is to the system. It is highly related to a person's perception of the system. This model is really only trying to predict overall time to solve a problem. If you wanted to get down to a finer grain, let's

TRAINING APPLICATIONS

NATURE OF COURSE	NATURE OF TRAINEES	NO. OF TRAINEES
OPERATIONAL PROBLEM SOLVING	MARINE ENGINEERS	>100 (~100/YR)
SWITCHBOARD DIAGNOSTICS	ARMY MAINTAINERS	>100 (~300/YR)
DIESEL GENERATOR DIAGNOSTICS	NUCLEAR OPERATORS AND MAINTAINERS	- (~100/YR)

Figure 2.

look at Figure 4. This model predicts what kind of actions people take to form a feasible set and make choices in that feasible set to decide what to test. One of the things we found from the literature and from our results is that people are not very good at forming a feasible set. There is a tremendous amount of information in the problem to help you form the feasible set, but people end up with a fuzzy feasible set. Some things are very clearly alternative solutions while others, the vast majority of things, are in the middle. With this model, we were able to predict how long it would take people, how many tests they would have to take, to find the problem and the nature of different kinds of aids used in the testing sequence. That was fairly successful. However, one thing that came to mind here was that maybe people don't think about a feasible set at all. As engineers, we tend to think about them, but maybe people in general don't think about them at all. So the next model, Figure 5, was the first one that has any AI flavor, sort of a very simple production system model. People are assumed to approach the problem with a set of heuristics and that's how they find their faults.

We found out that this model was actually pretty good. We could predict the type of action a person would pick with an agreement of over 90 percent using this model. Perhaps the best insight from this model was that it isn't so much people knowing what to do, it is a matter of them knowing when to do it. People have a tremendous amount of knowledge; they know all the rules in this particular task, but they aren't always sure when to apply those rules.

Figure 6 shows the next model in this whirlwind tour. We started looking at problems that were highly context related. We looked at a context people were familiar with and then one they were unfamiliar with. One thing that emerged is that people use contextual cues extremely strongly to solve their problems. This model basically says that people look at the face of the system, and if they can find anything familiar there, they act on it. By S-Rule we mean a symptomatic rule; they simply take a symptom and they map to a solution. There is a loop in Figure 6 that people tend to try to stay in, and they use their contextual clues to do that.

However, sometimes there's nothing familiar in what you're looking at on the face of the system, and then you should revert to a more structural approach. A lot of what we've heard so far in this workshop uses a structural approach. People are not as good at structural approaches as they are at state-oriented approaches. They're very good at recognizing patterns and images, but people will avoid having to get down and analytically solve a problem at almost any cost. When forced to, they will consider the structure and apply a topographic rule. So an S-Rule is just a mapping from observations of symptoms to a hypothesis and solution. A T-Rule is getting down and looking at the structure of the problem.

One of the things we found is that, while people are really loath to apply T-Rules, you can train them and they'll do it fairly well. So this distinction about the impact of context, how people tend to be context dominated, was a very important one. We found we could only be successful with some of the training things we tried by explaining them in context. People can be trained to consider structural information, but they don't naturally walk in the door with that inclination, so the training is very important.

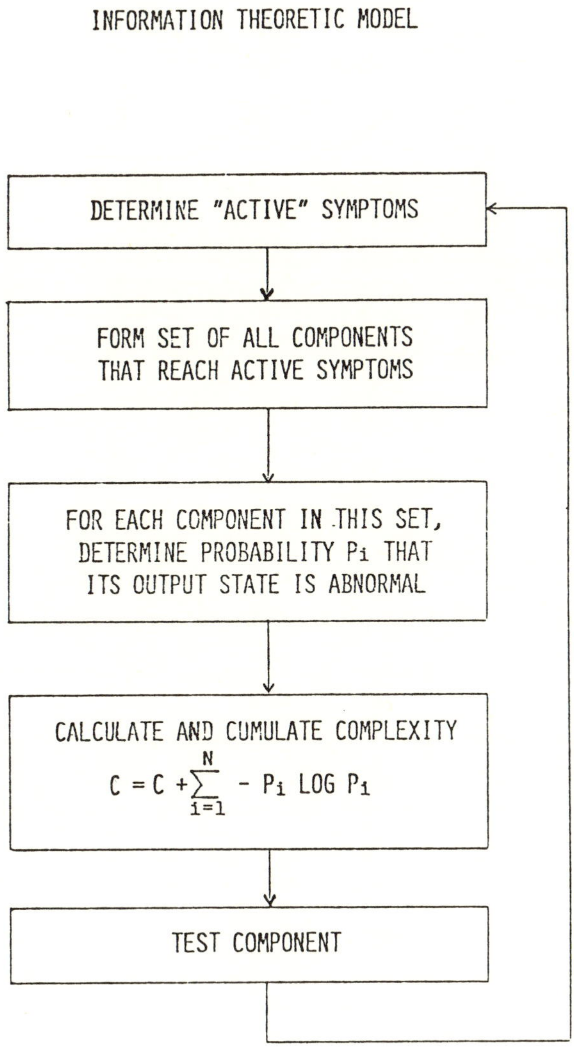
INFORMATION THEORETIC MODEL
DETERMINE "ACTIVE" SYMPTOMS
FORM SET OF ALL COMPONENTS THAT REACH ACTIVE SYMPTOMS
FOR EACH COMPONENT IN THIS SET, DETERMINE PROBABILITY Pi THAT ITS OUTPUT STATE IS ABNORMAL
CALCULATE AND CUMULATE COMPLEXITY
$C = C + \sum_{i=1}^{N} - P_i \log P_i$
TEST COMPONENT

Figure 3.

FUZZY SET MODEL

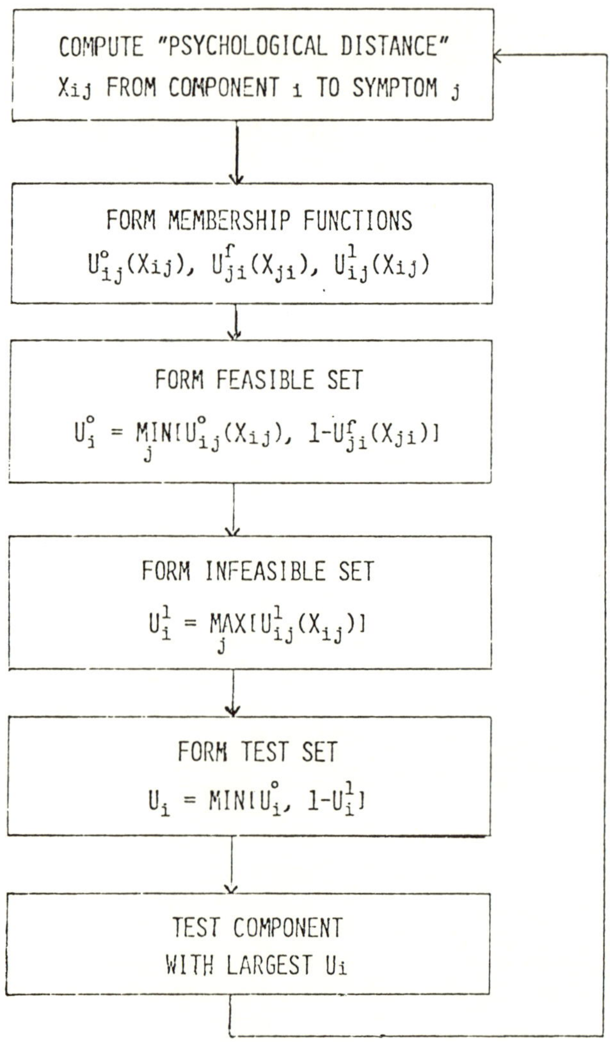

Figure 4.

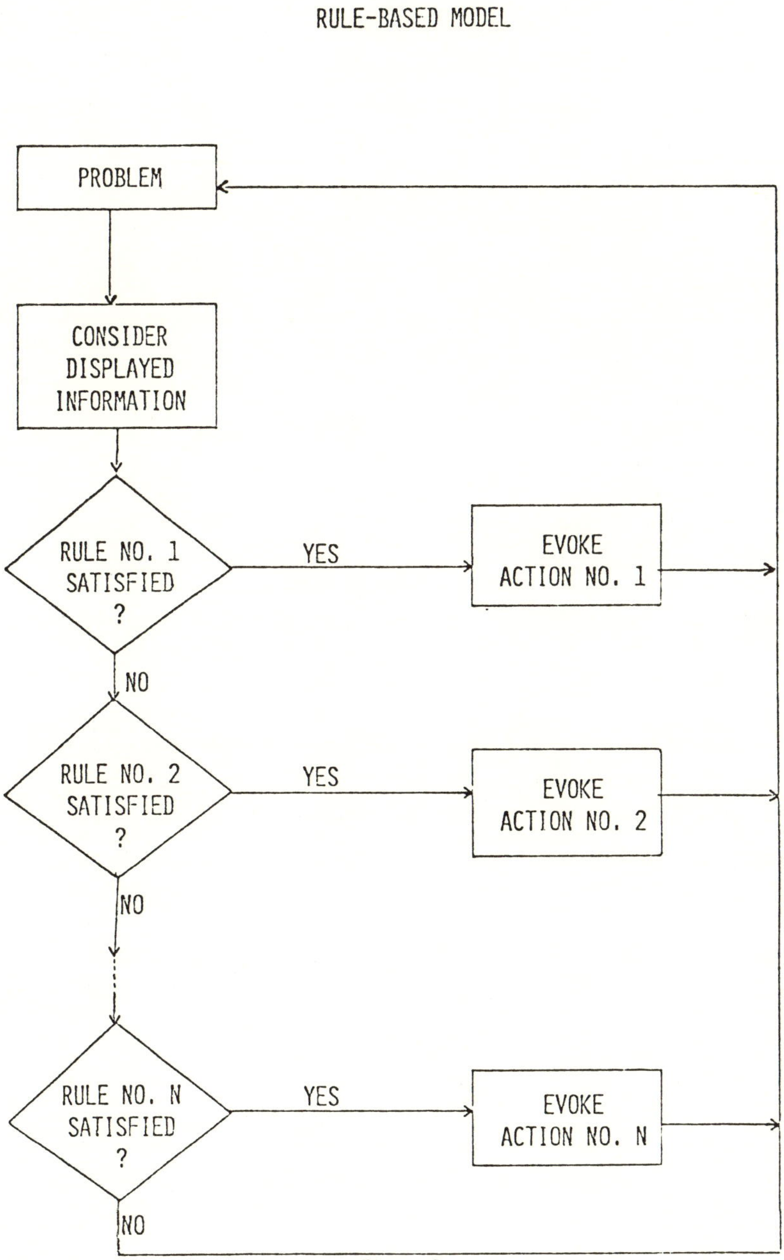
RULE-BASED MODEL
PROBLEM
CONSIDER DISPLAYED INFORMATION
RULE NO. 1 SATISFIED ?
YES
EVOKE ACTION NO. 1
NO
RULE NO. 2 SATISFIED ?
YES
EVOKE ACTION NO. 2
NO
RULE NO. N SATISFIED ?
YES
EVOKE ACTION NO. N
NO

Figure 5.

FUZZY RULE-BASED MODEL

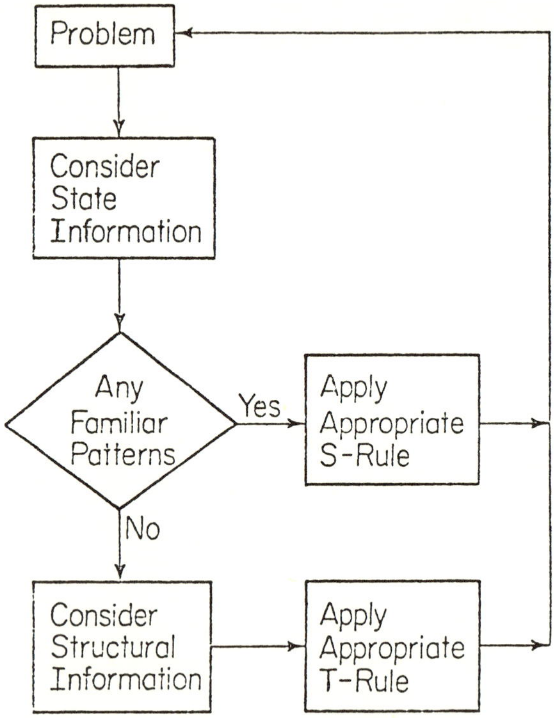

Figure 6.

Figure 7 considers the question, "How do people pick rules?" It turns out that if you analyze their sequences and protocols, they are somewhat inconsistent. So we decided to look at rules in different categories. To use a rule, you have to recall it, it has to be applicable, it has to be useful and, above all, it has to be simple. We assume that people have this "choosable" set and they'll pick rules in this way. The only reason for adding this to the problem, to the model, was to allow the possibility of things being somewhat qualitative and not being crisp. We found it was crucial to be able to represent and to predict what sequence of actions people would pick. At this point, we're not trying to predict whether they solve the problem or not, or how long it takes, we're trying to predict at each point in time, what will they do? That's a much more ambitious goal.

You may notice that I am basically willing to borrow from any discipline that will help me to solve my problem. Some people have commented that some of the things we've done are old AI. That doesn't bother me because I wasn't intending to do AI in the first place. Also, people have commented about the concepts and techniques being a mixed bag. That's quite all right, because mainly we're concerned with how you train and aid people. We're not concerned with how we advance the state-of-the-art.

Question: It seems to me there's an underlying assumption that all of problem solving is driven by rules. However, you could have just as easily asked the question, "How do you invoke concepts or procedures to solve a problem?"

Rouse: I'm glad you asked that, because that's the next model. Often problem solving isn't action-by-action; it can be procedures or scripts; it can be involved with dealing with particular environments; or it can be frames. As shown in Figure 8, for our next model we ended up taking the same model as we had in Figure 6, but we didn't use S-Rules and T-Rules. We just said there are some things you do related to the picture or to the face of the system you see, and there are some things you do related to a deeper knowledge of the system.

Figure 9 includes some of the things that the questioner just mentioned. At the highest level of recognition and classification, one of the problems is whether or not you are in a familiar environment. We've done studies, for example, where we take people who are airframe mechanics and give them avionics systems to troubleshoot. It turns out we can train them to do that pretty well, even though they don't know what the words or the systems mean. But certainly when they do that, they don't have an avionics frame. They may have a frame that is analogous. The basic notion of this whole model is that, at the highest level, when you run into a problem situation, you ask if you have a frame. If it fits at all, you invoke it and you assume you're in that environment.

At the next level down, there is planning. One thing we've found is that people would just love to avoid planning. And the easiest way to avoid it is to just do what you've done before. If people have a script of the problem that roughly fits, people will follow that script. If not, they may end up having to actually formulate a plan, and planning is a very formal process.

Down where you're actually doing things, you get to the point of looking for familiar patterns and again applying the S-Rules and the T-Rules. This model,

SELECTING RULES

U_R = MEMBERSHIP IN FUZZY SET OF <u>RECALLED</u> RULES

- DECREASES WITH TIME SINCE LAST USAGE
- INCREASES WITH NUMBER OF USES

U_A = MEMBERSHIP IN FUZZY SET OF <u>APPLICABLE</u> RULES

- INCREASES IF ALL ENHANCING FEATURES PRESENT
- DECREASES IF ANY DETRACTING FEATURES PRESENT

U_U = MEMBERSHIP IN FUZZY SET OF <u>USEFUL</u> RULES

- MIGHT INCREASE WITH EXPECTED REDUCTION OF FEASIBLE SET SIZE
- INVOLVES TRADEOFF BETWEEN SHORT-TERM AND LONG-TERM USEFULNESS

U_S = MEMBERSHIP IN FUZZY SET OF <u>SIMPLE</u> RULES

- DECREASES WITH NUMBER OF PROBLEM ELEMENTS TO CONSIDER
- INCREASES WITH NUMBER OF USES

U_C = MEMBERSHIP IN FUZZY SET OF <u>CHOOSABLE</u> RULES

$$U_C = \text{MIN}\,[U_R, U_A, U_U, U_S]$$

Figure 7.

MULTI-LEVEL RULED-BASED MODEL

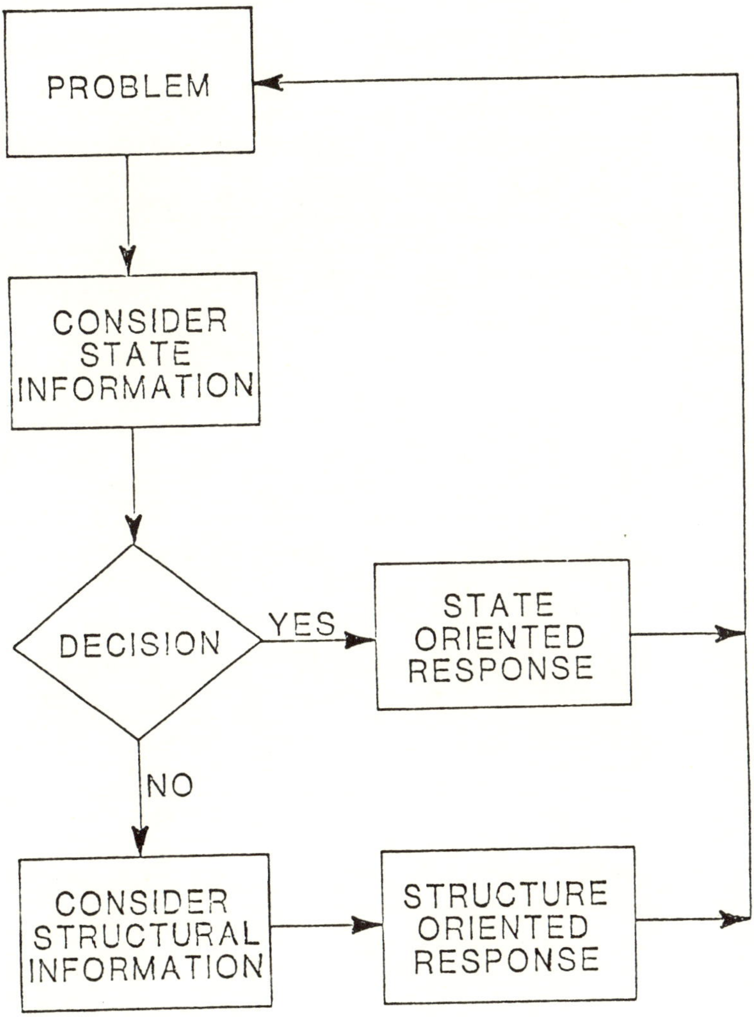

Figure 8.

DECISIONS AND RESPONSES FOR THREE LEVELS OF PROBLEM SOLVING

LEVEL \ PROCESS	DECISION	STATE-ORIENTED RESPONSE	STRUCTURE-ORIENTED RESPONSE
1. RECOGNITION AND CLASSIFICATION	FRAME AVAILABLE?	INVOKE FRAME	USE ANALOGY AND/OR BASIC PRINCIPLES
2. PLANNING	SCRIPT AVAILABLE?	INVOKE SCRIPT	FORMULATE PLAN
3. EXECUTION AND MONITORING	PATTERN FAMILIAR?	APPLY APPROPRIATE S-RULE	APPLY APPROPRIATE T-RULE

Figure 9.

the concept of which came out of an ARI grant, was operationalized out of our current ONR grant. We have it up and running in Pascal. It's now a process control operator and has about 250 or 300 rules. The rules aren't as important as the structure which deals with them. This model was designed to deal with dynamic environments, things which change in time. That would be the case if you were trying to operate a system and maintain it at the same time. We had to add a lot of these elements as soon as we got into the nature of dynamic environments. For example, we realized that people tend to find a pattern that triggers a script, and then follow that procedure almost independent of the information coming back.

The purpose in presenting all these models is to provide the basis for the following conclusions. Given these models and this series of experiments, we've learned a bit about people's limitations and abilities in problem solving in maintenance and operational diagnostics tasks. I'm going to give you a summary of these limitations, all of which are based on experimental results and our reasoning from the models.

I want to talk about three types of behavior. First, pattern recognition behavior. All of our results say that people definitely prefer to use pattern recognition. There's a very good reason for that. If we contrast pattern recognition with more analytic information seeking, we find it's much easier to get through life with pattern recognition. You can imagine if we had to build an expert system, for example, to get up and have breakfast in the morning, and it did everything analytically. It would have to rediscover all sorts of interesting things each day, such as, what is a fork and how do you get out the door. Well, people don't analytically figure those things out each day. There is a tremendous number of context specific pattern recognition rules, and people would definitely rather avoid doing analytic information seeking. There is one exception, one subpopulation, and that's researchers. They'd rather do the latter than admit that pattern recognition is there. We might be more successful, I guess, if we had all our researchers become mechanics.

One of the inefficiencies of pattern recognition, or the thing that makes it ineffective, is that people tend to be captured by almost familiar patterns. A lot of work on human error has talked about this, for example, the work done by Don Norman and Jim Reason. A good example, the other day I was driving downtown to go to a festival they were having in part of the city, and I drove by the exit that goes to work. Suddenly, I found myself at work. I said, "What am I doing here?" It was very disconcerting for my wife and daughter. Thus, patterns tend to capture you and that can present problems.

A corollary to this we've found is that people tend to be very reluctant to accept that the unfamiliar has occurred. I think we find that this is true of expert systems. They're very reluctant to admit that they don't know where they are. So, there are commonalities between people and systems, I suppose, but one of the things we've found is that it is important to try to train people so they will accept that the unfamiliar occurs and they have to deal with those problems differently. If they tend to force themselves into a context specific pattern, they can lead themselves astray.

We found another very interesting thing unintentionally. We thought if we taught people general principles of problem solving, and then could get them to admit they were in the unfamiliar, they could deal with the unfamiliar. We conducted various studies to try to promote that and found that, if you tell people about general principles, they tend to say, "Yeah, that sounds pretty reasonable." If you watch what they do, however, they don't necessarily act like that. What we found is that, if you get those general principles on-line, get the person in a situation where the principle applies, explain that principle right then and there, as he needs it, and explain it in a context that he's currently dealing with, people tend to conceptualize general principles themselves. In other words, if they see these things explained to them on-line as they're trying to troubleshoot this power plant or avionics system, then they start to generalize. You have to explain it in context to get them to understand it in general. Whereas, if you explain it in general, they shake their heads "yes," but they don't tend to use it.

If you think about it, that's not so surprising. I find if people give me an elaborate theory of human behavior or the nature of the universe, I always end up asking for examples so that they'll give me something concrete to hold onto.

Information seeking behavior, the second behavior I want to discuss, is more analytical. Assuming that we've got people in an analytical mode, what do we know about them? People don't tend to consider the full implications of all of the available information; instead, they focus on a portion of the information. They also don't tend to seek disconfirming information. If they've got a hypothesis, they are not going to look at the alternative. One specific thing we've found is that, when you're focused on the failure of your system, you tend not to look at what's still working, which may be important. You're thinking about failures.

When time-pressured, people adopt brute-force strategies. We've done things like time pressure them at a rate that is twice what they'd do self-paced. Impulsive subjects, assessed via the Matching Familiar Figures Test, make all sorts of errors in information collection (and we don't seem to be able to train them out of this). In contrast, field dependent subjects seem to be able to be trained out of it. Another characteristic of this behavior is a difficulty in identifying the feasible set.

We believed we could make people optimal by training them correctly. In one experiment, we were able to get 100 percent negative transfer training; so we could manipulate them, that was clear. But we're at the point in all of our studies, where we just want people to be acceptable. As long as they do nothing wrong, as long as they're productive, and what they're doing is heading toward a solution--if we can just get to that point, we're in a good situation. That attitude has tended to flavor a lot of the work we're doing now.

The third behavior I call meta knowledge, which isn't a very good term, but I couldn't think of a better phrase. I wanted to indicate some higher level things. One big problem we've encountered is that people very quickly learn <u>what</u>--they'll tell you all sorts of facts about the system; you can test them on their training, and they know an amazing amount of information about the system--they just don't know when. We find you put people into the environment, and they don't know which piece of all that information to use. The difference is between system knowledge and operational knowledge, having it in your head and being able to use it. People have difficulty with multiple goals, especially operational goals and maintenance goals. Many accident reports decribe situations where people have so focused on operations, they ignore the problem until it overwhelms them, or they have so focused on the problem, they forget to operate the system and it crashes.

Another thing we found is how people deal with risk. Often people know the facts, know when to do what they're supposed to do, and have been instructed on what the tradeoffs are in relation to the risks in the system. In one recent experiment, when subjects were put into the operational environment and everything was falling apart, they adopted very different risks from what we thought they were going to adopt.

What are the implications? There are three types: training, aiding, and common themes. With the "common themes" I'd like to emphasize, and I've heard it alluded to in this workshop, that we're getting to the point where it's hard to separate training and aiding. You can think about the same system actually serving both purposes. I'll come back to that, but first let's talk about training.

Given all this background, the first question in discussing implications for training is, do we want people to be able to deal with unfamiliar problems? The way we do that is to give them experiences in multiple problem domains. For example, in our training program right now for marine engineers, the first sequence of training they go through is fixing automobile engines, then aircraft engines, then marine propulsion systems. The idea is, when you try to teach them general principles of problem solving on the systems they're familiar with, they can't tear themselves away from the context. This is a hard concept to sell. When we first talked to the people who wanted this training program, they were skeptical about teaching these engineers about car engines. It worked out very well. It turns out car engines are very popular with people in general, and they think they're going to learn how to fix their car (sort of as a freebie) while they're there.

Another implication for training is that the balance between knowledge of "what" and "when" should be improved by shifting from passive to active training methods. Too many programs are organized toward passive training methods. You get a lecture or a film, and jam in a bunch of knowledge and facts. I remember when I was in basic training, and I got all this knowledge about what each airplane looked like and how much it could carry. It just wasn't useful to me. I was inundated with information, and it didn't do me any good unless I knew what to do with it. To do that, you shift from passive to active methods so people can be involved. One of the interesting things about active training methods for multiple domains is that, if, for example, we're training communications switchboard mechanics, we can't really have people go out and fix airplanes just because it's good for them. So we end up using simulators, and in this case AI has a lot to offer.

A third implication for training is that we can improve people's abilities to resolve tradeoffs and choose acceptable levels of risk by, again, active training methods with context-oriented feedback. Fourth, we can improve abilities to use available information by using on-line context-oriented explanations and guidance. For example, if they're switchboard mechanics and they're in the airplane propulsion portion of the training program and they're trying to figure out some problem with the airplane system, you explain the principles you're trying to get across in the context of what they're doing right at the moment.

What are the implications for aiding? One key thing, as I said earlier, is that we should design systems to support any productive strategy the user wants to choose, rather than just supporting the optimal strategy. We have to define what productive means in different domains, but as long as the person is moving toward a solution, then we shouldn't try to force him into a different kind of path. Interestingly, as long as the person is productive and doesn't have any of these other problems, he or she never sees the aid.

We can use the computer to evaluate the consistency and merit of hypotheses and plans. This is a difficult one to implement because, to get people to stop in the midst of problem solving and tell you what their hypotheses and plans are, may not be too realistic.

The next implication for aiding is important and pretty easy to do. It's this--determine and display implications of information obtained and actions taken. People do not take into account the full implications of the information they collect. The computer, for example, with its topographic knowledge can show them. It may not know what the best test is, at least not with respect to their strategy, but it can tell them the implications of what it just found out.

Next, monitor for inconsistent and erroneous actions. When detected, provide context-oriented explanations and guidance. We've found that, instead of trying to force people down the optimal path, think of it in terms of an acceptable envelope, and as long as they're going through their own world, but are within this envelope, that's fine. If they start to do inconsistent things, the computer should come back with a prompt in the context of what they're doing and explain why they're getting out of that envelope.

Neglected goals are also a very important thing. For example, an Eastern Airlines 401 crashed in the Everglades because all four people were absorbed in a light bulb failure, no one was flying the airplane. The airplane should have been smart enough to know it shouldn't spiral down into the swamp; it didn't have to know the swamp was there, but that spiraling was an unusual approach to an airport. The computer should be able to handle those kinds of things.

One final implication for aiding is more difficult to do for the computer, but should be doable. We tend to talk about supporting the solution of familiar problems. Why couldn't we also use the computer, at least in terms of some of these kinds of things, to support the operator in solving a problem when the computer has no expertise in that particular problem at all? In other words, some of the support functions should be generic and not tied tightly to particular feasible sets of problems.

Now to common themes. One is a notion of experience in multiple domains, the idea of different kinds of simulators that would support that. Active training methods get people involved and it's so inexpensive to do that now, it's a shame not to. In terms of motivation, it seems to me that for some of the programs we've observed, it would be a major success to get people to stay awake, and active training does that; people get involved and you get good results in the end. Explanations should be in context whether it's an aiding or a training explanation. Don't come back and tell someone you got error #43. Explain it in the context of what they have been doing. Of course that means the system has to know what people are doing, so it's a little more than just changing the format of the print-out statement. The system should also be flexible with respect to strategies people might choose. The last common theme is on-line monitoring and feedback and how we can do that.

On-line models for training and aiding (the ones that we are using lately) would, I think, classify as somewhat archaic AI models. So this addresses directly the approach of this workshop. There are three things I'd like to mention. First, what expertise would we like from these models? Because I'm driven by how to train and aid people, I'm not so concerned by what AI can do for me. I'm more concerned with telling them what I want. These things I'll suggest aren't necessarily easy. Second, what functions should be provided? Finally, there are several issues I want to summarize.

Let's consider the expertise of the on-line models. I would like on-line models to have expertise in contextual elements and relationships. We've also heard a little bit about expertise in principles of problem solving, but not a full range of what you might consider. For the purposes of training and aiding that I'm suggesting, I think it should also have expertise in human problem solving and limitations. So, you're not only going to have to talk to the person who's fixed the radio for 20 years, you're also going to have to talk to psychologists. The point is that we have to have the system understand the context, but also the human behavior that is likely to be observed in that context. To me, that's very important. Some of the aiding notions we've applied that were most successful were done only after we'd had a series of experiments to understand the behavior of the people in that environment.

What should these models do? It would be nice if they knew enough about people to determine the level of a particular individual's problem solving abilities and identify the most appropriate types of training and aiding. I don't know how you'd do it, but certainly if you could identify those impulsive people that sit at the keyboard, it would be very useful because they present a lot of problems, especially because you can't train it out.

Second, the models should monitor solution sequences to identify inconsistencies and errors relative to contextual constraints and principles of problem solving. We've got a program with NASA right now where this system monitors what the aircraft crew is doing, and it's not trying to tell them what to do or force them or give them optimal feedback; it's just trying to find out if they're doing things that are consistent with what that airplane is supposed to do. It turns out, as you may expect, the system has to know one heck of a lot about airplanes and what air crews do in airplanes to be able to do that. Finally, models should provide context-oriented explanations and guidance relative to anomalies identified and alternative courses of action.

To conclude, I have three issues that are important. One is assessing expert knowledge. We haven't been involved with this until recently, and a very interesting thing came out. We had subjects who were highly trained in a process control task, 32 subjects trained over many weeks, and they had previously had 3 years of engineering to be involved in this kind of task. We assessed what they knew about the system. What we did was to give them pictures and displays and ask them to explain what they would do here. Very extensive explanations of many pages were collected. What we concluded is that they were really expert in the system, they knew what to do, they knew approriate tradeoffs. Then, we had the fifth model I was showing you (Figure 8), playing relative to these subjects. This model received the same training as the subjects, it has these expert rules, and we wanted to see how they compare. It turns out that the model and the subjects do the same thing about 70 percent of the time. So we looked at when they don't agree. The best conclusion, after a lot of tedious analysis is that the experts told us different things when we asked them off-line than when we asked them on-line. The difference was not in specific knowledge, that is the factual knowledge, it was more in their values and the risks they were willing to assume or would try to avoid. In other words, what they told us from a factual point of view of how the widgets connect was good, and they seem to use this information. But how they traded off risks and how they dealt with the values of the different goals that were competing, such as, "Do I keep the system operating or do I shut off the system and protect the resources?" It was very different from what they said they would do.

Another issue is training vs. aiding. I've mentioned this before. I think we can exploit the same technology for both cases. In fact, you can imagine an elaborate scenario in which all new trainees gets a LISP machine when they check in, and it goes with them through training, goes out with them on the job, and in our scenario, it's very small and in their watch. This machine can transition from training to aiding and be involved with aiding them on their task, as well as involved with learning their task.

Finally, and this may be the most important point, is that a lot of what I've heard today and yesterday at this workshop seems to be oriented toward computerizing. I think we should be focusing much more on computer aiding, because if we can train people and aid them so we can be sure that they use productive strategies to solve problems, then we have people as resources to deal with other problems in the future. Especially when they run into a problem that no one anticipated. The difficulty here is that one strategy you could adopt would be to say, "Well, we'll just computerize 90 percent of it, and they'll know what to do." When they type in those symptoms, it just says "replace x," and they do it. The 10 percent of the time when there are really difficult problems, we'll let them do those. But, it turns out that 90 percent of the time they're not doing anything, and 10 percent of the time we're expecting them to react.

Let me give you one example of this problem in closure. In our current ARI project, we have operators monitoring automated communications networks, and they have to step in when some problem arises. Well, we thought it would be very nice after studying some systems like the Bell System, to have a lot of automatic re-routing so the system reconfigures itself when things fail. What we found is that we had to get rid of that option because, for most of the problems, it reconfigures and the operator never saw anything.

For the problems that were difficult, such as multiple failures, it would keep on reconfiguring, using up resources, until finally there was no solution that it could find after exhaustively searching. Then it would say to the operator, "It's all yours." I think we've got to keep the person involved. Those problems would never arise if the person was involved, at least at some supervisory level, rather than having an automatic system.

ABOUT THE AUTHOR

Dr. William B. Rouse is a Professor and Director at the Center for Man-Machinery Systems Research at Georgia Institute of Technology. He is also President and Principal Scientist at Search Technology, Inc. (applied R&D in computer-based training and aiding). Dr. Rouse is current President of IEEE Systems, Man and Cybernetics Society.

A GENERALIZED MODEL OF FAULT-ISOLATION PERFORMANCE*

Douglas M. Towne

Behavioral Technology Laboratories
University of Southern California

Introduction

This paper will briefly summarize a computer-based model of corrective maintenance performance, developed to generate realistic fault-isolation behavior. The model forms the core of a maintainability projection system which quantifies the times to isolate and repair a sample of faults in an existing or planned equipment. Since the projections are a direct result of the system design, the model can be used to assess the maintenance implications of design decisions concerning internal organization, packaging and modularization, and selection of external indicators, controls, and test points.

For each malfunction of interest, the model generates a sequence of tests, adjustments, disassembly/assembly operations and replacements which isolate and resolve the fault. The testing sequences generated by the model have been found to correspond well with those performed by maintenance technicians in identifying and resolving those malfunctions. The manual times to perform the projected actions are automatically retrieved from a data base of predetermined times for generic maintenance actions, derived from standard motion times. Applying the model to a substantial number of possible faults in a system yields a distribution of corrective maintenance times and such quantitative measures as Mean-Time-To-Repair (MTTR), and the probability of repair within a specified time.

Since the model projects the actions required to resolve each failure, the range and character of maintenance activities imposed by the system design may also be considered.

* This research was funded by the Office of Naval Research, Engineering Psychology Group, under contract N00014-80-C-0493. Mr. Gerald S. Malecki served as scientific officer.

System Representation

A specific equipment is represented in a manner which is logically complete, in that information is provided about the possible effects on each indicator of failures in each replaceable unit. The notation scheme, however, is intentionally 'fuzzy', i.e. it does not enumerate the symptom effects of each possible failure mode. Instead, the following is provided for each indicator affected by a replaceable unit:

a. If all possible failure modes in the unit affect the indicator in one way, then the symptom effect is specified.

b. If different failure modes in the unit affect the indicator in different abnormal ways, then a symptom equivalent to 'MIXED ABNORMALS' is specified.

c. If some failure modes affect the indicator, and others do not, then a symptom equivalent to 'MIXED NORMAL & ABNORMAL' is specified.

The case of no failure modes in a unit affecting an indicator is implicitly specified by omitting the indicator from the unit's fault effects specification.

This complete, but non-detailed, scheme allows for very compact specification of fault effects, and avoids the necessity to determine how each possible failure could affect an indicator.

Corrective maintenance sequences for faults in three different systems have been generated by the model to date, and compared to those of 87 technicians. It has been a surprising result that the maintenance sequences generated by the model correspond so closely to those actually performed by human technicians when the failure-effects data are so sparse. Adding more detailed symptom data causes the projections to differ markedly from observed performance.

It is important to note that this process for representing fault effects in the model's data base is not arbitrary, and that the uncertainty, or fuzziness, exhibited by the representation scheme reflects the extent to which fault effects are confounded as a result of the system design. When failures in a system produce effects which map closely to the replaceable elements, (i.e. the symptom effects of units do not vary for different failure modes) then that system's data base will reflect clear and easily identifiable symptoms. Unfortunately, most systems selected or devised as vehicles for research in fault isolation have been ones in which the fault effects are nearly ideal - each unit can fail in only one catastrophic way.

Ideally, a system would be designed in just this manner, so that the set of indicators affected by a unit is consistent, no matter how the unit fails. In reality it is often difficult to accomplish this, and the effects of failures in a unit may vary according to the failure mode. The maintenance performance projected by the model reflects the increased difficulty of fault isolation when the replaceable units can fail in complex ways.

Organization of the Model

The maintenance performance model is organized on two levels, data and program (see Figure 1).

Data. The data level consists of three types of information:

1) equipment-specific information, describing the equipment design:

- the names of the tests available in the system
- the indicators which are stimulated by those tests
- the names of the adjustment points and replaceable elements
- the possible effects of faults in the replaceable elements
- the non-conditional times to perform the tests, adjustments, and replacements (i.e. the portion not dependent upon previous actions)
- the times to perform necessary disassembly/reassembly operations
- the relative costs and reliabilities of the replaceable elements

Figure 2 presents an example specification of a microcomputer design.

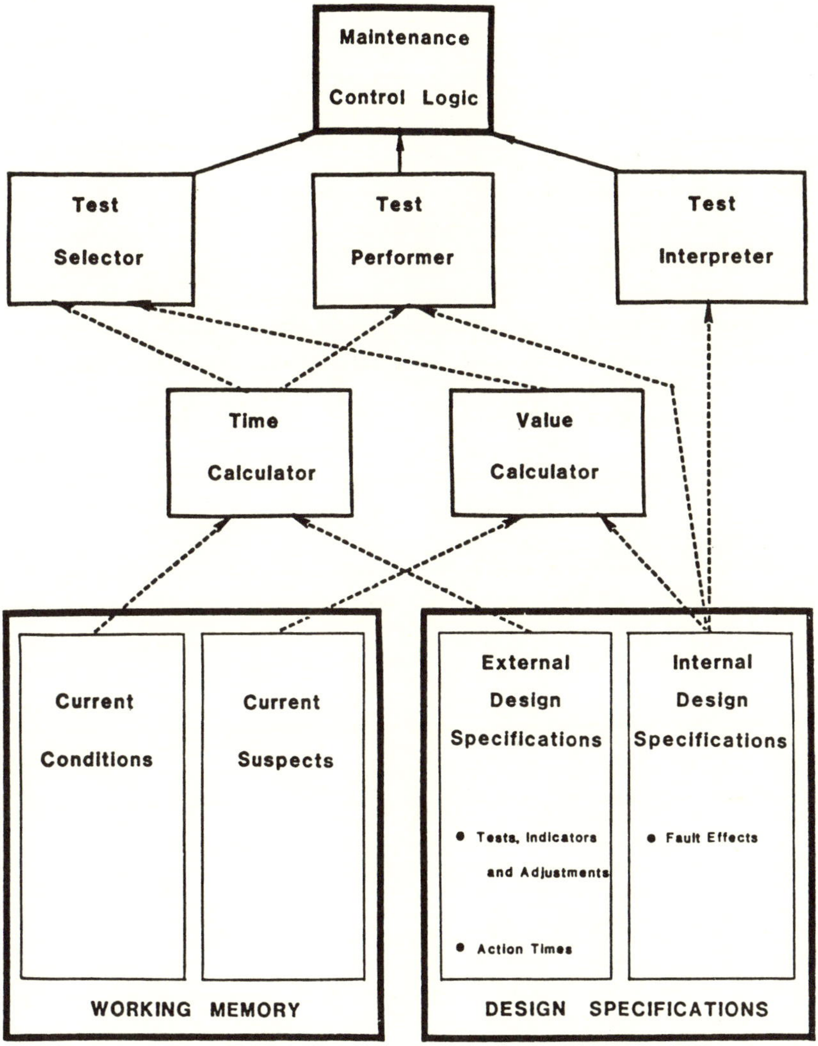

Figure 1. PROFILE System Organization

RU No.	Replaceable Unit Name	Repl. Time	Unit Cost	Fault-effects
(1)	POWER SUPPLY	196	329	7771778820100000087
(2)	CPU	43	5	7777788770000000007
(3)	ON-BOARD RAM	51	2	0007100070000000000
(4)	RAM CARD	37	195	0000200070000000000
(5)	DISK CONTROL BOARD	40	125	0707007870000000087
(6)	ANALOG BOARD	98	100	0707007870000000007
(7)	DISK MOTOR	166	25	0007000870000000007
(8)	DISK CABLE	71	25	0701007120010000077
(9)	PRINTER CHAR BOARD	40	220	0000000080000000000
(10)	PRINTER CABLE	23	20	0000000020000100000
(11)	PRINTER POWER SUPPLY	72	500	0000000087001000000
(12)	PRINTER INTERFACE BOARD	80	200	0000000080000000000
(13)	CRT	23	285	0019999900000001000
(14)	CRT FUSE	9	1	0019999900000011000
(15)	CRT CABLE	35	20	0019999900000000100
(16)	SYSTEM DISKETTE	14	5	0007000870000000000
(17)	MOTOR SPEED ADJUSTMENT	85	0	0007000870000000000
(18)	DISK HEAD ALIGNMENT	55	0	0007000870000000000
(19)	DISK HEAD TRAVEL ADJUSTMENT	69	0	0007001370000000000

RU SPEC'S

3 4 1 2 6 7 4 6 3 6 4 3 2 2 8 18 4 7 10 (relative failure percentages)

Test No.	Test Name	Test Time	Indicators Monitored
(1)	SYSTEM BOOT	36	1 2 3 4
(2)	RAM DIAGNOSTIC	301	1 3 5
(3)	CPU DIAGNOSTIC	78	1 3 6
(4)	DISK HEAD TRAVEL DIAG.	54	1 2 3 7
(5)	DISK READ/WRITE DIAG.	29	1 2 3 8
(6)	PRINTER TEST PROGRAM	65	1 2 3 4 9 10
(7)	MAINFRAME POWER TEST	57	11
(8)	DISK CABLE CONTINUITY	109	12
(9)	PRINTER POWER TEST	88	13
(10)	PRINTER CABLE CONTINUITY	57	14
(11)	CRT FUSE CHECK	109	15
(12)	CRT HEATER CHECK	88	16
(13)	CRT CABLE CONTINUITY	57	17
(14)	DOWNSTREAM VOLTAGE TEST	57	18
(15)	DISK ROTATION CHECK	24	2 19

TEST SPECIFICATIONS

Fault No.	RU No.	Fault Symptoms
(1)	1	1101322220100000011
(2)	2	1111999920000000001
(3)	4	0000200020000000000
(4)	6	0001000120000000000
(5)	17	0001000120000000000
(6)	7	0001000120000000001
(7)	10	0000000020000100000
(8)	16	0002000300000000000

FAULT SPECIFICATIONS

Figure 2. Representation of Computer System

2) working memory, which reflects the current status of a maintenance problem in progress. The primary contents of working memory are a) likelihood measures for each replaceable unit, and b) current values of various equipment conditions which can change during maintenance work.

The likelihood measures are derived from numerical scores, maintained for each possible fault or mis-adjustment. The score for a replaceable element reflects the difference between the symptoms already received in a problem and those which the element might have produced, if it were the failure. Consequently, a relatively low score indicates a close fit and a likely source of the symptoms received.

The equipment conditions reflect the status of various attributes of a system, such as the extent to which it has been disassembled. This information is maintained and accessed by the model to determine the time required to perform various possible maintenance operations.

3) parameter values, which express a) the urgency of the maintenance environment, and b) the availability of spares. These affect the model's use of hardware substitution as a means for effecting rapid equipment restorations.

Program. The computer program contains two levels of control mechanisms, although these are not clearly partitioned as separate entities. At the top level is what may be regarded as generic maintenance control and planning logic.

This control structure invokes the lower-level functions in a relatively fixed sequence, as follows:

```
REPEAT (for each fault examined)

    SELECT THE NEXT OPERATION.
      (and add its context-dependent performance time
       to the cumulative total)

    If Adjustment or Replacement was selected above:
      SELECT THE SHORTEST TEST WHICH MONITORS THE SYSTEM.
        (and add its performance time to the total)

      else  DETERMINE THE OUTCOME OF CONVENTIONAL TEST.
      (by fetching the symptom produced by the true fault)

    UPDATE THE LIKELIHOODS OF THE POSSIBLE FAULTS.

UNTIL no fault
```

Thus the model involves operators for selecting tests, performing them, and evaluating their outcomes, as described further below.

Test Selector

At each decision stage, the test selection algorithm forms an ordered set of n productive tests, with test 1 being the test of highest fault-isolation value, and n being a parameter set to less than, or equal to, the total number of tests available. The value of a test is computed as the ratio of the test's likely information value to its performance time. Both of these quantities are sequence-dependent and are re-computed at each stage. The definition of a 'test' is unconstrained so that any operation potentially capable of providing new information is considered for selection. Thus adjustments and replacements are included in this evaluation of what to do next.

The general rules applied to select the next operation consider all of the following:

- the relative reliabilities of the replaceable elements
- the costs of the replaceable elements
- the current likelihoods of the possible faults
- the times to perform the operations, in the present context
- the new information possibly obtained from the operations

Since only productive tests are included in the set, previously performed tests, and tests which have no new information to offer are not considered for selection. The values of the n possible tests are then normalized, and a test is selected probabilistically according to the relative values.

With n set to 1, the model selects the best available test at each decision point. The resulting testing sequences are potentially useful for instruction and performance-aiding, but are not maximally representative of performance by human technicians. With larger n, non-optimal tests are considered for selection. Since probability of selection is related to computed value, however, extremely poor tests are rarely selected by the model. The fault-isolation sequences of the model corresponded best with actual troubleshooting performance with n set equal to three.

The selected operation may be a replacement, as well as a test or adjustment, because replacements (followed by confirming tests) provide new information about the system. In early phases of problems, replacements are not usually attractive choices because they offer little information compared to other tests. In addition, their relative time investment is often large, since the time to obtain new information includes the time to access and replace the part plus the time to perform a confirming test. Later in problems, however, replacements may offer more information than the remaining available tests, for the time investment involved.

Like many human technicians, this decision logic may decide to replace an inexpensive part prior to obtaining complete proof of its failure, if the time to replace is low compared to the time required to complete the necessary confirming tests. Excessive behavior of this type by human technicians is termed 'Easter-egging' and is costly unless the replacement parts are extremely inexpensive. The maintenance model considers component costs to avoid Easter-egging, but it will resort to swapping moderately-priced suspected elements if the times of the other useful tests are excessive, and the maintenance environment is sufficiently urgent.

Following a replacement, the model performs the shortest available test which is sure to be abnormal if the fault persists. This is often chosen to be some test which previously yielded an abnormal result, although some other test could be selected if considerable reassembly is required. The model continues to generate maintenance operations until the assumed fault has been rectified by a replacement or adjustment, and normal system operation has been confirmed.

Test Performer

The test performance function simply appends the selected test to the ongoing sequence, along with any disassembly or reassembly operations necessary to satisfy conditions for performing the test, and adds the performance times to the cumulative total. Finally, it fetches from the data base the symptoms which would be obtained if that test were actually performed.

Test Interpreter

The test interpretation function compares the symptoms received from the selected test to the possible fault effects of the replaceable units. It computes a difference score for each unit, which varies according to the difference between the unit's possible fault effects and those received from the test performed. These values are then added to the cumulative distance scores, and normalized likelihoods are computed from the scores.

If the system's replaceable units can fail in multiple modes, the model may, at times, perform tests which turn out to yield no useful information. Suppose, for example, three units (A, B, and C) are suspected, based upon prior symptoms. Suppose further that only unit A could affect test 1, if it fails in a particular mode. If test 1 is performed, and an abnormal result is obtained, then the fault is known to be in unit A. If a normal result is obtained, however, nothing is learned except that part of unit A is operational. It is seen that normal results are useful for eliminating a unit from suspicion only if the element always produces an abnormal result on the indicator, when it fails, regardless of its failure mode. When replaceable units are functionally large, they tend to exhibit more failure modes, often including a mode in which there is no effect on indicators intended to monitor those units.

Consequently, the model finds normal symptom information to be less useful than abnormal symptoms, in many cases. Thus, if a designer were to revise the modularity and/or packaging of the replaceable units, the model would sense the fault isolation implications.

ABOUT THE AUTHOR

Dr. Douglas M. Towne is Director of the Behavioral Technology Laboratories, University of Southern California. He has performed research in troubleshooting and human task performance, optimization of serial-action task sequences, and development of computer-based training systems. Dr. Towne holds a Ph.D. in engineering from the University of Southern California.

THE PSYCHOLOGY OF TECHNICAL DEVICES AND TECHNICAL DISCOURSE

David E. Kieras

Department of Psychology
University of Arizona
Tucson, Arizona 85721

This paper is concerned with some issues in cognitive psychology that are relevant to the general question of what artificial intelligence techniques can do toward the solution of problems concerning equipment training and maintenance. Three topics will be discussed. The first is the nature of expertise in electronics, which is not very well understood. This is a problem because if the goal is to design an AI system that behaves like an electronics cxpert, or can help ordinary people become electronics experts, it is difficult to see how this could be done without understanding the nature of electronics expertise. The second topic is the relation between instructions and expertise. It would seem that there should be better ways of organizing operating instructions, but our intuitions can be seriously wrong. The third topic is technical documentation. Even in an AI computer-based system, the user will have to read and understand material in order to learn and carry out procedures. Here there is a striking opportunity for the application of AI techniques. There is a long history of success in AI work on language processing, and cognitive psychology has a substantial accumulation of theoretical and empirical work to contribute. Thus, solving some of the problems in technical documentation is a "target of opportunity" for the application of AI techniques.

The Nature of Electronics Expertise

There has been very little work done in experimental cognitive psychology on the nature of electronics expertise, although there are several important areas of expertise that have been investigated. The relevant form of electronics expertise is the kind acquired through years of interacting with electronic equipment for the purposes of maintenance and construction. There has been some work done in cognitive psychology with regard to electrical theory from the viewpoint of expertise in physics, or expertise acquired during engineering training. However, in neither case does this relate directly to the expert with "hands on" experience.

Here a brief description will be provided of some work that has been done on electronics expertise in my laboratory. More detail on these results can be found in Kieras (1982) and a forthcoming technical report.

In the first experiment, experts and nonexperts were asked to describe actual devices presented to them. The experts were typically individuals with several years of actual working experience with electronic devices. The nonexperts were students recruited in the usual manner done in psychology experiments. The subjects were asked to simply describe everything they could about the devices, from the point of view of one having to explain our technology to a technically sophisticated visitor from another planet. The subjects' verbal and motor behavior were recorded on videotape, which was then scored for content. The devices in these experiments ranged from everyday devices such as an alarm clock and a tape recorder, to devices familiar mainly to experts, such as a standard volt-ohm-milliameter (VOM), to devices unusual and peculiar even to experts. In a second experiment, to be described in more detail below, subjects operated pieces of equipment of varying familiarity from instructions, either mandatorily read, or optionally read.

The results of these experiments can be briefly summarized. First of all, expertise is very complex in that it is not just a knowledge of electronic circuitry, but also contains several other kinds of knowledge about electronic equipment. Experts have a great deal of what might be called "surface" information about electronic devices. This is information about what electronic devices typically look like, how they are constructed, and what the controls feel like when they are manipulated. All of the subjects, especially the experts, in the first experiment manipulated the controls on the devices at great length. Furthermore, many subjects recognized a device very quickly, apparently on the basis of just a few features. This was especially striking with some of the unusual devices, which experts would classify on the basis of a few global features, such as a centrally located meter, or a large calibrated dial. It also appears that expert subjects have a certain physical smoothness and fluency at interacting with equipment. For example, in the instruction-following experiment, experts were not only faster overall than nonexperts, but were very fluent at performing complex physical actions such as plugging in a cord. There were many cases of nonexpert subjects fumbling while trying to plug in an ordinary line cord. In contrast, experts perform very smoothly and efficiently. Experts also do quite a bit of exploration of the device and examination of small components.

In general, experts show a deep richness in their behavior, in that they can unpack their knowledge at any level of detail, but are nonetheless sensitive to the task domain. In the device description experiment, expert subjects would sometimes comment that, of course, they could provide a full description of how a piece of equipment operated, but they assumed that this was not wanted and instead provided descriptions of how to operate it. Other expert subjects went into great detail on small features such as the characteristics of the pilot light bulb on one of the devices.

Experts, however, could get confused, and were prone to make mistakes, although their overall performance was impressive. Where they got into trouble concerned cases of trying to go too far on the knowledge that they had available. For example, some experts were confused by a novel device which did not obey the convention that terminals on the left-hand side are input terminals. One such subject entirely misconstrued this device as a result. In other cases, expert subjects are able to pursue paths through a device operation task that nonexpert subjects simply do not have available, and when this path is in fact an incorrect one, the expert may end up being worse off. For example, one expert subject in the optional instruction condition of the second experiment attempted to carry out the task of measuring the resistance of a resistor with a volt-ohm-milliameter (VOM). The meter on the VOM had been set off of zero in order to have the subject carry out a slightly more complicated task. One subject did not notice this, and when the measurement on the resistor did not agree with the markings on the resistor, he proceeded to disassemble the VOM and test its batteries. After this fruitless effort, the subject discovered that the meter was off zero and then was able to complete the task. Thus, while experts are generally impressive in their performance, their knowledge can occasionally mislead them when the device does not correspond well to what they have been led to expect; meters are usually satisfactorily zeroed.

Thus, experts apparently think of devices in terms of the conventional surface features, such as appearance and layout, and have strong expectations about what is normally present on such a device, and the normal state of affairs. This kind of expectation-based knowledge has been described recently in cognitive psychology as *schema* knowledge, (see Rumelhart & Ortony, 1977). A schema is an organized piece of memory information that specifies or describes classes of objects in terms of their typical features. The notion is very similar to the concept of *frames*, but it is much older.

Furthermore, subjects show a sensitivity to patterns and expectations not only at the level of the entire device, but also its sub-parts and even its individual controls and connections. Thus, knowledge of devices must be organized in terms of a hierarchy of schemas. Thus, one can describe an expert's knowledge of a class of devices, such as radio receivers, as a hierarchy of subdevices, each belonging to a schematic class. Each one of these subdevices can then be described in terms of other subdevices, until eventually we get down to individual common components, both internal ones such as resistors and capacitors, and external ones such as switches and indicators.

In Tables 1, 2, and 3 is shown the possible contents of such a schema for a simple radio. In the radio schema, a radio is portrayed as being made up of three subdevices, namely a power supply device, a tuning device, and an audio output device. Each of these devices is in turn described by a schema, and with each such schema also appears schematic procedures for operating the device. For example, the power device is made up of a schematic power cord, power switch, and pilot light. The schematic procedure for operating the power device is to plug in whatever power cord the device uses, and operate whatever power switch the particular device has, and check whatever type of pilot light the device has. Any one particular device will have a particular instance of the class of power cords, power switches, and so forth.

By using general schematic knowledge of this sort, an expert could figure out how to operate a novel device. For example, he or she would know that a novel radio must have a power switch on it somewhere, and that the first stage in the operation of the radio will be to turn the power switch on. Moreover, if the device is a completely novel one, unique in the expert's experience, it will still be assembled from familiar subdevices.

Table 1

Schema for a Radio

```
STRUCTURE
  power-device
  tuner-device
  audio-device

LAYOUT
  box shape
  medium size
  tuner-device on front
  audio-device on front
  tuner-device right of audio-device

OPERATION
  IF (Goal is to listen to station X)
  THEN (Do power-device operation
        Do tuner-device operation
        Do audio-device operation)

HOW-IT-WORKS
  station sends signal to tuner-device
  tuner-device sends signal to audio-device
  audio-device sends sound to user
  power-device supplies power to tuner-device, audio-device
BEHAVIOR
...
```

Table 2

Subschema for Power-Device

```
STRUCTURE
  power-cord
  power-switch
  pilot-light

LAYOUT
  power-cord on back of device
  power-switch on lower front of device
  pilot-light on front of device

OPERATION
  IF (goal is to power-up)
  THEN (plug in power-cord
        turn-on power-switch
        check pilot-light)

  IF (goal is to power-down)
  THEN (turn-off power-switch)

HOW-IT-WORKS
  electricity from plug goes through cord to the
  power-switch which controls whether electricity
  goes to device.
BEHAVIOR
...
```

Table 3

Subschema for Tuner-Device

```
----------------------------------------------------
STRUCTURE
  antenna
  dial
  knob
  selector

LAYOUT
  dial on front middle of device
  large knob to right or below dial
  antenna on back top of device

OPERATION
  IF (goal is to select station X)
  THEN (turn knob until dial reads X)

HOW-IT-WORKS
  antenna sends signal to selector controlled
  by knob, selector chooses signal, sends to
  rest of device

BEHAVIOR
...
----------------------------------------------------
```

Thus, the expert will have a large variety of schemas which will partially match with the appearance of the device. The expert can recognize familiar configurations of controls on the front panel, and can eventually assemble a description of the device from the subschemas, and deduce how to operate it.

At this point, this schema-based description of knowledge of devices must be regarded as being speculative, rather than strongly supported by data. However, if a goal is to construct an AI-based system that knows about devices in general, such a hierarchical schema format for this knowledge may in fact be a very good idea, because this appears to be a good description of experts' knowledge.

The point of this work on the nature of expertise is that electronics expertise is not very well understood, so we do not really know what is important about it. For example, experts have detailed knowledge of the surface properties of electronic equipment. Is this important to being an expert? Perhaps there are some implications for the design of electronic equipment. In older equipment the relative positions of controls was largely determined by the requirements of the circuitry and the physical nature of the components that the knobs were attached to. But, the newer solid-state equipment makes it possible to arrange controls in essentially arbitrary arrangements. Is it possible that with modern electronics technology, experts are losing some important cues in their ability to interact successfully with equipment? Very little is known about such matters, and further research is very important.

Instruction Organization and Expertise

This section presents a very practical example of the danger of trusting one's intuitions with regard to expertise and the design of job-aiding systems. This question was addressed in the above-mentioned experiment on instruction-following in terms of the issue of whether there would be any relationship between the optimum instruction format and the expertise of the user and the familiarity of the device. Six devices were used, of varying familiarity: a portable AM-FM radio, a cassette tape recorder, a VOM, an oscilloscope and signal generator combination, a phi-phenomenon demonstrator, and a physiological stimulator. Again, the experts were people with several years working experience, and the nonexperts were ordinary student subjects.

The two instruction formats were intended to determine the truth of an obvious intuition about instructions: Step-by-step instructions should be inferior to an organized "menu" format which allows the user to choose the instructions they wish to read. Thus, instructions for operating a piece of equipment could be in the form of a simplistic list of the individual steps, or in a more "intelligent" fashion that would make it possible for a person who is familiar with the equipment to skip large portions of the instructions. This was accomplished with a hierarchical menu of instructions, which decomposed the operating procedure for the device into two or three levels of subprocedures. The very bottom steps in the hierarchy were the very same operating steps as used in the step-by-step instructions.

It is interesting at this point to predict what the effect of these instructions would be. Intuitively, and based on work conducted by Smith and Goodman (1982), one would expect that the menu instruction format would be generally better, both because of the greater structure it gives the instructions, and also because it would allow people to use their knowledge of how to operate the equipment. People who knew how to do a task would not have to be forced to read every individual step in the instructions.

In these results there was no overall advantage of menu instructions at all; in fact, the group who used the menu instructions were somewhat slower overall in completing the tasks. Table 4 shows the average total times to complete the six different tasks for the expert and nonexpert subjects using each instruction format type. The percentages show the percentage gain obtained by using the menu instructions, compared to the step-by-step instructions. If the device is familiar, which is more likely if the subject is an expert, the menu instructions are superior. However, if the device is unfamiliar, such as the VOM to the nonexperts, or the stimulator to the experts, instead of a net gain, we see either little gain, or a very substantial impairment in speed of completing the task.

Apparently, in this experiment, subjects who thought they knew something about the equipment would try to operate it on their own, reading little or none of the instructions, but would eventually discover that they had done something wrong. For example, one expert plugged the indicator light into the wrong jack on the stimulator, and spent a considerable amount of time trying to get it to light before deciding that "when all else fails, read the instructions."

Table 4

Mean Total Time for each Device, Instruction Format, and Expertise Group

	Device					
	Radio	Recrdr	VOM	Oscil	PhiDem	Stim
Nonexpert						
Step-by-step	224.3	216.3	270.8	604.3	260.4	359.5
Menu	100.9	158.2	462.8	723.6	196.9	378.0
% Gain	55%	27%	-71%	-20%	24%	5%
Experts						
Step-by-step	147.0	186.4	189.5	404.4	160.6	269.2
Menu	78.3	108.8	156.3	387.4	142.6	373.5
% Gain	47%	41%	17%	4%	11%	-39%

Thus, the intuitive superiority of menu instructions appears to be obtained only when the subject has considerable familiarity with the specific piece of equipment. Merely being an expert is not necessarily enough. It should be cautioned that this is not a definitive study on instruction format and presentation. But it does show that one's intuitions can not be trusted.

The Problem of Technical Documentation

Essentially every piece of equipment used in the military and industry is accompanied by a technical manual which usually is the only single comprehensive documentation on how the equipment works and how it is to be maintained and used. The volume of this technical documentation is astounding, and has increased very rapidly since the "high-tech" era in military equipment began. The procurement process for equipment is such that developing high-quality technical manuals generally receives low priority, and thus it is generally agreed that there are serious problems in quality of the manuals (Bond & Towne, 1979). Furthermore, the volume of the technical manuals and the problem of keeping them up-to-date are substantial problems just in themselves.

Clearly there will be some gains from replacing paper manuals with some form of computer medium. This might help solve some of the logistical problems. But the problems with the current manuals are mainly a problem of what the manuals _say_, not the medium in which they are prepared. Thus, in order to really have an impact on the quality of technical manuals, attention will have to be focused not on just their packaging, but also on their content.

Two major problem areas in technical manuals can be identified. The first is clarity; most manuals are muddled, densely written, and suffer from poor layout and design. The second is selection of content: Most manuals provide large amounts of detail on a variety of subjects, such as how the equipment works, how to install it, how to use it, and how to troubleshoot it. How much of the detail is necessary, and how much simply gets in the way? What is needed are tools for helping the writer ensure both greater clarity and a more usable selection of the content. Such an approach would provide a system like the Writer's Workbench developed at Bell Labs, but one that is considerably smarter. AI techniques can provide the necessary language processing technology, but what the system should _do_ needs to be determined by the basic research on comprehension processes.

It should be noted that developing a writer's aide system is practical because the material that has to be processed can be limited in complexity both syntactically and semantically, and some of the major writing problems can be identified with only a limited depth of understanding on the part of the program. In particular, such a system does not have to be able to parse any sentence, but rather only the sentences that a typical recruit must be able to parse; this is a much simpler problem!

Based on my own work, three problem areas where a writer's aide system would be of value can be described:

Selection of how-it-works content. We have conducted a series of experiments on the role of how-it-works knowledge in learning how to operate a piece of equipment. This is described in more detail in Kieras & Bovair (1983), and in additional reports now being prepared. The typical technical manual for a piece of equipment has extremely complex and extensive how-it-works information in it. For a device such as a shipboard radar set, the level of detail goes down to the individual resistors and capacitors in the circuitry. While it is clear that a ship-yard troubleshooter will need more information than a typical operator, it is not clear which information is actually needed for what kind of user. Perhaps if this could be determined, technical manuals could be much shorter and more to the point.

We have done a series of experiments in which people learn how to operate a simple control panel device, a sketch of whose front panel is shown in Figure 1. Subjects were asked to do two kinds of tasks: In one, they were to learn a series of operating procedures, in which the goal was to get the PF indicator light to flash. In the other, they had to infer these procedures without any explicit training. Two groups of subjects performed these tasks: the *rote* group did this learning or inferring with no information about how the device works. Another group, the *model* group, studied what we call a "device model." This consists of a block diagram, shown in Figure 2, along with roughly two pages of descriptive material that explain the block diagram. To make this technical information interesting and enjoyable for college student subjects, we placed this device in the context of "Star Trek." Subjects were asked to pretend that the control panel is for a "phaser bank" aboard the starship *Enterprise*.

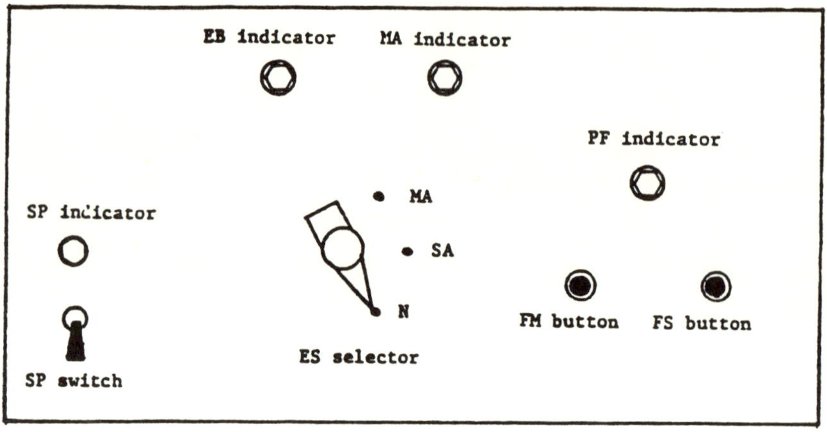

Figure 1. Sketch of the front panel of the artificial device.

Table 5 summarizes the effects in the learning experiment. We observed large improvements in learning how to operate the device; a typical effect size is 20%. Also, subjects with the device model are able to devise more efficient procedures than those instructed.

In the inference experiments, people with the device model are able to infer how to operate the device without any explicit instructions much more readily. The rote group discovers the procedures by lengthy trial-and-error, while model group subjects can infer the procedures almost immediately. These effects are especially strong when subjects must operate the device when it has simulated malfunctions of some of the internal components.

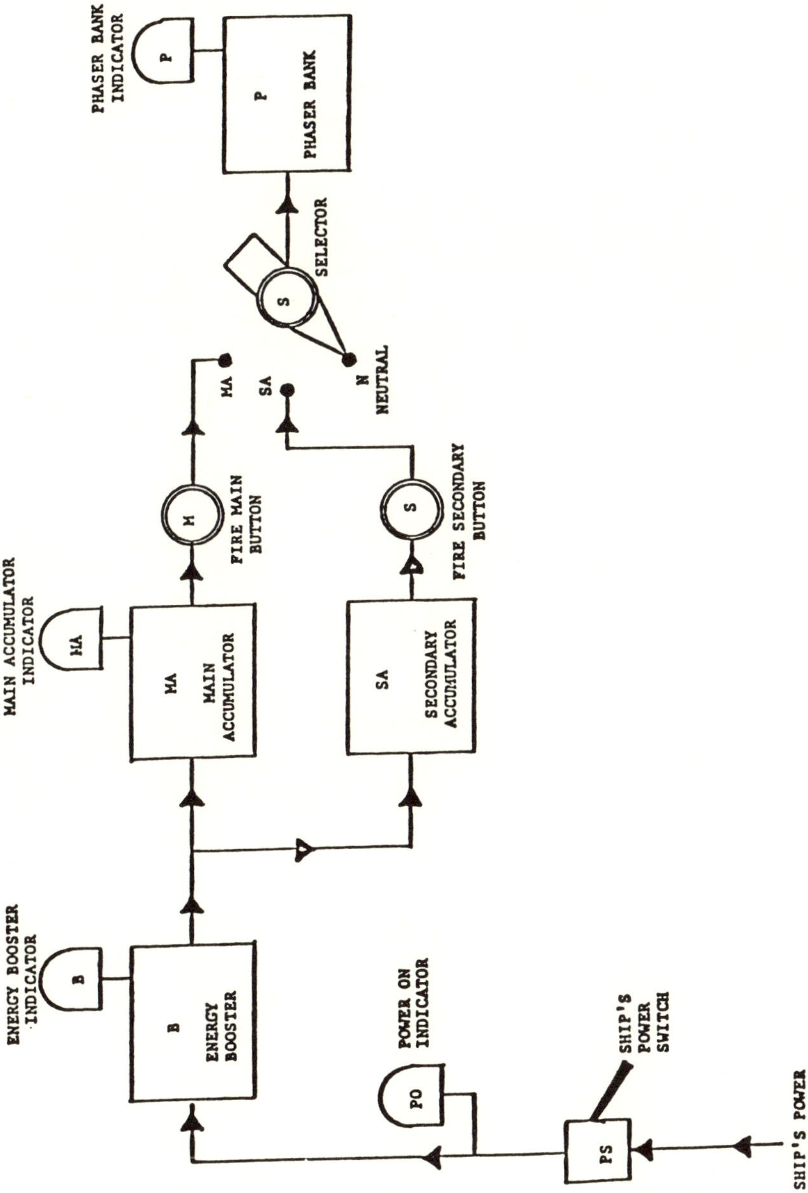

Figure 2. The block diagram studied by subjects in the device model condition.

TABLE 5

Summary of Results on Learning Procedures with and without a Device Model

Measure	Group		
	Rote	Model	Improvement
Mean Procedure Training Time (secs)	270	194	28%
Mean Correct Procedure Retention	67%	80%	19%
Proportion of "short-cuts" (more efficient procedures) done when possible	8%	40%	400%
Mean execution time of retained instructed procedures (secs)	20.1	16.8	17%

Finally, it is not the highly motivating fantasy context of the device model that was effective, but rather the _circuit topology_. This is the configuration of components, controls, indicators, and the connections between them. In short, it is the information contained in the block diagram for the device.

These results led us to a criterion that the important information to include in the how-it-works section of a technical manual is information about the circuit topology, especially with regard to the controls, that is specific enough to enable the user to infer the exact operating procedures or troubleshooting procedures for the device. Information that is not specific and relevant enough to support these inferences, such as metaphors or analogies, is simply not useful and could be excluded. In related work done with a simulation model, I have demonstrated that this circuit topology information is in fact adequate to account for the types of inferences that need to be made, and apparently for some of the details of human performance in this situation as well.

Thus, only certain how-it-works information is needed for users or troubleshooters of equipment. Since technical manuals usually go into extreme detail, more information is probably being included than is necessary. A possible application of AI would be a system that could help determine what portions of the how-it-works information is actually needed by analyzing which information is actually required to support inferences about operating procedures and the location of malfunctions. Such a system would be useful both in documentation preparation, and also as an on-line assistant that would access the full data base on the equipment and display only the relevant portions of it to the troubleshooter.

Since the problem is one of defining the information that is _relevant_ to a malfunction, rather than identifying the actual malfunction, this should be technically feasable with current AI techniques.

Procedural instructions. Another important type of material in technical documentation is information on _how to use_ the piece of equipment. This raises the question of how the user acquires a procedure from instructional prose. In the current theory of cognitive skills (Anderson, 1982), procedural knowledge can be represented as production rules, which are IF-THEN structures similar to those used in expert systems, but usually with a more elaborate and explicit control structure. In these terms, understanding written procedural instructions corresponds to translating the written prose into a production rule representation. If so, then the quality of procedural instructions corresponds to the ease of performing this translation.

In work done by Peter Polson and myself, we tried out this idea on a portion of IBM's training documentation for their Displaywriter word processor. An example is Figure 3, which shows a page of training instructions on how to delete items from the text. We simply carried out a very loose translation of the instructions into production rules. Even though these materials initially struck us as being of very high quality, we were amazed at some of the problems that this simple analysis revealed. For example, notice the statement roughly half-way down the page, in

MAKING DELETIONS

Production system	Training material
IF goal:delete text X THEN do step 1	The first revision requires that you delete the word "regular" and then add the word "large."
IF goal:do step 1 THEN move cursor to X(first) Note:deletion starts at X(first) do step 2	The first step to delete text is to move the cursor under the first character to be deleted. This tells the system where the deletion starts. MOVE THE CURSOR UNDER THE FIRST "r" IN "regular."
IF goal:do step 2 THEN press DEL do step 3	The next step is to press the DEL (Delete) key. PRESS THE DEL KEY (located above the CHG FMT key).
IF goal:do step 3 and prompt = "delete word" THEN type X(end) Note:cursor moves to X(end) Note:X(first) to X(end) highlighted do step 4 Note?highlighted characters will be deleted	When the system prompts, Delete what?, type the last character of the text to be deleted. WHEN Delete what? PROMPTS, TYPE: r The cursor moves to the last character. All the text from the first character through the last character is highlighted. You can see exactly what is going to be deleted before it is deleted.
IF goal:do step 4 and highlighted ≠ X THEN type CANCL add goal:TRY AGAIN	If the wrong characters are highlighted, press CODE + CANCL and try again. When the text you want to delete is highlighted, press the ENTER key.
IF goal:do step 4 and highlighted = X THEN press ENTER Note:highlighted word now deleted	PRESS ENTER. The highlighted word is deleted, and the remaining text on the line moves over to take its place.

MAKING ADDITIONS

The cursor is already at the point where you want to add the word "large," so you simply type the word.

TYPE THE WORD: large

Revising a Letter 8-3

Figure 3. A sample of training materials for a word processor, showing the informal production system translation.

which if the to-be-deleted material is not highlighted, the user is instructed to cancel and try again. In production rule notation this translates to adding a goal, TRY AGAIN, to the goal stack that has the problem that there are no production rules available that will satisfy it.

Thus, instead of simply acquiring these production rules, the user of this manual must first infer what the intended production rules were supposed to be, and then troubleshoot and debug them. Let me point out that although this particular flaw appears to be obvious now, it certainly was not obvious either to the preparers of this otherwise high-quality material, or to ourselves. There are many other examples in this one sample of material.

Perhaps an AI-based system can help with this problem by attempting to translate procedural instructions into production rules. If this translation is hard to accomplish, then the instructions are not clearly written. If the resulting production rules have obvious logical flaws in them, such as in the above example, then the instructions are not adequately clear. What needs to be done is the relevant research to determine whether procedural instructions that meet this criterion of easy and correct translation into production rules are actually easier for people to follow and to learn from.

Document clarity. The clarity issue is a complex one; it has been difficult to characterize the overall comprehensibility of a piece of prose. Although readability formulas have been in existence for many years, they have been under heavy attack recently both because of their lack of any theoretical rationale, and also because of failures to demonstrate substantial improvements in the comprehensibility or usability of material that has been made more *readable* by this criterion. Duffy and his associates at NPRDC (Duffy & Kabance, 1982; Duffy, Sass Curran, 1982) have conducted several experiments attempting to demonstrate that the comprehensibility or usability of technical documents can be improved, either by improving their readability formula scores, or by large-scale changes performed by professional documentation firms. This effort has not yet succeeded, which demonstrates that again one can not trust one's intuitions in this regard. When such counterintuitive empirical results are obtained, it is a strong signal that we do not understand the psychological issues involved. Much more research work is clearly needed. We are currently engaged in some preliminary work with simulated technical manuals for the above "phaser bank" device. This work suggests that certain types of changes in the manual can make substantial differences in how well subjects can use the manual to learn how to operate the device. These changes concern the details of the information-processing demands on the reader, rather than gross readability measures or document design changes.

Once the empirical situation is understood, an AI-based system could be developed that would provide some of the functions of systems such as the Writer's Workbench, but in a more useful and precise way. The information that is needed to specify such a system is the results from basic research on the comprehension of technical prose, which can reveal what actually impairs comprehension. Then a straightforward rule system organized around a powerful parser can be used to detect these comprehensibility problems. Again, while this is a target of opportunity for the application of AI, what is missing is the sound research base in psychology that would allow this technique to be of definite value.

Concluding Remarks

The above discussion has been intended not only to inform the reader about some of the psychological issues involved in the application of AI to maintenance situations, but also to inform non-psychologists of how important it is to get a grasp on the psychological problems involved. More specifically, many proposals for the application of AI in maintenance problems have as their goal the improvement of the working situation and productivity of some human being, such as the troubleshooter or maintenance technician. However, many of these efforts, especially those developed by AI researchers, do not take into account any information about the actual psychology of the user. For example, complex information display systems are being developed that might be completely useless because they will overwhelm the human information-processing capacity; complex maintenance-aiding systems are being developed that might turn out to be of little value when actually used in the field. An example of this problem is the finding described above that menu instructions are no better overall than step-by-step instructions and can actually be worse in certain situations. Considerable time and money can be spent on organizing procedural instructions into conceptual hierarchies, but unless the psychology of the user is considered, the result may actually be worse than simply copying existing instructions into a computer medium.

In short, application of artificial intelligence technology to maintenance problems without considering the powers and limitations of natural intelligence can easily be a fantastic waste of time and money. It should be noted that in many cases an evaluation can be conducted of whether a proposed AI system will be of value <u>before</u> the system, or even its prototype, is constructed. For example, the system can be mocked-up and tried out. An example of this approach is in my project concerned with developing an AI-based system to help the technical writer. Since I can specify the problems that such a system should be able to detect without actually constructing it, I can then mock-up the results of using such a system and compare this mock improved technical manual with an original technical manual. If I fail to get any improvement in the usability of the manual, I can conclude that even if the system was developed, its use would not be of any advantage. I can then make an informed choice about the desirability of spending resources on creating such a system. Clearly this approach could be used widely in the development of AI-based maintenance systems.

Acknowledgement

The work described in this paper is supported by the Office of Naval Research, Personnel and Training Research Group, under Research Contracts N00014-81-C-0699, N00014-83-K-0224, NR 667-453, NR 667-513, and, in collaboration with Peter Polson, University of Colorado, by the IBM Corporation.

References

Anderson, J. R. (1982) Acquisition of cognitive skill. *Psychological Review*, *89*, 369-406.

Bond, N. C. & Towne, D. M. (1979) Troubleshooting complex equipment in the military services: Research and prospects. Technical Report No. 92, Behavioral Technology Laboratories, University of Southern California, December.

Duffy, T. M., & Kabance, P. (1982) Testing the readable writing approach to text revision. Naval Personnel Research and Development Center, Technical Report.

Duffy, T. M., Sass, D., & Curran, T. E. (1982) Job reading tasks and the design of technical text. Paper presented at the meeting of the American Education Research Association, New York.

Kieras, D. E. (1982) What people know about electronic devices: A descriptive study. Technical Report No. 12 (UARZ/DP/TR-82/ONR-12). University of Arizona, October 1.

Kieras, D. E. & Bovair, S. (1983) The role of a mental model in learning to operate a device. Technical Report No. 13 (UARZ/DP/TR-83/ONR-13). University of Arizona, March 1.

Rumelhart, D. E., & Ortony, A. (1977) The representation of knowledge in memory. In R. C. Anderson, R. J. Spiro, & E. Montague (Eds.), _Schooling and the acquisition of knowledge_. Hillsdale, N. J.

Smith, E. E. & Goodman, L. (1982) Understanding instructions: The role of explanatory material. Bolt Beranek and Newman, Inc., Technical Report No. 5088, July.

ABOUT THE AUTHOR

Dr. David Kieras is a Cognitive Psychologist at the University of Arizona. His research interests include reading comprehension, procedural knowledge, human-computer interaction, and simulation modeling of cognitive processes. The focus of his current research concerns representing the same cognitive processes used to acquire procedural knowledge from written material in the form of computer simulations. Dr. Kieras received a Ph.D. in experimental psychology at the University of Michigan in 1974.

ARTIFICIAL INTELLIGENCE APPROACHES TO MONITORING SYSTEM INTEGRITY

Roy A. Maxion

Institute of Cognitive Science
University of Colorado
Boulder, Colorado 80309

ABSTRACT

This paper introduces the concept of artificial intelligence-based (expert) systems [6] for enhancing system availability through system integrity monitoring and system diagnosis. Such expert systems use knowledge and inference mechanisms to solve problems which would ordinarily require the expertise of the best human practitioners in the field. We demonstrate the seriousness of failure and explain why several traditional methods of ensuring system availability, reliability, and maintainability fail in certain important cases, e.g. intermittent failures. An outline of the human diagnostic problem-solving process is presented with a computational analog. A symptom-based expert diagnostic system(*) is introduced with its early and successful results in fault prediction.

Overview

Never mind if the implications of high-technology complexity haven't influenced your recent consciousness; they will. With the steady advance of technology, and the accompanying redoubling of sophistication and complexity in our electronic world, failures in complex systems are manifesting themselves in increasingly insidious ways. A high-technology information industry is evolving in which powerful processing techniques are now required to support hardware systems. The job market, too, is taking an increasingly technological orientation requiring workers to have complex skills and extensive training.

One cogent result of this is the recognition that human diagnosis of complex systems and their concomitant failures is strongly influenced by equipment complexity [1, 2]. Given a complexity threshold, human diagnostic skills will soon become ineffectual and the mean time to a diagnostic decision will increase without bound. Because current methods of design and diagnosis are being challenged by the spectre of massively automated involution, building complex systems whose reliability and availability approach 100% will require further innovations to fault-tolerant computing.

* The implementation described here was done at the Xerox Corporation, Palo Alto, California.

The Problem of Failure

How serious is the problem of failure? You probably don't know, because, as in most installations, you have ceased to view failure as an unusual event. You refer to failure more in comparative terms than descriptive ones: "The disk is not as bad as it was last week." We chart our pain from one day to the next and feel better or worse by comparison, ignoring the presence of failure when it falls below what we believe is a tolerable level.

The seriousness of computer failure can be equally grave from both fiscal and social viewpoints, particularly with computers moving out of clean-rooms and into uncontrolled environments. In many applications -- for example, in spacecraft, air traffic control, nuclear and process plant control systems, and hospital patient monitors -- failure can have catastrophic effects. Even barring catastrophe, severe consequences such as protracted downtime, wrong results, security breeches, or inadvertant unauthorized accesses to data and equipment may occur as a result of failure. From the point of view of the user, computer failure is most often seen as downtime. Downtime can be broken down into several constituents, the most salient one being spoiled work time, either in terms of work that cannot be done on a faulty machine or work that must be repeated due to system failure. To make at least one of these examples concrete, it is reported that one US airline suffers revenue losses in excess of $36,000 for every minute that their reservation system is down [3].

In addition to user-perceived costs of failure, the vendor also bears a substantial burden in the field service domain. As the computer industry moves into an age when customers demand availability and reliability approaching 100%, manufacturers will be forced to carefully examine the trade-offs among the several avenues of failure, diagnosis, and recovery available to them. Service costs for computer systems of all types are rising at a rate of about 25% per year [4], a rate much greater than that of hardware costs. As the growing complexity of computer systems outstrips the troubleshooting abilities of technicians, the problems of computer downtime and reliability will explode spectacularly. Highly skilled technicians will be increasingly scarce as the battle for technical manpower heats up. Who should bear responsibility when computer failure leads to revenue loss, property damage, or personal injury? There is a host of legal problems to consider and it is likely that litigation and regulations will be on the rise as computers and the consequences of their failures proliferate. Clearly, reliability and maintainability will be the principal issues for computer systems of the eighties.

Availability, Reliability and Maintainability

Availability, the probability that a system will be able to perform its mission when required, is a system parameter of paramount importance for influencing operational readiness. Availability is a function of system mean time to failure (MTTF) and mean time to repair (MTTR). Reliability is the probability that a system will perform a required function under specified conditions for a predetermined period of time. It is the significant variable influencing MTTF. Once a system has failed, concern focusses on maintainability and MTTR. Maintainability is the probability that a failing system will be restored to operational readiness within a given period of time.

The two general typical approaches to solving reliability problems are often termed fault avoidance and fault tolerance. The goal of fault avoidance, reducing the possibility of failure, is most often attained through cautious, conservative design and the use of high-reliability components. Nevertheless, even after the greatest of care, faults will still occur and the result will be system failure and a subsequent need for diagnosis. In fault tolerant systems the use of redundancy (extra time or extra components) provides the information required to obviate the effects of failures. The field of fault-tolerant computing has designed and implemented a spectrum of clever and sophisticated techniques, most of which are anticipatory in that a particular (type of) fault must be conceived of in the designer's mind before any implementation of preventive, fault-tolerant measures can occur. Siewiorek and Swarz [5] give an excellent review of such reliability and availability techniques as fault detection (e.g. duplication and fail- safe logic), masking redundancy (e.g. error-correcting codes and N-modular redundancy with voting), and dynamic redundancy (e.g. backup sparing, reconfiguration, and graceful degradation).

A class of failures particularly resistant to standard fault-tolerant techniques, known as the so-called "5% problems" because vendor diagnostics are so unusually ineffective in locating these recalcitrant faults, account for nearly 40% of all service costs according to an industry rule of thumb. These problems consist primarily of three failure types: (1) intermittent failures, transients which exhibit symptoms of failure for only a short time before returning to normal; (2) device interaction failures in which devices function well independently, but interactions among multiple devices create problems; and (3) command sequencing failures in which only a certain sequence of commands will cause difficulty. A significant factor in isolating these types of problems is the time spent by technical personnel in attempting to understand and replicate field failures, especially in the face of little evidence other than operator description or complaint.

Summarizing, the current state of fault-tolerant computing is good. Reliability and availability have improved by some hundreds of per cent over the last decade. Nevertheless, failures will still occur and they will still have to be dealt with by whatever means are available after fault-tolerance has done its job. The implication is not a pleasant one. Ironically, in fact, some fault-tolerant techniques appear to be working against us. Since techniques in fault-tolerant computing are now quite advanced and since the integration level of most modern equipment is so high, the failures that do slip through are more and more likely to be in the previously mentioned class of 5% problems -- but that percentage will doubtless rise, since only the truly recalcitrant problems will remain. Many fault-tolerant methods, though quite effective, have merely worked as masks or filters, taking care of the "trivial" problems automatically and leaving the really perverse ones to humans. Due to various limitations of human cognition, non-experts are poorly equipped to solve these abstruse problems. As consumer demand for high reliability and high availability systems mounts, manufacturers will need to be ever more watchful over the scarce (and expensive) resource of expert diagnosticians. Artificial intelligence has the potential to address these problems in significant ways.

Maintainability is influenced primarily by design and diagnostic factors. A system that is well designed for testability will provide -- at least -- increased observability and controllability of internal signals, as well as error reporting and logging facilities. These design factors, among others, provide crucial information for the diagnostic process, irrespective of whether the diagnosis is being performed by human or machine. In the final analysis, machines will sometimes fail no matter how carefully designed or constructed they may be. At that point the quality of the diagnostic process and its concomitant tools is the principal determinant for restoring operational readiness.

Diagnosis

Since diagnosis portends to be a central issue in this exposition of how special techniques can positively influence the availability equation, let us briefly explore its implications. "Diagnose" is a word that comes from the Greek, meaning to identify a condition by its signs, symptoms, or distinguishing characteristics. The general problem of diagnostic systems is to discriminate among the possible states of the object under scrutiny, and to determine which one actually exists.

For either human or machine, that constitutes a problem-solving task of considerable magnitude. Humans have a number of important limitations in inferring the process that generated a particular set of results, i.e., diagnosis. Machines, in their current approaches, are almost hopelessly inadequate. Typical computer diagnostic programs suffer from incompleteness, complexity, poor fault models, combinatorial explosion due to circuit fanout, limited test sets, compute time, and the plethora of usual errors introduced by human programmers. Consequently, until methodologies improve, humans are needed as an interpretive and problem-solving link in the diagnostic process.

Humans, however, are subject to some serious limitations of their own. Many of these may be overcome by use of machine aids, taking advantage of the best that machines and humans each can offer. Consider first that diagnosis, as a problem-solving task, has an a priori requirement for a nontrivial collection of cognitive skills. While general cognitive abilities are not of major impact in solving simple problems, they gain in import as problem complexity increases. Perceptual and spatial abilities have been shown to be strong determinants in problem-solving behavior [25]. Cognitive style is another significant factor [26]. Reflective, field-independent persons tend to be better problem-solvers than impulsive, field-dependents. Another important factor is human short term memory span, which has been linked to one's ability to successfully recall and execute problem-solving strategies requiring conservation and transitivity [27]. Ideational fluency, the ability to generate a large number of ideas or hypotheses in response to a particular problem situation, is an important part of creative problem-solving [29]. A diagnostician must be able to generate and explore multiple explanations about the causes of an event, and be able to predict the implications of events.

Good problem-solvers are also affected by various personal and affective characteristics. For example, they constantly deal with situations involving missing information where frequent strategy shifts are needed in the face of changing data. This requires a high tolerance for ambiguity. Finally, good problem-solvers have a high self-concept of ability [28], a high achievement motivation, and less fear of failure than their counterparts.

If all that weren't enough to seriously reduce available technical talent or attempt to embody in a machine model of diagnostic reasoning, there are additional factors which specifically affect diagnostic problem-solving [24]. The net effect of evidence, for example, can be different depending on how it is perceived; an object or situation is judged to be more or less salient as the surrounding circumstances change. This means that the significance of failure symptoms may go unnoticed under certain conditions, but not others. Focus effects, such as how a question is posed, are influential, too. Consider the question "how is a tree like a man?" as opposed to the question "how is a man like a tree?" When evidence is distributed into several categories it can become diffuse, its effectiveness being distorted, even though probabilistically its meaning remains unchanged; humans often misinterpret diffuse data. In the face of missing information, people will seize on almost any cue -- often a negative one -- in an effort to explicate what is probabilistically untenable. Anchoring and adjustment strategies [23] demonstrate that people anchor on what is perceived to be favorable evidence for a particular situation, then adjust their judgements according to the total evidence available. Such a strategy can depend on whether one is evaluating a hypothesis or its complement, on the number and specificity of alternative hypotheses, and on perceptions of missing evidence. Diagnosis is also sensitive to temporal relations which can be very complex, but not necessarily indicative of causality. Finally, attention is a factor in diagnosis, since diagnosis itself shifts attention to new evidence, thereby directing the search for information and causality.

As can be quite easily discerned from this short discussion, diagnosis is a complex phenomenon which, at least in the near future, may well defy our best attempts at description, let alone machine modeling or simulation. It is good to get a perspective on the difficulty of the problem facing us before we launch headlong into a program of possibly endless frustration in attempting to solve all the problems of diagnosis, whatever the methodology. Now we are left in the awkward situation of having a few humans with relatively good -- but little understood -- diagnostic skills; and relatively bad -- but well understood -- machine implementations of diagnosis. Though a long and deep research program would doubtless produce many interesting results (and should indeed be carried out), there are some things which can be done now to improve the plight of diagnosis and make headway against the problems of failure. Prominent among these are various applications of artificial intelligence methodologies, notably expert systems and human-machine cooperative systems, which can help overcome many of the human limitations in diagnosis. The remainder of this paper will focus on suggested applications of artificial intelligence technology and the results of an experiment utilizing one of the new approaches.

Expert Systems

The primary objective of fault-tolerant computing is to minimize the average cost of a fault in terms of time and equipment by achieving some explicitly stated goal or intent in the face of an unanticipated, but well understood failure. Similarly, the field of artificial intelligence (AI) is directly concerned with the problem of expressing and automatically converting possibly ill-specified intent into effective action. Problem-solving methods exist for choosing and specifying an intended action from within a hierarchy of levels, moving from highly abstract assertions to detailed machine instructions. When an unanticipated problem arises at one level in the hierarchy, the possibility exists for "understanding" what was actually intended at some high level, and finding a new, lower-level means for achieving correct action. Many artificial intelligence domains assume uncertain and incomplete knowledge of the environment, using what IS known to infer a more completely specified situation. Though this would constitute an extremely ambitious endeavor, suggestions have indeed been made wherein that kind of AI system architecture could be utilized. Ideally, some sort of "fool-tolerance" [7] should extend into all phases of system operation as suggested by AI opportunities at the human interface in Figure 1 [8].

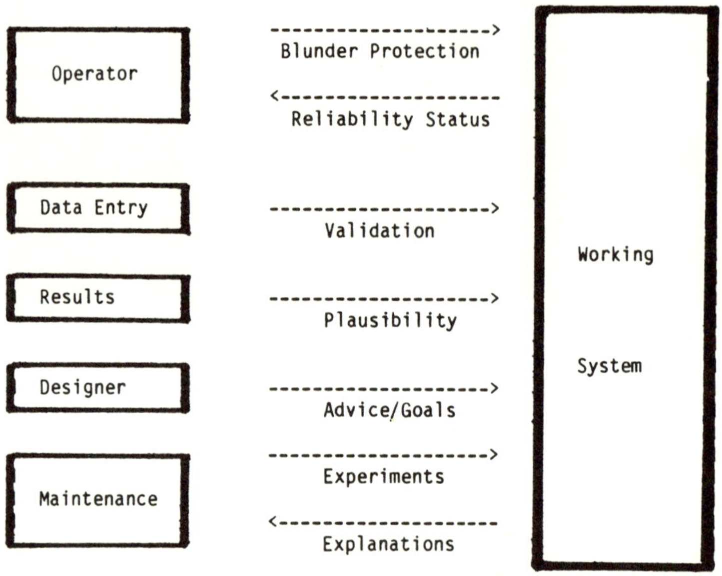

Figure 1. AI Opportunities at the Human Interface

This paper will concentrate on a few conceptually simple tools that would significantly impact the maintenance function. The ultimate goal of these tools is to provide a level of performance for troubleshooting (and monitoring) that is comparable to that of an experienced engineer. We would like to take advantage of the heuristics that experts utilize in the tasks of fault detection and diagnosis, discerning multiple fault conditions, distinguishing among transient, intermittent, and permanent faults, and taking appropriate action for system recovery, even if in a degraded mode. An expert diagnostic system so composed could function both as a technician's assistant and as an on-line monitor. With the use of expert systems -- software systems that encapsulate the skill and reasoning power of human experts -- substantial reductions in downtime, maintenance time, and costs can be realized by automating the diagnostic process. In some cases faults can be predicted!

An expert system uses artificial intelligence techniques to make inferences based on domain-specific knowledge supplied by experts. In typical expert systems the expertise that the system brings to bear on a problem is represented as a large collection of rules (hence the often-used moniker, rule-based system) usually based on empirical associations. One example of such a rule might be "IF the display flickers, THEN examine the power supply." Domain experts, such as senior technicians, may be consulted about problems known to occur in a computer system; their solutions and knowledge are codified into a set of condition-action rules which subsequently drives a program for inferential reasoning about the specified domain. Paraphrasing [9], the individual rules are usually specified as IF-THEN statements, each rule representing some small portion of the problem-solving or decision process. Each rule specifies a conclusion that follows from a given set of premises. The rules are usually in the form: if <condition> then <action>, with the conditions composed of conjunctions or disjunctions of terms. These premises either refer to facts given to the system or to the conclusions of previous rules using such facts. The conclusion of one rule could be used as a premise for other rules. In such a manner the simple rules comprising the program can be chained together to describe complex decision processes. Thus a rule-based system can be "data-directed," meaning that the flow of control is determined by the data rather than by rigidly fixed statements of program code.

Rule-based expert systems have several important properties that make them suitable for certain classes of application. They can focus on and handle significant amounts of detail, and their continual re-evaluation of the control state lends an environmental sensitivity unmatched in canonical procedural approaches. They are well-suited to real-world, multi-dimensional environments whose events and actions are richly interconnected. The rule vs data organization of the system allows the separation of data examination from action or data modification. Rule systems are highly modular and allow easy addition of new information, hence easing the chore of knowledge acquisition. A complete treatment of rule-based systems is in [10, 12].

The extent of activity in AI applications is considerable and increasing rapidly in the US and in Europe. AI applications have penetrated medical practice, chemical and biological research, and a number of scientific domains. These include analytical chemistry [13], protein x-ray crystallography [14], molecular genetics [15], mathematics [16], geological exploration [17], and automatic configuration of computer systems and their peripheral components [19].

Expert systems lend themselves to several generic tasks that experts commonly perform. Each of the tasks listed below [from 11] are part and parcel of the job of an intelligent monitor for complex systems whose task it is to monitor real-time data, interpret it, and prescribe correct responses accordingly. Notice that in real-world environments, not only are these tasks ubiquitous, but all of them can be construed as diagnosis.

Hence the importance of understanding this diagnostic phenomenon.

> Interpretation: The analysis of data to determine its meaning.
>
> Diagnosis: The process of distinguishing or identifying a (fault) condition based on an examination of symptoms.
>
> Monitoring: The continuous interpretation of signal data to recognize predetermined signatures and events or to synthesize them based on the data stream.
>
> Planning: creating programs of action to be carried out toward the achievement of various goals
>
> Prediction: forecasting future events based on reasoning about time, time-ordered data, and models of cause-effect relations among data.

A conception of an expert system that acts as a diagnostic monitor of a computer hardware system must, in some sense, perform in all the roles just mentioned. The work described here has been more grounded in the non-planning tasks, since they are more tractable for initial implementation. In particular, monitoring is regarded to be the most important part of complex system diagnosis because the signals received by the monitor demon provide the lion's share of clues for subsequent problem-solving. Before describing the architecture of the system, let us examine some typical domain-specific behaviors of human diagnostic problem-solving. This is entirely reasonable to do, since it is essentially a computational model of human expertise that we are eventually attempting to construct.

Expert Diagnosticians

An expert diagnostician must have an expert-level background in hardware system diagnosis and should be equally versatile at conversing with human agents as with the target system. He should be able to interpret the available data and provide a summary of system status. He should be able to recognize unusual events and make suggestions for corrective action, if necessary. He should be able to give advice on adjusting various system parameters based on system status and diagnostic or monitoring goals. He should be able to detect possible measurement errors and maintain a set of expectations and goals for future evaluation while being able to shift focus based on newly received data.

Observation of diagnostic problem solvers in action [20, 21] reveals that diagnostic judgement is based on gross chunks of conceptual knowledge as opposed to detailed knowledge of the domain architecture. This knowledge appears to procedurally organized as if-then rules which allow rapid focus of attention on relatively few diagnoses, and the avoidance of large searches. It contains associated levels of uncertainty and is retrieved with great facility, usually in response to an external confusion or misconception. Most diagnosticians first generate a list of potential (possibly competing) hypotheses and then choose from this list by considering the most common diagnoses first. The second step is to gather problem-relevant data and form a (reasoned) plan for hypothesis testing. The observed behavior is then explained within the context of available data and finally an experiment is conducted to confirm or deny the present hypothesis or to distinguish among competing hypotheses. It should be clear that diagnostic problem-solvers bring with them a certain amount of general, domain-nonspecific problem-solving knowledge; this is known as the kernel. Not surprisingly, our diagnostic system architecture follows this regimen fairly closely as shown in Figure 2.

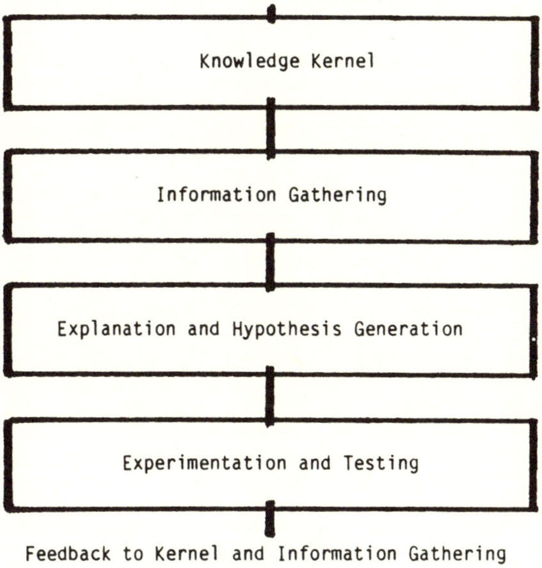

Fig 2. Diagnosis Cycle

Diagnostic Approaches

In general there are two major approaches to system diagnosis, both of which can effectively exploit artificial intelligence techniques. They are called specification-based and symptom-based diagnosis. In a specification-based approach [22] system design specifications are used to predict the types of faulty behavior that might occur in the system. Diagnostic tools are then developed, based on this behavior.

A variation of the specification-based technique is sometimes called discrepancy detection [23]. This method looks for mismatches between the values expected for a given operation and the values actually detected. This has the advantage that faulty behavior can be defined as any behavior that is incorrect, as opposed to focusing only on stuck-at logic lines.

The specification-based methods avoid many of the drawbacks of traditional diagnosis such as being bound by large fault trees and fault dictionaries or being focused exclusively on stuck-at-one or stuck-at-zero types of faults. However, both variations mentioned here are noticeably poor at resolving intermittent failures.

The symptom-based approach, also distinct from traditional simulation and fault insertion, employs tactics for capturing the times and locations of observed errors. It contrasts normal system behavior (which can be characterized automatically) with error behavior, usually by discovering or analyzing trends in data. This method is based on the observation that modules typically exhibit periods of sporadic unreliability before final failure. Observation and detection of these trends makes it possible to predict certain hard failures prior to catastrophe. (For predicted failures, preventive maintenance can be performed or spare parts can be ordered in advance.) It has an important advantage that the other approaches do not: the ability to discover and locate intermittent failures. Intermittents are the poorest understood, most troublesome types of failures, because they do not stand still for the scrutiny of the traditional diagnostician. Additionally, intermittents frequently result from system interactions that are too complicated to discover in specification-based approaches. The symptom-based methods are the ones with which we are presently experimenting; the following discussion is based partly on our experiences.

Symptom-based diagnosis is always founded on some sort of monitoring. Two useful methods are real-time monitoring and retrospective analysis. The present approach uses both. The outputs of simple, feature-focused devices, unobtrusively implanted in the system, are monitored. The temporal resolution and the parametric granularity are dynamically varied by an intelligent analysis system. In our distributed environment a single machine, called a diagnostic server, is responsible for monitoring (and controlling) all systems on a network, including itself. If this server goes down there is a mechanism for automatically starting some other machine on the network to take over its function. The only distinction among machines is in the software; only one machine at a time runs the special monitor and control software. Collecting and amalgamating the outputs of these monitors (e.g. for disk controllers or network traffic) yields what is viewed as a syndrome or signature. These signatures form the bases for automatically characterizing the normal behavior of the entire system, as well as its individual components, and for detecting deviations from normalcy.

Notice that these concepts embody the usual view of a pattern classification paradigm. From this perspective the monitors are feature extractors and their amalgamated outputs constitute a feature vector. The range of outcomes for each monitor defines a feature spa . Classes of failure phenomena can produce signatures associated with clusters in the feature space. When monitored system characteristics deviate from normalcy, the signature is checked against a feature cluster and an appropriate recovery scheme is invoked.

Recovery can be interpreted in many ways. If the failure is intermittent and potentially serious, the failing part of the system can be dynamically taken off line or an operator/user can be notified. A less radical approach would be to first confirm the observed effects by automatically selecting or constructing a test program, based on signatures and knowledge-based information, and administering the test to confirm or deny specific hypotheses about the failure. When the test results are analyzed, a more intelligent decision can be made by the system as to the direction in which diagnosis should proceed, or which type of recovery should be invoked. (Naturally, implementors must exercise care in selecting automated recovery procedures.)

A symptom-based diagnostic approach is heavily dependent on a constant flow of information. One rich source of information relevant to diagnostic problem-solving can be provided through error logging and status reporting. When a diagnostic program cannot recreate an error event it is often because diagnostics do not stress the system in the same way that the operational program does. Error logging can capture information about the state of the system at the moment of error, thus providing clues to the source of the error. Error logging can also provide the data which makes automatic trend analysis possible. A program can periodically scan the error log looking for patterns. This kind of analysis can be further enhanced if the analysis program can make requests for certain tests to be run either concurrent with normal execution or stand-alone. Trend analysis can be used in all systems, even those with little error detection logic. The establishment of a trend or a systematic occurrence can be of tremendous value in reducing the time spent on system diagnosis.

Any of these approaches to system integrity and availability using techniques of automated diagnosis and monitoring requires a sophisticated arrangement for information gathering and feedback. The intelligent monitor needs to gather and assess specific information from (possibly) remote sites at varying degrees of resolution, both in terms of the number of measured parameters and in terms of temporal granularity (to avoid information overload). Hence comes a requirement for automatic abstraction techniques for data reduction. There is also a requirement for the ability to control certain aspects of the remote systems, such as the execution of tests and the return of their results, including the identification of these results as distinct from the data of normal operations.

Implementation, Status, and Results

Such a system is now partially implemented as part of a phased design of a collection of individual tools that run in a mutually cooperative mode. The system has been run for eight months on a network of over two hundred computers. The symptom-based monitoring strategy is working well. Even in its current, unrefined state, it has enabled the prediction of several system failures. (Lead time of one week to one day; accurate to one day.) It has been used to collect data for the assurance of a new architecture and it has unexpectedly discovered intersystem clock discrepancies. Experiments are in progress for real-time monitoring of various parameters of network traffic as viewed by individual machines, as opposed to network-wide measurement.

The system operates both in real-time and retrospective modes, the latter involving a posteriori analyses of detailed log data. For the convenience of technicians and observers, a dynamic graphic display can show relations among selected monitor results. Dynamically variable information gathering and feedback is functioning and measurable parameters can be dynamically selected at arbitrary resolutions. Test programs can be sent to remote systems via the local area network and, remotely, can be automatically loaded and run with the results being delivered back to the controller. It is anticipated that in the future the system's knowledge base will be automatically updated with the results and rules induced from monitored behavior.

Conclusion

This paper has described the general and ubiquitous environment of diagnosis, and has sketched several issues in diagnostic reasoning due to human cognitive limitations. It was shown that understanding and modeling the diagnostic process will be difficult, but not impossible. A description of a partially implemented diagnostic architecture was given. This implementation has produced significant results in diagnosis and fault prediction, as well as being an excellent vehicle for suggesting new directions for investigation. Work is in progress in constructing a real-time, dynamic, computer-based laboratory for studying the diagnostic behavior of humans and of model systems, including aspects of rule acquisition.

Techniques from artificial intelligence, applied to the diagnosis of general complex systems (not just computers), can significantly ameliorate the problems associated with increasing complexity and decreasing availability. It is probable that no single method presented here will solve a majority of the problems of system diagnosis; rather, a meld of these techniques will most likely be evolved as each technique becomes better understood in its own right.

The approaches outlined here will be best utilized in conjunction with the advanced understanding of such concomitant issues as man-machine interactions, user models, limitations on human cognition, and exploitation of certain especially human capabilities like pattern recognition and pattern discovery. The methodologies presented here are not panaceas; nor are they particularly inexpensive. However, they are being developed and used in several laboratories and have already proven effective in the detection, diagnosis, and prediction of system failure.

References

[1]
Rouse, W. B. [1978]
Human Problem-Solving Performance in a Fault Diagnosis Task
IEEE Transactions on Systems, Man, and Cybernetics, Vol. SMC-8, No. 4, 258-271.

[2]
Wohl, J. G. [1982]
Maintainability Prediction Revisited: Diagnostic Behavior, Systems Complexity,
and Repair Time
IEEE Transactions on Systems, Man, and Cybernetics, Vol. SMC-12, No. 3.

[3]
Hightower, Kenneth [1982]
Experience With UAL's Apollo System
Lake Arrowhead Workshop on Practical Approaches to High Availability of Computer Systems
Lake Arrowhead, California: September 1982.

[4]
Computer/Electronic Service News [1982]
September/October 1982.

[5]
Siewiorek, Daniel P. and Robert S. Swarz [1982]
The Theory and Practice of Reliable System Design
Digital Press: Bedford, Massachusetts.

[6]
Feigenbaum, E. A. [1977]
The Art of Artificial Intelligence: Themes and Case Studies of Knowledge Engineering
IJCAI-5, 1014-1029.

[7]
Goldberg, Jack [1975]
New Problems in Fault-Tolerant Computing
An Int. Digest, 5th IEEE FTCS, Computer Society, Paris, France.

[8]
Goldberg, Jack [1983]
Interface Between Conventional Fault-Tolerance and Expert System Techniques
IEEE Workshop: Applications of Artificial Intelligence to Fault-Diagnosis and Fault-Tolerance
San Juan, Puerto Rico: January 12-14.

[9]
Waterman, D. R. and F. Hayes-Roth [1978]
An Overview of Pattern-Directed Inference Systems
In Pattern-Directed Inference Systems
Academic Press: New York.

[10]
Davis, R. and J. King
An Overview of Production Systems
In E. W. Elcock and D. Michie (eds.)
Machine Intelligence 8
[11]
Stefik, Monk, et al. [1982]
The Organization of Expert Systems; A Prescriptive Tutorial
Xerox Palo Alto Research Center Technical Report VLSI-82-1
Palo Alto, California.
[12]
Waterman, D. R. and F. Hayes-Roth [1978]
Pattern-Directed Inference Systems
Academic Press: New York.
[13]
Buchanan, R. G. and Feigenbaum, E. A. [1978]
DENDRAL and Meta-DENDRAL: Their Applications Dimension
Artificial Intelligence, Vol. 11, 5-24.
[14]
Engelmore, R. S. and H. P. Nii [1977]
A Knowledge-Based System for Interpretation of Protein X-Ray
Crystallographic Data
Stanford Computer Science Department Technical Report HPP-77-2.
[15]
Stefik, M. [1978]
Inferring DNA Structures from Segmentation Data
Artificial Intelligence, Vol. 11, 85-114.
[16]
Lenat, D. B. [1977]
The Ubiquity of Discovery
Artificial Intelligence, Vol. 9, 257-286.
[17]
Duda, R. O., et al. [1978]
Development of the Prospector Consultation System for Mineral Exploration
SRI International: Final Report Projects 5821 and 6415.
[18]
Simon, H. A. and G. Lea [1974]
Problem-Solving and Rule Induction: A Unified View
In L. Gregg (Ed) Knowledge and Cognition
Lawrence Erlbaum: Hillsdale, New Jersey.
[19]
McDermott, J. [1980]
R1: A Rule-Based Configurer of Computer Systems
Carnegie-Mellon University Technical Report CMU-CS-80-119.
[20]
Maxion, Roy A. [1982]
Unpublished paper.
Xerox Corporation and University of Colorado.

[21]
Gorry, G. A. [1973]
Computer-Assisted Clinical Decision-Making
Methods Information in Medicine, Vol. 12, 45-51.
[22]
Davis, R. et al [1982]
Diagnosis Based on Description of Structure and Function
Proceedings of the National Conference on Artificial Intelligence
Pittsburgh, Pennsylvania.
[23]
Genesereth, M. [1982]
Diagnosis Using Hierarchical Design Models
Proceedings of the National Conference on Artificial Intelligence
Pittsburgh, Pennsylvania.
[23]
Kahneman, Daniel, Paul Slovic, and Amos Tversky (Eds.) [1982]
Judgement Under Uncertainty: Heuristics and Biases
Cambridge University Press: Cambridge.
[24]
Einhorn, Hillel J. and Robin M. Hogarth [1983]
A Theory of Diagnostic Inference: Judging Causality
Center for Decision Research, Technical Report
Graduate School of Business
University of Chicago: Chicago, Illinois.
[25]
Witkin, H. A., D. R. Goodenough, and P. K. Oltman [1977]
Psychological Differentiation: Current Status
Educational Testing Service Research Bulletin RB-77-17
Princeton, New Jersey.
[26]
Rouse, William B. [1982]
Cognitive Style as a Correlate of Human Problem-Solving Performance in Fault Diagnosis Tasks
IEEE Transactions on Systems, Man, and Cybernetics, Vol. SMC-12, No. 5, 649-652.
[27]
Case, R. [1978]
A Developmentally Based Theory and Technology of Instruction
Review of Educational Research 48, 3, 439-463.
[28]
Bloom, B. S. [1976]
Human characteristics and School learning
McGraw-Hill: New York.
[29]
Torrance, E. P. [1967]
Scientific Views of Creativity and Factors Affecting its Growth
In J. Kagan (Ed.)
Psychology in the Making: Histories of Selected Research Problems
Alfred A. Knopf: New York.

Part III

DOD Programs and Projects

AFHRL PROGRAM FOR ARTIFICIAL INTELLIGENCE APPLICATIONS TO MAINTENANCE AND TRAINING

Brian Dallman

Air Force Human Resources Laboratory

The young science of artificial intelligence has not yet produced a technology that can be used to solve real world problems in a consistent manner; however, within the next 10 years it is expected that practical application of some forms may be commonplace. The time is ripe for military laboratories to start stimulating and guiding research in the development of systems which would extend the capabilities of the military forces. AFHRL is initiating a program to participate in the development of AI technology as it applies to maintenance aiding and training. Measurable outcomes could include lower mean time to repair, a greater operational readiness, and a stabilized corporate experience base resistant to personnel attrition. Other benefits could include enhanced personnel productivity, greater training efficiency, and decreased task loading on weapon systems personnel.

This program has three principal goals. First, the program will apply AI technology to real Air Force problems in the maintenance aiding and training domains through an integrated system. The rationale for this integrated system has been documented by Richardson (1983). The principal initial demonstrations will be conducted as a part of AFHRL's Integrated Maintenance Information System (IMIS) program (Johnson, 1982). The second goal is to establish a capability for the conduct and examination of artificial intelligence research. AI is a multidisciplinary field with the principal contributions being made by cognitive psychologists and computer scientists. Because of the scarcity of experts, it will be necessary to educate Air Force personnel about AI and maximize the sharing of resources and information. This can be accomplished through jointly funded research activities and participation with AI researchers as in the case of the Intelligent Computer-Assisted Instruction Network. The third goal will be to assist/consult with other Air Force organizations in the development and exploitation of the evolving AI technology. As the technology becomes more refined and personalized, it will also become more distributed. There will be a need for contacts for information and assistance.

This program is jointly sponsored by the Logistics and Human Factors Division and the Training Systems Division of AFHRL. As currently envisioned, the core applications efforts will be to build and demonstrate Intelligent Maintenance Aiding and Training software systems for IMIS. Supporting these core efforts will be basic research and technology development studies.

The IMIS proposal is to provide all necessary automation to flight line personnel in one compact, user-friendly device. It would have common data bases, user interfaces, reporting requirements, displays, hardware, etc. It is envisioned to be capable of aiding, training, and supporting personnel. It would display procedural data, aid in troubleshooting, present training material tailored to the specific person and task requirements, as well as aid in personnel decisions.

It will eventually be capable of changing its internal knowledge representation based on an analysis of its data bases. IMIS will achieve this end state through an evolution that is contingent on advances in AI technology. Research is required in areas such as expert diagnostic systems, knowledge representation, information extraction, intelligent computer-assisted instruction, and machine learning.

The three elements of the core program are to (1) perform an extensive planning, coordination, and experience acquisition activity, (2) develop an intelligent test bed, and (3) design and develop the prototype IMIS AI applications. Other demonstrations outside of IMIS are being considered. These include small portable ICAI systems and intelligent instructional design, development, and evaluation tools.

The basic research and technology development efforts will facilitate the development of the intended applications and assist personnel in maintaining currency with other related research programs. In the basic research areas, we envision performing supporting studies in natural language interfaces, cognitive modeling of learning and memory functions, and developing models of human diagnostic processes. The technology development efforts will be oriented toward the application of the results of basic research studies that have promising outcomes.

Figure 1 provides an initial pictorial description of the program architecture. Following this are brief descriptions of proposed efforts.

REFERENCES

Johnson, R. C. Integrated Maintenance Information System: An imaginary preview (AFHRL-TP-81-18). Wright-Patterson AFB, OH: Air Force Human Resources Laboratory, Logistics and Technical Training Division, September 1981.

Richardson, J. J. Artificial intelligence: An analysis of potential applications to training, performance measurement, and job performance aiding (AFHRL-TP-83-28). Lowry Air Force Base, CO: Air Force Human Resources Laboratory, Training Systems Division, September 1983.

FIGURE 1. INTELLIGENT SYSTEMS TECHNOLOGY FOR MAINTENANCE AND TRAINING

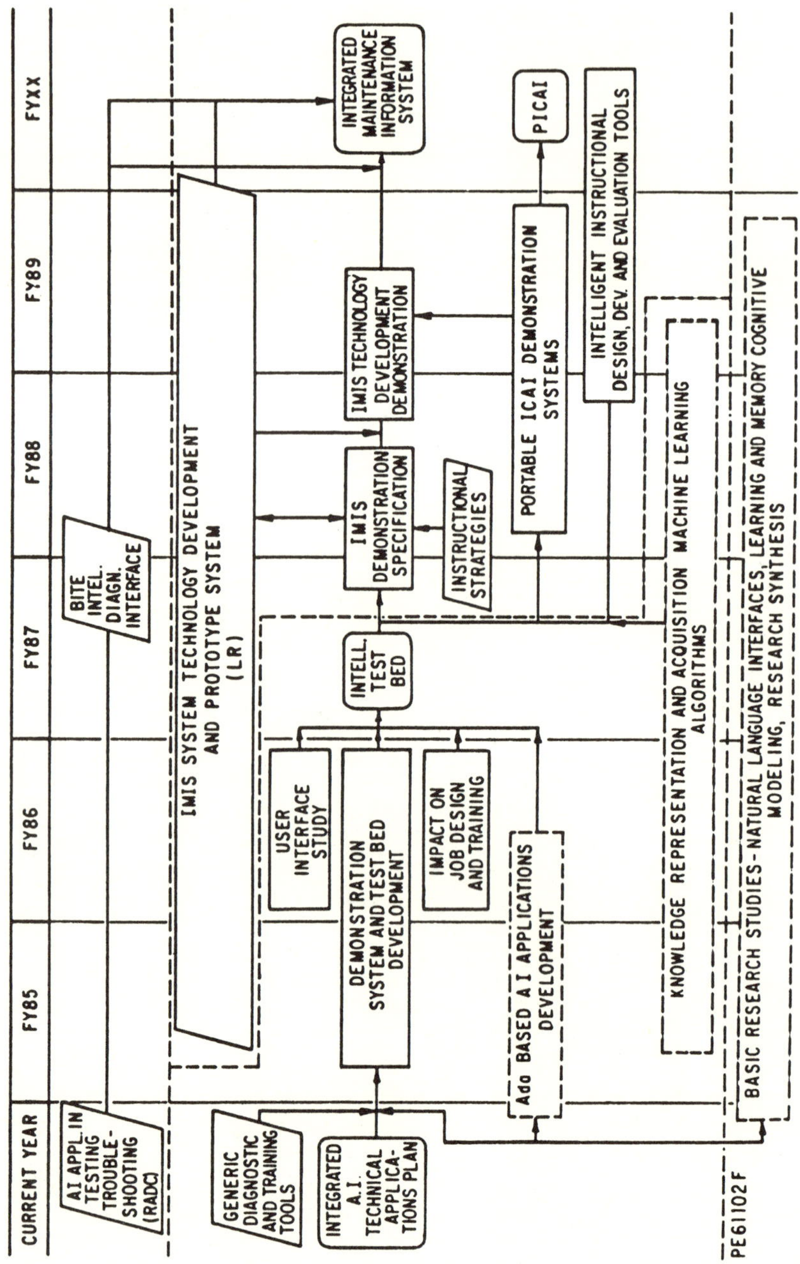

Artificial Intelligence Applications for Ada

PROBLEM:

Since Ada recently became the DoD standard computer language, ideally it should be used for all programming applications within DoD. However, there are some applications for which Ada is not currently practical. One of these areas is artificial intelligence. In DoD, the majority of programming for AI applications is done in LISP. Consequently, if LISP remains the primary AI language, then Ada's usage and acceptance in a critical new area of software engineering will be severely limited and DoD's effort to establish a common high order language will be hampered.

OBJECTIVE:

To develop an extension of the Ada language which will provide the capabilities for AI programming applications. This extension can involve possibly only an Ada package or collection of packages.

APPROACH:

This project involves three distinct tasks. The first task is to identify the capabilities a language must provide to meet AI programming needs. This needs assessment will be accomplished by studying the capabilities provided by existing AI programming languages such as LISP or PROLOG. AI researchers will also be queried for their input on necessary capabilities for AI that have not been sufficiently provided by the existing AI languages.

Once a list of requirements has been developed, Ada will be evaluated to determine if it is capable of meeting those requirements. If Ada simply cannot meet the needs of AI programming, then the project is over. But if Ada can in fact meet some of the AI needs, then work will continue to design and develop a super-set of Ada which provides AI programming capabilities.

PRODUCTS:

* Survey of Requirements of Programming Language
* Evaluation of Ada Respecting AI Programming Language Requirements
* Possible Super-set of Ada Providing AI Programming Capabilities

AFHRL Plan for the Application of Intelligent Systems Technology

PROBLEM:

The application of artificial intelligence (AI) techniques to maintenance and training is a high-risk activity in part because of the scarcity of scientific personnel who are experienced in the field. By adequately planning efforts and coordinating activities, these risks can be reduced.

OBJECTIVES:

1. Acquire hands-on experience with AI-based systems for maintenance diagnostics and training.

2. Develop a detailed, prioritized research and development plan for the near-term initiatives.

3. Develop a general planning document for establishing an artificial intelligence technology base.

APPROACH:

Acquiring hands-on experience with expert systems technology designed for maintenance diagnostics will involve the implementation of an experimental system on the AFHRL/ID VAX 11/780. Issues associated with the use of expert systems technology for maintenance aiding and training roles within the Air Force will be identified and explored. Coordination activities have included a joint-services workshop on AI applications to maintenance aiding and training. The technical papers and the exchange of information will be used to develop the detailed research plan and the functional description for the next program effort--an intelligent test bed system.

PRODUCTS:

* Proceedings of Workshop on AI in Maintenance

* Research Development and Application Plan

* Functional Specification for Demonstration System

Artificial Intelligence Basic Research Studies

PROBLEM:

Basic research issues that are likely to emerge in the application of artificial intelligence principles will need to be studied. Problem solving strategies that can be adapted in artificial intelligence software must be designed. Knowledge representation techniques will have to be developed. Designing expert systems software needs to be done. A study that clearly describes computational linguistic patterns would break down the research task considerably.

OBJECTIVES:

1. To investigate and clarify basic knowledge representation, heuristic generating, and expert systems software techniques.

2. To better define the structures, meanings, and situations that form natural language environments in training and job aiding settings.

APPROACH:

Target four in-house or contract studies that emerge as a result of the findings at the end of the planning stage. Issues that may be particularly relevant will be in the areas of expert knowledge representation, heuristic techniques, and natural language processing.

PRODUCTS:

* Four technical papers on such topics as Knowledge Representation, Open-Ended Heuristic Software, Comparison of Expert Systems, and AI Linguistics

Intelligent Test Bed for Maintenance Aiding, Training, and Organizational Support

PROBLEM:

Little research has investigated the integration of different intelligent computer systems (i.e., expert diagnostic systems and intelligent CAI). Determining both the practicality and the necessary resources for AI applications is an important need in the development of an integrated maintenance aiding, training, and organizational support system.

OBJECTIVES:

1. To assess the feasibility of developing an integrated system and determining research requirements for the prototype IMIS demonstration.

2. To determine cost and time requirements for the development of the prototype system.

3. To build a test bed for resolving some issues before the prototype design planning.

APPROACH:

The integrated system will be built using state-of-the-art intelligent computer-assisted instruction and expert systems technology. The concept is to have the components of the integrated system share the knowledge representation of the target weapons subsystem. This sharing is a principal concern for the successful cost effective application of intelligent systems technology. Other key issues are the user interface design for the system, low cost knowledge representation and acquisition methods, effective development methods, effective development tools, and the impact of intelligent systems on job roles and training requirements.

PRODUCTS:

* Intelligent Test Bed System for Research Activities

* Functional Specification for Prototype IMIS System AI Demonstration

Artificial Intelligence Technology Development Studies

PROBLEM:

Many of the techniques for acquiring and representing knowledge in AI systems need refining. The cost to create and maintain the knowledge domain of a system could be reduced if machine learning models could be applied.

OBJECTIVE:

The objective of this effort is to refine knowledge representation and control techniques, knowledge acquisition procedures, and explore the application of machine learning systems.

APPROACH:

Likely candidate approaches for further development will be identified. Focus will be on causal models, flexible problem solving strategy, temporal contiguity, large knowledge base maintenance, and computer-aided design/computer-aided manufacturing CAD/CAM interfaces. Small projects will be funded, each addressing one of these areas.

PRODUCTS:

* Refined Software Techniques/Strategies

Prototype Intelligent Maintenance Aiding, Training, and Organizational Support Capabilities for IMIS

OPPORTUNITY:

Intelligent systems technology enables machines to perform complex tasks such as diagnostic troubleshooting that normally are considered to require intelligence. Intelligent computer-assisted instruction (ICAI) provides highly tailored human tutor-like instructional experiences for students. By integrating diagnostic troubleshooting and ICAI capabilities into IMIS, a sophisticated system for Air Force maintenance aiding, training, and organizational support can be built to increase measurably operational readiness.

OBJECTIVE:

To build a prototype maintenance aiding, training, and organizational support function for IMIS based upon artificial intelligence techniques. Functionally, support functions will assist maintenance technicians of varying abilities in troubleshooting complex subsystems of a weapons system, provide task relevant training, assist in making personnel action recommendations, and performing trend analysis on weapons system performance.

APPROACH:

Phase I will consist of a systems definition study based on the results of early demonstration efforts and current research/application of AI.

Phase II initial efforts will focus upon the creation of generic tools to enable the IMIS AI applications to be built for the selected weapons system. Where possible, existing tools developed as part of related efforts will be adapted. A likely target system for the prototype IMIS may be an avionics system of the proposed Advance Tactical Fighter. A maintenance information system interface will be used to extract subsystem data, synthesize findings, and update the IMIS knowledge representation.

Phase III will perform the implementation, operation, test and evaluation for the IMIS at an operational site.

PRODUCTS:

* IMIS Softare and Hardware Specifications
* Generic Building Tools
* Prototype Applications

ABOUT THE AUTHOR

Mr. Brian Dallman is a Research Psychologist for the Training Systems Division of the Air Force Human Resources Laboratory. Since 1973, Mr. Dallman's responsibilities with the laboratory have included the development and evaluation of the PLATO IV system within the Air Force vehicle maintenance courses; the development of the student progress management component of the Advanced Instructional System (AIS); the evaluation of the AIS; and the development of the interactive graphics simulation system for the Air Force's maintenance training simulation program. Currently, he is a member of the TRIADS--a joint services computer-based instructional system group--and is also responsible for preparing the Air Force's program to develop and apply artificial intelligence technology to maintenance aiding and training.

DEPOT LEVEL PROBLEMS IN THE TESTING OF PRINTED CIRCUIT BOARDS

Dr. Rob Milne

Air Force Institute of Technology
Wright-Patterson Air Force Base

Introduction

The Air Force today has a severe problem in the automatic testing of analog cards. Most automated test programs run a structured series of tests requiring many hours. Even after several hours of testing, the program has reduced the fault to as many as 10 potential components. In most cases, it is not possible to reorder the tests. As a result, there is no way to indicate to the system that the last test is the one which is most likely to identify the fault.

At the Air Force Institute of Technology (AFIT), we are working with Warner-Robins Air Logistics Center (WRALC) to develop an expert system for the diagnosis of faults in analog circuit cards. WRALC has a large depot of Automated Test Equipment (ATE) which runs virtually 24 hours a day, 7 days a week. Their problems include inflexible programs which proceed in sequence even if it is believed the failure to be located would be found by one of the last tests to be run. Some of these programs take 3½ hours to run.

One of the "biggest problems" cited by one of the WRALC people is that the ATE doesn't catch all the failures. In many cases, some conditions of some components are never tested. This leads to frequent RETOKs (or Re-test OK). Many cards circulate through the system, failing at one level and succeeding at another. Ingenuity must be applied to manually detect the failure in this case. Ambiguity is another problem, (e.g., the F-15 AIS normally isolates to one component, but can provide as many as 15 suspected parts); memory devices are especially prone to high ambiguity isolation. In these situations, the operators often rely on a "trial and test" approach to find the actual fault.

Another problem is that the program may isolate to a string of components which theoretically would all be replaced. With some hybrids costing $300-$3,000, this creates a significant parts expense. Even replacing a string of cheap parts would require significant maintenance time. Finally, the ATE does not isolate chassis problems (e.g., wires in the chassis). Some cards have very long wires, which are optimized to be "points" in the circuit.

Another major problem is that the test equipment is very slow, requiring many hours to test a single board. The programs are not easily modified and very little documentation exists. Because test documents are binding though, there is very little one can do to change the tests. After all this testing, they may have missed the problem or may have isolated it to 5 or 6 components. They must then employ highly trained labor to find the exact fault. It was felt that a system which could isolate errors to one component quickly and accurately would present a considerable savings to WRALC.

The current system consists of a test card mounted on an ATE. This device then runs a predetermined set of tests, in the form of an Atlas program (Atlas is the standard language for all Air Force ATE) over the card. If a specific test is unsuccessful, the intervening components are identified to be replaced. The tests are not independent of each other. As a result, each card must go through the entire series of tests (taking as long as several hours). Actually, some tests are independent of others, but no one seems to know which ones.

The Proposal

It is proposed to replace the current software with a program employing AI expert system and heuristic search techniques. This program will base its testing on a schematic diagram of the circuit board and the list of test specifications which were originally used to write the Atlas test programs. This program will use this data and a simulation or model of the functioning circuit card to allow more detailed and guided testing. The ordering of the tests shall be independent and every effort made to identify the unique component which is faulted.

The Expert System

The system we will develop will be a "structure and function" expert system. That is, its knowledge will be the structure of the system and the function of each subsection. It will base its reasoning first on the structure of the board. When it can no longer isolate the fault based in the structure, it will reason about the function of the isolated region and what may have caused the particular problem. We believe this to be a standard architecture which future maintenance systems should use. Specifically, two sets of information should be used. First is the structure of the circuit and the possible testing points. The program compares the value at each point with the desired value and attempts to isolate the region where the fault is.

Second is the function of each subsection. The group of components work to achieve a certain output. It is desired to reason about how this output is formed and how it may be incorrect based upon its overall function. In most circuits it is possible to isolate to subcircuits of about 10 components.

Our system will contain the following sections:

The test harness. This will be the existing ATE.

The test board. This will be the board which is being tested. It will be connected only to the ATE. Initially, this will be the CP power supply card from the F-15.

The model board. This will be a computer model of what the board would be like if it were properly functioning. This does not have to be a full simulation of the board, but only needs to contain the proper values for all points on the board under the anticipated test conditions. It is hoped that past simulations developed at WRALC will aid in this. This model will be consulted for each test to determine whether the board is at fault at any intermediate node.

The reasoning module. This will be the main program. It will control which tests are performed, in what order, and which faults have been identified. The reasoner will control the ATE via Atlas code over the appropriate interface (RS232C). It will keep a history and explanation of each test as well as the status on each component of the card. The reasoner will be responsible to keep test records, histories, and reports for later analysis.

The circuit diagram. The schematic diagram of the circuit board will be entered in the form of a network. The reasoner will use this to guide its tests and the focus on potentially bad components.

The user interface. The user shall have the capability of ordering the tests, selecting individual portions of the board to test, and demanding explanations of why a certain component is considered bad.

The Basic Algorithm

The user interface will first initialize the system and perform the safe to turn on tests. The user will then select the particular tests or ordering of tests. The users shall be able to inspect the current list of tests and easily edit this list. The user may also set the level of interaction required at each test. An easy to use interface is preferred. Each test will know what tests must be performed before itself. This sequence will be maintained by the system.

The reasoner will then conduct the first test on the list. It will direct the ATE to perform the tests using Atlas code and wait for the result. If the result is different by more than the tolerance from the desired result, further diagnosis will be conducted. If the user has requested, a report will be made on each test. If the test is successful, the components which are known to be functioning will be marked in a component status entry in the schematic model. Note that a successful test does not mean that the component works over all of its specifications. The reasoner will continue through the list of tests to be performed until the list is exhausted.

Before the tests the following data needs to be established. The schematic needs to be represented in the form of a network. Frames could be used to allow the flexibility of properties, inheritance, and procedural semantics for each component. The hierarchical nesting of these could be used to establish substructures on the card. Secondly, the Test Requirements Document (TRD) needs to be used to identify the tests which must be performed. The most automatic method of doing this will need to be exploited. At the very worst, existing Atlas programs can be examined to identify the basic tests and values expected. The Atlas code to perform these tests will need to be developed, both for the standard tests and the internal diagnostic tests. The simulation will need to be developed based upon the schematic and the TRD values initially, but including a one time simulation of the board. It is intended that the internal testing of the board will be conducted only for the values used in the original tests, so we will know in advance what input values will be needed. As a result, other values can be computed off-line.

If a test fails, at the appropriate time for finer diagnosis, all possible paths between the inputs and the outputs can be identified. This can be done by a simple network search algorithm. Initially, this list of paths will be generated by brute force. It is hoped that later some good heuristics can be devised to provide a smaller set.

Each of these paths is then checked with the status of each component on the path. Paths or subpaths of all valid components are then eliminated. All other components are marked as suspect. If only one component is labeled bad, then no further testing is done at that level. If there is already a bad component, it will be assumed that this is the reason for the failure. This is an initial assumption only and will be replaced later.

At the end of each test, a set of production rules will run. These rules will look at the results of all the tests to date and embody the knowledge of the expert diagnosticians. They will see if any standard problems have arisen and use these to conclude as to the real fault or further guide the search.

A new set of tests is then devised to test each of the paths. Preference is given to global tests which can test all or part of the subpaths. If there are none, then the paths are ordered according to how likely they are to be wrong. The first (next) path is explored from the input end to the output end. At each subnode, the current value is obtained from the ATE. If it is different from the simulation board for the same conditions, then it is marked bad and we are finished with this test. Otherwise, the next node is checked. A later test may mark a questionable node as "okay."

Once the initial framework has been developed and proven, it is intended that a more elaborate search strategy can be explored. There is much interest in the AI world in this area and programs such as SOPHIE, ARBY, DELTA, DART, STAMP, and NDS may influence how this is implemented.

When all tests have been completed, or when the user requests, the status of all components is reported. All bad components are noted as well as all components still marked "questionable" and those marked "okay." It is assumed that current methods are so slow and inefficient that the extra search and lack of optimizations in this approach will be tolerated.

When the tests have been isolated to one group of components, the deep reasoner will be called into action. It will first look at why the test was wrong. In general, there are only a few classes of failure for each test. Examples are:

there may have been no output, output was high, output was low, or output was only slightly out of tolerance. Most current systems do not distinguish between these cases.

If the output is only slightly out of tolerance, then the system will check for the presence of trim resistors. This is a common type of failure.

If the output is off considerably, deeper reasoning needs to be employed. In most systems today, the technician attempts to change the active components in the call-out group and see if the problem is fixed. If not, he changes all the components. The system will be limited by the type of information which the test harness can collect. It will try to use all information it has to decide on the most likely failure.

Eventually, we hope to reason about the failures from "first principles." For example, we know that a capacitor appears as an "open" at low frequency and a "short" at high frequency. If a high pass filter is not allowing the signal to be generated at high frequency, we can reason this way:

1. The signal should be present at high frequency.
2. If the capacitor is a short, the signal is present.
3. The signal is NOT present at high frequency.
4. The signal IS present at low frequency.
5. Conclude: the capacitor is not correct.

In this paper, we have outlined a structure and function expert system for the diagnosis of faults in printed circuit boards. The state of the art is such that we know how to perform the isolation to a group of components. The state of the art now needs to develop the techniques to decide which of a group of components is actually faulted.

As a final note, the state of the art in AI and the state of the art in operational testing are very different. Before AI can really help the testing community, it will be necessary to advance the operational state of the art.

ABOUT THE AUTHOR

Army Captain Robert W. Milne is an Assistant Professor of electrical engineering at the Air Force Institute of Technology, Wright-Patterson Air Force Base. He is also Director of the AFIT Artificial Intelligence Laboratory and a consultant to the Army AI program. Capt. Milne holds a Ph.D. from the Department of Artificial Intelligence at the University of Edinburgh and a B.S.C. in electrical engineering and computer science from the Massachusetts Institute of Technology. He has published professional papers in the field of artificial intelligence and is a member of the American Association of Artificial Intelligence and the Association of Computational Linguistics.

EXPERT SYSTEMS IN MAINTENANCE DIAGNOSTICS FOR SELF-REPAIR OF DIGITAL FLIGHT CONTROL SYSTEMS

John Davison

Air Force Flight Dynamics Laboratory

A couple of weeks ago, the Flight Dynamics Laboratory (FDL) of Wright-Patterson Air Force Base met with our sister laboratory, the Avionics Laboratory, to exchange some ideas on artificial intelligence. I briefed them on this workshop program and they were surprised to learn that FDL was going to demonstrate a maintenance diagnostics system this spring. They had not planned to do this until 1987. They suggested that I contact Dr. Richardson and this workshop and communicate some of these ideas as they think this demonstration is a well kept secret of the work we've been doing. However, I might add that we've been too busy working to advertise.

I'd like to cover three basic components of this program. One is an overview and the progress of the program starting off with the battle damage statistics that are supplied to us by aircraft battle damage repair people. These statistics are the drivers that influence the self-repairing program. They are gathered primarily from Southeast Asian data, updated from the Falklands conflict and Israeli data. Secondly, I would like to talk briefly about the self-repairing concept, and thirdly, the status of our expert system for maintenance diagnostics.

Figure 1 assumes a four-to-one damage/loss ratio for a status of the fleets during surge. The dramatic part about the top line is that after the second day, as you can see, 68 percent of all the aircraft are out of commission. That's not due to attrition alone; we have aircraft that are awaiting maintenance and in battle damage repair. Those are pretty alarming statistics.

If we examine aircraft losses by functional area, we see that flight control is a large contributor along with fuel and fire explosion and propulsion system. In aircraft damages by functional area of the return, flight control is again a large contributor, around 18 percent. However, when we look at the percentages of the aircraft returning with damage (see Figure 2), propulsion, fuel, power, and, of course, structural damage are the real drivers. I don't know why structure isn't 100 percent, I think everything has to go through the structure. I think this graph was based on small arms fire only. When we look at the repair time it takes to turn the plane around, we see that flight control occupies the majority of the median time to repair. Figure 3 shows that even with the advent of digital electronics and the complexity of the flight control systems, we're still only at 11 percent of the cost in the digital electronics. The drivers are still in the equipment areas, for example, in the servos.

As you'll see in Figure 4, the self-repairing system is broken into three general areas. The first is the survivability of the aircraft where we're concerned with real-time configuration in case of system faults and battle damage where we reconstruct the forces and moments using the remaining surfaces. For the quick

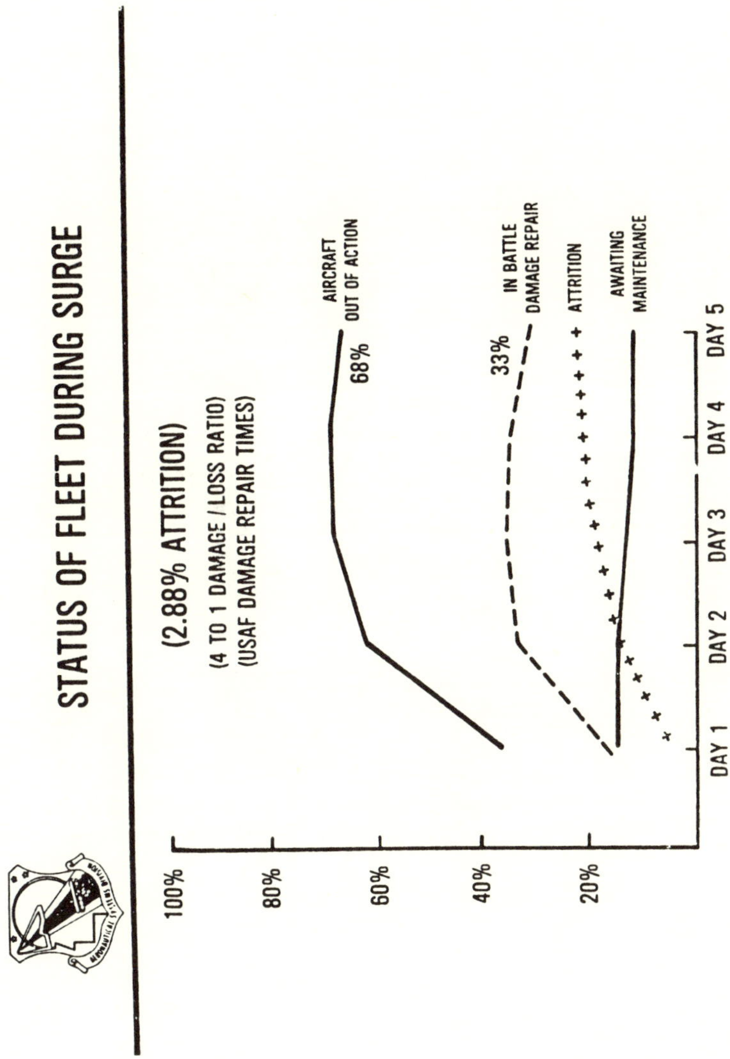
STATUS OF FLEET DURING SURGE
(2.88% ATTRITION)
(4 TO 1 DAMAGE / LOSS RATIO)
(USAF DAMAGE REPAIR TIMES)
100%
80%
60%
40%
20%
DAY 1
DAY 2
DAY 3
DAY 4
DAY 5
68%
AIRCRAFT OUT OF ACTION
33%
IN BATTLE DAMAGE REPAIR
ATTRITION
AWAITING MAINTENANCE

Figure 1.

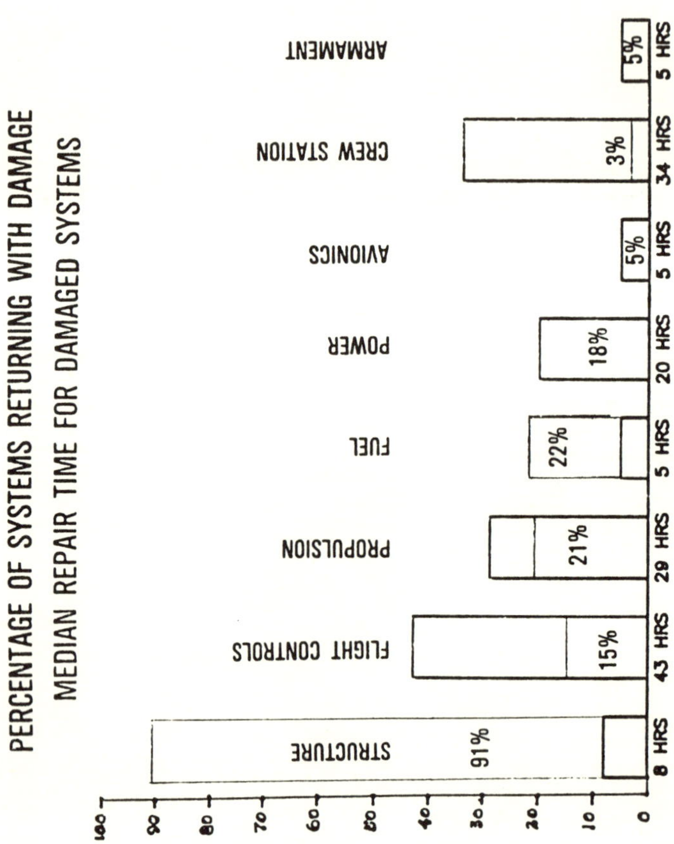
PERCENTAGE OF SYSTEMS RETURNING WITH DAMAGE
MEDIAN REPAIR TIME FOR DAMAGED SYSTEMS
STRUCTURE
FLIGHT CONTROLS
PROPULSION
FUEL
POWER
AVIONICS
CREW STATION
ARMAMENT
91%
15%
21%
22%
18%
5%
3%
5%
8 HRS
43 HRS
29 HRS
5 HRS
20 HRS
5 HRS
34 HRS
5 HRS
0
10
20
30
40
50
60
70
80
90
100

Figure 2.

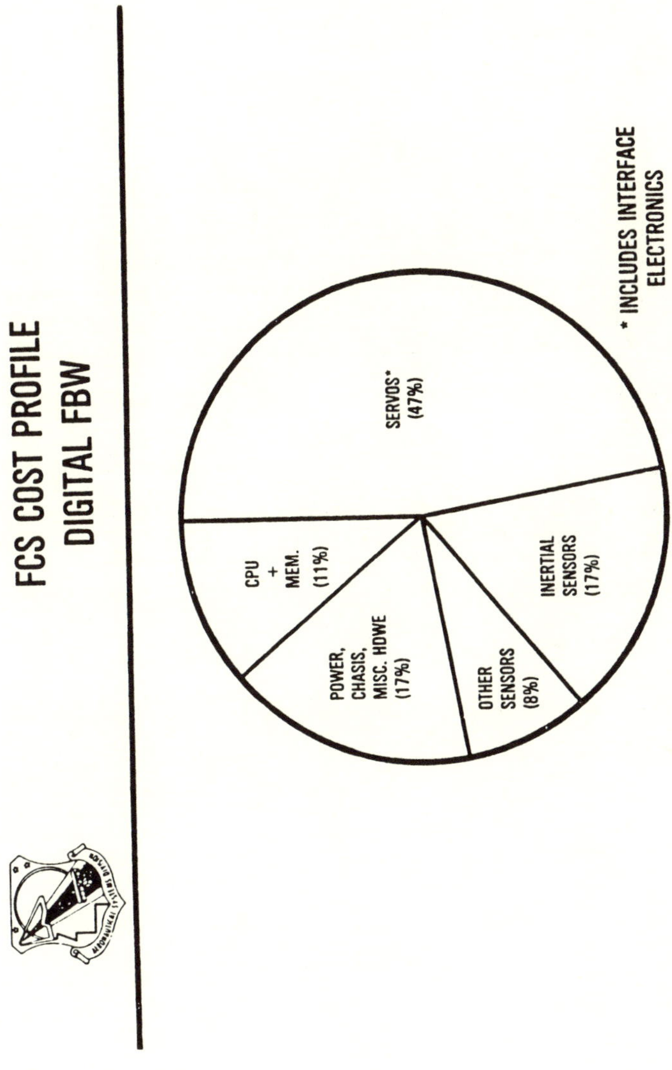
FCS COST PROFILE
DIGITAL FBW
SERVOS* (47%)
INERTIAL SENSORS (17%)
OTHER SENSORS (8%)
POWER, CHASIS, MISC. HDWE (17%)
CPU + MEM. (11%)
* INCLUDES INTERFACE ELECTRONICS

Figure 3.

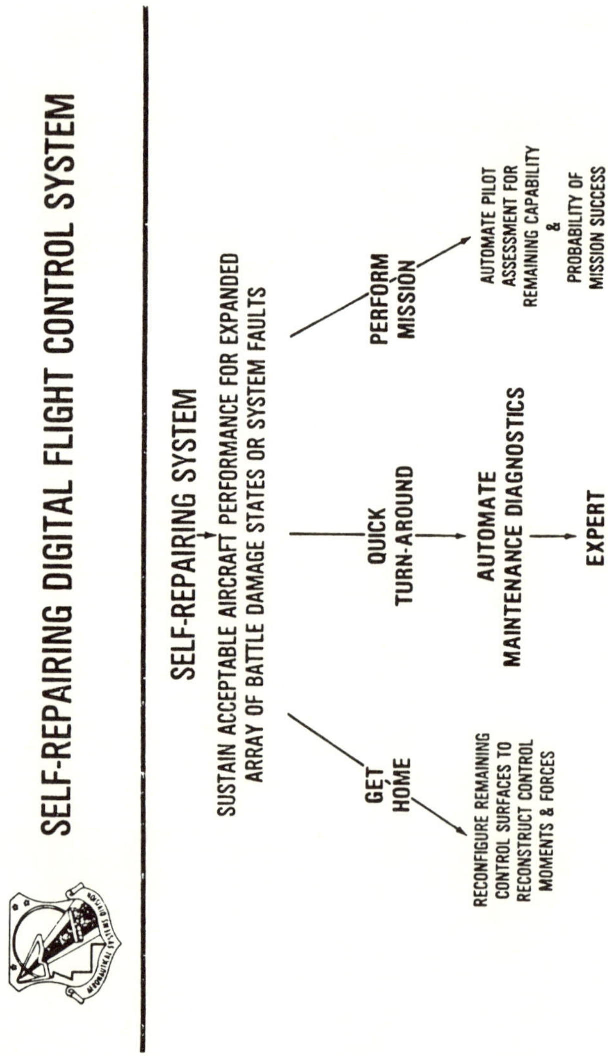
SELF-REPAIRING DIGITAL FLIGHT CONTROL SYSTEM
SELF-REPAIRING SYSTEM
SUSTAIN ACCEPTABLE AIRCRAFT PERFORMANCE FOR EXPANDED ARRAY OF BATTLE DAMAGE STATES OR SYSTEM FAULTS
GET HOME
RECONFIGURE REMAINING CONTROL SURFACES TO RECONSTRUCT CONTROL MOMENTS & FORCES
QUICK TURN-AROUND
AUTOMATE MAINTENANCE DIAGNOSTICS
EXPERT SYSTEMS
PERFORM MISSION
AUTOMATE PILOT ASSESSMENT FOR REMAINING CAPABILITY & PROBABILITY OF MISSION SUCCESS

Figure 4.

turn around of the aircraft, we're looking at automatic maintenance diagnostics and we're using an application of expert systems. Because we can detect and classify these failures, we want to let the pilot know what capability remains, not just what has failed.

To take a general look at our system in a single channel, the blocks in solid lines in Figure 5 would be a standard flight control system. The key in this system is our system impairment detection classification function. This feeds into a drop-in module where we remix the flight control laws and send them back to the flight control computer without changing those flight control laws at all. As long as we're able to do that, as I mentioned, we give the pilots a real-time status of what are the operational capabilities. For example, we might tell them that with the remaining capability they can only pull 4½ G's as opposed to 6½.

In our maintenance diagnostics, we think that we're going to follow the TAC two-level maintenance concept so that we can data-link figures back to the forward base. If the pilot has a servo that has failed or experienced damage, the mechanic will be waiting with a part at hand as the plane taxis up. However, it's really not our idea that maintenance begins in the air. Other people have been doing it for a long time. We do think that we have a little different approach to the problem, though. This is where we get into our maintenance diagnostics computer. In our approach, the troubleshooting expert is paramount. We're also going to use in-flight faults, the situation data, and we're going to incorporate the technical orders and the illustrated parts breakdown in our maintenance diagnostics computer.

The general components of the expert system are the same. As you'll see in Figure 6, in the knowledge base we use the heuristics and the rules of logic and in the situation base we use current data, historical facts, and background information. That's also where we put all our flat file data for all the prioritized possible faults. It goes directly into our maintenance computer, and that computer interrogates the maintenance person. For example, we're experiencing in-flight faults and, let's say we had a problem in the pitch axis, it would drop us right into the pitch axis diagnostics. Part way through the diagnostics the computer may ask maintenance if the follow-up potentiometer in the pitch actuator has been checked. If the maintenance person punches the "no" button, the next question would be, "Do you know where it's at?" If the "no" button gets punched again, we bring up the illustrated parts breakdown technical order file and draw a tone over the follow-up pot to indicate exactly where it's located. Then we explain how to go about checking that and clear the system.

We're looking at two possible applications. For new applications, we'd like the computer to be autonomous and reside in aircraft. Right now, we're trying to impact existing aircraft like the F-15 and the F-16 (Figure 7).

Question: I have a problem: Why would you do that when it's sent in subject to battle damage?

Davison: It can be stand-alone, or because it is stand-alone, we can roll another one up in front if it does have battle damage. But we don't want to get into the redundancy, triplex and quad of everything in airplanes. It can be easily substituted.

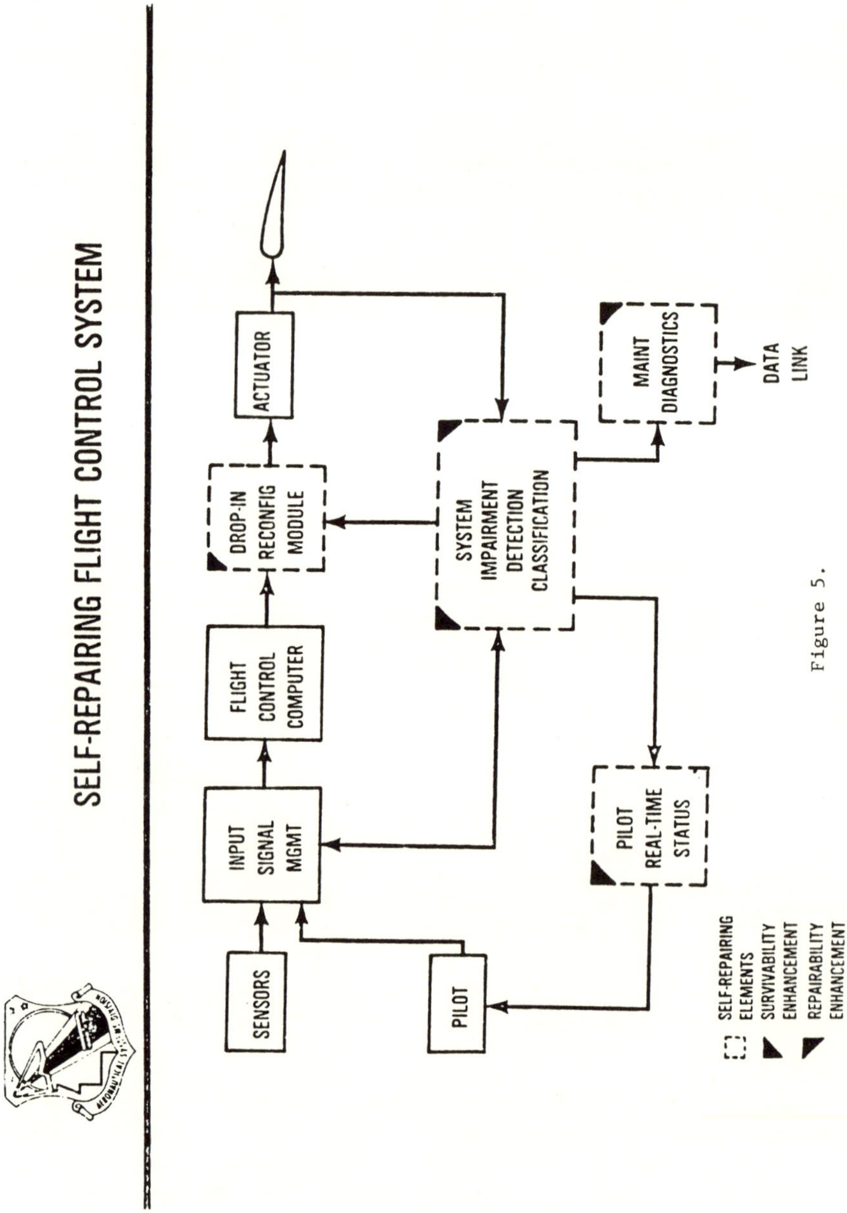
SELF-REPAIRING FLIGHT CONTROL SYSTEM
SENSORS
INPUT SIGNAL MGMT
FLIGHT CONTROL COMPUTER
DROP-IN RECONFIG MODULE
ACTUATOR
PILOT
SYSTEM IMPAIRMENT DETECTION CLASSIFICATION
MAINT DIAGNOSTICS
DATA LINK
PILOT REAL-TIME STATUS
SELF-REPAIRING ELEMENTS
SURVIVABILITY ENHANCEMENT
REPAIRABILITY ENHANCEMENT

Figure 5.

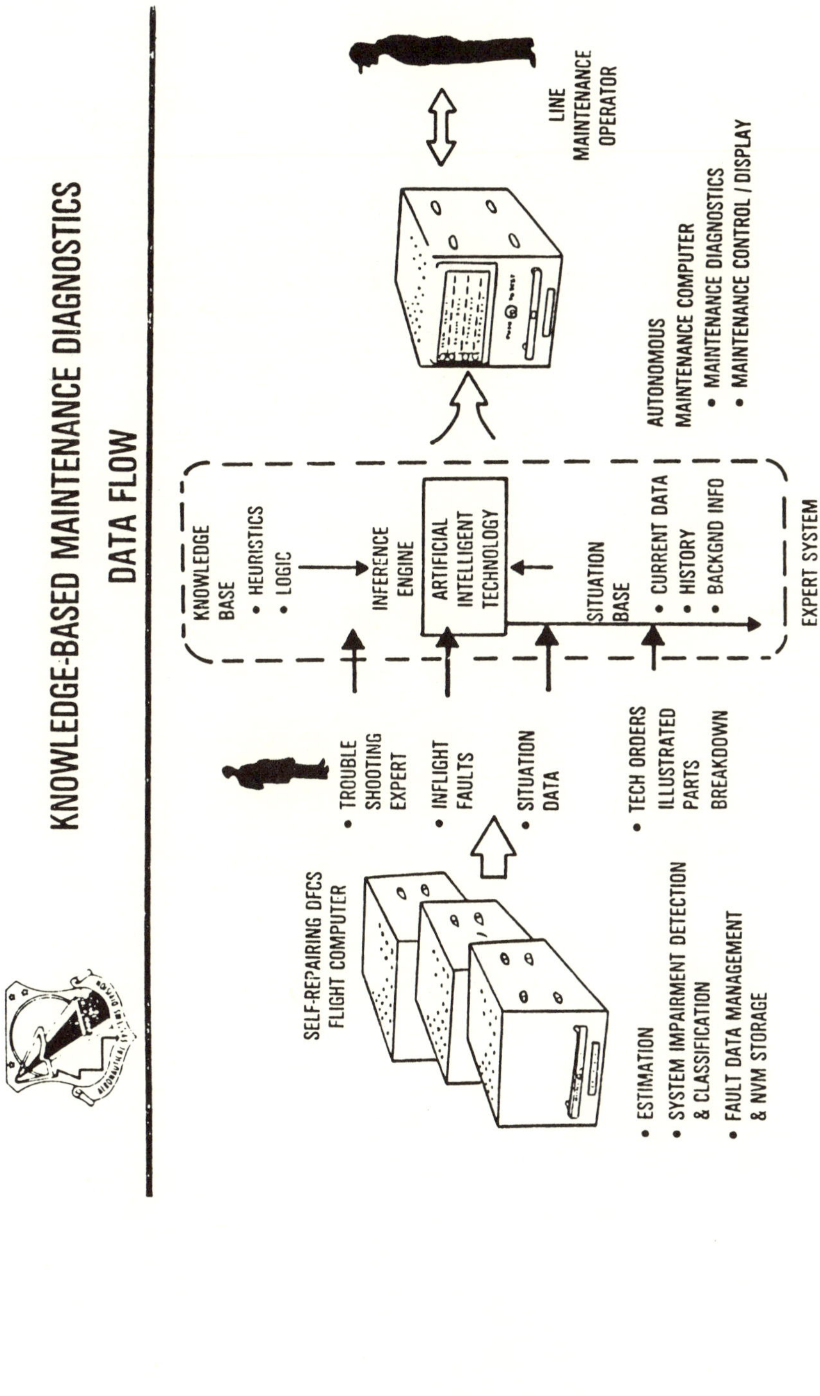

KNOWLEDGE-BASED MAINTENANCE DIAGNOSTICS
DATA FLOW
SELF-REPAIRING DFCS FLIGHT COMPUTER
• ESTIMATION
• SYSTEM IMPAIRMENT DETECTION & CLASSIFICATION
• FAULT DATA MANAGEMENT & NVM STORAGE
• TROUBLE SHOOTING EXPERT
• INFLIGHT FAULTS
• SITUATION DATA
• TECH ORDERS ILLUSTRATED PARTS BREAKDOWN
KNOWLEDGE BASE
• HEURISTICS
• LOGIC
INFERENCE ENGINE
ARTIFICIAL INTELLIGENT TECHNOLOGY
SITUATION BASE
• CURRENT DATA
• HISTORY
• BACKGND INFO
EXPERT SYSTEM
AUTONOMOUS MAINTENANCE COMPUTER
• MAINTENANCE DIAGNOSTICS
• MAINTENANCE CONTROL / DISPLAY
LINE MAINTENANCE OPERATOR

Figure 6.

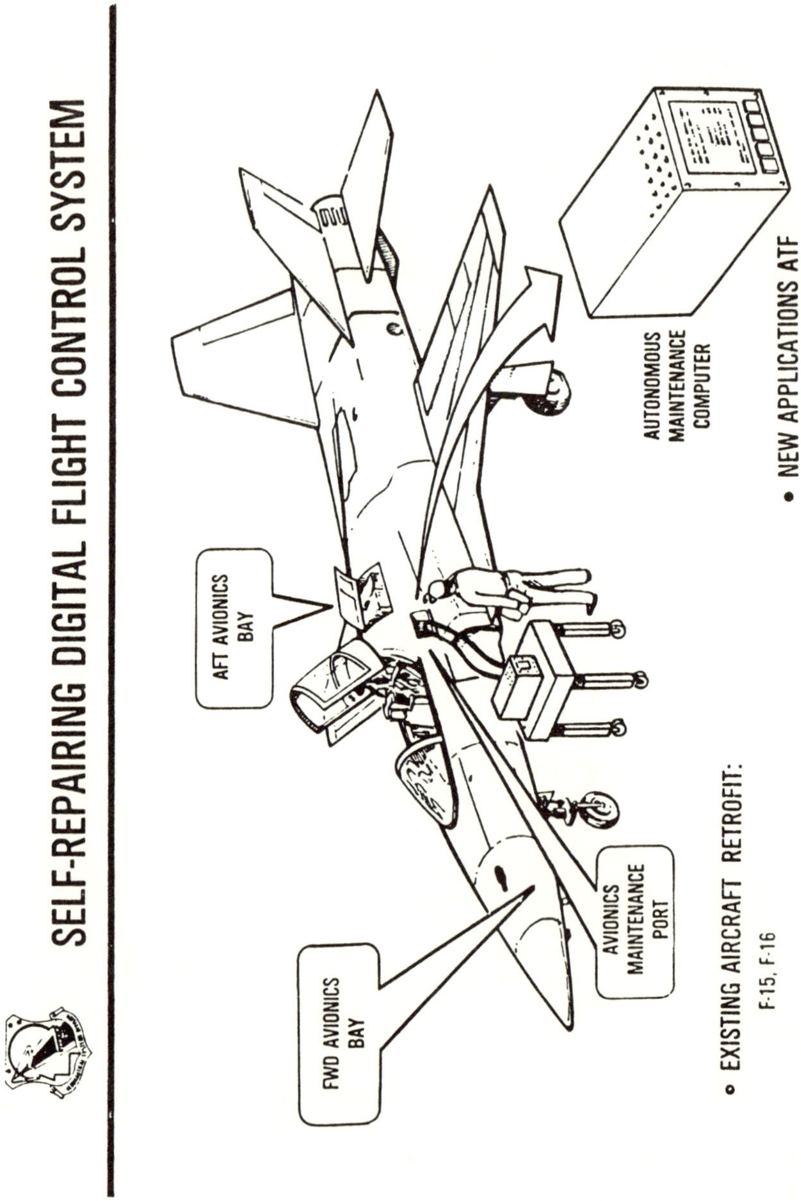
SELF-REPAIRING DIGITAL FLIGHT CONTROL SYSTEM
FWD AVIONICS BAY
AFT AVIONICS BAY
AVIONICS MAINTENANCE PORT
AUTONOMOUS MAINTENANCE COMPUTER
• EXISTING AIRCRAFT RETROFIT:
F-15, F-16
• NEW APPLICATIONS ATF

Figure 7.

I heard a lot of conversation this morning about the quality of maintenance personnel and the problems involved with troubleshooting the system. Let me tell you that flight control systems are complex. There's digital, quad, fly-by-wire systems, and I don't care if you're a control engineer or a mechanic, when you open up that panel and try to troubleshoot that system, it's like a hog looking at a wristwatch. I mean, you don't know where to begin. We think this self-repairing system is the only way we can circumvent that problem.

We think we're really a little bit ahead of the game because we've relied on General Electric and have a contract with them to develop this system. We're riding on the coattails of their DELTA system, the locomotive system for maintenance diagnostics. This is supported with both Air Force funds and IR&D funds. In order to develop their DELTA system, it took them 12 months to get a 50 rule feasibility demo model. It took another year to bring it into lab prototype and a third year to a field prototype model--that's at around 500 rules. To get into a 1200 rule system, it's 4 years and about a megabyte of memory.

Figure 8 shows where we are right now. We're going to use the F-18 because it's the only production digital fly-by-wire system available now. We're going to develop a 50 rule system and demonstrate this in the coming spring. We're moving this technology into our AFTIF-16 and by March of 1986, we hope to have a 1200 rule system developed and in place.

To wind this up, we want to look at both the on-board diagnostics and be able to data link this data back to the forward base. This will provide rapid assessment of fault and damage. We want to incorporate all the technical orders into the flight hardware. We want to impact that median repair time of 43 hours (rf. Figure 2) and reduce it by a factor of five. By incorporating those technical orders in there, we eliminate a ground-support function, so we don't have to divert to the large fixed infrastructure-type bases. We can divert anywhere, the maintenance people can rendezvous with the airplane and hopefully perform maintenance that would normally be performed at the depot level.

<u>Question</u>: I don't understand why you call it self-repairing?

<u>Davison</u>: Well, we're reconfiguring the flight control laws. Regarding self-repairing, we're talking about the system level. We're not using artificial intelligence to reconfigure the system; that's another presentation.

<u>Question</u>: Doesn't the maintenance person still make the replacement?

<u>Davison</u>: Yes, but we're saying that we can do away with the unscheduled maintenance and continue to fly by being able to detect, isolate, and recover from any failure in the system.

Thank you.

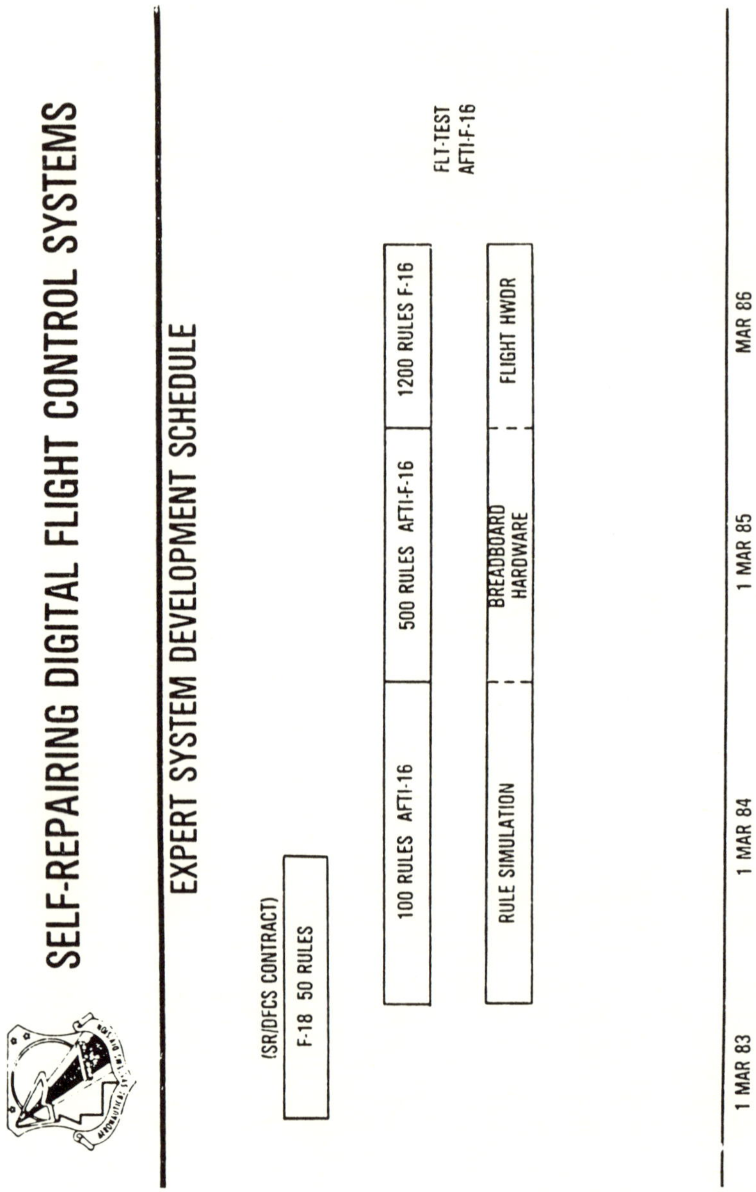
SELF-REPAIRING DIGITAL FLIGHT CONTROL SYSTEMS
EXPERT SYSTEM DEVELOPMENT SCHEDULE
(SR/DFCS CONTRACT)
F-18 50 RULES
100 RULES AFTI-16
500 RULES AFTI-F-16
1200 RULES F-16
FLT-TEST
AFTI-F-16
RULE SIMULATION
BREADBOARD
HARDWARE
FLIGHT HWDR
1 MAR 83
1 MAR 84
1 MAR 85
MAR 86

Figure 8.

ABOUT THE AUTHOR

John W. Davison is a Project Engineer in the Flight Control Division of the Air Force Wright Aeronautical Laboratories Flight Dynamics Laboratory. He is responsible for project planning and technical management of R&D programs dealing with flight control system reliability and safety. During the mid-1970s, Mr. Davison served as lead engineer for reliability and safety analyses of the Laboratory's C-141 All Weather Landing System flight demonstrator. He was subsequently instrumental in focusing emphasis on the need for development of software reliability prediction methods. He currently directs laboratory activities in self-repairing flight control, a concept involving in-flight reconfiguration and advanced maintenance diagnostics based on expert system concepts.

ARTIFICIAL INTELLIGENCE CONTRIBUTIONS TO TRAINING AND MAINTENANCE

Joseph Psotka

U.S. Army Research Institute

Abstract

Artificial intelligence is rapidly becoming a practical and useful technology for training and maintenance. This paper provides an introduction to its uses in maintenance training, drawing on current research funded by the Army. After a description of this work, a call is made to fund more exploratory research, expand the base of competent professionals in the field, and begin the complicated process of evaluating this new technology in order to diagnose its failings and hasten its development.

Introduction

My sincere thanks and appreciation go to our hosts for this workshop on artificial intelligence and maintenance training. The timing could not be more appropriate as the very many fine activities described in this volume testify. The development of training systems, particularly maintenance systems, is about to be complicated in quite new and, in many respects, unanticipated ways. Artificial intelligence (AI), knowledge-based systems, and expert systems for training and maintenance are becoming an overnight success after some 20 years of hard effort. We must prepare ourselves to use them wisely. The complicated issues that have been raised in connection with computer-based instruction in the past (cf. Orlansky, 1983) are all reissued in new guise: there is, after all, a continuity between this new application of AI and the older (but still developing) forms of CBI and simulations. We must be careful. Yet, the promise is also so clear that we must be prepared to act quickly and not squander a very real opportunity.

What is Artificial Intelligence?

The phrases "artificial intelligence," "knowledge-based systems," and "expert systems" are used interconnectedly throughout this paper. None of them have precisely defined meanings. AI is the most generic of the three, since it involves activities like pattern recognition and voice synthesis and recognition that are generally not central to knowledge-based systems and expert systems. Expert systems are the mind of any AI program. An expert system incorporates inside a computer all the rules of action or thought a human expert has about any well-defined domain of knowledge or skill. For instance, John McDermott's Vax configuration program incorporates 500 rules extracted from a professional who was paid very highly for just knowing these rules. It must have been very disappointing to find out that a lifetime of expertise could be summed up in so few rules.

Knowledge-based systems are all expert systems, and they are the best known and understood kind of expert system. Very little is known about how to use expert system technology for training highly practiced skills and automatic skills like driving tanks and shooting, but arcade and video game technology is rapidly pushing in this direction.

All of these AI applications employ the symbol manipulation powers of the new generations of computers to solve problems. Problem solving seems to be at the heart of all expert systems. Expert systems technology provides a way to extract knowledge from an expert and place it into computer symbolic forms (in a process called knowledge engineering) and then use that knowledge base to solve problems. Problem solving in this context has a very broad definition, covering things ranging over algebra problems, medical diagnosis, mechanical or electrical maintenance and troubleshooting, all the way to training field generalship or even running an automated tactical operations center.

Opportunities for the Army

Three rapidly evolving developments make the time ripe for applying artificial intelligence approaches to the Army's severe training and instruction problems. The major development is rapidly improving hardware that has produced personal LISP machines at low cost (20 - 30K) and the power of last year's mainframes. The second development is in the application of "expert systems" technology to a host of real world problems (ranging from medical diagnosis to mineral prospecting) that have demonstrated the utility of artificial intelligence techniques in very dramatic style. Finally, current state-of-the-art in computer- based training and instruction has advanced to the stage where the leap to using "expert systems" approaches is practical and possible: the basic knowledge is there to model soldier, task, and instructor characteristics with fidelity in a machine.

These technological windows of opportunity are opening in time to address some pressing Army needs and challenges. The Army of the 1990s is increasingly a high-technology Army and this is imposing tougher new demands on its soldiers. Maintenance training needs to become much more sophisticated and individualized. The distributed battlefield of the future will also make unprecedented demands on the cognitive decision making skills of its soldiers. They need to be prepared intellectually to make fast, appropriate decisions and use complicated strategies and technologies in order to win the war. What better way exists than to use high technology in order to train soldiers effectively to use high technology on the battlefield?

Previous Work

During the past several years, ARI has engaged in a concerted program of research and development to prepare for this activity. Work on computer-based instructional systems has progressed on several fronts, ranging from the hand-held, talking, technical term tutor to a computerized videodisc instructional system (SDMS). Training and simulation work has progressed from 3-D computerized systems like AMTESS to the current proposals for AI-based maintenance tutors. The groundwork for specific artificial intelligence applications has been carefully laid with a 1M per year jointly funded ARI/ONR program supporting basic research in artificial intelligence applications to maintenance and training. This work has reached the advanced development stage where several projects can lead to working demonstrations in the next few years if the critical funding is made available.

Current AI Applications

The Army is in the middle of several initiatives that have the potential of providing significant funding to AI research and development in general, and maintenance training research in particular. Let me try to provide a brief overview of these programs.

- ARI will provide funding to several AI activities, to be described in more detail later in this paper.
- ARO is in the process of selecting a U.S. institution of higher learning with graduate level programs to develop a capability for research, education, and training in AI to help fill Army needs.
- TRADOC has formed a General Officer Steering Committee to oversee the development of an overall Army AI action plan by November 30, 1983.
- DCSRDA in concert with several other Army agencies, including DARCOM, HEL, TACOM, ETL, and ARI, has developed specific demonstrator projects, including:

    1. Reconnaissance Vehicle;
    2. Ammunition Supply Robot;
    3. Intelligent Display;
    4. Expert Medical System;
    5. Intelligent Maintenance Tutor.

All of these activities are providing high level and very visible support to AI research and development within the Army. It is certain that these plans will amount to something significant, so we can look forward to a period of productive research and development.

Current Academic and Commercial Efforts

Although there are plans for applying AI techniques to Army problems, we must examine the larger world of academic and commercial development for examples of how these systems work and what training purposes they might serve.

The best known and most mature developments of expert systems for problem solving have occurred in medicine: CADUCEUS by Myers and Pople at CMU, and MYCIN by Shortliffe at Stanford. Both systems are designed for decision making and diagnosing diseases to help an expert physician interpret a case. This is an important point because it has led people to believe that expert systems can only help experts of a similar kind (in this case doctors) do their job better. That is basically a faulty conclusion: expert systems can both act as consultants to experts, and they can replace experts. However, most of us do not yet have to worry: there are some rather severe restrictions on the kinds of expertise that can be entered into expert systems. Medicine provides virtually a prototype for this kind of expertise.

1. The knowledge domain must be bounded and well defined. It must be small enough to be manageable; yet large enough so that conventional, linear algorithms and programs will not work.

2. The problem or task domain is intellectual rather than dependent on sensory or motor skills. The problems are defined by a large number of interacting variables that require human knowledge to resolve.

3. At least one and preferably more human experts exist who can solve the problems. These experts must be able to verbalize their reasons in forms that can be converted to rules; that means they cannot rely on common sense for an answer; or if they do, then someone must be able to analyze their cognitive processes into rules.

Medical expertise clearly fits these constraints. Political savvy probably does not. And many areas of expertise fall in between.

CADUCEUS has a very broad expertise. It covers hundreds of diseases in internal medicine. It takes into account thousands of symptoms and lab tests. It does professionally well against diagnostic tests of its abilities. The home computer will truly be here when this fine program is available for everyday use. However, this represents the result of 10 years full-time commitment by an expert internist and the help of many colleagues and students.

MYCIN is much narrower, but deeper. It deals only with the diagnosis and treatment of organisms that infect blood or cause meningitis. In direct tests, it has achieved performance comparable with experts in the field (Buchanan, 1981). Furthermore, it has spawned a whole family of expert systems.

By taking away the specific medical knowledge domain, a shell of essential or empty MYCIN has been formed, called EMYCIN. Given a new problem domain, EMYCIN provides help in constructing an expert system to solve the problems. EMYCIN assumes an appropriate representation format for the new knowledge base (production system rules) and goal-directed backward chaining as the appropriate inference mechanism. Production systems are simply collections of IF-THEN rules. Goal-directed backward chaining is the same process you use when you decide to get 40 dollars out of the bank because you are going to dinner. Other forms of knowledge representation and other inference mechanisms are available, but these have so far proved to be most useful.

Combining EMYCIN with new knowledge domains has yielded useful expert systems for pulmonary diseases (PUFF), blood clot diseases (CLOT), structural analysis (SACON), filling in and debugging these expert systems (TEIRESIAS), and explaining and tutoring these systems (GUIDON).

GUIDON (Clancey, 1981) is of special interest to us as this expert system is for instruction and training. In a project funded by ARI, Clancey at Stanford's Heuristic Programming Project has converted MYCIN into NEOMYCIN. NEOMYCIN reconfigured the rules in MYCIN so that they became more psychologically plausible as the basis for reasoning diagnostically. This allows GUIDON to provide test cases to students, allow them to analyze NEOMYCIN's diagnoses, and by interpreting the students' analyses, build up student models of their knowledge base and diagnostic reasoning abilities. Obviously, GUIDON represents a very large step forward in individualizing instruction and getting the computer to become a tutor.

A discussion of intelligent computer-aided instruction (ICAI) and tutorial systems would be utterly inadequate without mention of the dramatic and pioneering work of John Brown and his colleagues at Xerox PARC. In a now lengthy series of impressive tours de forces, Brown (1983) and company have provided imaginative demonstrations of how to change our mind set about computers in instruction. His fundamental thesis is that these sophisticated symbolic environments provided in personal LISP stations or Smalltalk environments can expand the use and effectiveness of learning-by-doing through discovery and apprenticeship.

Learning-by-doing environments can provide a tremendous opportunity for students to learn about themselves and their own thinking processes (metacognition) and their learning strategies. As an example, Brown and Burton capitalized on the current computer games mania by creating a computer coach for PLATO's "How the West Was Won" called simply WEST (Brown & Burton, 1982). WEST can watch two people playing each other and decide on its own when to interrupt politely. It can then point out to a player that, if he had only paid more attention to his opponent's moves, he might have discovered a strategy he did not possess. The obvious strength of this coach is that it can make use of the skills of the opponents without having to create unique scenarios for tutoring. It can in fact facilitate peer tutoring. ARI is sponsoring work to continue some aspects of this research and development.

Finally, I want to describe briefly a project called STEAMER (for a more detailed view, see Jim Hollan's contribution to this workshop). STEAMER has tried to integrate some of this research and development to provide intelligent computer-based instruction in propulsion engineering. This work arose directly from SOPHIE, another Brown, Burton, and de Kleer project (1982) providing explanatory qualitative models for training electronic troubleshooting for a relatively simple amplifier circuit.

In the first phase of STEAMER (Orlansky, 1983), a learning-by-doing environment was created with a sophisticated graphics interface that simulated thousands of components in a naval steam propulsion plant. This graphics package is a major product for instruction by itself. It may now be used within this Lisp environment for other kinds of instruction, or other LISP environments, such as LOOPS, may be converted to perform similar functions. This part of STEAMER provides a unique audio-visual instructional aid, and it is being used just for that purpose in a Navy setting.

The second phase of STEAMER is now underway to build a computer coaching facility into the same environment. Two strikingly different approaches are being used. One carries out a sequential dependency analysis of appropriate steps in any procedure of running the plant, i.e., this meter must be checked before that valve is opened. This leads to the sort of tutorial feedback that says, "Sorry, you should have checked A before doing B; you just blew up the ship."

The second form of tutorial tries to avoid the complexities of understanding the functioning of each single component and tries to create a deeper conceptual understanding of the causal connections among things. For instance, it may provide a moving graphic of a steam valve that can be controlled with all its functioning parts in display. A student can manipulate this model in gross ways, like increasing the pressure at a point and see, visually and dynamically, what the consequences are. Hopefully, this kind of learning, while it does not provide engineering competence, does provide the kinds of mental models that allow expert technicians to operate and troubleshoot the system effectively.

None of these ICAI projects have been evaluated in any rigorous fashion. In a sense, they have all been toy systems for research and demonstration. They have all raised a good deal of excitement and enthusiasm about their likelihood of being effective instructional environments. With the dramatic decreases in computer hardware costs we have recently seen, delivery vehicles for systems like these in the $10,000 range are a reasonable estimate. Clearly, it is the judgment of many that implementations of these systems in a variety of environments will prove to be highly cost effective. The real difficulty in making application decisions is in foreseeing the role that they will play as stepping stones to the future: to imbedded training devices; on-the-job computer aids for maintenance; personnel assessment devices that simulate real tasks; and to devices that actually carry out real tasks, such as imbedded maintenance or robotic control. For even if these systems are not yet cost effective, the only cost effective way of eventually deploying these systems may be to start using primitive and even unwieldy systems now. This is a difficult but very real problem.

Cognitive Science Technology

The productive application of artificial intelligence to training and instruction rests heavily on the technology base of understanding provided by good cognitive science research. This research is advancing rapidly to provide a richer theory of learning that can actually be used in ICAI environments. Two provocative components of this research provide some insight into how ICAI can be used to provide superior instruction and training. The first component to be described will be an analysis of misconceptions, and the second will be the use of learning strategies.

Misconceptions

Consider the path a projectile will take after emerging from a curved tube at high speed. For both shapes in Figure 1 the correct answer is a straight line, tangent to the curve. Notice that more people said the exit path would be curved for the spiral tube than the semicircular tube. It is as if the extra turns were more likely to impart their curved "momentum" or "force" to the moving object. In fact, this bears some similarity to medieval impetus theory and Aristotelian ideas about motion. Other evidence strengthens this suggestion. For instance, similar misconceptions can be found for dropping things from airplanes, tossing coins, and other problems with moving objects. The striking fact about this finding is that all these people are high school graduates who have taken physics.

The second area of misconceptions deals with equations (Figure 1). Any relationship that can be represented algebraically can be expressed in words. Clement, Lochhead and Soloway (1980) report that 37 percent of a group of engineering students wrote 6S=P for "There are six times as many students as professors." Apparently, one source of this problem is that students deal with the equal sign as a static rather than a functional symbol. It is easy to imagine a room with 6 Ss and 1P and use the faulty equation to describe it. It is much more difficult to understand that this description calls for an operation--multiplication of P by 6--to achieve the goal of equalizing the P side of the balance.

Both misconceptions proclaim that simple errors may arise from complex and detailed systems of thinking that may in fact be transitional to more complete ways of understanding a knowledge domain. That is to say, the errors may not just be random, but arise systematically from erroneous ideas or misconceptions that people hold about an area of knowledge. Just such a view of errors has been studied within arithmetic by Brown and Burton (1982) and used as a diagnostic aid for prescribing remedial instruction.

The analysis of such misconceptions is proceeding in other knowledge domains. Identifying a misconception is a very difficult, time-consuming task; but it is well worth the effort because instruction can then be explicitly designed to deal with it and produce longer lasting and more immediately effective instruction. From the perspective of the present talk, it also has the powerful advantage that this kind of analysis is just right for ICAI systems that have to be explicit about their diagnostics and forms of remediation.

Learning Strategies

Cognitive science is contributing important knowledge about how formerly mysterious components of thinking, like intuition, inference, and problem solving, are carried out. More important, there is every indication that

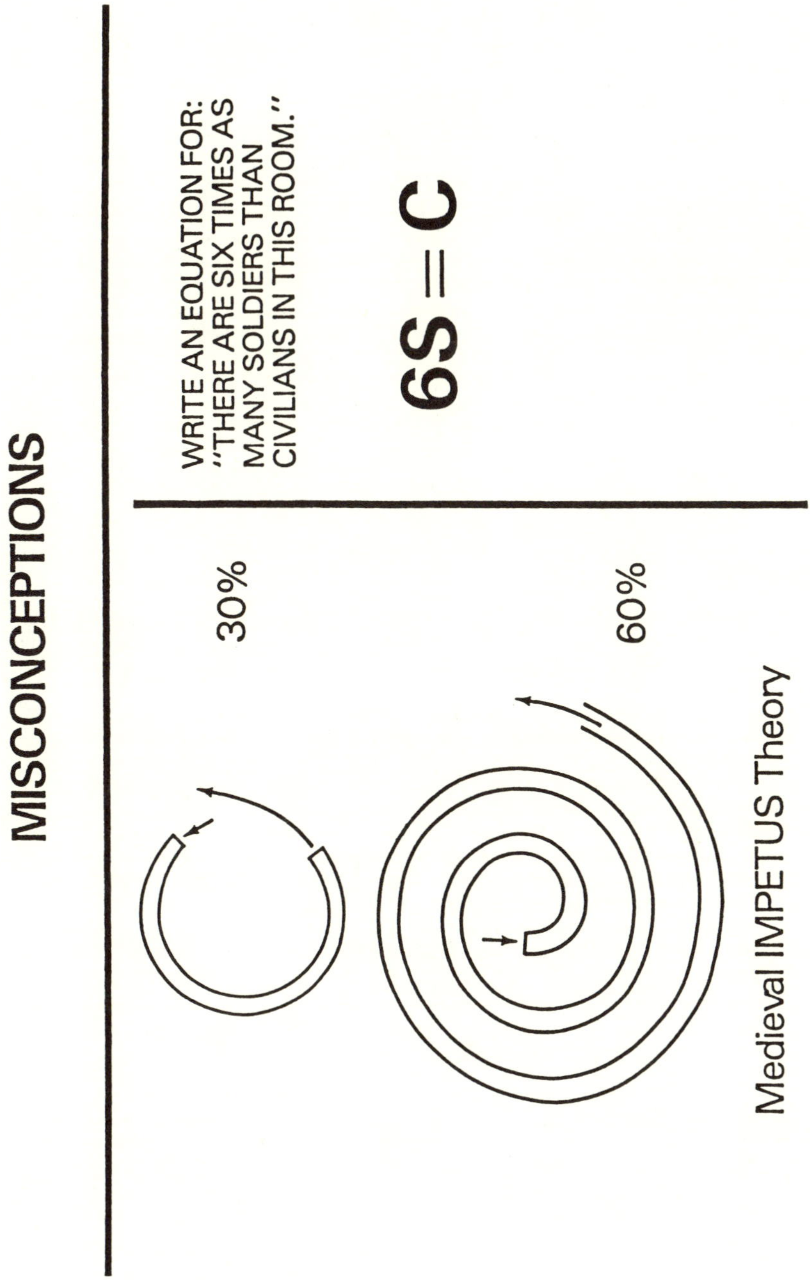
MISCONCEPTIONS
30%
60%
Medieval IMPETUS Theory
WRITE AN EQUATION FOR:
"THERE ARE SIX TIMES AS
MANY SOLDIERS THAN
CIVILIANS IN THIS ROOM."
6S = C

Figure 1.

these mental processes can be taught explicitly, although not easily (Nickerson, 1983; O'Neil, 1977). It may take the special audio-visual and explanatory powers of a sophisticated computer system to realize the full potential of the learning and teaching strategies that are being uncovered.

A short paper like this can only begin to give a flavor for the vitality of the research going on in this area, and its importance for ICAI. Much of the important work deals with working out the details between experts and novices, in terms of the strategies and heuristics they use, the structure of their knowledge, and guiding metaphors and analogies of their thought. By understanding these relations it is hoped that procedures for speeding up the expert-novice transition can also be found.

Experts carry out many of their activities automatically, below their general level of awareness, with little cognitive overhead or interference with other tasks. Speeding up the automaticity of these procedures in novices is something that can be done by computer after an effective cognitive task analysis. ICAI can help decompose tasks into manageable components so that not only are the tasks easier to learn, but the general skill of breaking things into bite-sized chunks can also be learned and used in many novel situations.

Most intellectual processes are not subject to awareness or introspection. This has the unfortunate effect that most of us are not well aware of how good our memory is; how many rehearsals it takes to remember a telephone number; what our misconceptions about physics, public policy, or people are; how well we can use imagery, analogies and metaphors; and a host of other mental skills. The study of metacognition is exploring how to make these facts of our mental life visible to us, so that we can begin to change and improve them.

Visual representations (graphs, charts, tables, working sketches, even cartoons) are all relatively underused when people try to learn and understand new material. Computers, with their dramatic display capabilities provide an environment that opens up rich new possibilities for using these tools to enhance our understanding and create new ways to learn.

Finally, learning without computers is often all too passive. Intelligent CAI can help ask the questions that test the boundaries of our understanding; provide counter examples to explode the limitations of overly narrow comprehension; make new connections among the things we know; and provide a flexible and generally supportive but challenging environment in which learning can take place.

Conclusion

To do all this, the computer would indeed become a tutor, and replace to some extent those who would now be trainers and teachers. However, this development is still a long way off. Until then, however, ICAI systems will be able to take on an increasingly heavier burden, becoming more intelligent as the growth in technological power, cognitive science, and artificial intelligence applications permits. This may be a Pollyannic vision of the future, but it is certainly one that must be taken into account in analyzing current directions and policies for training technology.

NOTE: The views expressed in this paper are the author's and do not necessarily reflect RI's official policy. Arpanet address: Psotka @ NPRDC. Mail address: Attn: PERI-IC.

References

Brown, J. S., & Burton, R. R. An investigation of computer coaching for informal learning activities. In Sleeman, D. and Brown, J. S. (Eds.) Intelligent tutoring systems. London, England: Academic Press, 1982.

Brown, J. S., Burton, R. R., & de Kleer, J. Pedagogical, natural language, and knowledge engineering techniques in SOPHIE I, II, & III. In Sleeman, D., & Brown, J. S. (Eds.), Intelligent tutoring systems. London, England: Academic Press, 1982.

Brown, J. S. Learning by doing revisited for electronic learning environments. In White, M. A. (Ed.), The future of electronic learning. Hillsdale, NJ: Lawrence Erlbaum, 1983.

Buchanan, B. G. Research on expert systems (Report # CS-81-837). Stanford, CA: Dept. of Computer Science, Stanford University, 1981.

Clancey, W. J. The epistemology of rule based expert system: A framework for explanation (Report # CS-81-896) Stanford, CA: Dept. of Computer Science, Stanford University, 1981.

Clement, J., Lochhead, J., & Soloway, E. Positive effects of computer programming on students' understanding of variables and equations. Proceedings of the National Association for Computing Machinery Conference, Nashville, October 1980.

Feigenbaum, E. A., & McCorduck, P. The fifth generation. Reading, Massachusetts: Addison-Wesley, 1983.

Nickerson, R. S. Computer programming as a vehicle for teaching thinking skills. The Journal of Philosophy for Children, 1983, 4, 42-48.

O'Neil, H., Jr. Learning strategies. New York: Academic Press, 1977.

Orlansky, J. Have we increased the productivity of training? Proceedings of the Society for Applied Learning Technology, July 13-14, 1983.

Stevens, A., & Steinberg, C. Project STEAMER (NPRDC Tech. Note 81-21). San Diego: Navy Personnel Research and Development Center, 1981.

ABOUT THE AUTHOR

Dr. Joseph Psotka is team leader of the Army Research Institute's Computer-Based Systems Development Team. In this position, he is involved with the application of artificial intelligence to answer the Army's needs in combat, doctrine, training and instruction. Previously, he was Senior Associate at the National Institute of Education and taught at the University of Waterloo. Dr. Psotka received his Ph.D. from Yale.

NAVAIR's AI PROGRAM FOR ATE

Dr. Randall Shumaker

Naval Air Systems Command

I'm going to be doing two things today. I'm going to be summing up a few of the things I've heard at the workshop, but I'm also going to talk about the Naval Air Systems Command (NAVAIR), Naval Research Laboratory (NRL), and Naval Air Engineering Center (NAEC) program in automatic test program generation. Part of the key to understanding some of the decisions we make in this program is the fact that even though it's very big, a ship only has so much room inside, only has so many people on it, and is very far away from land most of the time. This environment is the key to some of the things NAVAIR does in maintenance.

The key to the Navy's problem is that virtually all of the Navy's avionics testing at sea is done automatically. That is, there are no people involved. There are several reasons for that, not the least of which is there is no room for all those people that you need to do the testing. We test over 600 different pieces of avionics (that is black boxes) and if you multiply boxes by cards inside, you see we have a very serious problem because we have a very limited amount of space.

Additionally, test programs are costly--they range from $100,000 to over $3,000,000, and these figures may be conservative. Other problems include long delivery times, long execution times, and, worst of all, inflexibility--whatever you get--is it. Your only other choice is to start over again and write another program. Use of ATE for diagnosis implies replacement of all indicated fault modules, regardless of the fact that it is likely that only one is actually bad.

For this program, we picked a target of opportunity--some area of AI that looked like it was mature enough to really have a chance of producing a practical product in a reasonable amount of time. The one area that has shown some practical success from our standpoint is knowledge-based systems and it appears to be applicable to the electronics area. Electronics is well defined, we have machinery on which it can operate, and we saw maturing in the knowledge-based systems, so we chose to try to put all those together to generate test programs. I will be talking a little bit more about our particular strategy later, and I'd like to get some feedback on that.

Our knowledge-based system (KBS) approach is shown in Figure 1. The key for us is that we own the ATE already and are not going to be dealing directly with people. What we'd like ultimately to do is have the expert system deal only with the automatic test equipment, generate questions to the ATE and it provides measurements back. In effect, we have insulated ourselves from the human-machine problem, because the Navy's mode of diagnosis for avionics does not involve interaction with people. An extension of this might have application to training, but that's not our prime goal. That is, we're going to permit ourselves to do things in a dirty way, use it if it works, as opposed to making it clean enough to work with people.

KBS APPROACH

- NO EXPLICIT LOGIC TREE - TREE IS EXPANDED (TEST + PATHS GENERATED) AS NEEDED
- "RULES" IN IF-THEN FORM IMBED KNOWLEDGE ABOUT WHAT TO DO
- CAN HANDLE BAD DATA, AMBIGUITY AND "SOFT" OR MULTI-VALUE LOGIC
- CAN IMPROVE ITS OWN PERFORMANCE
- CAN EXPAND CAPABILITY BY ADDING RULES (E.G.: NO SOFTWARE REWRITE NEEDED)

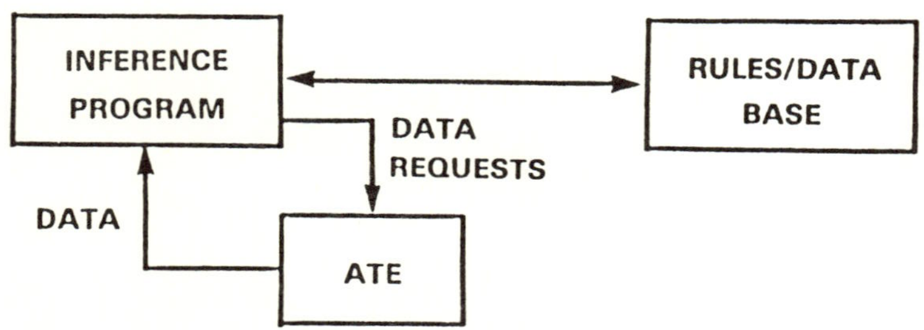

Figure 1.

We propose three modes of using a KBS test-generator. Now you may find these less than optimum from the standpoint of AI. The first mode that we've chosen is off-line generation of test programs. That is, the ATE runs on test programs generated off-line by the KBS. What we'd like to demonstrate is that we can generate test programs that are no worse than manually generated test programs, and are either cheaper to produce or can be produced in less time. I think this is a pretty safe thing to do. A typical turnaround time for a test program is 18 months. So if we can do it in less than 18 months of elapsed time, then we will have made our first milestone. Doing it cheaper than the cost of manually generated test programs is, I think, also feasible. You can buy a lot of computer time for a million dollars.

The second mode of this program would be to have the KBS on-line to the ATE; that is, operate interactively with the ATE. I think this is a much more ambitious goal, because contrary to things you have heard before at this workshop, the computer time is almost immaterial in the testing procedure. It's the set-up time of the instruments and the measurement time of the instruments that is time consuming. The computer itself is idle virtually all the time. It executes a few instructions to command setups and measurements, and then it reads, evaluates, and moves on. However, when we start searching large rule bases and putting things together, it may turn out that computer time becomes a significant part of the testing time. We may be able to eliminate 30 percent of the tests and more than make that up in computer time. That's one of the unknowns of this program. If we're just trading a slow knowledge-based system for raw speed in testing, then we haven't really gained anything and that's something that will have to be to be determined.

The final mode of this program would be a fully autonomous test system that gets a functional description of the equipment to be tested and operates without any intervention. In other words, the KBS "knows" what it's dealing with and it tests completely. I think this is a very ambitious goal. We've staged our plans in order to achieve success, because from my standpoint as a manager, I have to keep providing products and achieving milestones to continue the program. I can't wait for the millennium in 20 years. I'm going to be talking about a bit of philosophy on that later on and once I start doing that, I'd like to get interactive with the audience and see what happens.

We think knowledge-based systems are suitable for the electronics domain, because it's a well established field. For one thing, it's made by people. We design things, we presume that they worked once, and that knowledge is a big plus. You can't always say that about general types of diagnostic problems. Sometimes things could never have worked, and in that case it's very hard to fix them. We think we can reduce the time to generate test programs, and our goal is to do no worse in diagnostic capability than manually generated test programs, and we hope, much better.

One subtle difference here between some approaches I have heard and our approach is that we're not trying to capture an expert diagnostician's procedures. We're trying to capture an expert test programmer's methodology. There is a subtle difference because the test programmer is presented with a whole body of information about how something is supposed to operate--the block diagrams, the schematics, the test points--and is producing a testing sequence without having a particular example of the device to go by. Thus, the test programmer has to traverse all possible paths for the diagnosis. To initially generate test programs, we are going to be emulating the performance of test programmers rather than test technicians. Later on, we assume that that can be generalized into acting as a technician. We think we have a reasonable chance of doing this because we only intend to fault diagnose to the module level, not the component level, which is a considerably more difficult problem.

In the Navy maintenance procedure, you remove a suspected box at the aircraft. You bring that box in and put it on one piece of test equipment which diagnoses a module or modules to be changed, which then theoretically puts the box back into service. Replaced modules are then put on a different tester and tested as a separate step. Thus, we will never be diagnosing to the component level in one step and we get our successive refinement almost mechanically as a byproduct of the maintenance strategy. We pull the box out of the aircraft system, we take a subsystem of that as our next level, and then in a third step, down to the component level.

We hope that adding Units Under Test (UUT) to an expert system will be easier than starting all over again. In other words, we're going to pick a UUT, try to generate automatic test programs for that, and the hope is (and we think this is within reason) the next one will be far easier, with many reusable rules. If it isn't easier, we haven't done anything, all we've done is written test programs in a different way. That is interesting to a certain degree, but doesn't have any economic value for our purposes. So we're assuming that it's going to be easier.

We would like to think that ultimately the knowledge-based systems that we develop would be fast enough that they would not require a separately compiled test program. The target is to develop systems that are both usable on existing generation of test machines and can be incorporated as part of future testing systems.

I would like to re-emphasize that we don't have to deal with the users in the present maintenance methodology, so we're not concerned with a friendly interface at present. As presently envisioned, there is no human user in our systems. This saves worrying about color graphics displays, keyboards, and all sorts of other aspects of dealing with people. So we can take shortcuts in the design of the system that can give us some advantages.

Comment: You may also want to point out why analog systems were selected.

Shumaker: We have chosen to look at analog boards first for a good reason. There's no automatic way of generating analog test programs at the present time. All the ways that have been proposed and evaluated seem to work wonderfully well for small numbers of components, but don't work very well at all for practical numbers of components. We have automated means of producing test programs for digital systems. There are lots of reasons for it, but the bottom line is that analog circuits are much harder to test than digital circuits. We rely strictly on human input for analog systems. The level of abstraction you can get with knowledge-based systems means that we don't have to deal with the circuit at the component level. I saw someone propose using a simulation in parallel with operation of the system to compare for faults. We've tried it, and it doesn't work very well because you need a very large computer to hope to keep up with even the simplest analog system. We'd like to look at the circuit at a much higher level.

The plan is to have some sort of inference engine working on several different sets of rules in a boot-strapping and hierarchical way. The first set of rules would be generic: how does the ATE work, what sort of instruments are available on it, how do you set them up? The second set would be general rules about how to troubleshoot electronics equipment: what sort of measurements are permissible and what sort of measurements are not permissible? It's basic knowledge about how devices work and how they can be measured in an electronics system.

To the generic rules, we propose to add class specific rules. There are 600 different types of avionics that we test, but they fall into general classes. There are power supplies, radars, communication devices, and the like. Conceptually, many of these things are very much the same in that the overall functions and block diagrams are the same. You can impart certain kinds of generic information about how things of this type work.

For each specific UUT, we propose to add specific data. Some of this may be specific peculiarities of this particular unit, or they may be just performance data, functional description in the form of a block diagram and schematics.

We propose to first demonstrate vertically, that is, to pick a UUT as a target and work on that. However, a critical part of the project is to expand that by showing that it is relatively simple to add new UUTs of a particular class. It seems intuitive that we should be able to do that, but, it may not work out for a variety of reasons. If that's the case, then we're simply writing test programs in a different way rather than getting any boot-strapping effect. At this time, we think that the boot-strapping effect will be there.

I'll give you the sales pitch for this--why AI for automatic test? From our standpoint, it has a very high payoff and we measure that payoff in terms of economics. We spend a lot of money on testing and test programs, so it has a very high economic payoff potential. It has the potential to reduce testing time, as the testing of any particular UUT is done at least twice in the normal mode of operation. We test once to fault diagnose, we replace the modules and then we test again. A unit does not go back into service until it successfully completes the test sequence. That means that even if you have just that one iteration, two complete test times are required. When somebody said earlier it takes 2 hours to test a unit, it's not just 2 hours--it's actually 4 hours. Some units don't retest as "good," so there's another iteration. Thus, we're talking about large multiplier effects on getting these things to work.

We think there's a great potential for getting better fault isolation. That's not clear yet because we are stuck with the built-in test points. So it's not clear that we can do better than a very good test programmer can do although there is a good possibility that we can do better than the average test programmer. This remains to be seen. We think the risk of complete success is high but manageable due to the step-by-step approach planned. When I say it's never been attempted, I mean it's never been attempted in a production environment. We do have a target machine and target applications.

Our proposal is to transition this in a 4 to 5 year period into use with ATE. Now I think that's a fairly ambitious thing to do. We're not just going to demonstrate the concept, we'd like to have a product that can be transitioned into service. We're going to take some theoretical shortcuts that others may not strictly approve in order to improve efficiency. One problem with the whole method is that you need a very large data base even to get started. For the first UUT, you need the whole generic data base, plus information for that class, plus information for that specific one. The trouble is then, we're going to have a big investment before we find out that it can't or can work. We're taking a chance, but the risk-to-benefit ratio is very high and makes the risk worthwhile. A big plus is that electronics is well defined and we know we have a target audience. Success would be a true breakthrough in the way maintenance is done for the Navy and for others as well.

The program will theoretically start in 1985, but in fact it's under way right now with some background work and some baseline studies. To those not familiar with government that seems like a very long time; to those who are inside, this is a relatively short amount of time to begin a project. We've set ourselves some specific milestones we're reasonably confident we can meet. First, we'd like to demonstrate a functional KBS for at least one UUT by the end of fiscal year 1986. We would like to add to that additional classes of UUTs and demonstrate better-than-human capability for ambiguity reduction by the end of the program. That's NAVAIR's program for intelligent automatic testing and I will be glad to answer any questions anybody might have about that.

Comment: In the real world of developing test program sets for analog modules, writing the program is not the painful part. The painful and expensive part is designing the adapter that has to convert the limited capabilities of the ATE to the peculiar requirements of the module. Once it's designed, the program utilizes it and that's fine. When you go into interface and check out that program, it is the circuitry and the adapter that causes the most cost.

Shumaker: There are always lots of ways to go wrong. For us, a test program set consists of two parts: (1) an adapter that goes from the unit you want to test to the ATE, which has a big patch panel, and (2) a program which activates signal generators and measurement instruments and acts through that patch panel to talk to the unit. The adapter can be quite complicated. In fact, it may be more complex than the thing it's testing. In other cases, it may be fairly straightforward, just making the pins match up. The test program is a separate issue. The adapter problem is a constant, regardless of test method. An additional use of AI may be in interface fault diagnosis and maintenance of the ATE itself.

We can't do anything about the interface, we're stuck with that. We would hope that in future years, some more standardized way of attaching to the outside world would be developed. For digital if you use a 1553 bus or some other kind of bus, you may have hooks in the interior of the system and may be able to eliminate many interface problems, but not all. The real world of military testing is that we have things in service that are vacuum tube technology, discrete transistors, small-scale integration, medium-scale integration, and, very shortly, large-scale integration. All of those will continue to exist in parallel for a long time, in the 20 year time frame. So anything we develop can't require re-doing everything that we have already. We have to be able to accommodate a broad range of technologies, and the present way of doing that is through these adapters. We can start to plan for the future, and some people mentioned Consolidated Support Systems (CSS) as one sort of plan. They can crank that in for future generations. I feel this system is applicable to old ones through generation of test programs and new ones through on-line diagnosis. Unfortunately, we're not in a position to say, "Let's throw all this out and start over again." It's just not a practical way to go.

Question: Do you have a measure for trying to test the program productivity of the Navy, like how many lines are coded a day?

Shumaker: I don't have that, but if we had that figure, we probably wouldn't tell anybody. Fred Liguori may have some comment on that.

Liguori: It varies a lot because complexity is the biggest multiplier, and that can go from one to a hundred. We're getting paid by lines of code and it's very easy to add lines of code. Efficiency sometimes causes you to turn out a higher price for code because you cut a lot of the garbage out.

Question: Yes, I know it's a poor method but it's the one that is used, as you know. How are you going to measure improvement?

Shumaker: The way I'm going to measure improvement, as I have stated, is that it takes less testing time when the thing runs, not more. If my measure was that my knowledge-based system produces more lines of ATLAS than a manually generated one, then I could absolutely ensure that I'd succeed.

Initially, the measure that we're going to use is very crude, it says, "If a manually generated generator costs three million dollars and I can do this for less than three million, then this is a better way to do it." Or, "If it takes me 18 months turnaround at a given cost to get one and I can get one in 1 month turnaround, then I also have an improvement"--either cost or time; we hope both.

I think we can improve both and that's how we're going to know. I'm setting an initial performance goal for the program itself about equal to what good test programs can produce. We can probably do better, especially since we can modify these on the fly. Right now, when you get a test program, you are stuck with it. If you want a better one, if it doesn't work up to the specifications, you go back and you get another one written and you pay the same prices all over again. Whereas with this sort of system, we'd have a lot more flexibility in improving it in a relatively short term.

Comment: Another point that I would like to make is that one of our big problems is assessing when the product is done. And, how good is that product? It's a totally subjective thing right now. With a mechanized way, or at least semimechanized way, we know if the process is sound that the product will be relatively sound. So our "policing" problem, which is quite large, could become another cost saver.

Shumaker: You can tell that you're listening to an engineer instead of a scientist--I think there's a distinction in approach. We're worried about pragmatic things like costs and elapsed time. We're not worried about purity. If I have to kludge this up to make it work better, I'll buy that as long as it, in fact, does work better in the end. That kludge may or may not make contributions to the science of AI, but that's not going to be important to us. What we hope to do is adapt things to our application that will work. And, if we succeed, its going to be wonderful for everybody else in getting funds because a lot of people will decide this is a very good thing to do.

Comment: About 15 percent of the tasks related to program development go to validation--not a trivial amount. And one of the reasons for that is because of the subjectivity of the design. Once again, if you have a model approach, a quasi-machine approach to producing a product, the validation itself should become a simpler task.

Shumaker: Notice that if you had one of these AI systems functioning, and it could have access to the CAD/CAM data base, it could serve as a very useful design tool. Right now somebody reads the manuals and writes a program from it. The full range of raw data that are actually available are not used. With this system, you could propose a particular design and see what sort of test program and what sort of ambiguity levels resulted while there is still time to make changes. With the present method, by the time we get it for test program, the design is done. If we found a wonderful modification for the unit while developing the test program, it would be impossible to get it in because it's too late by that time. So, something like this system could serve as a very useful design tool and improve maintenance just by its ability to be used during design.

Question: You mentioned that you've done a cost benefit analysis and traded off the costs vs. the payoff risk factor. Do you actually qualify that or document it; is that a logical analysis?

Shumaker: It was not done in strict quantifiable terms. We spend $3 billion a year for support equipment and we said, "Spending a million a year to save some of that is probably a good investment." We spend a tremendous amount of money and we also know that we're starting to get into trouble keeping up with changing technology. The old methods worked well when they were developed and they still work. But today we have many more things to test and the technology is outstripping us. When Very Large-Scale Integration (VLSI) starts getting into equipment, we are going to be totally overloaded. We are being crushed right now and we need a different approach to make this work. That's the reality that our system is based on. I can only provide a qualitative answer, but considering the amount of investment at present and the procurement budget, the ratio is very high.

Question: Do you plan to give some of the tasks in this program to industries?

Shumaker: The management plan is not yet complete. I view it as a shared project between NAEC (they're in charge of automatic test equipment for the Navy) and NRL which has the mandate for artificial intelligence. Each one of them thinks that they are best qualified to do the whole job, but the truth is that a combination of their special talents is needed. I believe that they are going to need outside help to do it, there aren't enough people in those two places that can work on this to cover the whole project in the time allotted. There will be many industry opportunities. There is enough money and time to do this job if we are careful, but there's also not enough if we don't do it right.

Comment: I have a couple of questions about your host. You said you wanted to capture expertise with a test programmer rather than a test diagnoser. A priori, it seems to be an odd thing to do. I think the expertise of the test programmer is much more sophisticated than that of the expert diagnostician.

Shumaker: Well, what I mean by that is there is a qualitative difference. My initial target is not a diagnostician, but something that generates diagnostic procedures. And this requires a different way of thinking about testing. If you are sitting there with your instruments and testing a unit, you might do things considerably differently than if you were writing a set of instructions for somebody else to do the same troubleshooting. There is a different perspective involved.

Question: But to write a set of instructions for someone else to do it is much harder than having the procedure adapt as the measurements come on. Wouldn't you like to have a fault drive the search? Otherwise you have to process all possible faults.

Shumaker: That's correct, but to allow TPS generation to allow use of existing equipment, that is the compromise we make. I think, and anyone is free to contradict me, that the kind of product that can reliably generate on-line diagnostics for general classes of things is a decade away at least and more likely 15 years or more, whereas something that can generate reasonable test programs is probably a lot closer. I picked a target based on the philosophy that if I'm going to get money long enough to make the ultimate thing work, I've got to show some product in near term. Test programs are the product I've chosen. This is not going to be a delivered product in 5 years; it will be a demonstration of the feasibility of producing such products. However, we are not locked in. We intend to spend this year really getting to the details and may modify the approach. But as it stands, it was sold on this particular approach.

Question: You said that there are already automatic procedures for generating the test programs for digital?

Shumaker: Yes, digital systems are in some sense easy, at least with the kinds of systems that we have deployed now. What you do is get a gate equivalent for the whole thing, feed it to a program, and let it crank away overnight or for days generating test patterns which are designed to exercise all possible data paths. If you put in this pattern, some predetermined pattern comes out the other end. If not, the pattern gives an indication of the fault. I don't want to attack the digital problem because the critics can say, "Well we are doing all right now, you are only projecting a problem." I predict that there will be a problem with digital, too, once the number of gates exceeds some critical level. But the analog is currently an unsolved problem and will work in any event, so it's a useful way to go.

Comment: It seems to me that although the digital problem is obviously a heck of a lot simpler, the fact that the digital problem has this economical solution to it right off the bat shows that this approach is a good idea.

Shumaker: Digital systems are qualitatively different from analog. One reason is that digital systems are deterministic, analog systems are not necessarily so. Every component in the circuit could be out of tolerance and the end to end performance still be within specification; the opposite can also be true. So there is a qualitative difference that means you have to move to a different level to isolate faults. The simulation methods pick a point and propagate the errors to find faults. Well, if all the components are within 10 percent tolerance, you don't get very far before all measurements become meaningless. You need to think about it in a different way for practical size circuits.

I would now like to give you some perspective of some things I've heard at this workshop. I'm very much open to dialogue and audience participation. Some of these things are purposely meant to make you mad, make you yell at me. It is my job to act as the intermediary between the people that carry out the work and the people that have the money; nobody likes what you're doing. Making those two sets of people match up is often difficult. You have to have a lot of tolerance for long time delays--there's funding time and there's real time. For example, a program that was sold last year doesn't start for another year. What does one do in the meantime? Sometimes you have some seed money to put in, but other times you'll be sitting and waiting while everybody else is, at least in theory, getting ahead of you.

I hear a lot of discussion about what is and isn't AI. The consensus about AI that I got from this workshop is that it's either too hard or it's SMOP. Does anyone know what SMOP is? SMOP is "small matter of programming." A lot of people say, "Here's my scheme, now all somebody has to do is write the software for this, and you've got it made. I gave you all that you need to know." So there's the concensus--it ranges from "This is impossibly difficult and I don't know how to proceed" to "I've just given you the answer, all you have to do is put it together."

Another conclusion from what I've heard is that if something runs, it's not AI. Once you actually get it going, it's out of the realm; once the magic is gone, it's no good. Also if it's not pure, it's not fun. That is if you have to go to mixed mode and heuristics, then it suddenly loses all its glamour and becomes an uninteresting problem from a theoretical standpoint. This last point is something that doesn't bother me, but that's because I'm "contaminated." I'll go for mixed mode if I have to make it work.

Now, I'm not a licensed program manager, I got into that accidentally. I am a licensed philosopher with a Ph.D., and I'm also a registered professional engineer--which I don't ususally say around software people because it marks me. I think that avionics maintenance is an excellent target project because values and costs are very high. Sixty percent of the faults on aircraft are avionics, not the air frame, not the propulsion, not tires. The avionics are the key to modern weapon systems. Some aircraft have 30 million dollars of electronics on board. Having to keep extra spares because the turnaround time is slow makes people want to talk to me if I tell them I can do something about it. Present methods are near the limits of their capability; that is, they work fine and were very good choices at the time, but they're saturated and don't work well with either the volume of the equipment we have or the complexity of the equipment we have now.

Equipment is now much more reliable; that is, the components are much more reliable. However, we in the military have chosen to spend our reliability of components to get more complexity, not to get system reliability. To take a very crude example, an ARC-5 from the WWII era, a simple AM transceiver, had a mean time to failure of maybe 50 to 100 hours. Well it's got five vacuum tubes in it and we can fix it fairly fast. Now, I could build an ARC-5 using integrated circuits that would have 100,000 hours mean time to failure. But I don't do that. What do I do? I build a super, covert communication spread spectrum transceiver that has much more capability, but a lower mean time to failure. That's how the military has chosen to spend increased reliability of components and I see that trend continuing. Very Large-Scale Integration (VLSI) with very high reliabilities in components is not going to be spent to make existing radars or acoustic processors more reliable; it's going to be spent to make even better ones that have the same kind of failure rates that we have now within a factor of two or three.

I think the expert systems are mature enough to have a real chance to be engineered in something. They're not ready for general use and have a lot of faults, but I think the level of maturity is enough to let us do some practical things. I see spin-offs of that, even though it's imperfect, having real live experiment on real live things is going to give a lot of information to the theorists and it's going to give us a lot of data that we might not otherwise get. If it works we'll get more data than if it doesn't, but in the failing we'll also generate a lot of information. So, it's a definite plus either way.

I also picked this area because AI has sex appeal. Most of the practitioners, however, don't have sex appeal. When they go to sell a program they don't fare well. There's a good reason for that, because you have to know what the users want to use it for and what their real problems are. If you say, "In 25 years we'll have the optimum system," they'll say "See me in 24 years." I think one thing the universities have not done well is know to whom they're selling. They have a hard time relating to the actual problem. You need to research your market the same way an industrial firm does. You can't pick your own problems and then expect people to embrace it all the time. Sometimes you can hit it lucky, but most of the time you won't.

In my case, I've said it will probably take 10 to 15 years for a fieldable, practical, workable system. That's too long a time to sell a program, because nobody's going to allow that amount of time without results. First of all, five generations of military people are going to go through the Pentagon in that time, and no individual manager wants, or can take, the responsibility for such a decision. So you've got to have intermediate milestones that make sense. If you want to maintain a high level of interest you have to have some tangible spin-offs, even if they're dirty and even if you don't want to do it. And "interest" means "funding" in this context.

I'd be glad to entertain any discussion.

Comment: It seems like sort of the heart of the approach is the idea that you can build a system that is general or has the plugs in it to make it general. But it strikes me that the expert system work so far doesn't have any success stories for general purpose anything.

Shumaker: Well, the ATE needs a lot of rules on how to use an ATE, so there's a generic aspect to whatever I plug in. How particular kinds of components work--they work the same way whether in a power supply or an RF amplifier or anything. Those kinds of general things will work the same. I propose to describe these things in a block diagram sort of form for a high level initial diagnosis and only go to descriptions of the nodes once we've got it isolated to a general area. That's the same way a technician might do it. The functional description of an RF amplifier is going to be the same whether it is in a radar or in a high frequency receiver or in anything else. Those are the generic things I think will be transferrable.

Question: I think that makes a lot of sense, but my question is where in the field of currently successful AI products is there anything like that?

Shumaker: I don't know that there are any. I don't think that this will require an AI breakthrough. I suppose its an act of faith to say that we think that the field is narrow enough and well enough known that a truly general purpose system is not needed to achieve usable results. The success in the medical field gives me confidence in that. Ninety percent of the facts about how the human body operates aren't known, but 100 percent of what makes electronics operate is known.

Comment: It strikes me that your analogy to the medical field fails because you want a medical diagnostic system that you can come in with a reel of magnetic tape and suddenly it knows how to diagnose diseases for Martians. You want a system that you put in the description of a different widget and out comes the automatic test programming.

Shumaker: Well, that would be the ultimate. I'm willing to hand code for my initial examples. I think the generic base is going to have to be hand done, the more specific class base is going to have to be hand done, and at least the first UUTs are going to have to be hand done. Ultimately, I'd like to see a CAD/CAM data base produce the specific descriptions. I think that's perfectly feasible. The kinds of things that I feel are necessary to build as rule base in the data base are just exactly the things that are in the users' manual--block diagram, functional description, schematics. And I think that if not automated ways, at least convenient ways of coding that can be found.

Comment: For example, in an ATLAS program the preamble is the same 95 percent of the time regardless of what box you're talking about. So, you get 100 or 200 lines of code and there is no reason to start from zero every time. There's the generality.

Shumaker: Our philosophy on this is that the test program is not going to start from zero every time and say what should be done first. The way I envision the actual product working is that some initial set of measurements to establish some kind of initial data base will be done, and then we go into a "think mode," if you want to look at it that way. Why should it start from zero every time? Presumably there will be historical gain in these kinds of things, that is, once we've tested a certain number of units, then we can get smarter in doing them. The test programmers don't have that advantage, because generally they don't have one of the actual products or a prototype to work from. Whereas we will be able, theoretically at least, to update this as we go along.

ABOUT THE AUTHOR

Dr. Randall Shumaker is the NAVAIR Technology Manager for maintenance technologies and flight deck equipment. Currently he is a lecturer at George Washington University in control systems, microcomputer applications and software development. Dr. Shumaker holds a Ph.D. in computer science from the University of Pennsylvania, and an M.S. degree in electrical engineering.

ARTIFICIAL INTELLIGENCE APPLICATIONS TO AUTOMATIC TEST EQUIPMENT

Jerry L. Kunert

Naval Air Engineering Center
Lakehurst, New Jersey

Abstract

The Naval Air Engineering Center (NAEC) under the sponsorship of the Naval Air Systems Command has initiated a program to develop and demonstrate artificial intelligence (AI) applications to automatic test equipment (ATE) for sharply improved Navy aircraft support operations. This paper will discuss the NAEC AI program and why such a program was initiated. The Naval Air Engineering Center acknowledges the technical support and guidance from Dr. Randall Shumaker (Naval Air Systems Command, AIR-310G) and the Navy Center for Applied Research in Artificial Intelligence.

Describing the Need

The maintenance of Navy aircraft weapon systems is of vital importance to the Navy. Modern and future Navy aircraft depend heavily upon weapon systems for a wide variety of successful missions. Aircraft weapon systems are continuously incorporating new technologies and have proliferated and grown in complexity of performance and structure. However, these systems are only of use when they are available and functioning properly. Maintaining these systems is also an increasingly difficult problem due to the increasing complexities of the systems themselves, and to personnel problems such as severe shortage of qualified personnel, low operation skill levels, and low educational levels. It is quite apparent that fault diagnosis and repair of aircraft weapon systems are becoming serious and increasing operational readiness problems.

Temporary Relief

Presently, automatic test equipment is playing a major role in the Navy's maintenance program for operational readiness of its aircraft. A typical ATE system is comprised of a test operator, an automatic test system (ATS), a test program set (TPS), and the unit-under-test (UUT). ATE is designed to analyze UUT behavior in a variety of ways, but with a minimal number of tests. Ideally, ATE performs these tasks with minimum dependence on and in smooth interaction with the test operator; or as defined by MIL-STD-1309B, dated 30 May 1975:

> "Equipment that is designed to conduct analysis of functional or static parameters to evaluate the degree of performance degradation and may be designed to perform fault isolation of unit malfunctions. The decision making, control, or evaluation of functions are conducted with minimum reliance on human intervention."

In terms of utopia ATE, the test system should be such where the test operator simply hooks the UUT up to the test system, pushes a start button, then sits back and watches the ATE perform UUT behavioral analysis.

However, ATE has encountered many obstacles hampering full aircraft weapon systems support in the Navy's maintenance program. Many of these obstacles involve reasoning in the design of the hardware or software, or in the operation of ATE itself. The hardware and software or technical problems are grouped into two categories:

1. The development of ATS to support a wide variety of UUTs whose complexity is rapidly growing.

2. The development of TPSs with sufficient insight to provide diagnostic capability for all conceivable field failures.

The operational problems of ATE can be divided into two major subdivisions of management and personnel. The management problems are related to workload characteristics and inefficient real time reporting of maintenance problems. The major personnel problems faced by the Navy maintenance program are:

1. A decreasing educational level of ATE operators in view of the continuous growth of weapon systems and ATE complexities.

2. A high turnover rate among Navy personnel resulting in a nearly impossible training situation in which inexperienced operators are being employed to replace skilled operators.

Fault diagnosis in ATE is driven by a TPS which takes weeks, months, or even years to become fully developed and critically lags the deployed UUT it supports. Although the Navy developed ATE with horizontal functional support as a goal, each specific type of UUT requires its own TPS which ranges in cost from $10K to $3M (nonrecursive costs). Surprisingly, the costs of TPSs are the primary drivers for the extravagant costs of ATE systems. Another note related to this matter, most ATE systems have reached full capacity loads of TPSs but have yet to complete horizontal support! A final physical-related problem of TPSs is the length of test time; the test time for a typical ATE system ranges from 10 minutes to 2 hours, and the run is repeated until redundant results are obtained. Generally, the isolated fault is an ambiguous group of components due to variable results obtained during the test runs.

An "open loop" approach is the method used in conventional TPSs; that is, the test operator does not know how to interpret abnormalities, programs, or hardware failure. Before a TPS is developed by a programmer, he prepares a fully explicit logic tree which provides a flow chart analysis of the test procedures. However, most logic trees are very deterministic where all of the decisions are either two state (Yes or No) or final; and they do not provide rational explanations to the test operator as to why such a decision was made or what the programmer's reasoning was. It is apparent that the programmer assumes that the test operator can deduce such facts from the logic trees; however, due to lack of documentation, these facts become implicitly lost in the logic trees.

These ATE problems have created an urgent need in the Navy to investigate and develop new technological approaches which will sharply improve ATE aircraft support operations for today's ATE and future generations of ATE.

A Proposed Technology

A review of the problems associated with ATE support operations shows a need to capture the knowledge of expert level test operators and TPS developers in some sort of medium which will transfer the knowledge to Navy maintenance personnel. Artificial intelligence technologies are capable of fulfilling such a need. Artificial intelligence provides both a development methodology and a set of implementation techniques appropriate for addressing complex problem areas, especially those beyond the reach of conventional methods. Any ATE benefitting from the application of AI technologies would become versatile, more flexible to adapt to unanticipated events, and would provide more effective guidance to the test operator.

Artificial intelligence is a new generation of computer science, although it is 25 years old, that is rapidly growing in interdisciplinary interest and practical importance to the Navy as well as industry. AI is concerned with the development of intelligent computer systems; that is, computer systems that exhibit the characteristics we associate with intelligence in human behavior. Within most scientific disciplines there are several distinct areas of research, each with its own specific interests, research techniques, and terminology. In AI, these specifications include research on language understanding, vision systems, problem solving, AI tools and programming languages, automatic programming, and several others. Many artificial intelligence researchers believe that insights into the nature of the mind can be gained by studying the operation of such programs. Whether or not they lead to a better understanding of the mind, there is every evidence that these developments will lead to a new, intelligent technology that may have dramatic effects on our society. Experimental AI systems have already generated interest and enthusiasm in industry and are being developed commercially. These experimental systems include programs that:

1. solve some complex problems in chemistry, biology, geology, engineering, and medicine at human expert levels of performance;

2. manipulate robotic devices to perform some useful repetitive, sensory motor task;

3. answer questions paced in simple dialects of English.

However, doing arithmetic or learning the capitals of all the countries of the world are certainly activities that indicate intelligence in humans. Can it be said that a computer that performs these tasks knows or understands anything? This philosophical point has been through many discussions. Although some activities other than numerical calculation and information retrieval have been accomplished by programs, many key thought processes, like recognizing people's faces and reasoning by analogy are still puzzles. These are performed so subconsciously by people that adequate computational mechanisms have not been postulated for them.

Like the different subfields of artificial intelligence, the different behaviors discussed are not all independent. Separating them out is just a convenient way of indicating what current AI programs can do and what they cannot do. Most AI research projects are concerned with many, if not all, of these aspects of intelligence. Here are a few of these different subfields of AI.

Knowledge-Based Systems, also referred to as expert systems, have produced a very general architecture for representing various kinds of knowledge, explicitly, and interpreting this knowledge as needed to perform useful work and explain its processing steps.

Automatic Theorem Proving is a mature body of knowledge for formally deducing facts and theorems from more primitive quantities which model aspects of interest in the application domain.

Automatic Programming is concerned with producing executable computer programs directly from requirements specifications, instead of higher level procedural specifications.

Game Playing and Heuristic Speech are perhaps the oldest subfields and have studied problem solving in simple but well-defined game contexts and developed many problem solving and search strategies now used in various AI subfields.

Machine Vision focuses on the difficult task of automatically interpreting sensor-produced images using computers.

Information Representation and Processing is the empirical study of representing and processing all forms of information by natural and artificial systems.

Robotics is concerned with integrating high-level planning and perception capabilities into mobile, electro-mechanical implementations capable of physically interacting with the natural environment.

Natural Language Processing seeks to provide computers with the ability to communicate with users directly in natural human languages.

There has been much activity and progress in the 25 year history of artificial intelligence. And there is more activity now than ever. AI is a relatively well funded discipline, principally in the United States, by the Defense Advanced Research Projects Agency (DARPA) and other government activities. There are active AI research groups in other countries, including Japan, Canada, Britain, France, Germany, Australia, Italy, and the USSR. Increasing research support is coming from the private sector where interest in using and marketing AI programs is on the rise. The real shortage is people; there are only a few AI research groups in universities and corporate laboratories; in terms of the number of people involved, the field is quite small.

Knowledge-Based Systems

Knowledge-based systems (KBS) have presented the highest potentials for AI applications to ATE due to their unique abilities. KBS are a subfield of AI directed towards specific problem domains such as maintenance through the logical application of rules developed by experienced personnel and stored in a special data base. KBS are composed of a collection of rules called the rule base, a collection of facts called the knowledge base, and an executable program called the inference engine. The rule base is what gives KBS the ability to make decisions and recommend actions. Rules are of the form:

IF SITUATION 1 EXISTS,
THEN PERFORM ACTION A

Hence, the rules are referred to as situation-action pairs.

The inference engine's program is basically a search and pattern match. It scans the rules in an efficient way, searching for a rule whose premise (the IF part) matches the current state or facts from the knowledge base under consideration. If a match is found, the consequent (the THEN part) is executed. The actions can be anything from manipulating the knowledge base on the rule base itself, to querying or advising the user.

A description of the MYCIN system can provide a clearer picture of KBS and can provide an insight to one of NAEC's proposed AI applications an intelligent test generator for Navy avionics. The MYCIN system was developed by Stanford University to provide consultative advice on diagnosis and selection of therapy for patients with infectious diseases. It conducts an interactive dialogue with a physician to collect information or facts from which it infers the diagnosis and selects an appropriate therapy. Besides being capable of explaining its reasoning to the physician, MYCIN employs a knowledge acquisition subsystem which helps physicians expand or modify the rule base.

The medical knowledge, or rule base, in MYCIN contains several hundred production rules (IF-THEN format) representing human expert level knowledge about the domain. The IF part of the rule, called the premise or the lefthand side, states the conditions that must be present for the production to be applicable; and the THEN part, called the action part or the righthand side, is the appropriate action to take. During the execution of the production system, a production whose premise is satisfied can fire or have its action part executed by the inference engine.

The knowledge base, or collection of facts, data, or short-term memory buffer, is the focus of attention of the production rules. The premise of each production in the rule base represents a condition that must be present in the knowlede base before the production can fire. The actions of the rules can change the knowledge base, so that other rules will have their premises satisfied. The knowledge base structure may be a simple list, a very large array, or more typically, a medium sized buffer with some internal structure of its own. In the MYCIN case, the knowledge base is constructed by acquiring a patient's record files and queries to the physician for information or facts describing the conditions or sympotms of the infectious disease.

The mechanism used to draw conclusions based on the rules in the rule base and the data for the current case is the system's reasoning process or inference engine. In the MYCIN system, rates are involved in a backward chaining fashion that results in an exhaustive depth-first search. Backward chaining, also referred to as goal driven, expectation driven, or top-down thinking, requires looking at the action parts of the rules to find out what conditions would make them fire, then finding other rules whose action parts conclude these conditions, and so on. In other words, the inference engine starts from a goal of what is to happen and works backwards, looking for evidence that supports or contradicts the hunch.

The representation of knowledge as production rules and the ability to explain specific rules allow MYCIN to interact with the physician in a manner that permits the system to acquire and apply new knowledge. When a physician is dissatisfied with the system's performance on a particular case, MYCIN is able to explain how it made the erroneous conclusions and to guide the physician while he is determining the source of reasoning; the physician elects to enter new rules or alter existing rules. He enters his requests through a nearly natural language interface.. Once this new rule or alteration is accepted and understood by the system, the next consultation will make use of it and alter its recommendations accordingly. This ability permits the system to interact directly with the domain personnel without intervention of the programmer.

KBS Versus Algorithm-Based Systems

Prior to the availability of knowledge-based systems, the only way to represent and organize knowledge was through the use of algorithm-based systems. These systems possess the following characteristics:

1. Deterministic and do not have redundancy.
2. Sharp distinction between code and data.
3. Opaque algorithms, thus difficult to modify or analyze.

4. Lack the ability to reason about or explain the techniques and mechanism that they employ.

Knowledge-based systems are a body of knowledge and simple mechanisms for applying knowledge whenever possible and useful. This feature is possible due to the rules that make up the rule set. KBS are applied to problem areas that rely on the judgment of human experts; in other words, where problems are complex and require the application of high-level rules that are judgments and evaluations of solutions. In contrast to algorithm-based systems, KBS have the following characteristics:

1. Knowledge is redundant, so the absence of one fact does not necessarily prevent the system from arriving at a result by another route.

2. A sharp distinction exists between the body of knowledge and inference engine.

3. Transparent algorithms with independent rules which allows for modifications and analysis.

4. Provision of explanations to describe the reasoning path used to arrive at a given goal.

Many problems are amenable to algorithm-based systems, but many are not; those that are not require experts to evaluate and assess situations, then make judgments based on those assessments. The selection of KBS over algorithm-based systems is basically a tradeoff between the ease of modification and intelligibility offered by the former, and the fast execution speed and low data base space requirements offered by the latter.

Potential KBS Applications to ATE

The application of knowledge-based systems can close the "open loop" test approach by developing input/output dialogue with the system user. The development of such an application would be similar to the interactive dialogue used in the MYCIN system. The following features are proposed from such an application of knowledge-based systems:

1. Has the capability of explaining its actions and reasoning processes with respect to an interaction with the user or to a solution it produces.

2. Has the capability to acquire new knowledge, modify existing knowledge, and expunge erroneous or useless knowledge.

Another application of KBS is for fault diagnosis of UUTs. First, the knowledge-based system determines what tests need to be performed and instructs the ATE or user to execute the tests. The fault diagnosis procedure is fired by developing a set of facts which describes what the system knows about the UUT. This set of facts are composed of:

1. Facts that describe the UUT and its problems or systems. The facts are acquired by the KBS, producing a sequence of queries to the test system or user.

2. An auxiliary facts table that provides finer details or specific details describing the UUT such as operational specifications, components, failure history, and failure propensity.

Next, the knowledge-based system transfers the set of facts to its knowledge base to develop a preliminary list of tests to be performed. Residing in the knowledge base is a set of rules that were experimentally verified facts of the UUT. The rules are segregated into smaller subsets according to their required tests or as more commonly known, their hypotheses. This structure will aid in establishing a depth-first search strategy. Finally, the KBS associates the initial facts to the relevant subsets from the knowledge base and associated hypotheses.

Now, the KBS instructs the ATE to execute the tests while maintaining interactive dialogue, thereby replacing the traditional ATE software that runs a battery of brute force exhaustive tests. Test evaluation would be accomplished by embodying the knowledge of expert diagnosticians. The KBS would evaluate the test results and either determine the problem directly, and the need for additional tests which would likewise be performed and evaluated, or supply its conclusion in near natural human language to the system user.

Conclusion

It is quite apparent that knowlege-based systems propose broad applicability in test program generations. Already, the following capabilities have been shown to be available from the KBS approach of test program generation:

1. No explicit logic tree is required in advance as with the traditional TPS approach. The logic tree is expanded (tests plus paths generated) as needed.

2. The rules are in the production rule format which imbed knowledge about what to do.

3. The KBS approach can reach a conclusion under uncertainty and when it encounters bad, ambiguous, or corrupted data.

4. By means of continuous interactive dialogue with the test operator or ATE, the KBS approach can improve its own

performance or expand by adding rules to the logic tree (e.g., this eliminates the need for software rewrite and ATE software center modifications).

5. The KBS reasoning for obtaining a diagnosis is not lost in the generation process due to KBS ability to provide a rational explanation to the test operator.

However, the Naval Air Engineering Center acknowledges the fact that it is undertaking a high risk project but one that is tenable. The following key points support such a declaration:

1. The KBS approach has never been attempted.

2. The initial knowledge base needed is large.

3. The electronics field is sufficiently well defined to make success possible in reasonable time.

And should success prevail, a breakthrough in electronics (analog, digital, and hybrid) maintenance would become inevitable.

REFERENCES

Avron Barr & Edward A. Feigenbaum, The Handbook of Artificial Intelligence, Volume I and II, William Kaufman, Inc., 1982.

Anthony Coppola & Lorraine M. Gozzo, "Artificial Intelligence Applications to Testability," Proc. of AUTOTESCON '82, pp. 138-142.

Jerry Kunert, "ATE Applications of Artificial Intelligence," Proc. of AUTOTESTCON '82, pp. 84-87.

Nils J. Nilsson, Principles of Artificial Intelligence, Tioga Publishing Company, 1980.

ABOUT THE AUTHOR

Mr. Jerry L. Kunert is currently the Senior Project Engineer for computer-aided maintenance aids in Navy aircraft support operations at the Naval Air Engineering Center, Lakehurst, New Jersey. He is chair of the IEEE Automatic Test Program Generation Subcommittee. He has made presentations on artificial intelligence applications at AUTOTESTCON 81, 82, 83 and the IEEE AI-Fault Tolerance Workshop. Mr. Kunert received a B.S. in electronics engineering from Monmouth College.

MODEL-BASED PROBABILISTIC REASONING FOR ELECTRONICS TROUBLESHOOTING

Richard R. Cantone

Navy Center for Applied Research in Artificial Intelligence
U.S. Naval Research Laboratory - Code 7510
Washington, DC 20375

ABSTRACT

The Navy A.I. Center is currently developing a series of increasingly sophisticated expert consultant systems for guiding a novice technician through each step of an electronics troubleshooting session. One of the goals is to automatically produce, given a set of initial symptoms, a binary (*pass/fail*) decision tree of testpoints to be checked by the technician. This paper discusses our initial approach using a modified game tree search technique, the *gamma miniaverage method*. One of the parameters which guides this search technique - the cost of each test - is stored *a priori*. The two other parameters that guide it - the conditional probability of test outcomes and the proximity to a solution - are provided by a dynamic model of an expert troubleshooter's beliefs about what in the device is good and what is bad. This model of beliefs is updated using probabilistic "*test-result → plausible-consequences*" rules. These rules are either provided by an expert technician, or approximated by a model-guided *Rule Generator*. The model that guides the generation of rules is a simple block diagram of the Unit Under Test (UUT) augmented with component failure rates.

1. Introduction

The Navy A.I. Center is currently developing a series of increasingly sophisticated expert consultant systems for guiding novice technicians through each step of an electronics trouble-shooting session. This paper describes the current, Mark I implementation. The basic design of this implementation grew out of a series of preliminary conversations with our domain expert - a master technician. Using a Tektronix Model 465 oscilloscope as a potential Unit Under Test (UUT) for particular examples, these discussions focused on the general *types* of information used in troubleshooting electronic equipment. To achieve an implementation in a reasonable amount of time, we chose for inclusion a proper yet important subset, namely:

A Priori:
- circuit topology
- cost of individual tests
- relative component failure rates
- component replacement costs

A Posteriori:
- conditional probability of test results
- proximity to a solution

In the remainder of this introduction (Section 1) we describe their importance in electronics troubleshooting, and briefly how they have been incorporated in the current implementation. The final section (Section 4) of this paper briefly discusses how other important types of information (e.g., component function) could be added to the current system. The body of this paper (Sections 2 and 3) describes in detail the current system - a novel application of heuristic search guided by a rule-based reasoning component that makes use of both traditional, expert-supplied rules and rules approximated by a novel, model-guided Rule Generator.

In principle, a technician can isolate the faulty components of an electronic device with an exhaustive search by testing every discrete, low level component (e.g., resistor or transistor.) This simple linear search can find all faults and in fact is often done when there are relatively few components to test. When there are a great many discrete components, the technician can take advantage of the hierarchical organization that designers generally impose upon complex and sophisticated circuits. In this tree-like organization the top-most branches represent the major subsystems, such as the power supply, while the bottom leaves represent the discrete components, such as the individual resistors and transistors. This organization of the search space permits the technician to consider, at each level of abstraction, relatively few components. The system, as well as others (e.g., [Davis, 1982b] and [Genesereth, 1982]), attempts to mimic the troubleshooter by starting the search for faults at the top of the component hierarchy, and then slowly moving down to lower and lower levels.

At each level in this abstraction hierarchy tree the troubleshooter must decide where to test first, and then based on the outcome of that test, where to test next, etc. In the computer programs that guide Automatic Test Equipment (ATE) these decisions are stored in a binary (*pass/fail*) decision tree. Each node in the decision tree represents the *best* test to make next, given the test outcomes represented by the arcs which lead to it from the root node. The root node represents the initial symptoms. This is similar to the decision trees produced by artificial intelligence *game tree* search algorithms, such as the A* algorithm and the alpha-beta minimax algorithm (see [Nilsson, 1980] for an excellent discussion of these algorithms.) In these decision trees each node represents the best move for a player to make next. The arcs which lead to each node represent his opponent's responses to his earlier moves.

The A* algorithm can find an solution tree which is optimal (in cost) for and/or trees, but requires a depth-first search to termination (eg., by looking ahead until a faulty component is found.) When there are many possible tests in a circuit (or many possible moves in a game) the A* algorithm can be impractical* and a shallow, suboptimal search strategy may be required. The *Alpha-beta*

* Even in this case, where there are only two branches at each "and" node (i.e., *pass/fail*), it has in fact been shown that the general problem of finding an optimal solution tree is NP-hard (see [Hyafil and Rivest, 1976] and also [Loveland, 1979].)

minimax method can allow this to be done efficiently, yet the alpha-beta method does not take into account the cost of each test. While the cost of moves in a game may be inconsequential, the cost of a test in troubleshooting can be crucial.

Still another problem with using *any* minimax method for this application is the built-in assumption that the "and" branches in the and/or search space are decided by an *opponent*. In physical systems, such as electronic devices, the "and" branches are governed by nature, or chance, and can be estimated using conditional probabilities. This observation by Slagle and Lee motivated their creation of the *gamma miniaverage method* [Slagle and Lee, 1971]. In the miniaverage method, the backed-up value of an "and" branch is not a maximum, but a weighted average - weighted by the conditional probabilities associated with each branch. It allows for efficient pruning of the search space with cut-offs, similar to *alpha-beta* cut-offs, called *gamma* cut-offs. The method can also allow for termination of the search when the expected cost of continuing the search exceeds the cost of simply replacing the suspect components.

While the cost of each test can often be estimated *a priori*, two other parameters that guide the gamma miniaverage method - the conditional probability of a test outcome, discussed above, and a static evaluation function, which estimates the proximity to a solution - are based on the results of earlier tests. Even with only 2 possible outcomes (i.e., *pass/fail*) for a test, for n possible tests there may be as many as 3^n possible combinations to consider (since each test could either *pass*, *fail*, or not be made.) Rather than require that values for these two parameters be established *a priori* for all possible combinations of test results, the system estimates these values through rule-based *simulation*.

Figure 1 shows the overall structure of the rule-based reasoning component, which is the heart of the system. Test results, real or hypothetical, are introduced one at a time to the Inference Engine. Given a test result, the Inference Engine uses a single, triggered rule to update a dynamic, *a posteriori* model of an expert technician's *beliefs* about what in the UUT could be bad and what should be good.

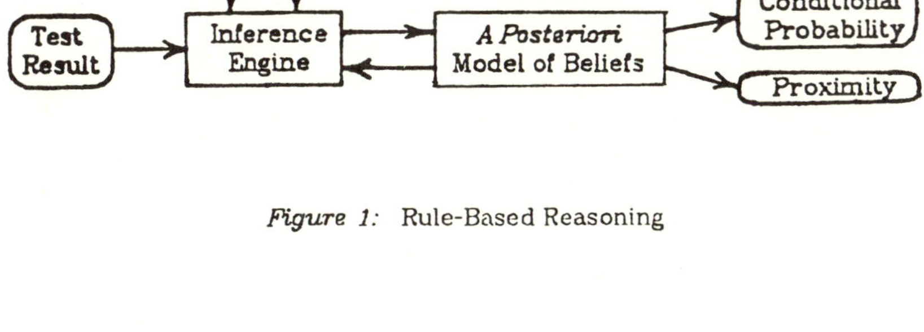

Figure 1: Rule-Based Reasoning

In the traditional *expert systems* approach, the rules used to update these beliefs would come from a stored, *a priori* collection of expert-supplied *symptom → possible-cause* rules. Randall Davis [1982a, 1982b] has pointed out that the task of extracting a separate rule from the expert for every conceivable symptom that might arise in a sophisticated piece of electronics equipment is unrealistic. Because of this, Davis stresses the importance of an alternative means with which to reason - a *model* of the system being diagnosed. Davis argues that expert systems should have *both* compiled rules (which he calls "compiled experience") and the ability to reason from a model. The system incorporates these two knowledge sources through its small expert-supplied, device-specific *a priori* rulebase, and a model-guided, device-independent *Rule Generator*.

The Rule Generator can dynamically produce rules, with the same syntax as the compiled rules, by consulting an *a priori* model of the UUT. The model of the UUT that has been implemented, thus far, is an *augmented block diagram** - augmented in the sense that it contains such non-traditional information as component failure rates. Although the rules that the system generates from its model may be less accurate than expert-supplied rules, the generated rules can fill in whatever gaps exist in the expert-supplied rulebase, and then only when needed. The motivation for this design was a statement by our domain expert that in troubleshooting any sophisticated piece of electronic equipment, including equipment with which he is very familiar, a set of block/schematic diagrams is indispensible. He also says that given a *good* set of such diagrams he can troubleshoot essentially *any* piece of analog electronics. The Rule Generator tries to capture this generality by producing *approximations* of the rules which normally make up "compiled experience."

The rules in the system, both compiled and generated, are probabilistic (or, more properly, evidential) rules of belief. Each rule is triggered by a single test result. The consequences of each rule are probabilistic assignments of guilt or innocence, given this one particular finding, to various components and lines in the UUT. These probabilistic assignments are used by the system's inference engine to update the system's *a posteriori* model of beliefs about what in the UUT is good and what is bad. Since the system does not make use of a "single fault assumption" that at most one of the UUT's components is faulty, for each component and line the system gathers *both* evidence that is it good *and* evidence that it is bad. And, because of the uncertainty inherent with approximated probabilities, the probabilities associated with these two mutually exclusive possibilities may not necessarily sum to 1. The system combines evidence from separate, independent sources (i.e., test results) using Dempster's Rule [Shafer, 1976]. Dempster's Rule does allow for a sum less than 1, yet reduces to the traditional Bayesian approach when the sum is exactly 1.

Dempster's Rule works fine for combining evidence from sources that are *independent*. But because of circuit connectivity, test results are not always independent. In the system, non-independent test results are defined as those that are taken from a common path in the UUT circuitry. The interpretation assigned by the inference engine given two non-independent results depends upon whether the tests passed or failed and upon which result is upstream or downstream from the other. For example, if two non-independent results are

* Fault isolation and testability analysis based upon block diagrams has come to be known as *logic modeling* or *logic model analysis*. One notable example of this is the STAMP system [Simpson and Balaban, 1982] which makes use of information theory to generate, in a proprietary manner, binary decision trees of the type generated by the NRL system.

both bad (good), then only the more useful - the upstream (downstream) result - is retained and interpreted by the inference engine. As another example, when one *passed* test result later clears away the blame from some component - assigned as a result of an earlier *failed* test result - that blame is *removed* from the component and the original *failed* test result is re-interpreted in light of this new information. This form of non-monotonicity has been implemented using the basic truth maintenance facility in the electronics simulation system EL [Stallman and Sussman, 1979].

The current system is made up of two basic components. Section 2 of this paper discusses the probabilistic rule-based reasoning component that guides the heuristic search component discussed in Section 3. Section 4 is a discussion of future plans.

2. Probabilistic Rule-Based Reasoning

The rules in the system incorporate probabilistic measures of belief. Probabilistic measures of belief, or certainty factors, have played an important role in such successful rule-based expert consultant systems as MYCIN [Shortliffe, 1976] and PROSPECTOR [Duda et.al., 1979]. The expert consultant system for electronics fault isolation ARBY [McDermott, D. and Brooks, R., 1982] totals "amounts" of evidence for and against hypotheses, but since these "amounts" are not related to probabilities, it does so in a very ad hoc manner [Brooks, R., 1982].

Probabilistic measures of belief can play an important role in troubleshooting electronic devices. For example, consider the simple circuit depicted by Figure 2,

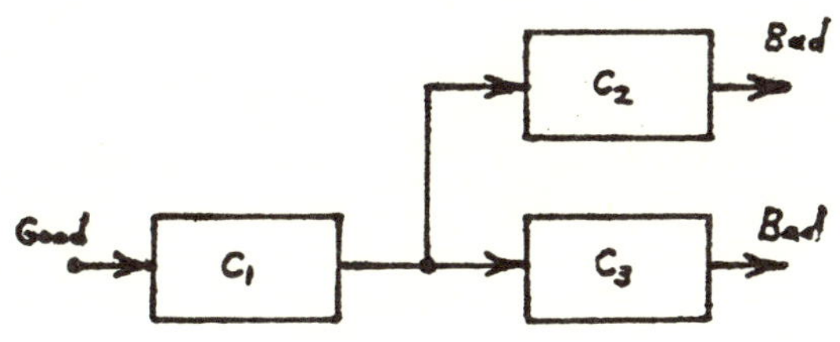

Figure 2

where it is known, through testing, that the input is good and that both outputs are bad. One explanation for these test results could be that both components C_2 and C_3 are faulty. While this is possible, and should not be ruled out, the possibility that C_1 is broken is much more *probable*.

Also, consider the slightly different circuit depicted by Figure 3, where it is known that the input of C_1 is good, the output of C_2 is bad, and the output of C_3 is good. Since the output of C_3 is good, its input must be good, which also means that one of the outputs of C_1 is good. This give *some* evidence that C_1 is good. (If it were known that *both* of the outputs of C_1 are good then we could be *completely* certain that C_1 is good.) So, in this case, C_1 is slightly *less* suspect than C_2, since there is some evidence that C_1 is good while there is none at all that C_2 is good.

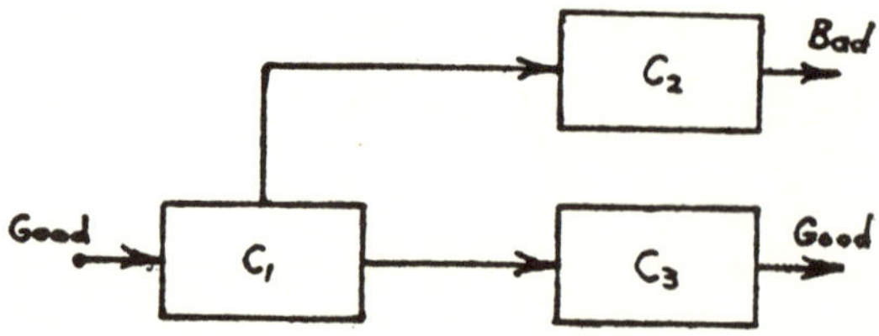

Figure 3

2.1. The Inference Rules

In expert consultant systems, relative measures of belief, such as those discussed above, have been quantized using *antecedent* → *plausible-consequences* rules. In the system there are two types of rules - rules for *passed* tests and rules for *failed* tests. Also, each rule has two parts - one suggests consequences about components, while the other suggests consequences about other test-points in the circuit. The basic syntax of the rules is described using the following rule schemata:

Rule-1a *If* there is evidence with probability x that an output of a component is bad*, *then* if there are n components which could have caused this bad output, then for each such component there is evidence (with probability $\frac{x}{n}$) that this component is broken.

Rule-1b For each input I of each of the n components indicated by Rule-1a, *if* m of these n components feed line I, *then* there is evidence (with probability $\frac{m \cdot x}{n}$) that I is bad.

Rule-2a *If* there is evidence with probability x_i that output O_i of a component with n outputs is good, *then* for each line that feeds this component, through some path, there is evidence (with probability $\sum_{i=1,n} \frac{x_i}{n}$) that this line is good.

Rule-2b *If* there is evidence with probability x_i that output O_i of a component with n outputs is good, *then* there is evidence (with probability $\sum_{i=1,n} \frac{x_i}{n}$) that this component is good.

These schemata have actually been used by our domain expert as a guide for writing device-specific rules for the Tektronix 465 Oscilloscope, with the probabilities in parentheses merely suggestions.

Rather than requiring that domain expert provide the system with such rules for every one of perhaps thousands of test-points in a UUT, the system's *Rule Generator* can approximate missing rules using information stored in the system's *a priori* model of the UUT. If information is missing from the model,

* Here, a "bad" input or output line just means that the signal on the line is not the same as when the entire UUT is good.

the Rule Generator will use the probabilities within the parentheses in the schemata above as defaults. The types of information presently stored in the *a priori* model of the UUT and used by the Rule Generator are: the circuit structure (e.g., topology), sub-structure, and relative component failure rates. For example, the Rule Generator can approximate a Rule-1a rule by making use of information about:

- *Topology:* The grossest estimate of n is the total number of components in the entire circuit. This can be cut down significantly, using simple signal tracing, by considering only those components that lie upstream from the bad output.
- *Component Failure Rates:* The probability $\frac{x}{n}$ is a default probability. The failure rate of each component is used as a weighting factor. For example, if one of the n components has exactly twice the failure rate of each of the other $n-1$ components then the probability of the evidence assigned to it would be $\frac{2x}{n+1}$ and $\frac{x}{n+1}$ for each of the others.

The Rule Generator can custom tailor a Rule-2b rule using information about:

- *Component Sub-Structure:* Some of the outputs of a component could be more informative than others. For example, output i may be affected by 90% of the component's internal sub-components. By making use of such information, the probability assigned is a weighted average rather than a simple average.

2.2. The Inference Engine

All the rules are triggered by a test result. When a new test result is entered into the system, the inference engine first looks in the small rulebase, which comprises compiled experience, for a rule that is appropriate. If there is none, it will call upon the Rule Generator to generate one. With either the retrieved or generated rule, the inference engine can then update the *a posteriori* model of beliefs about what in the UUT is good and what is bad.

In updating the model of beliefs, there are two cases that the inference engine must consider. The new test result could either contribute new independent evidence that should be *combined* with earlier evidence; or it could provide new information upon which earlier plausible inferences should be *revised*.

Combining New Independent Evidence

At any point in time, we may have evidence, say for a particular component C, that indicates with probability x_1 that C is good and y_1 that C is bad. Since exact values for x_1 and y_1 are difficult or impossible to calculate, x_1 and y_1 are simply estimated lower bounds on the true, Bayesian probabilities (i.e., $z_1 = 1-(x_1+y_1)$ may be greater than 0.)

When a new piece of independent evidence is introduced concerning C, the new evidence can be combined with the old evidence using Dempster's Rule [Schafer, 1976].* For example, suppose that new evidence suggests, with

* One notable use of Dempster's Rule has been by Garvey for integrating sensor information [Garvey, 1981]. It has also influenced Friedman's Extended Plausible Reasoning [Friedman, 1981].

probability x_2, merely that C is *good*. The uncertainty z_2 associated with this evidence is simply $1-x_2$ (since, in this case, $y_2=0$.) According to Dempster's Rule, the updated probabilities x_3 (good), y_3 (bad), and z_3 would then be computed as follows. First, using a cross product, let:

$$x'_3 = x_2 \cdot x_1 + x_2 \cdot z_1 + z_2 \cdot x_1$$

$$y'_3 = z_2 \cdot y_1$$

$$z'_3 = z_2 \cdot z_1$$

$$N = (x'_3 + y'_3 + z'_3)^{-1}$$

and then, through re-normalization:

$$x_3 = N \cdot x'_3$$

$$y_3 = N \cdot y'_3$$

$$z_3 = N \cdot z'_3$$

There are similar equations for combining new evidence that C is bad.

For example, suppose that at some moment the total probability that component C is good is $x_1=1/3$ and $y_1=1/3$ that C is bad (with $z_1=1/3$.) If new evidence is introduced with certainty $x_2=1/3$ that C is good (and with $z_2=2/3$), then the updated probabilities would be $x_3=1/2$ that C is good and $y_3=1/4$ that C is bad (with $z_3=1/4$.)

The associativity and commutativity of Dempster's Rule are very important in this application since the results of independent tests should be independent of the order in which the tests were made. The Rule's sound treatment of uncertainty is also important here, since in troubleshooting *exact* probabilities are often difficult or impossible to calculate.

Revising Earlier Plausible Inferences ("Shifting Blame")

Inferences made earlier in a troubleshooting session might need to be re-evaluated in light of new information. For example, Rule-1a rules distribute the blame for a fault among n components. If m (for $m \leq n$) of these are later cleared by a *passed* test result, then the blame assigned to these m components should be removed from them and re-distributed among the other $n-m$ components. Similarly, when the plausible blame attributed to some line L (by an instance of Rule-1b) is later *confirmed* by a *failed* test result, then the blame that had been assigned to the m components that line L feeds (by the corresponding instance of Rule-1a) should be removed* and re-distributed to the other $n-m$ components using a *new* instance of Rule-1a - one triggered by the *new* test result.

This form of non-monotonicity has been implemented using the basic truth maintenance system incorporated in the electronics simulation system EL [Stallman and Sussman, 1979]. Borrowing the terminology of Stallman and Sussman, at each moment an assertion can be believed with some certainty, and labeled *in*, if there is some well-founded support behind it (i.e., a test result);

* Although that blame is removed from these components, the components are not cleared since this test result provides no evidence that they are good, but merely that one of their inputs is bad.

otherwise it is labeled *out*. An assertion that is less than completely certain can move from *in* to *out* by the introduction of contradictory evidence that is completely certain. To implement this capability we store with each discrete piece of evidence that is less than completely certain the test result and rule that originally introduced it to *in*. This is the only information necessary for removing and re-evaluating the plausible consequences of a rule in light of new information.

3. Deciding the Best Test

The *a posteriori* model of beliefs has two basic purposes. Firstly, the system can present to the user a list of suspect components, ordered by their current probability of being faulty. This can either be done at any time, upon request from the user; or automatically, when the maximum such probabability exceeds some user established threshold. Secondly, the system can use the model of beliefs, in a *hypothetical mode*, to help decide the best test for the user to make next. If there are no initial symptoms the best test model of beliefs can be used to construct, *a priori*, a binary decision of best tests to be performed at each step of such a troubleshooting session. If there *are* initial symptoms, a custom tailored binary decision tree which takes these initial "test results" into account can be computed at the beginning of the troubleshooting session (or dynamically recomputed if the user later contributes, through his own initiative, other test results.)

The best test is basically that test which, for its cost, will bring the system closest to isolating the fault to a single component. Since there are two possible outcomes of each test (i.e.,*pass* or *fail*), the system must consider both of them separately. It does this by simulating the effect that each such outcome would have on its model of beliefs. A heuristic static evaluation function is applied, in each case, to the model of beliefs to estimate how far the system would then be to having isolated the problem to one faulty component.

We have applied the gamma miniaverage method in a straight-forward manner (and refer the reader to [Slagle and Lee, 1971] for a detailed discussion of the method itself.) The nodes in the search tree represent, on alternating levels, the possible tests that can be performed and the potential outcomes o_i of the possible tests. A static evaluation function G applied to an outcome node on the frontier of the search represents the loss, or cost, of terminating at that point. The value of the static evaluation function G which we have empirically chosen is the size of the component ambiguity set (the still suspect components.) G could also represent the total cost of replacing all of the components in the ambiguity set, if this data were known.

To calculate the backed-up value of the "and" node which represents the cost R of terminating the search after performing test T_k, the static values $G([o_i,T_k,E])$ for each possible outcome o_i of T_k (where $[o_i,T_k,E]$ represents the model of beliefs after outcome o_i of test T_k is incorporated into the model of beliefs E) are combined with the cost C_{T_k} of performing test T_k and the conditional probabilities $P_{T_k}(o_i\,|E)$ that test T_k will have outcome o_i (given the evidence E that has been accumulated thus far) using the formula

$$R(E,T_k) = C_{T_k} + \sum_i P_{T_k}(o_i\,|E)\cdot G([o_i,T_k,E])$$

An approximation of the *a posteriori* probability $P_{T_k}(o_i\,|E)$ is maintained in the system's *a posteriori* model of beliefs (see, for example, rule schemata Rule-1b and Rule-2a.) The value of $G([o_i,T_k,E])$ is calculated by statically evaluating the *a posteriori* model of beliefs. The risk R basically represents the total of the actual cost and the potential cost if the troubleshooting session were to be terminated at that point.

Since we want to choose the test T_k of minimum risk $R(E,T_k)$, the backed-up value of the "or" node which represents this decision is

$$R(E) = \min_k R(E,T_k).$$

To allow for multiple levels of look-ahead, and a better estimate of the best test, this backing-up process can be repeated as many levels as resources permit. Not only can these backed-up miniaverage values be used for estimating the best test to make next, but using gamma cut-offs, this search can be done efficiently.

4. Future Work

The algorithms have been implemented in Franz LISP on a VAX 11/780 computer and produces reasonably good decision trees for block diagrams that include series, parallel, and feedback circuits. For example, in the case of a simple series circuit where all test costs are equal, the system reduces to the standard half-split method (i.e., binary search.) In the more realistic case of a 2-dimensional circuit, where there is a real ambiguity about where the "middle" is, the system performs much better than the half-split method. In the next few months this basic system will first be applied to troubleshooting a standard oscilloscope, the Tektronix Model 465, and its performance will be evaluated by our domain expert. To test the generality of the system, it will then be applied to troubleshooting a sophisticated piece of military electronics, such as the WLQ-4 Intercept Receiver.

We will also be adding a learning component, in the style of the Self-Improving Diagnostics system SID [Hughes Aircraft Corp., 1980], to retain and periodically refine generated rules. The probabilities within a rule, initially assigned by the Rule Generator, would be changed to reflect the actual distribution encountered by the system over time.

A more difficult improvement that we will be exploring is a more *informed* Rule Generator. We will attempt to incorporate an ability to reason with knowledge about component *function* (in addition to circuit topology and component failure rates.) Also the Rule Generator should know *when* to use assumptions that narrow the set of possible faults (e.g., that faults are *always* upstream from a bad line) but are *not always* correct (see [Davis, 1982b]).

Acknowledgements

We would like to thank our domain expert, master technician Mr. Mark Hulbert, for his time and patience; Prof. Kenneth De Jong, Prof. Michael Gaynor and Dr. James Slagle for their advice; Dr. Randall Schumaker (NAVAIR) for directing our attention toward the problem of automatic test program generation (ATPG), and Dr. Jude Franklin, especially, for introducing us to the general problem of electronics troubleshooting.

References

[1] Brooks, Ruven, personal communication (June, 1982).

[2] Davis, Randall, "Expert Systems: Where are we? And where do we go from here?", pgs. 3-22, *The AI Magazine*, III, Number 2 (1982a).

[3] Davis, Randall, et. al.,"Diagnosis Based on Description of Structure and Function", in *Proceedings of the 1982 National Conference on Artificial Intelligence (AAAI-82)*,(1982b).

[4] Duda, R.O, Hart, P.E., Konolige, K. and Reboh, R., "A Computer-Based Consultant for Mineral Exploration," Artificial Intelligence Center, SRI International, Menlo Park, CA (Sept., 1979).

[5] Friedman, Leonard, "Extended Plausible Inference," *Proceedings, International Joint Conference on Artifical Intelligence (IJCAI-81)*, (August, 1981).

[6] Garvey, Thomas D., et. al., "An Inference Technique for Integrating Knowledge from Disparate Sources." in *Proc. IJCAI-81.*, (August, 1981).

[7] Genesereth, Michael R., "Diagnosis Using Hierarchical Design Models," in *Proc. AAAI-82*, (August, 1982).

[8] Hughes Aircraft Corp., "Knowledge Based Systems (KBS) Study for Advanced MATE Systems," HAC Report No. FR80-75-869 (May, 1980).

[9] Hyafil, Laurent and Rivest, Ronald L., "Constructing Optimal Binary Decision Trees is is NP-Complete," pgs. 15-17, *Information Processing Letters*, **5**, 1 (May, 1976).

[10] Loveland, Donald W., "Selecting Optimal Test Procedures from Incomplete Test Sets," in *Proc. First Intern. Symposium on Policy Analysis and Information Science*, Duke University, Durham, N.C., pgs. 228-235 (June, 1979).

[11] McDermott, Drew and Brooks, Ruven, "ARBY: Diagnosis with Shallow Causal Models", in *Proc. AAAI-82*, (August, 1982).

[12] Nilsson, Nils J., *Principles of Artificial Intelligence*, Tioga Pub. Co., Palo Alto, CA (1980).

[13] Shafer, G., *A Mathematical Theory of Evidence*,Princeton University Press, Princeton, NJ (1976).

[13] Shortliffe, Edward H., *Computer-Based Medical Consultations: MYCIN*, American Elsevier Pub. Co., New York, NY (1976).

[14] Simpson, William R. and Balaban, Harold S., "The ARINC Research System Testability and Maintenance Program (STAMP)", in *Proc. 1982 IEEE AUTOTESTCON Conference*, Dayton, Ohio (October, 1982).

[15] Slagle, James R. and Lee, Richard C.T., "Application of Game Tree Searching Techniques to Sequential Pattern Recognition," p. 103-110, *Communications of the ACM*, 14, 2 (February, 1971).

[16] Stallman, Richard M. and Sussman, Gerald J., "Problem Solving About Electrical Circuits," in *Artificial Intelligence: An MIT Perspective*, Winston, Patrick Henry and Brown, Richard Henry (eds.), The MIT Press, pgs.33-91 (1979).

ABOUT THE AUTHOR

Mr. Richard Cantone is currently engaged in designing expert systems, primarily for electronics troubleshooting, at the Navy Center for Applied Research in Artificial Intelligence. Prior to this, he worked at Rutgers University on various AI applications, including the expert medical diagnosis system, EXPERT. Mr. Cantone received his Master's degree in computer science with a concentration in natural language processing at New York University in 1978.

IMPLICATIONS OF ARTIFICIAL INTELLIGENCE FOR A USER DEFINED TECHNICAL INFORMATION SYSTEM

Robert J. Smillie

Navy Personnel Research and Development Center

Introduction

A colleague of mine, Bob Johnson at AFHRL, has developed a scenario about the Air Force technician of the not-too-distant future. In the "Sgt. Bayshore scenario" (Johnson, 1981), a female flight-line technician uses a portable delivery device to obtain technical information for maintaining and repairing aircraft. The information, accessible with the delivery device, is updated daily to reflect the latest changes and revisions to the stored information. The device provides technical information, including troubleshooting strategies, in video and audio outputs. Training information adapted to meet the needs of the individual user is available on request. Voice recognition permits direct interaction with the information data base. Available display options include step-by-step procedures and animated graphics. Although the delivery device is stand-alone and portable, there is a communications link that provides direct access to a central data bank. The inclusion of AI allows the technical information system to (1) evaluate all troubleshooting data to revise and update troubleshooting strategies and (2) determine appropriate training when training mode is engaged. Is this different from what I call a User Defined Technical Information System (UDTIS)? Probably, only by degree.

What Is a UDTIS?

UDTIS is obviously an electronic, computer-based device related to Stanley Kubrick's 2001's HAL. Size is unknown, but UDTIS has contained within it or has access to all the technical and training information of the particular operational system for which UDTIS covers. UDTIS may have multiple screens to permit simultaneous viewing of different types of technical information. Display characteristics are unknown, but it does present the technical information in a form that the user readily understands. The degree of interactiveness is also unknown, but UDTIS is more than user friendly. UDTIS has to "know" the background and capabilities of the user and has to "anticipate" the needs of the user.

What UDTIS Is Not

UDTIS is not:

1. A fully automatic device that finds 100 percent of the faults. It is a maintenance aid that integrates information from all sources--historical records, built-in test equipment (BITE), automatic test equipment (ATE),

etc.--to guide the technician through various heuristic paths until the most likely cause of the fault is found.

2. A device that factors man out of the loop. Embedded training and enrichment is a must. The intent is to provide the technician with information required to do the job at hand, while at the same time, continue to provide constantly changing training and technical information based upon the growing skills and knowledges of the technician. UDTIS has to facilitate transition from a novice technician to a skilled experienced technician.

3. A device that makes all the troubleshooting decisions for the technician. UDTIS does provide logical alternative troubleshooting paths based upon evaluation and integration of all troubleshooting data, regardless of source.

AI Implications for UDTIS

In UDTIS, AI may be required for:

1. data retrieval

2. data presentation

3. user performance monitoring

4. problem solving

5. training

Data retrieval. UDTIS has to be an efficient data retrieval device. Since it would be impossible to design a system with unlimited capabilities, a UDTIS type approach has to account for some basic assumptions about the range of users. How will users who vary within an experience level, as well as across experience levels, access the information in UDTIS? More importantly, how will information be stored and linked in UDTIS in order to provide the user with the correct data when requested? The information data base for any one system covered by UDTIS will be large. Besides the source data, UDTIS will have to have historical files on all the fielded systems, i.e., if a direct communications link is not possible, then it will be necessary to update the UDTIS historical files via additions to the memory modules in a very timely manner.

The incorporation of a natural language parser that could analyze all user input requests, in order to provide UDTIS the file tag it needed to retrieve specific information, would ease the requirement on the user to remember file tags. An alternative to a comprehensive parser is an "interactive expert" within UDTIS. The "expert" could process the initial input and continue to query the user until a match was made between the user request and the file tag for the specific information. The implication for the "expert" is the use of menus, e.g., the Knowledge Management System (KMS) (Information Technologies, 1983). Although a menu-driven system requires unambiguous input to retrieve information, the KMS structure guides the user through a hierarchical use of menus, i.e., choices, until the correct information is found. KMS has a flexibility that allows novices to browse through the data while an experienced user can jump to the specific information. Perhaps, the incorporation of an AI natural language parser within a menu-driven structure would provide for those situations where the menu approach fails.

Data presentation. UDTIS has to have the capability of providing technical information in formats compatible with several different levels of users. The Air Force's Computer-Based Maintenance Aids System (CMAS) (Thomas, 1982) is presently studying the need to provide multiple tracks of technical information to users. By having a wide range of format options available, the user can have the technical information presented according to his specific needs. In essence, the user designs his own technical manual. Since all technical jobs have to be performed according to an established standard, there will be a requirement to develop a core track of minimal technical guidance, e.g., a checklist. From this track, however, detailed and versatile tracks can be developed. Assuming that there will also be some selection criteria and possibly initial training requirements, the most detailed track can be determined.

With AI it would not be a simple matter of depressing a "help" key and obtaining more detailed information. Rather, the "system expert" in UDTIS would have to help determine why the user is having a problem and provide the appropriate information. Historical files of the user would have to be maintained and updated continuously in order for the UDTIS "expert" to provide technical information tailored to the particular user. In the display of troubleshooting information, UDTIS would have to have the capability of integrating source data in order to create a format compatible with individual user requirements.

User performance monitoring. For UDTIS to retrieve and display information in a form that is compatible with the user's needs, it will have to maintain accurate files of all users. While an ultimate in this area would be a device that constantly monitors task performance, UDTIS will, at least, have to record what types of technical information the user requested in previous encounters in order for UDTIS to "learn" what level of detail each user requires during subsequent interactions with the technical information. With the inclusion of training information, UDTIS can monitor training progress and integrate that information with the user's level of detail requirements for technical information to develop a complete model of each user's skills and knowledge.

UDTIS has to be more than a device where the user can tailor the information to satisfy his needs. UDTIS has to be able to analyze past interaction to ensure all relevant information is made available to the user. When the match between this relevant information and the user's perceived needs differ, UDTIS should have the capability to provide all the relevant information, covertly, if necessary.

Problem solving. UDTIS has to facilitate troubleshooting. Research into the troubleshooting process (e.g., Hunt & Rouse, 1981) has suggested that efficient fault isolation requires the use of both domain-free and domain-specific cognitive skills. With the domain-free skill, a strategy is formulated for initiating the fault isolation process to determine where to test. The domain-specific skills are used within this strategy to determine how to test. The results obtained from the domain-specific tests are used to modify the domain-free strategy.

The requirement for AI appears to be in the area of domain-specific skills. After a domain-free strategy is formulated to determine where to test, the UDTIS domain-specific program has to decide:

1. What test needs to be performed?

2. How to perform the specified test.

3. How to interpret the results in order to modify the domain-free strategy.

With AI to analyze user capabilities during task performance and user progress in embedded training, the formulation and modification of domain-free strategies become continually changing processes. Applied to the domain-specific area, this same information can be used to determine (1) what tests are within the capabilities of the user and (2) what level of detail is required to ensure the user performs the test correctly.

The use of AI for troubleshooting implies that there is an "expert troubleshooter" in UDTIS. The expert is more than a compilation of all the past faults and how they were corrected. It has to be heuristic. It has to integrate all the available information about a set of symptoms in order to determine the testing path that will provide the most effective information to eventually arrive at the suspected fault.

Training. As a tutoring device, AI in UDTIS can be very effective. UDTIS will have to build a unique model of each user and continually change that model as the user becomes more proficient in system knowledge and troubleshooting capabilities. Assuming that UDTIS can be used to achieve a goal of fully capable technicians who can maintain the system for which they are responsible, the tutoring requirement becomes very important.

Development of a user model will have to account for both task performance and training progress. The model will have to evolve through repeated interactions of the user with UDTIS. In task performance, UDTIS will have to collate and analyze the methods each user employs as he troubleshoots. With this information, the model of the user can be changed to reflect how well the user's performance improves or deteriorates. In addition, when the performance information is integrated with training progress, the potential for a more complete and accurate model of the user is greater than if a model was built on either training or performance information alone. With the development of an accurate model, UDTIS can be used to identify incorrect use of and missing principles in the user's application of domain-free and domain-specific skills.

Once identified, UDTIS can design an individualized training program and provide individualized guidance during the troubleshooting process.

To facilitate the learning and maintaining of troubleshooting skills, UDTIS can also be used to provide feedback to the user upon completion of a troubleshooting task. Once the faulted system has been corrected, UDTIS can evaluate the user's performance and provide immediate feedback on the quality of that performance. To evaluate performance implies that UDTIS maintains a model of an expert to which individual user performance can be compared. With the availability of an expert model, the actual troubleshooting performance can be interrupted if UDTIS "determines" that the user is pursuing an inappropriate fault isolation path. The problem, then, is that UDTIS will have to determine if and when it is "appropriate" to interrupt actual task performance.

Finally, in both troubleshooting and nontroubleshooting task performance, UDTIS can be used to determine when the presented information should be enriched. Enrichment is the addition of information to provide the user with a more thorough understanding of (1) the task being performed or (2) that part of the system being troubleshot or repaired. In other words, training information is embedded in the technical information. UDTIS would have to determine when, where, what, and how enrichment can be added.

Summary

UDTIS is an electronic, computer-based maintenance aid containing all the technical and training information relevant to a particular system. Incorporation of AI allows UDTIS to integrate automatic testing data and training progress with the technical information to modify heuristic troubleshooting strategies. UDTIS is not the ultimate in ATE or maintenance aiding, nor does it replace training.

Since the user is the focal point for UDTIS, AI can assist the user in the definition of that system by:

1. Providing complete information, even if the user does not realize initially that more information is required than requested.

2. Presenting the information in a format that is matched to the user's capabilities for the task at hand.

3. Maintaining a dynamic model of the user for modifying presented technical and training information.

4. Incorporating an expert troubleshooter to evaluate and guide performance.

5. Providing an expert trainer to design an appropriate training program that has both overt and covert components.

REFERENCES

Hunt, R. M. & Rouse, W. B. Problem-solving skills of maintenance trainees in diagnosing faults in simulated powerplants. Human Factors, 1981, 23, 317-328.

Information Technologies. Knowledge management system: An overview. Pittsburgh, PA: Author, September 1983.

Johnson, R. C. Integrated maintenance information system: An imaginary preview (AFHRL-TP-81-18). Wright-Patterson Air Force Base, OH: Air Force Human Resources Laboratory, Logistics and Technical Training Division, September 1981.

Thomas, D. Computer-based maintenance aids system: Preliminary development and evaluation of a prototype (AFHRL-TP-82-84). Wright-Patterson Air Force Base, OH: Air Force Human Resources Laboratory, Logistics and Technical Training Division, September 1982.

ABOUT THE AUTHOR

Dr. Robert J. Smillie is a Research Psychologist with the Navy Personnel Research and Development Center. At NPRDC, he has been involved in the development, implementation, test, and evaluation of a job performance aid-based integrated personnel system. His interests include the development and application of job performance aid technology for troubleshooting and nontroubleshooting maintenance tasks. As a member of the Human Factors Society study group, he was involved in developing a comprehensive long-range human factors plan for the U.S. Nuclear Regulatory Commission. Dr. Smillie received his Ph.D. in human factors from North Carolina State University.

STEAMER: AN OVERVIEW WITH IMPLICATIONS FOR AI APPLICATIONS IN OTHER DOMAINS

James D. Hollan

Navy Personnel Research and Development Center
San Diego, CA 92152

The great promise of the application of artificial intelligence software and hardware technology to the solution of problems in a variety of domains is a refrain that one hears often these days. As someone involved with research questions related to applying cognitive science and AI technology to training and other areas, I am both encouraged and fearful of the attention AI is currently receiving. I am encouraged because I too see tremendous promise in the technology and in the types of explicit computational accounts of cognition emerging from AI and the other cognitive sciences. I am fearful though that people will not be sufficiently informed to be able to distinguish what is currently possible from the promise and that something akin to the history of computer-based instruction might obtain. In this talk, I will attempt to accomplish the following:

- discuss the underlying ideas which motivated us to initiate the Steamer effort.
- attempt to give you a feel for the current status of the project.
- discuss some of the issues that have been raised by the effort.
- provide a glimpse of the directions we plan to pursue in the future.
- discuss the implications of Steamer for the application of AI to other domains.

(Further text not available at time of publication)

Invited presentation at the *Joint Services Workshop on Artificial Intelligence in Maintenance: Automatic Testing, Maintenance Aiding, and Training*, Institute of Cognitive Science, University of Colorado, Boulder, Colorado, October 4-6, 1983. Arpanet address: hollan@nprdc. Mail address: Future Technologies, NPRDC, San Diego, CA 92152.

ABOUT THE AUTHOR

Dr. Jim Hollan is the leader of a cognitive science research group at the Navy Personnel Research and Development Center. He is also a teaching faculty member at the University of California at San Diego and a member of the UCSD Cognitive Science Laboratory.

Part IV

Commercial and Industrial Development Projects

APPLICATION OF ARTIFICIAL INTELLIGENCE TO EQUIPMENT MAINTENANCE

John H. Hinchman and Michael C. Morgan

General Dynamics
Electronics Division
San Diego, CA

ABSTRACT

All military services are confronted with increased training costs, reduced training budgets and a widening gap between the skills of entry-level personnel and the abilities required to maintain increasingly sophisticated systems. Institutional training is being minimized, and more emphasis is placed on on-the-job training. This requires a greater reliance on built-in test equipment and organic automatic test equipment support. Unfortunately, automated testing (built-in or off-line) does not unambiguously fault-isolate all of the time. The result is a high rate (up to 30%) of removal and replacement of non-faulty assemblies. Reduction of the number of suspected faulty assemblies within an ambiguity group requires manual troubleshooting. The manual troubleshooting procedure used to fault isolate to a single assembly typically involves an exhaustive method of remove-replace-retest. This manual troubleshooting method is expensive in terms of both test time and logistics support. A computer-based Intelligent Maintenance Aid (IMA) offers a solution to this problem.

1. INTRODUCTION

All military services are confronted with increased training costs, reduced training budgets and a widening gap between the skills of entry-level personnel and the abilities required to maintain increasingly sophisticated systems. Institutional training is being minimized, and more emphasis is placed on on-the-job training. This requires a greater reliance on built-in test equipment and organic automatic test equipment support. Unfortunately, automated testing (built-in or off-line) does not unambiguously fault-isolate all of the time. The result is a high rate (up to 30%) of removal and replacement of non-faulty assemblies. Reduction of the number of suspected faulty assemblies within an ambiguity group requires manual troubleshooting, an exhaustive method of remove-replace-retest. This manual troubleshooting method is expensive in terms of both test time and logistics support. Our premise is that a solution lies in improving on-the-job training and job performance aids. We need to provide tools at the job site that will enable maintenance personnel to pick up where automated diagnostics leave off; thus, fault isolation and repair can be completed in a direct and efficient manner. Our approach combines enhanced job performance aiding and on-the-job training by means of a computer-based troubleshooting "coach," the Intelligent Maintenance Aid (IMA). The IMA possesses the knowledge of an expert maintenance technician and aids in fault diagnosis and fault isolation. The IMA also acts as teacher, having the capability to explain recommended actions and lines of reasoning.

2. INTELLIGENT MAINTENANCE AID

Automated test, whether built into hardware or performed off-line by special equipment, does not unambiguously fault-isolate all of the time. Our project addresses the problem of manual troubleshooting and the job performance aids that are needed by maintenance technicians in the field. Our overall approach (Figure 1) is to provide the technician with an intelligent advisor, or troubleshooting coach, that will assist in developing strategies for productive fault diagnosis and isolation. To be useful and cost-effective, these tools must have friendly interfaces, for the expert maintainer who participates in developing an application package as well as for the maintenance technician. The software must be self-tutoring to obviate specialized training and possess a supportive query mechanism.

In recent years, knowledge-based systems and system-building tools developed by researchers in artificial intelligence have been exposed to the general public. The success of programs that perform medical diagnosis (MYCIN, CADUCEUS), develop a VAX computer configuration based on customer requirements (R1 or XCON), or locate mineral deposits (PROSPECTOR), offers promise for other applications where expert practitioners are in short supply. One of those applications is the diagnosis and isolation of faults in electronic equipment.

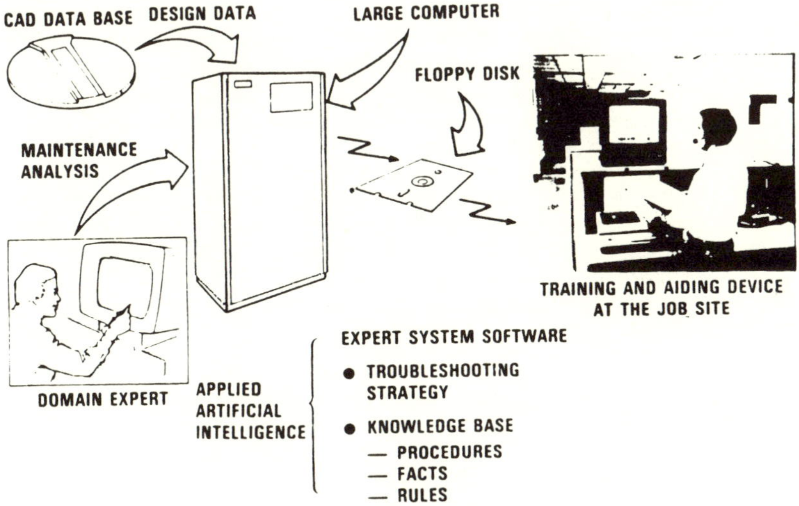

Figure 1. Computer-Assisted Fault Diagnosis

Requirements Definition – In establishing the parameters of our IMA, we first cataloged the features and capabilities of a number of existing expert systems (e.g., MYCIN, R1, DART) and expert system-building tools and languages (e.g., EMYCIN, OPS-5, ARBY). Most expert systems share a common three-part architecture:

1. Knowledge base of domain facts and heuristics
2. Inference procedure for using the information in the knowledge base for problem solving
3. Global data base, or working memory for keeping track of input data and history and status of the consultation

The key feature of this architecture is the clear separation and distinction between the knowledge base (data) and inference mechanism (control). This separation results in a high degree of extensibility; rules and facts are not intertwined within some control structure and can therefore be easily modified, added or deleted. When rules in the knowledge base include a measure of strength-of-belief or strength-of-evidence (usually represented by a numerical attribute), we have a means of handling inexactness. This is particularly useful in troubleshooting where fault isolation does not necessarily follow deterministic procedures, but rather each new finding contributes evidence to a line of reasoning. When an audit trail is maintained during a consultation, we have a means for examining the assertions (similar to popping data off a stack) that guided a particular line of reasoning. This would be difficult to do without a separation of knowledge from the inference mechanism. This explanation feature is not only useful when building a system, but also provides the basis for a training feature as well.

With few exceptions, existing systems have primitive human interfaces, both for the system builder and the end user. The reason for this is that the majority of expert systems software has been developed in an academic environment and represents research findings as opposed to production software. In most cases, the developers and target users were PhD-level (or MD) practitioners. Because of these interfaces, most systems require a go-between (knowledge engineer) to elicit and transfer the facts and rules from a domain expert to the system knowledge base. This approach to knowledge acquisition is costly and time-consuming. We need friendly interfaces that will allow expert maintainers to interact directly with the knowledge base with a minimum of training. Similarly, for our end user (the maintenance technician), the system should be self-tutoring. In addition to an explanation capability, the system should be able to assist in the "how" of gathering a new finding if necessary.

In our study of troubleshooting strategies, we find that we must consider the following as our IMA evolves:

a. Multiple Failures – The simplifying assumption of single failures, applied in some systems, results in severe performance limitations when viewed with real world expectations.

b. Temporal Reasoning – Unlike most current diagnostic systems, we are not dealing with a snapshot in time. For example, in medical diagnosis the consultation makes use of patient history and the results of recent tests. In our world of troubleshooting, our "patient" changes during the consultation. That is, during a troubleshooting session, it is not uncommon to do things like isolate a circuit, break a feedback loop or ground an input. When these changes in configuration occur, some of the assertions made previously will no longer be valid. It is necessary, then, to be able to distinguish between things that are true for all time and those facts and rules that are valid during certain event intervals.

c. Cost of New Findings – The fault isolation process usually involves reducing a candidate list of suspects to a unique problem source. We often need to gather additional data (run a diagnostic test, make a measurement) in order to reduce the list of competing hypotheses (suspects). In deciding which test to run or which measurement to make, we must consider the cost of obtaining the new finding. Here, cost is defined in terms of the time required to gather the new finding; however, cost could have other dimensions as well. For example, a prescribed action could have destructive consequences or a particular measurement may require the borrowing of assets, thereby incurring cost to the loaner. In any case, we must have a choice mechanism for requesting the new finding that will give us the most information at the least cost.

d. Top Down – Bottom Up Control Structure – For efficiency in diagnosis, we want to reduce the search and decision space as rapidly as possible. The approach is to reduce the top level problem (fault symptom) to a succession of smaller problems. This method of hierarchical decomposition is particularly well suited to electronics maintenance in that hardware is designed and described hierarchically and most troubleshooting strategies include a "divide and conquer" approach. An efficient implementation in this case is to combine two search strategies by going from the bottom up (data-driven search or forward chaining) to obtain findings that are helpful in reducing the hypothesis space used in a top-down approach. In a top-down search, hypotheses are asserted that in turn generate subgoals or hypotheses at another level of refinement (goal-directed search or backward chaining).

The ARBY system-building tool, developed by Smart Systems Technology, met most of our requirements and is documented well enough to allow changes and modifications. We procured an ARBY license, installed the software on our VAX 11/780, and began building our prototype at the end of the first quarter of 1982. The following paragraphs describe our prototype IMA.

Development of Prototype Expert System – For the target of our prototype, we selected the diagnostic task of reducing fault ambiguities in the microwave stimulus interface (MSI) of the F-16 Avionics Intermediate Shop. The MSI provides an RF stimulus over a frequency range of 10 MHz to 18 GHz to a unit under test by routing, modulating and amplifying the inputs from two frequency sources (Figure 2). The MSI has analog and digital circuitry, a feedback loop, and RF switches, thereby providing a good mix of troubleshooting problems. Examples of ambiguity groups encountered by a maintenance technician when a diagnostic test fails are presented in Figure 3. When the test fails at step 300430, and if the failure is not frequency-dependent, the technician must determine which one of eleven subassemblies has failed. The instructions to the technician at this point (from the Technical Order) are to start at the top of the list for

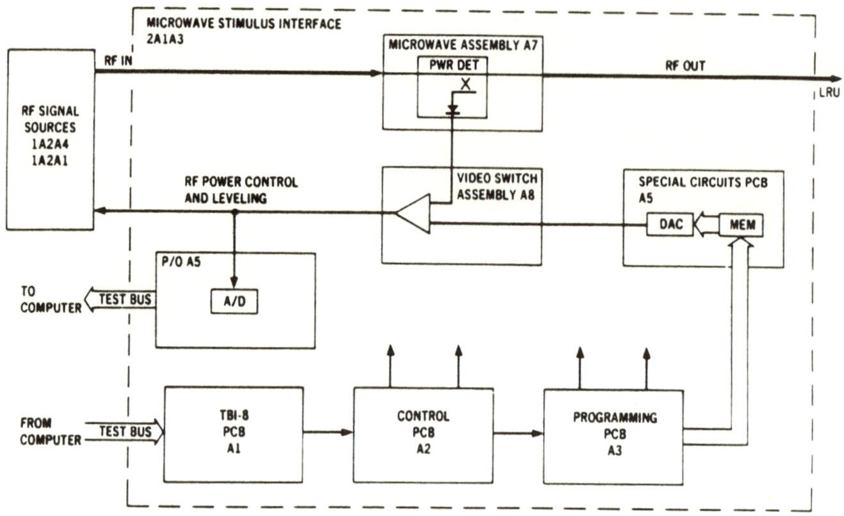

Figure 2. Problem Domain

the indicated ambiguity group and remove and replace subassemblies, rerunning the diagnostic test after each replacement until the faulty component is identified. The goal of the IMA is to help the technician to arrive at an unambiguous solution with a minimum (best case is one) of removals and replacements.

We will begin the description of our prototype with an overview of the system-building software, and follow with a sample consultation with the prototype aid.

The system-building tool we are using to develop our IMA can be viewed as a high-order language for defining both the rules that a system needs to know and the units of interaction used by the system during the process of diagnosis and fault isolation. Written in an extended dialect of Franz Lisp, the software has two principal components: The Inference Manager and Human Interface Manager. The Inference Manager is responsible for maintaining hypotheses that explain current findings. The Human Interface Manager isolates and controls the units of interaction, called interaction frames, used to gather new findings. The key feature in the Lisp extension is a mechanism to define data types. Data types provide a structure for defining the vocabulary and the configuration of the system. Once the typing is established, the system designer is forced to be consistent. This has proved to be an invaluable check, ensuring consistency of arguments in the rule structure. All inferences are accomplished using a deductive retriever module designed for the manipulation of relational databases. The declarative and procedural knowledge is represented by predicates (lists of symbols having a logical value of true or false) and forward and backward inferencing.

Step No.	Trouble	Probable Cause	Remedy
300430	1. Leveling loop inoperative at ('F') MHz. Could not reach ('Z') dBm within ± 0.5 dBm after 12 attempts		
	a. Frequency at time of failure less than 2 GHz	1. Six position coax switch	Remove and replace six position coax switch 2A1A3A7S1
		2. 10-2000 MHz RF synthesizer	Refer to RF Synthesizer 1A2A4 Manual Troubleshooting paragraph (Section II)
		3. RF switch panel	Remove and replace RF switch panel 1A2A5
	b. Frequency at time of failure less than 500 MHz	1. Low frequency directional coupler detector	Remove and replace low frequency directional coupler detector 2A1A3A7DC2
	c. Frequency at time of failure greater than 2 GHz	1. 2000 MHz–18 GHz synthesized signal generator	Remove and replace RF synthesized signal generator 1A2A1
		2. Six position coax switch	Remove and replace six position coax switch 2A1A3A7S14
	d. Frequency at time of failure greater than 10 GHz	1. Six position coax switch	Remove and replace six position coax switch 2A1A3A7S15
		2. SPDT RF switch	Remove and replace SPDT RF switch 2A1A3A7S16
		3. KU band amplifier	Remove and replace KU band amplifier 2A1A3A7AR3
	e. Persisting failure of frequency dBm not specifically covered by steps a through d above	1. Six position coax switch	Remove and replace six position coax switch 2A1A3A7S2
		2. SPDT RF switch	Remove and replace SPDT RF switch 2A1A3A7S3
		3. SPDT RF switch	Remove and replace SPDT RF switch 2A1A3A7S5
		4. High frequency coupler detector	Remove and replace high frequency coupler detector 2A1A3A7DC1
		5. Six position coax switch	Remove and replace six position coax switch 2A1A3A7S4
		6. Six position coax switch	Remove and replace six position coax switch 2A1A3A7S6
		7. SPDT RF switch	Remove and replace SPDT RF switch 2A1A3A7S23
		8. SPDT RF switch	Remove and replace SPDT RF switch 2A1A3A7S30
		9. SPDT RF switch	Remove and replace SPDT RF switch 2A1A3A7S7
		10. SPDT RF switch	Remove and replace SPDT RF switch 2A1A3A7S8
		11. SPDT RF switch	Remove and replace SPDT RF switch 2A1A3A7S9
100220	2. Excessive attenuator insertion loss at ('F') MHz Measured insertion loss not within maximum acceptable level of 10.0 dBm	a. Programmable attenuator	Remove and replace programmable attenuator 2A1A3A7AF1
		b. Programmable attenuator	Remove and replace programmable attenuator 2A1A3A7AF5
		c. SPDT RF switch	Remove and replace SPDT RF switch 2A1A3A7S7

Figure 3. Ambiguity Groups for Manual Troubleshooting

In building the knowlege base for a diagnostic consultation, there are three tasks that the domain expert must perform:

1. Identify the fault-related findings
2. Define hypotheses to explain the given findings
3. Provide the means to gather more information when appropriate

Findings are simply assertions of predicates. At the top level, for example, an initial finding might be the frequency at which a certain diagnostic test failed. Based on the frequency at the incidence of failure, a predicate is asserted in the knowledge base. The hypothesis manager then attempts to find hypotheses, which are now subgoals, to explain the given findings. Once a subgoal is validated, it becomes a finding for the next level of refinement. The validated subgoal can also remain at the current level, as a finding in a compound hypothesis needed to explain some other hypothesis.

To refine hypotheses, we must have the ability to gather information as the consultation evolves. This capability is provided by the Interaction Frame mechanism that solicits information as needed. The most common way in which an interaction frame is triggered is when a backward chaining rule is trying to validate a subgoal. After an interaction frame has been run, new assertions are present based on the information supplied by the user. Examples of Interaction Frames (IFs) built for MSI troubleshooting are illustrated in Figures 4 and 5. The IF of Figure 4 is called early in the consultation to narrow down to a particular ambiguity group. Figure 5 shows the IF that recommends checking one of the frequency sources.

Currently, interaction frames consist of 10 fields:

1. ifargs – Arguments of the IF that allow the passing of parameters to the IF. An example is the "switch" argument of Figure 5 that enables one IF to refer to a specific switch depending upon which actual switch is in the call.
2. qtemplate – The template that contains the question that is asked of the user when the IF is run. Variables passed as arguments (ifargs) are placed in the message where an argument match occurs.
3. description – Provides additional information to the user, if needed, regarding the requested action.
4. goodanstest – Define the acceptable user response.
5. clarification – The answer to a user "why" query. Tells the user why the information is needed.
6. assertions – The predicates to be asserted depending upon the answer supplied by the user; e.g., referring to Figure 4, if the user answers the question with 2, meaning the frequency at incidence of failure was between 500 MHz and 2 GHz, then the predicate (freqfailform between500MHz2GHz) is asserted in the data base and becomes a new finding. Note that any word marked by ? is a pattern-matching variable.
7. forms – Expressions that invoke the IF. Instantiation of the form during the inference process causes the frame to run.
8. how – Enables the user to ask assistance in acomplishing the task associated with the IF.
9. cost – A qualitative measure of the cost to accomplish the IF task.
10. comment – Used by the system designer to comment on the purpose, results or side effects involved with the frame.

Defining Rules – The system designer defines two types of rules:

1. accounts-for rules
2. evidence rules

```
.. ....what-freq-if
.1 ifargs: ()
2 qtemplate: ('What was frequency at time of failure?

        1. Less than 500 MHz.
        2. Between 500 MHz and 2 GHz.
        3. Between 2 GHz and 10 GHz.
        4. Above 10 GHz.
        5. Persistant failures, not specific to frequency.

Enter menu selection.
')
3 description: ('We need to know the frequency at time of failure.')
4 goodanstest: (member *1 '(1 2 3 4 5))
5 clarification: ('I need this to continue and the frequency is included in the DIAG
6 assertions: (((eq *1 1) (call (new-finding (freqfailform less500mhz))))
             ((eq *1 2) (call (new-finding (freqfailform between500mhz2ghz))))
             ((eq *1 3) (call (new-finding (freqfailform between2ghz10ghz))))
             ((eq *1 4) (call (new-finding (freqfailform above10ghz))))
             ((eq *1 5) (call (new-finding (freqfailform persist-var-freq)))))
7 forms: ()
8 how: ()
9 prereqs: ()
10 cost: 1
11 comment: (())
```

Figure 4. Example of a High-Level Interaction Frame (IF) Used Early During a Consultation Session to Narrow Down the Faulty Component Within an Ambiguity Group

```
switch-status-if
1 ifargs: (switch)
2 qtemplate: ("Check status of " @switch " and report 'good' or 'bad'.")
3 description: (" ")
4 goodanstest: (memq *1 '(good bad))
5 clarification: (" ")
6 assertions: (((eq *1 'good) (switch-check ?switch good))
              ((eq *1 'bad) (switch-check ?switch bad)))
7 forms: ((switch-check ?switch ?status))
8 how: ()
9 prereqs: ()
10 cost: 20
11 comment: (())

w>a
nil
-> (ifed  panel-status-if)
panel-status-if
1 ifargs: ()
2 qtemplate: ("Check status of the rf switch panel and report if 'good' or 'bad'.")
3 description: (" ")
4 goodanstest: (memq *1 '(good bad))
5 clarification: (" ")
6 assertions: (((eq *1 'good) (panel-check rf-switch-pan good))
              ((eq *1 'bad) (panel-check rf-switch-pan bad)))
7 forms: ((panel-check ?dev ?status))
8 how: ()
9 prereqs: ()
10 cost: 5
11 comment: (())
```

Figure 5. Interaction Frames (IFs) Used to Isolate the Faulty Component for Failures Between 500 MHz and 2 GHz

Figure 6 has examples of accounts for rules and evidence rules. Accounts-for rules have the form:

(accounts-for ?hypothesis ?finding ?given)

In Figure 6, the accounts for rule afl-2 states

"The hypothesis that the probable cause of failure is switchl accounts for the finding that the frequency at incidence of failure was between 500 MHz and 2 GHz."

Accounts-for rules are used to generate hypotheses. The refinement process is aided by the second class of rules, the evidence rules:

(evidence ?choicename ?option /comment/ ?amount)

In Figure 6, the evidence rule evl-2 states:

"There is strong evidence (weight of 100 points) that the probable cause is switchl if switchl switch-check shows switchl is bad."

This illustrates part of the implementation for handling inexactness. If, at this level of refinement, a faulty switch 1 would only provide weak or suggestive evidence (such as when there are competing suspects), the number of points for strength-of-evidence would be considerably lower than 100. The choice mechanism of the inference procedure keeps track of the evidence during refinement. Evidence rules are usually backward chaining rules. A backward chaining rule is stated by (<-consequent antecedent) with the antecedent becoming a subgoal. The antecedent is the form that is associated with an interaction frame. If there is an instantiation of this form, an IF will be invoked.

Sample Consultation – The trace of an actual diagnostic session between a user and the intelligent advisor is presented in Figures 7 and 8. The user responses are indicated after the prompts > or w >. The principal purpose of this simplified example is to demonstrate the rich query mechanism available to both the user and the designer. The first query is the step number at which the diagnostic test (DIAG MSI) program failed. The user knows that DIAG failed at step number 208210 and selects the frequency associated with that step.

Upon specification that the frequency at incidence of failure was between 500 MHz and 2 GHz, the advisor now has three hypotheses (obtained from afl-2, afl-3 and afl-4) to explain the failure.

The goal now is to reduce the number of hypotheses. To accomplish this, evidence rules are examined, together with the cost of obtaining the evidence. Since the cost of the panel-status-if is lowest (cost=5), it gets run first (Figure 8). In response to this request, the user entered "reason" in order to look at the current goal stack. There are two stacks currently active; one reasoning that the panel is bad and the other reasoning that the panel is good. Entering "1 why" here allows us to examine goal stack #1, indicating that the supergoal is the consequent part of the rule evl-4. Since it is a backward chaining rule, the antecedent part of the rule proves the supergoal; i.e., the predicate (panel-check rf-switch-pan bad). This, of course, is what the IF is attempting to deduce.

The next input from the user was an up-arrow, meaning move up the goal stack. This shows that a test of the panel was selected to gather evidence in favor of accounts-for rule afl-4 (prob-cause rf-switch-pan).

```
af1-2
(accounts-for (prob-cause s1) (freqfailform between500mhz2ghz) t)

ev1-2
(<- (evidence ?c (prob-cause s1) |check switch| 100)
    (switch-check s1 bad))

ev1--2
(<- (evidence ?c (prob-cause s1) |check switch| -100)
    (switch-check s1 good))

af1-3
(accounts-for (prob-cause rfsynth2ghz) (freqfailform between500mhz2ghz) t)

ev1-3
(<- (evidence ?c (prob-cause rfsynth2ghz) |check rfsource| 100)
    (rfsource |2GHz| bad))

ev1--3
(<- (evidence ?c (prob-cause rfsynth2ghz) |check rfsource| -100)
    (rfsource |2GHz| good))

af1-4
(accounts-for (prob-cause rf-switch-pan) (freqfailform between500mhz2ghz) t)

ev1-4
(<- (evidence ?c (prob-cause rf-switch-pan) |check panel| 100)
    (panel-check rf-switch-pan bad))

ev1--4
(<- (evidence ?c (prob-cause rf-switch-pan) |check panel| -100)
    (panel-check rf-switch-pan good))
```

Figure 6. Examples of Accounts-for Rules (af 1-2, af 1-3, af 1-4) and Evidence Rules (ev1-2, ev1--2, ev1-3, ev1--3, ev1-4, ev1--4). See text for further explanation

```
-> (consult)
1. At which step does DIAG MSI fail?

        1. 208210
        2. 211450
        3. 212610
        4. 216150
        5. 600585

Enter corresponding menu number.

>1
2. What was frequency at time of failure?

        1. Less than 500 MHz.
        2. Between 500 MHz and 2 GHz.
        3. Between 2 GHz and 10 GHz.
        4. Above 10 GHz.
        5. Persistant failures, not specific to frequency.

Enter menu selection.

>2
New finding: (freqfailform between500mhz2ghz)


Choosing (hypothesis (freqfailform between500mhz2ghz) t)          [choice21]
among
(OPTION 0 (prob-cause rf-switch-pan) ((af1-4) ()) ())
(OPTION 0 (prob-cause s1) ((af1-2) ()) ())
(OPTION 0 (prob-cause rfsynth2ghz) ((af1-3) ()) ())

Outcome of choice21
Losers :
()
Winners:
((OPTION 0 (prob-cause rfsynth2ghz) ((af1-3) ()) ((total) ()))
 (OPTION 0 (prob-cause s1) ((af1-2) ()) ((total) ()))
 (OPTION 0 (prob-cause rf-switch-pan) ((af1-4) ()) ((total) ())))
```

Figure 7. A Sample Consultation from a Diagnostic Session for the Microwave Stimulus Interface

```
Choosing (hypothesis (freqfailform between500mhz2ghz) t)          [choice21]
among
(OPTION 0 (prob-cause rfsynth2ghz) ((af1-3) ()) ((total) ()))
(OPTION 0 (prob-cause s1) ((af1-2) ()) ((total) ()))
(OPTION 0 (prob-cause rf-switch-pan) ((af1-4) ()) ((total) ()))
Trying test (iframe panel-status-if (tup))

3. Check status of the rf switch panel and report if 'good' or 'bad'.
?reason
1  --fumbled DPTHING--
(stack for goal (panel-check rf-switch-pan bad))
2  --fumbled DPTHING--
(stack for goal (panel-check rf-switch-pan good))
w>1 why
^ Supergoal: (evidence choice21 (prob-cause rf-switch-pan) ?_17 ?f)
1 Rule: ev1-4
>>>> GOAL: (panel-check rf-switch-pan bad) <<<<
w>^
^ Supergoal: (**Evaluating choice (OPTION 0 (prob-cause rf-switch-pan)
                              ((af1-4) ())
                              ((total) ()))
                **)
>>>> GOAL: (evidence choice21 (prob-cause rf-switch-pan) ?_17 ?f) <<<<
w ^
^ Supergoal: (**Searching for Hypothesis to Account for (freqfailform between500mhz2ghz)
               given t **)
Why this rule has succeeded so far:
1 af1-4
>>>> GOAL: (**Evaluating choice (OPTION 0 (prob-cause rf-switch-pan)
                                          ((af1-4) ())
                                          ((total) ()))
                            **) <<<<
w u
 good
... ufetch returned t

Trying test (iframe switch-status-if (tup s1))
```

Figure 8. A Sample Consultation from the Trace of a Diagnostic Session for the Microwave Stimulus Interface

```
4. Check status of s1 and report 'good' or 'bad'.
=good
... ufetch returned t


Outcome of choice21
Losers :
((OPTION -100 (prob-cause rf-switch-pan)
          ((af1-4) ())
          ((total ev1--4 panel-check68) ()))
 (OPTION -100 (prob-cause s1) ((af1-2) ()) ((total ev1--2 switch-check73) ())))
Winners:
((OPTION 0 (prob-cause rfsynth2ghz) ((af1-3) ()) ((total) ())))
No further abduction for (FINDING (freqfailform between500mhz2ghz)
                                   ()
                                   ((choice21
                                     (OPTION 0 (prob-cause rfsynth2ghz)
                                               ((outcome75 af1-3) ())
                                               ((outcome75) ()))))))
Hypothesis level 1
Score: 0.

      1   (freqfailform between500mhz2ghz) completely accounted for by
            (prob-cause rfsynth2ghz)
    [1]
w 1 why
**Hypothesis element** 0 (prob-cause rfsynth2ghz)

Justification
1 (outcome chosen (prob-cause rfsynth2ghz)
           choice21 (hypothesis (freqfailform between500mhz2ghz) t)
           0)
2 af1-3
w 1 why
outcome75 (outcome chosen (prob-cause rfsynth2ghz)
          choice21 (hypothesis (freqfailform between500mhz2ghz) t)
          6w
```

Figure 8. A Sample Consultation from the Trace of a Diagnostic Session for the Microwave Stimulus Interface (Continued)

Typing "q" at the prompt w > returns the advisor to the state of waiting for a response to the question initially posed by the IF. By responding "good" at this point, the advisor deduces that the switch panel is not at fault.

There are two hypotheses left at this point. Once again, more information is required and the IF with the lowest cost is invoked. By responding "good" after request 4 (Figure 8), the user has stated that switch 1 is working. This concludes the consultation. The advisor does not ask about the third possibility because it has concluded, by process of elimination, that the failed element is the RF synthesizer.

The above example illustrates how the designer can use the query mechanism and the goal stack to validate lines of reasoning. Similarly, the technician can turn to the query mechanism for help in obtaining new findings ("how"). For example, rather than remove and replace switch 1, the technician is instructed to determine switch status by running a software diagnostic.

3. SUMMARY

We have established the basic requirements for a computer-based Intelligent Maintenance Aid (IMA) for electronic equipment. We have a prototype system running, with knowledge base development directed toward realistic problems. The issues of multiple failures, temporal reasoning and cost of findings are extremely important in fault diagnosis and have been considered in the design of our system. Future work is required to reduce the cost of building the knowledge base and to provide improved interfaces, both for the domain expert and the maintenance technician. When fielded, the IMA will increase productivity in the maintenance shop while reducing the incidence of replacement of non-faulty assemblies.

ABOUT THE AUTHOR

John H. Hinchman, Engineering Staff Specialist with General Dynamics Electronics Division, is responsible for research and development in applied artificial intelligence. His research interests involve the application of artificial intelligence technology to the domain of electronics maintenance. He has developed a prototype expert system for diagnosing and isolating faults in electronic equipment and has produced user friendly interfaces for job performance aids using computer graphics, videodisc technology, speech synthesis, and speech recognition. Awarded an M.S. from the Florida Institute of Technology in 1970, Mr. Hinchman has published technical papers in system design and data collection and analysis.

KNOWLEDGE BASED TOOLS FOR ELECTRONIC EQUIPMENT MAINTENANCE

Thomas Lee Williams

Smart Systems Technology, Suite 300
6870 Elm Street
McLean, VA 22101

Abstract

The sophisticated weapon systems on which our national defense depend pose considerable maintenance problems. Increased training costs, reduced training budgets, and a widening gap between the skills of entry-level personnel and the abilities required to maintain such weapon systems suggests the need for improved job performance aids and on-the-job training. Knowledge based tools for electronic equipment maintenance offer a novel approach to this problem. In this paper we present our experience at Smart Systems Technology over the past eighteen months in building knowledge based maintenance aids for electronic equipment. The presentation begins with a discussion of ARBY in the context of the Network Diagnostic System, and concludes with an overview of the Knowledge Engineering Language.

1. Introduction

The tremendous maintenance problem presented by the sophisticated weapon systems on which our national defense depends is well known and widely documented. Increased training costs, reduced training budgets, and a widening gap between the skills of entry-level personnel and the abilities required to maintain such weapon systems suggests the need for improved job performance aids and on-the-job training. Knowledge based tools for electronic equipment maintenance offer a novel approach to this problem. In recent years knowledge based systems have been successful in tasks as disparate as medical diagnosis (CADUCEUS) and VAX computer configuration (R1). The success of these projects offers promise for other applications where expert practitioners are in short supply, and electronic equipment maintenance is a leading candidate.

At Smart Systems Technology we have been building knowledge based tools for equipment maintenance over the past eighteen months. Our first project, supported by General Dynamics Electronics Division, involved the design and implementation of ARBY [1], a programming environment for the construction of knowledge based maintenance aids. As part of that effort we implemented an intelligent advisor for aiding maintenance technicians in troubleshooting faults in the F-16 Avionics Intermediate Shop, a system that is continuing to evolve at GDE [2].

Over the past year, with the support of Shell Development Company, we have been developing the Network Diagnostic System (NDS), a knowledge based system for the isolation of multiple failures in a nationwide communications network [3]. As a result of our experience with NDS, and the earlier work with General Dynamics, we have more recently undertaken, again with the support of Shell Development Company, the implementation of the Knowledge Engineering Language (KEL), a new knowledge based systems implementation language inspired by ARBY, but modified on the basis of practical experience. The remainder of this paper is a presentation of the evolution in our approach to knowledge based aids for electronic equipment maintenance. The presentation begins with a discussion of ARBY in the context of the NDS project, and concludes with an overview of KEL.

2. A Case Study

The Network Diagnostic System is a knowledge based maintenance aid that assists a human technician in diagnosing multiple faults in a nationwide communications network (COMNET). Our effort in this project focused on understanding the effort required to implement an expert system and on identifying missing features in the existing technology. In the process of implementing NDS it was necessary to extend existing expert systems technology dealing with multiple and intermittent failures. The domain was chosen on the basis of prior domain experience with trouble shooting electronic equipment, the availability of a domain expert, and by expected benefits from the eventual operational system. Criteria considered during the scoping of the project were that it require less than one person year of effort, that it be a non-trivial application, and that it avoid excessive uninteresting detail.

2.1 The problem

COMNET is a geographically distributed communications network supporting a variety of application systems. The application software runs on a central computing facility and is accessed remotely by users throughout North America via interactive terminals. The communication path from each user terminal to the central computer is a circuit (called a 'virtual wire') composed of both digital and analog electronic devices. The field repairable units, i.e. the components which can fail and be repaired, include telecommunication processors, statistical multiplexors, modems, telephone circuits, frequency divisional multiplexors, RS-232 cables and computer terminals (see fig. 1.).

Diagnostic inference in COMNET draws upon several different types of knowledge. The topology of the network, and in particular the virtual wire which has failed, is fundamental in guiding the diagnostician's search for the fault. In general the diagnostician will try to exploit hierarchical search methods. To optimize the search the diagnostician must know which diagnostic tests are available, what their information content is in terms of which components they test, and their cost. Actual physical devices have limited test points which are chosen by the designer, not the diagnostician. As a result, diagnosis is often driven by the availability of test points and diagnostic tests. There is the additional factor of accessibility for certain tests. In cases where the diagnostician does not have the required access to perform desired tests he must proceed as far as possible on the basis of incomplete or partial information, often resorting to alternative types of knowledge, such as frequency of failure data.

COMNET can fail in several modes and in general the single failure and non-intermittency assumptions do not hold ([4,5]). Because the function of the various components in a virtual wire are closely inter-related, it is often the case that one failure will lead to, or cause, other dependent failures. For example, a statistical multiplexor may be inadvertently reset, and as a result it will reset the baud rate on a remote modem with which it communicates. Multiple failures can also be independent. When a user cannot access an application system he may tamper with the terminal, RS-232 cables and/or the modem. As a result, there could be, in addition to the original failure, several unrelated independent failures. The presence of telephone circuits introduces frequent intermittent failures due to noise in the telephone equipment, and such intermittent failures can collaborate with unrelated

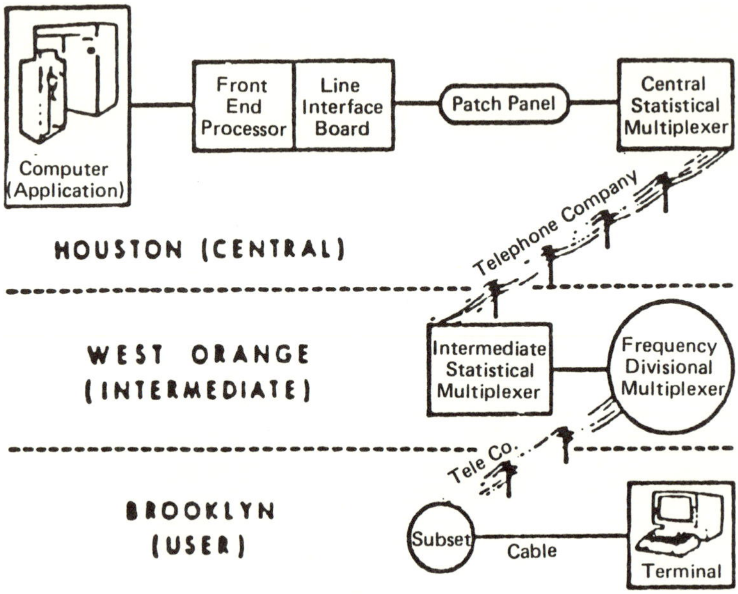

Figure 1. COMNET

failures elswhere in the network to generate multiple independent failures. It is also possible for repair operations to fail, further restricting the assumptions the diagnostician can reasonably make.

2.2 ARBY

Because our problem was one of fault isolation within an electronic system, we chose ARBY as our implementation vehicle for NDS. ARBY was designed by Drew McDermott and Ruven Brooks for Smart Systems Technology specifically for applications in electronic fault diagnosis. For a more detailed discussion of ARBY see ([6]).

Fault isolation problems are represented in ARBY as heuristic search through a space of successively more refined hypotheses as to where the fault is located. Each hypothesis has associated with it an evidence weight which is a numerical measure of the current evidence for or against that hypothesis. Evidence weights are used in choosing among competing hypotheses, as will be described shortly. The evidence for and against the various hypotheses is obtained from the available diagnostic tests.

Terminal hypotheses are hypotheses which assert that the fault is in a field replaceable unit (FRU). When ARBY has isolated down to a terminal hypothesis it invokes a repair operation for the corresponding FRU. Since each diagnostic test yields information about certain components, the tests, or more accurately the evidence derived from them, partitions the set of terminal hypotheses into subsets that are viewed as intermediate hypotheses. The possible evidence will again partition the set of intermediate hypotheses, and this process is repeated until a hierarchical structure has been defined on the hypotheses. This hierarchical structure is the starting point of the refinement graph which facilitates hierarchical search techniques, greatly improving the efficiency of the search.

The hypothesis refinement algorithm, shown in figure 2., proceeds as follows. At each stage in the search there is a current hypothesis. The current hypothesis is replaced by its set of refinements, as determined by the hypothesis refinement hierarchy. A choice is then made among the competing hypotheses based on relevant evidence. If the chosen hypothesis is a terminal hypothesis, the appropriate repair operation will be invoked. Otherwise, the chosen hypothesis is an intermediate hypothesis, in which case it becomes the new current hypothesis, and the refinement process is repeated. If, at any point, there is insufficient evidence to choose among competing hypotheses, the set of competitors is returned as an ambiguity group. After a repair operation has been performed, the termination test is executed. If this test is satisfied, the ARBY consultant terminates. Otherwise it assumes there are more faults and continues isolating.

When a choice must be made among several competing hypotheses, evidence rules which increment or decrement evidence weights of one or more of the competing hypotheses will be activated. Evidence rules define how evidence, i.e. the outcomes of diagnostic tests, affect the evidence weights of relevant hypotheses. In the event that multiple evidence rules could be activated at a choice point, the ARBY control mechanism will choose the evidence rule that will have the maximum impact on the decision with the minimum cost. The impact of the decision is defined in terms of the redistribution of evidence weights on the competing hypotheses. As soon as a clearly superior hypothesis emerges, it is chosen, eliminating the need to run additional evidence rules and reducing the overall cost. The algorithm is shown in figure 3.

The cost of an evidence rule is defined in terms of the diagnostic tests that must be performed to activate that rule. If a particular test has already been run, the cost to an evidence rule requiring it is zero. Otherwise the cost of a rule is the cost of any tests it requires, plus the cost of any prerequisite tests. Tests will not be re-run unless changes in the environment, such as the replacement of a component, require it.

Interaction with the human diagnostician is handled through interaction frames. Associated with each diagnostic test is an Interaction Frame which contains information as to how that test is performed. The information is organized hierarchically in increasing detail so the human diagnostician can request additional information as required. The Interaction Manager also provides an explanation facility to explicate the diagnostic inference up to any arbitrary point.

2.3 NDS

The Network Diagnostic System is a knowledge based maintenance aid implemented in ARBY which assists a human technician in isolating and repairing faults in COMNET, described in section 2.1. NDS uses a refinement graph constructed from eleven terminal hypotheses and eight intermediate hypotheses (see figure 4). Most of the diagnostic tests, of which there are twelve including the termination test, are loop-back tests which test subsections of the virtual wire. The rule base, including evidence rules and interaction frames (see [1],[6]), consists of approximately 150 ARBY rules. The current version of NDS required approximately four person-months of knowledge engineer and one person-month of domain expert. In the diagnostic expert's opinion the present level of performance of NDS is comparable to an intermediate level diagnostician. The rate at which new rules were added increased significantly toward the end of the project, due to increased understanding of the diagnostic process

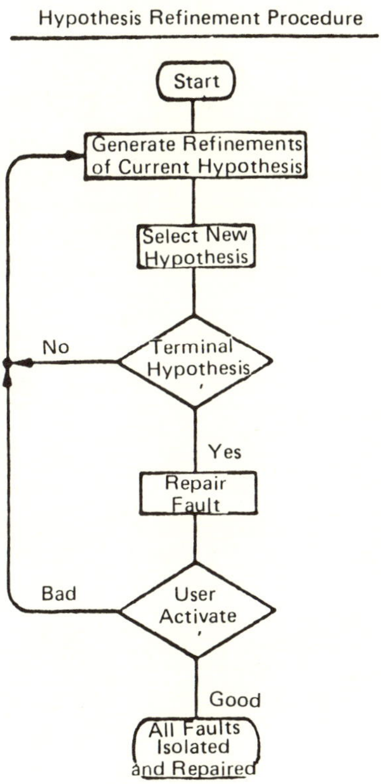

Figure 2. Hypothesis Refinement

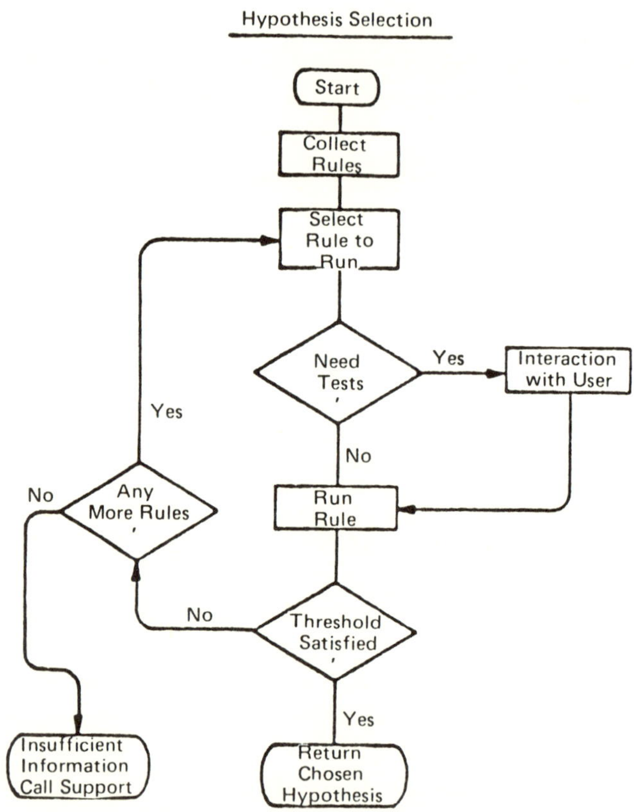

Figure 3. Hypothesis Selection

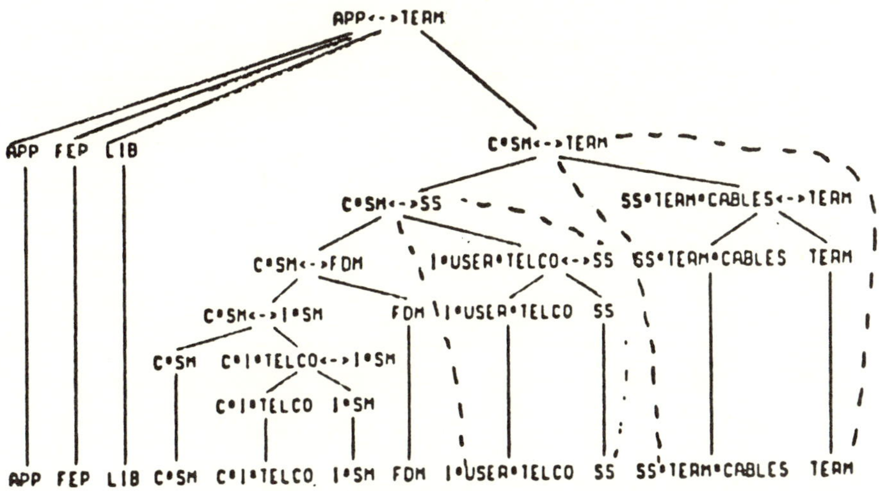

Fig. 4. NETWORK HYPOTHESIS STRUCTURE

by the knowledge engineer and increased understanding of the implementation method by the domain expert.

The NDS project demonstrates the feasibility of constructing expert systems for isolation and repair of multiple faults in electronic systems. The project also points out two hurdles to large scale deployment of expert systems in commercial environments. First is the labor intensive nature of current knowledge engineering practice. In many commercially desirable domains the expertise required is extremely valuable and of limited availability. Ultimately it will be necessary to develop methods for at least partially automating the construction of expert systems. In this vein we are currently exploring algorithms for automatically generating the refinement hierarchy for ARBY based consultants. Second is the absence of a commercial quality expert system implementation vehicle which is a stable, supported product and which runs on the variety of machines in use in the commercial sector. We are also actively working to overcome this second hurdle by designing and implementing KEL, a Knowledge Engineering Language descended from ARBY, and studying the requirements for porting it to machines such as the IBM 4300 and the new generation of microcomputers.

3. KEL

Our experience with ARBY suggested enhancements to the system at both a conceptual and pragmatic level. The underlying problem structure representation of ARBY proved extremely well suited to diagnostic inference, and has been substantially retained in KEL. The implementation has changed considerably to facilitate a much simpler, faster, and more portable system. There are two general, or philosophical, respects in which KEL differs from ARBY. First, KEL is intended to be a knowledge engineering workbench for construction of knowledge based maintenance aids. Since we have found that certain basic features of control in diagnostic inference vary from domain to domain, we have made these features parameters of the system. KEL is, in a sense, a language schema which must be instantiated by specific values for certain parameters. These parameters include the threshold function used in selecting the next hypothesis, the choice function used in selecting rules, and the strategy for pursuing multiple failures.

A second difference between KEL and ARBY, and most other expert systems languages for that matter, is its relationship to LISP, the implementation environment. Most systems of this type create a new software environment on top of LISP. The basic functionality of LISP is available at the new level, but only through a potentially obscure and often inconvenient interface. Since we have found routine access to most of LISP's functionality to be essential in constructing knowledge based systems, we have taken a different approach. KEL extends the functionality of LISP through the introduction of additional data and control structures suited to diagnostic applications, but does not create a new environment which in any way isolates the knowledge engineer from LISP. LISP and KEL fully interact, using LISP's conventions.

The requirements that motivated the design of KEL are quite similar to those behind ARBY. First, it is essential that the system continue diagnosis even in the absence of complete and reliable evidence. Second, the system must be able to isolate and repair multiple failures. In practice, these two requirements are necessities. They also imply a third condition; that the system be capable of representing sequences of events, and use its knowledge of previous stages in a diagnosis to guide future behavior. For example, when faults remain after isolating and repairing a fault, the diagnostician needs to know what previous tests have been performed and their values in order to know whether the state of the device has changed, and how. Finally, the system should minimize the overall cost of diagnosis by optimizing its evidence gathering strategy.

KEL, like ARBY, is based on the state transition model, with hypotheses corresponding to states, and refinements corresponding to transitions. The state transition algorithm uses evidence rules to allow a best first strategy, and backtracking to accomadate partial knowledge. Special data structures, called registers, are used to represent sequences of events and control user interactions. The next section describes KEL in more detail.

3.1 KEL Data Structures

Since KEL is fully integrated with LISP, all the data structures and operations available in LISP are available in KEL, including atoms, lists, strings, numbers, arrays, etc. There is an additional data structure, called the register, that behaves like a LISP variable in that it can store values. There are two differences, however. First, in addition to operations for setting and retrieving the values of registers, there are explicit PUSH and POP operations that allow registers to behave like stacks. By PUSHing successive values of a diagnostic test onto a register it in effect becomes a history of that test, previous values being accessible by a generalized GETR routine. The second difference is that registers can be defined as input or evidence registers, in which case they are assigned additional information necessary for conducting interactions with the user. This information includes a message requesting that a test be performed, the cost of the test, and explanations as to how and why. If, when an evidence register's value is accessed, it is undefined, the information associated with the evidence register is used to conduct a user interaction. The value input by the user becomes the new value of the evidence register. Otherwise the current value of the evidence register is returned. An example of a register definition is shown in figure 5.

```
(DEFREG   USER-ACTIVATE

RANGE    '(MEMBER T NIL)
COST     10
MESSAGE  "PLEASE INPUT THE VALUE
         OF THE USER-ACTIVATE TEST"
WHY      "I NEED TO KNOW WHETHER SERVICE
         HAS BEEN RESTORED"
HOW      "INSTRUCT THE USER TO
         TRY TO LOGON"

);  CLOSE REFREG
```

Fig. 5. A KEL Evidence Register Definition

3.2 KEL Control Structures

There are two special control structures in KEL; states, which are implemented as LISP functions, and a State Transition Control construct, STC. STC is a combination of an iteration construct and a conditional branching construct. In LISP terminology, a blend of DO and COND. The syntax for the STC expression is:

```
(STC

     <termination-clause>

     <transitions>

     <rules>

     <interpretation-function>

).
```

The <termination-clause> is a two element list consisting of a termination condition and a value to be returned upon termination, as in the Franz Lisp DO construct. The <transitions> expressions is a list of transitions, or function calls, that can be made from the current STC clause. Each transition has a label by which it is referenced within the STC clause, and a preference weight that may be used by the transition selection algorithm in selecting the next transition to evaluate. <rules> is a list of antecedent-consequent rules, the antecedents being arbitrary LISP expressions possibly containing KEL evidence registers, and the consequents being assignment statements that alter the weights associated with the active set of transitions.

In keeping with the philosophy of a knowledge engineering workbench, there is no fixed interpretation to the STC expression. Its interpretation is determined by the <interpretation-function> passed in as the last argument. If this argument is not provided, a standard system default interpretation function is used. The virtue of this approach is that the same STC expression can have different interpretations within a diagnosis depending on how it is used. For example, the diagnosis can switch from best-first to depth-first, or change its threshold operator in the state transition algorithm. The basic functions of the interpretation function are to: 1) determine the termination condition for the STC expression, 2) select the next transition to evaluate, and 3) select the next rule to evaluate when needed. Examples of intermediate and repair states are given in figure 6.

```
EXAMPLE KEL STATE
(DEFSTATE   CSM-SS   ()
(STC

[  (L1               (CSM-FDM)          0)
   (L2               (IUT)              0)
   (L3               (SS)               5)
   ]
[ (`LOOP-BACK:TERM-SS                   (SETW L3 'MIN))
  ( (NULL `LOOP-BACK:TERM-SS            (SETW L3 'MAX))
  ( `LOOP-BACK:CSM-FDM                  (SETW L1 'MIN))
  ( (AND `LOOP-BACK:TERM-SS
         `LOOP-BACK:CSM-FDM)            (SETW L2 'MAX))
  ]
  [ (OR `USER-ACTIVATE `LOOP-BACK:CSM-SS)   T ]
  ); CLOSE STC
  ); CLOSE DEFSTATE
```

```
EXAMPLE KEL REPAIR STATE

(DEFSTATE TERM ()

(MSG   "THE FAULT IS IN THE TERMINAL"   CR
       "CALL THE TERMINAL REPAIRMAN"   CR
       "TYPE 'DONE' WHEN THE REPAIR HAS
       BEEN COMPLETED"   CR)

(READ)

(RE-INIT-REGS '(ONLY LOOP-BACK:TERM-SS
                     LOOP-BACK:CSM-SS
                     LOOP-BACK:CSM-TERM
                     USER-ACTIVATE))

); CLOSE DEFSTATE
```

Figure 6. KEL State Definitions

3.3 Future Work on KEL

Application of the knowledge based approach to maintenance aiding is still in its infancy. There are many significant accomplishments to be made before knowledge based maintenance aids come under wide spread use. In conclusion, we mention some of them with respect to our experience with ARBY and KEL.

Ultimately, the time consuming process of hand coding human expertise must be automated. A solution along these lines would consist of a KEL like general interpreter that accepts representations of devices as input and 'evaluates' them with respect to evidence, isolating and repairing faults. Lacking such a general solution, semi-automatic means of constructing the knowledge bases currently required by KEL are essential. In the same spirit, more of the bookkeeping associated with building a KEL based diagnostic system should be automated. For example, KEL should keep track of which test results are anomalous, and, after invoking a repair operation, automatically reset the corresponding evidence registers to undefined and continue the search for additional faults from the appropriate point. And finally, with respect to the human interaction facility, KEL should allow mixed interaction in which the technician can volunteer information which KEL will respond to appropriately. Although the first objective is ambitious and not likely to be forthcoming in the short term, progress on the latter three goals is within reach.

4. References

1. McDermott, D. and Brooks, R. "ARBY: Diagnosis With Shallow Causal Models". Proc. of the National Conference on Artificial Intelligence, Pittsburgh, Pa., 1982, 278-283.

2. Williams, T. and Hinchman, J. "A Knowledge-Based Maintenance Aid for Diagnosing Faults in Electronic Equipment", Prodeedings of AUTOTESTCON, 1983.

3. Williams, T., Orgren, P., and Smith, C., "Diagnosis of Multiple Faults in a Nationwide Communications Network", Proceedings of IJCAI, 1983, Karlsruhe, West Germany.

4. Davis, R., et al. "Diagnosis based on Description of Structure and Function". Proc. of the National Conference on Artificial Intelligence, Pittsburgh Pa., 1982, 137-142.

5. Genesereth, M. "Diagnosis Using Hierarchical Design Models". Proc. of the National Conference on Artificial Intelligence, Pittsburgh, Pa., 1982, 278-283.

6. McDermott, D. and Brooks, R. ARBY Manual. Smart Systems Technology, Falls Church, Va., 1982.

ABOUT THE AUTHOR

Mr. Thomas L. Williams, Vice President and Senior Knowledge Engineer of Smart Systems Technology, has been involved with projects to develop a knowledge engineering language (KEL), diagnostic expert systems, and other knowledge-based power tools. Dr. Williams holds an M.S.E. in computer and information science and is a Ph.D. candidate in computer and information science at the University of Pennsylvania.

DELTA: AN EXPERT SYSTEM FOR DIESEL ELECTRIC LOCOMOTIVE REPAIR

Piero P. Bonissone and Harold E. Johnson, Jr.

Knowledge Based Systems Program, and
Flexible Automation Systems Program
Corporate Research and Development
General Electric Company
Schenectady, NY 12345

ABSTRACT

In recent years, expert systems have become the most visible and the fastest growing branch of Artificial Intelligence. General Electric Company's Corporate Research and Development has applied expert system technology to the problem of troubleshooting and the repair of diesel electric locomotives in railroad "running repair shops." The expert system uses production rules and an inference engine that can diagnose multiple problems with the locomotive and can suggest repair procedures to maintenance personnel. A prototype system has been implemented in FORTH, running on a Digital Equipment PDP 11/23 under RSX-11M. This system contains approximately 530 rules (roughly 330 rules for the Troubleshooting System, and 200 rules for the Help System), partially representing the knowledge of a Senior Field Service Engineer. The inference engine uses a mixed-mode configuration, capable of running in either the forward or backward mode. The Help System can provide the operator with assistance by displaying textual information, CAD diagrams or repair sequences from a video disk. The rules are written in a representation language consisting of nine predicate functions, eight verbs, and five utility functions. The first field prototype expert system, designated CATS-1 (Computer-Aided Troubleshooting System - Version 1), was delivered in July 1983 and is currently under field evaluation.

INTRODUCTION

In the last few years, expert systems [7-9] have become the most visible and the fastest growing branch of Artificial Intelligence [1,5,12,14]. The objective of these systems is to capture the knowledge of an expert in a particular problem domain, represent it in a modular, expandable structure, and transfer it to other users in the same problem domain. To accomplish this goal, it is necessary to address issues of knowledge acquisition, knowledge representation, inference mechanisms, control strategies, user interface, and dealing with uncertainty.

There are various approaches to the representation of the expert's knowledge, spanning from logic [11], to semantic network [3], frames [10] and production rules [6,13]. Each representation has its own advantages and disadvantages, and this paper will limit itself to the description of an expert system implemented using production rules.

Rule-based expert systems consist of a body of knowledge (knowledge base) and a mechanism (inference engine) for interpreting this knowledge. The body of knowledge is divided into _facts_ about the problem, and heuristics or _rules_ that control the use of knowledge to solve problems in a particular domain.

The facts represent atomic pieces of evidence describing the problem to solve. They can be generated at the beginning of the session, by asking the user a fixed sequence of questions that establish the current problem at hand. Facts are also generated throughout the session as a direct result of system inference, and as additional questions are asked of the user.

The rules are conditional statements expressed in a subset of English, thus easy to understand. Each rule consists of a situation recognition part (premise) and an action part (conclusion). The situation part expresses some condition on the state of the data base, and at any given point it is either satisfied or not. The action part specifies changes to be made to the data base whenever a rule is satisfied.

The inference engine is an interpreter of the facts and the rules. Its task is to monitor the facts in the data base and execute the action part of those rules that have their situation part satisfied. The inference engine can operate forward (event-driven) or backward (goal-driven). In the forward mode, it tries to arrive at a goal, starting from the available facts. In the backward mode, it selects a goal and then verifies whether or not the supporting facts are present or can be inferred.

PROBLEM AND PROPOSED SOLUTION

The General Electric Company's Corporate Research and Development has applied expert system technology to demonstrate the system's feasibility in the area of troubleshooting. To test these techniques, the problem selected was the repairing of diesel electric locomotives in "running repair shops": railroad maintenance personnel must detect and repair a large variety of faults that have partially disabled a diesel electric locomotive. The a priori information available to them is the list of "symptoms" reported by the engine crew. More information can be gathered in the shop, by taking measurements and performing tests that may consume excessive "shop time" if performed by inexperienced personnel.

The result of this development effort is a rule-based expert system, DELTA (Diesel Electric Locomotive Troubleshooting Aid) [2], which guides the troubleshooter in his task, enforcing some disciplined troubleshooting procedures that will minimize the cost and time of the corrective maintenance.

A prototype system has been implemented in FORTH, running on a Digital Equipment PDP 11/23 under RSX-11M. (The system also runs on a PDP 11/70 under RSX-11M-PLUS and in emulation mode on a VAX 11/780 under VMS.) This system contains approximately 530 rules, partially representing the knowledge of a Senior Field Service Engineer. Roughly 330 rules are devoted to the fault diagnosis and repair procedures, i.e., the Troubleshooting System, while about 200 rules form the Help System. The Troubleshooting System uses a mixed-configuration inference engine based on a backward chainer and a forward chainer, as illustrated in Figure 1. The Help System, uses the forward chainer of the same inference engine to respond to requests for information from the expert system. When the user hits the "HELP" key, the system provides additional information, such as the location and identification of locomotive components, replacement part classification, and description of repair procedures. To accomplish this task, the system uses CAD files stored in TEKTRONIX line graphics format and VIDEO pictures stored on a laser video disk.

A pictorial description of a session with this expert system is illustrated in Figure 2. A fixed sequence of questions is used to gather the initial facts about the locomotive problem, such as unit number, model year, reported symptoms, etc. An associative information table provides additional facts, such as unit standard features, unit history of failures, model failure propensity, etc. All these facts constitute the starting point for the troubleshooting process.

The set of rules (heuristics) that embeds the empirical knowledge about the diesel electric engine is functionally partitioned into knowledge spaces such as mechanical system, electrical system, etc. Within each knowledge space, the rules are subdivided according to hypotheses (fault areas), such as Operator Error, Engine Unable to Make Power, etc.

A set of meta-rules (a smart index of the knowledge partitions) retrieves from the various knowledge spaces the subsets of rules associated with all the hypotheses that could be relevant to the initial symptoms. This collection of hypotheses constitutes a preliminary diagnosis. Working in a backward mode, the interpreter tries to prove or disprove each hypothesis, based on both initial facts and additional facts inferred by the system or asked of the user.

The result of this process is a final diagnosis that indicates the successful hypotheses (faults) and their corresponding corrective actions (repairs).

INFERENCE ENGINE

This expert system is based on a mixture of control strategies, since its inference mechanism can work in either forward or backward mode (Figure 1).

When the initial facts are input by the user, the META-RULES load a set of HYPOTHESES and a set of IFF-RULES, IF-RULES and WHEN-RULES (see discussion of rules below).

The BACKWARD INTERPRETER then tries to evaluate each hypothesis with the given set of rules and current facts. The evaluation of a hypothesis (goal) is a three-step process. First, the system scans the list of facts to verify whether the hypothesis is already known to be true or false. If this is the case, then evaluation terminates. Otherwise, the system scans the conclusion of each rule to determine whether the hypothesis could be proved by at least one rule. In such a case, the system recursively evaluates each clause (sub-goal) in the premise of that rule. Finally, when no hypothesis (or argument) can be directly inferred by a rule, the system requests information from an external source (either the user or a sensor).

During this deductive process, new evidence (NEW FACT) needed to prove a hypothesis could be inferred by the BACKWARD INTERPRETER or input by the USER/SENSOR. When NEW FACT is written in the list of facts, the FORWARD INTERPRETER is activated. This interpreter scans the META-RULES, IFF-RULES, IF-RULES and WHEN-RULES, trying to execute any rules containing NEW FACT in their premise.

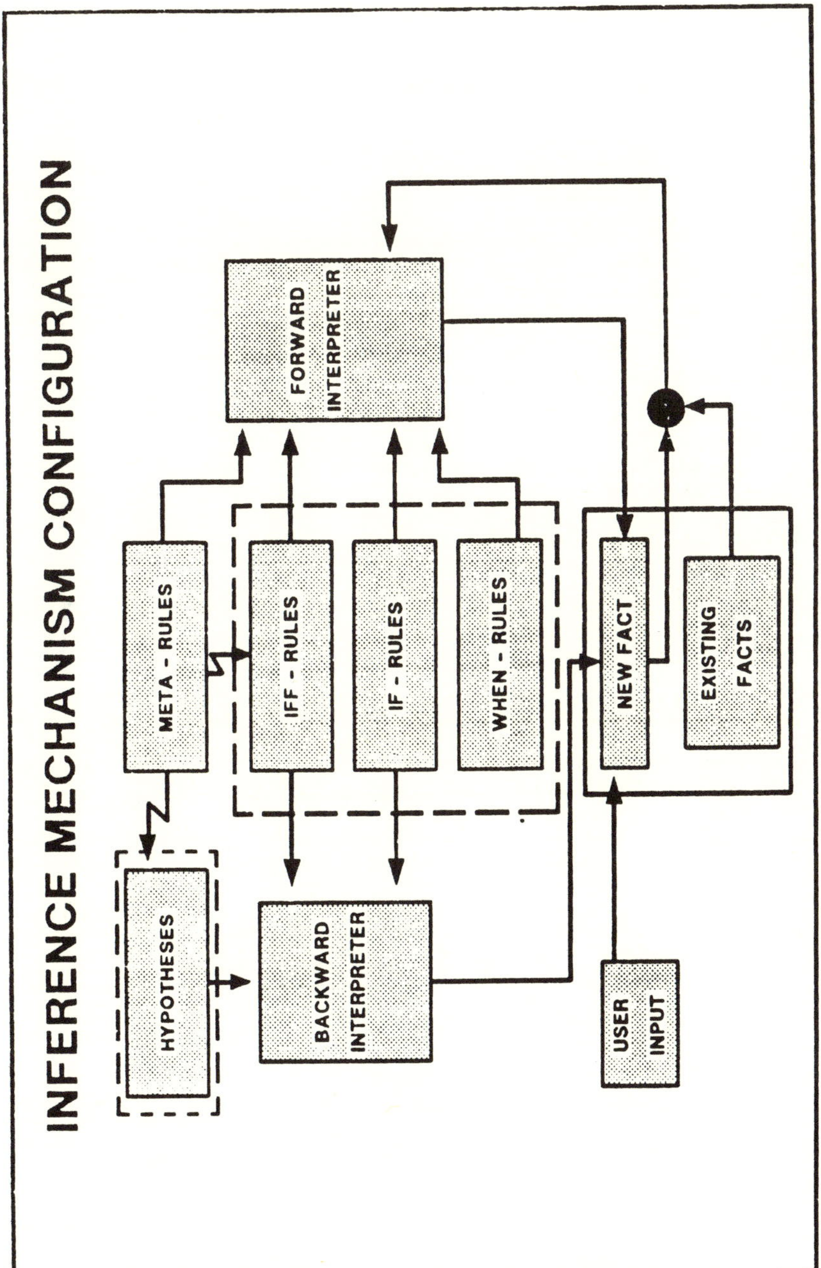
INFERENCE MECHANISM CONFIGURATION
FORWARD INTERPRETER
META - RULES
IFF - RULES
IF - RULES
WHEN - RULES
NEW FACT
EXISTING FACTS
HYPOTHESES
BACKWARD INTERPRETER
USER INPUT

Figure 1.

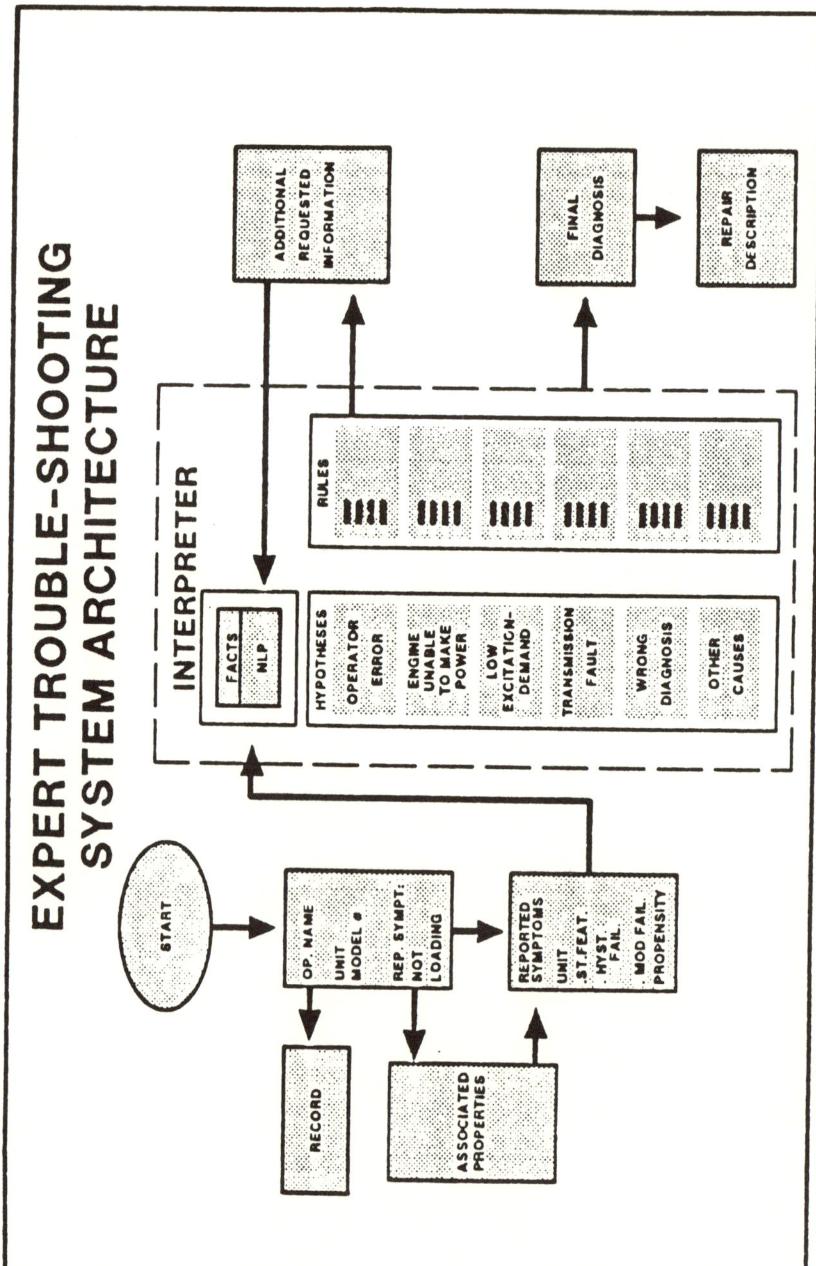
EXPERT TROUBLE-SHOOTING
SYSTEM ARCHITECTURE
START
OP. NAME
UNIT MODEL #
REP. SYMPT.: NOT LOADING
RECORD
ASSOCIATED PROPERTIES
REPORTED SYMPTOMS
UNIT
ST. FEAT.
HYST. FAIL.
MOD FAIL. PROPENSITY
INTERPRETER
FACTS
NLP
HYPOTHESES
OPERATOR ERROR
ENGINE UNABLE TO MAKE POWER
LOW EXCITATION-DEMAND
TRANSMISSION FAULT
WRONG DIAGNOSIS
OTHER CAUSES
RULES
ADDITIONAL REQUESTED INFORMATION
FINAL DIAGNOSIS
REPAIR DESCRIPTION

Figure 2.

The META-RULES verify whether or not some new knowledge (new set of hypotheses and corresponding IFF-RULES, IF-RULES or WHEN-RULES) is required and whether or not the existing knowledge should be reorganized, by reordering the set of current hypotheses, as a result of the presence of NEW FACT.

The IFF-RULES and the IF-RULES try to find some new evidence that can be inferred directly, based on the presence of NEW FACT. The new evidence could later provide a shorter path in the deduction process. These rules can be accessed by both the backward and forward chainers. IFF-RULES are "if-and-only-if" type rules (if A then B, and if not-A then not-B). IF-RULES are "if-then" type rules (if A then B).

The WHEN-RULES attach properties and activate procedures associated with NEW FACT. These rules can only be accessed by the forward chainer, thus preventing the backward chainer from using them to establish some goal. WHEN-RULES are "when-then" type rules (when A then B).

If any of the above rules has a fully satisfied premise (since no explicit rule-chaining or user-prompting is allowed during the evaluation of rules in the forward mode), then the FORWARD INTERPRETER executes that rule, writes another NEW FACT, and iterates again. This forward-chaining process stops when no rule can be executed by the FORWARD INTERPRETER, and control is returned to the BACKWARD INTERPRETER.

The BACKWARD INTERPRETER will continue its deductive process, until a hypothesis is proved or the entire set HYPOTHESES has been exhaustively evaluated.

REPRESENTATION LANGUAGE

The rules that form the knowledge base of the Troubleshooting System and the Help System are written in a special representation language. This user-extensible language currently contains:

- nine predicate functions to describe the conditions of the premise of each rule,
- eight verbs to describe the actions and inferences in the conclusions of each rule,
- five utility functions to interact with the user and display alphanumeric, graphic or pictorial information.

Each rule is a conditional statement describing the logical implication:

(premise) $\xrightarrow{cf}$ (conclusion)

The weight "cf" is the certainty factor, a number between -1 and 1, which indicates the strength of such implication. This number is used to control the propagation of uncertainty in rule-chaining, to control the combination of different pieces of evidence supporting the same conclusion, and to evaluate the overall degree to which a premise is satisfied.

Each premise is an intersection of clauses. Therefore, a premise is satisfied if <u>all</u> its clauses are also satisfied. In this case, the intersection of clauses corresponds to a boolean AND. However, this operation could be extended to a fuzzy intersection, e.g., MIN, if the truth-value of the clauses can take values within the interval [-1,1].

Each clause is defined by a predicate function and an argument composed of a 3-tuple <object attribute value>. Each clause is satisfied if its predicate function returns a true-value when applied to its argument.

Each conclusion is a disjunction of actions that are executed once the premise of the rule has been satisfied. Each action is defined by a verb and an argument.

Moreover, there are five utility functions that can be present in the premise or in the conclusion of the rule. These functions are transparent to the rule interpreter, in the sense that they do not affect the truth-value of the premise and do not modify the list of facts. The purpose of these functions is to help the user with text, graphics or video-images. These functions form the basis of a rule-driven help system.

A listing of the predicate functions, verbs and help-functions is provided in Appendix I. Appendix II illustrates three rules of the Expert System, describing a fault in the locomotive fuel system, and two rules of the Help System describing related available information.

CONCLUSION

The first field prototype of this expert system has already been implemented in a rugged unit, packaged by COMARK, containing a PDP 11/23 (running RSX-11M and an enhanced version of fig-FORTH), a 10 mega-byte Winchester disk, a VT100 terminal and a Selanar graphics board. A SONY laser-video-disk player and an additional color monitor complete the configuration of this field prototype system. The system has already shown promising results since its recent delivery to the General Electric Company's Locomotive Operation in July 1983. The mixed-mode configuration of its inference engine performs very well. The FORTH implementation proved to be easily transportable to small microprocessor-based systems while maintaining fast execution speed. The man-machine interface is very user-friendly and allows the user to interact with the system via menu selections or simple (single keystroke) answers such as: Yes, No, Unknown , Why?, Help.

During the next six months, the locomotive troubleshooting system will be tested in the field to verify the accuracy of its knowledge base and the reliability of the hardware configuration. In the following phase of this project, the knowledge base will be expanded to approximately 1200 rules, to cover, with increased depth, a larger portion of the problem space.

REFERENCES AND RELATED BIBLIOGRAPHY

[1] A. Barr, E. A. Feigenbaum, "The Handbook of Artificial Intelligence" vol. 1 and 2, William Kaufmann Inc., Los Altos CA, 1982.

[2] P. P. Bonissone, "Outline of the Design and Implementation of a Diesel Electric Engine Troubleshooting Aid", Proceeding of Expert System 82, pp. 68-72, Brunel University, Egham, England, September 14-16, 1982.

[3] R. J. Brachman, "On the Epistemological Status of Semantic Network", in "Associative Networks, Representation and use of Knowledge by Computers", pp. 3-50, Academic Press, 1979.

[4] E. Charniak, C. K. Riesbeck, D. V. McDermott, "Artificial Intelligence Programming", Lawrence Erlbaum Associates, Hillsdale, NJ, 1980.

[5] P. R. Cohen, E. A. Feigenbaum, "The Handbook of Artificial Intelligence" vol. 3, William Kaufmann Inc., Los Altos CA, 1982.

[6] R. Davis, B. Buchanan, "Production Rules as a Representation for a Knowledge-Based Consultation Program", Artificial Intelligence, vol. 8, pp.15-45, 1977

[7] R. Davis, D. Lenat, "Knowledge-Based Systems in Artificial Intelligence", McGraw-Hill, 1982.

[8] F. Hayes-Roth, D. Waterman, D. Lenat, "Building Expert System", Addison Wesley, Reading, MA, 1983.

[9] D. Michie, "Expert Systems in the Micro Electronic Age", Edinburgh University Press, UK, 1979.

[10] M. Minsky, "A Framework for Representing Knowledge" in "The Psychology of Computer Vision", pp. 211-277, McGraw-Hill, 1975.

[11] N. J. Nilsson, "Principles of Artificial Intelligence", Tioga Press, Palo Alto, CA, 1980.

[12] Y. Pao, G. W. Ernst, "Context-Directed Pattern Recognition and machine Intelligence Techniques for Information Processing", IEEE Computer Society Press, 1982.

[13] D. Waterman, F. Hayes-Roth, "Pattern-Directed Inference Systems", Academic Press, NY, 1978.

[14] P. H. Winston, "Artificial Intelligence", Addison Wesley, 1977

[15] P. H. Winston, B. K. Horne, "Lisp", Addison Wesley, 1981.

APPENDIX I

Description of the nine types of predicate functions used in the FORTH implementation:

(1) EQ: evaluates the argument, and returns a true-value if the argument was proven true (EQual).

(2) EVAL-ALL: forces an exhaustive evaluation of the argument and returns a true value if the argument was proven true at least once during its evaluation.

(3) NE: evaluates the argument and returns a true-value if the argument was proven false (Not Equal).

(4) NC: evaluates the argument and returns a true value if the argument was either proven false or unknown (Not Confirmed).

(5) ND: evaluates the argument and returns a true value if the argument was either proven true or unknown (Not Disconfirmed).

(6) ASK-Y: prompts the user with a particular question (the comment associated with the clause), writes the argument as a new fact (with an attached certainty-factor indicating the user's response) and returns a true-value if an affirmative response was input.

(7) ASK-N: like ASK-Y, but returns a true-value if a negative response was input.

(8) UDO: requires the user to perform a given action (the comment associated with the clause), waits for a confirmation from the user, writes the argument as a new fact and returns a true-value if the action was confirmed.

(9) MENU: displays a menu of choices, prompts the user for a specific menu entry selection, writes the selection as a new fact and returns a true value if a legal entry was selected. This function has three components:

MENU-T: displays the title of the menu
MENU-E: displays a menu entry
MENU-S: prompts the user for an entry selection

Description of the eight types of verbs used in the FORTH implementation:

(1) WRITE: writes the argument as a fact in the list of facts.

(2) CLR: deletes from the list of facts any existing fact which matches the argument.

(3) EVAL: activates the backward chaining interpreter, trying to verify the argument.

(4) EVAL-ALL: activates the backward chaining interpreter, performing an exhaustive verification of the argument.

(5) ASK: prompts the user with a particular question (the comment) and writes the argument (with an an attached certainty factor indicating the user's response) as a fact in the list of facts.

(6) UDO: requires the user to perform a given action (the comment), waits for a confirmation and writes the effect of the action (the argument) as a fact in the list of facts.

(7) STOP: displays a termination message (the comment) to the user and terminates the session, disregarding any pending tasks.

(8) MENU: displays a menu of choices, prompts the user for a specific menu entry selection and writes the selection as a new fact. This verb has three components:

MENU-T: displays the title of the menu
MENU-E: displays a menu entry
MENU-S: prompts the user for an entry selection

Description of the five utility functions used in the Forth implementation:

(1) DISPLAY: displays a message to the user.

(2) PAUSE: displays a message and waits for an acknowledgment from the user.

(3) SHOW: displays a CAD file (graphic picture) or an alphanumeric file on the user's terminal.

(4) SCREEN: clears the graphic plane of the user's terminal.

(5) VDSHOW: displays a video-image (still frame or film sequence) on the auxiliary monitor.

APPENDIX II

Sample of three rules in the Expert System related to a fault in the fuel system.

```
Rule 760
   there is a fault in the fuel system at idling speed
   and readings were taken from locomotive fuel pressure gage
IF:
   EQ  [ ENGINE SET IDLE ]
      Is the engine at idle?
   EQ  [ FUEL PRESSURE BELOW NORMAL ]
      Is the fuel pressure below normal? {Less than 38 psi?}
   EQ  [ FUEL-PRESSURE-GAGE USED IN TEST ]
      Did you use the locomotive gage?
   EQ  [ FUEL-PRESSURE-GAGE STATUS OK ]
      Is locomotive gage known to be accurate?
THEN:
   WRITE  [ FUEL SYSTEM FAULTY ]  1.00
      establishes that there is a fuel system fault.
End of rule 760


Rule 1270
   the locomotive fuel-pressure gage is OK
IF:
   UDO  [ FUEL-PRESSURE-TEST-GAGE STATUS ATTACHED ]
      Attach a known good pressure gage.
   ASK-Y  [ FUEL-PRESSURE-TEST-GAGE READING SAME-AS FUEL-GAGE ]
      Is test-gage reading the same as locomotive-gage reading?
THEN:
   DISPLAY  [ FUEL-PRESSURE-GAGE STATUS OK ]
      The locomotive-pressure-gage is OK.
   WRITE  [ FUEL-PRESSURE-GAGE STATUS OK ]  1.00
      establishes that the locomotive-pressure-gage is OK.
   WRITE  [ FUEL-PRESSURE-GAGE STATUS ALREADY TESTED ]  1.00
      establishes that the locomotive-gage has been tested.
End of rule 1270


Rule 1460
   there is at least one faulty fuel system component
WHEN:
   EQ  [ FUEL SYSTEM FAULTY ]
      The fuel-system is faulty
THEN:
   DISPLAY  [ FUEL SYSTEM FAULTY ]

      There is a fuel system fault.

   WRITE  [ FUEL PROBLEM SOLVED ]  -1.00
      establishes that the fuel problem is not solved.
   EVAL-ALL  [ FUEL SYSTEM-COMPONENT FAULTY ]
      is evaluating for a faulty fuel system component.
End of rule 1460
```

Sample of two rules in the Help System describing available information relevant to the subgoal of verifying the accuracy of the fuel pressure gage.

```
Rule 5190
   you want to see the Fuel Pressure Test Gage Menu
WHEN:
   EQ  [ FUEL-PRESSURE-TEST-GAGE MENU HELP ]
       Request FUEL PRESSURE TEST GAGE Menu
THEN:
   CLR  [ FUEL-PRESSURE-TEST-GAGE MENU HELP ]
       Forgets Request
   MENU-T  [ FUEL-PRESSURE-TEST-GAGE SELECTION INVALID ]  1.00
       This Menu contains information of the
       FUEL PRESSURE TEST GAGE

       These are your choices:
   MENU-E  [ FUEL-TEST MENU HELP ]  1.00
       I want to go back to FUEL TEST Menu
   MENU-E  [ FUEL-PRESSURE-TEST-GAGE PICTURE HELP ]  1.00
       CAD Picture of pipe plug where test gage should be attached
   MENU-E  [ FUEL-REGULATING-VALVE VIDEO HELP ]  1.00
       VIDEO Picture of regulating valve where pipe plug is located
   MENU-E  [ GOAL: BACK TO EXPERT OR STOP ]  1.00
       End of help.  Back to our problem
   MENU-S  [ FUEL-PRESSURE-TEST-GAGE SELECTION FINISHED ]
       Please enter your selection by number:
End of rule 5190


Rule 5210
   you want a VIDEO picture of fuel regulating valve
WHEN:
   EQ  [ FUEL-REGULATING-VALVE VIDEO HELP ]
       Request Picture of regulating valve where pipe plug is located
THEN:
   CLR  [ FUEL-REGULATING-VALVE VIDEO HELP ]
       Forgets request
   VDSHOW  [ 16120 16120 0 ]

   WRITE  [ FUEL-PRESSURE-TEST-GAGE MENU HELP ]  1.00
       We want to use Fuel Pressure Test Gage Menu
End of rule 5210
```

ABOUT THE AUTHOR

Dr. Piero P. Bonissone is a Systems Engineer with the General Electric Research and Development Center. He has carried out research in AI, expert systems, simulation, fuzzy sets, interactive graphics and process control. He also leads the development team for the Diesel Electric Locomotive Troubleshooting Aid (DELTA), and is an Adjunct Assistant Professor of electrical computer and systems engineering at the Rensselaer Polytechnic Institute in New York. Dr. Bonissone holds a Ph.D. in electrical engineering and computer science from the University of California at Berkeley. He has published over a dozen articles in the area of expert systems, decision analysis, and interactive interfaces.

THE ACE EXPERIMENT: INITIAL EVALUATION OF AN EXPERT SYSTEM FOR PREVENTIVE MAINTENANCE

Frederick D. Miller, David H. Copp, Gregg T. Vesonder and John E. Zielinski

AT&T Bell Laboratories, Whippany, NJ

1. Introduction

ACE (Automated Cable Expert) is a knowledge-based system designed to direct preventive maintenance activities in the local telephone network. ACE was developed at AT&T Bell Laboratories to demonstrate and evaluate the potential for using expert systems technology in cable maintenance.

The paper will describe the role of ACE in the maintenance process and will discuss the methods used to evaluate ACE's performance in the field. Some general issues for the evaluation of expert systems also will be considered.

2. ACE as a Maintenance System

Most of the expert systems described at this workshop (for instance [1] and [2]) are consultative systems that provide advice to craftpersons who are repairing malfunctioning equipment. ACE plays a different role in the maintenance process. ACE selects equipment for preventive maintenance by analyzing historical data on problems in the loop telephone plant. ACE suggests preventive maintenance that should be performed to reduce the likelihood of customers experiencing cable-related problems with their telephone service.

Additionally, ACE differs from most previous expert systems in that it gathers information to analyze from a database system, rather than through interaction with users or domain experts. ACE has access to a database where the operating telephone companies store telephone cable repair activity records. ACE uses these data to determine the existence of faults, their probable nature and cause, and their severity. ACE relays this information to users who determine when problems will be repaired.

ACE's analysis task is ordinarily assigned to an "analyzer" who uses reports from the database system. These analyzers have widely varying expertise concerning the telephone plant and computer based analysis. Given both the volume of data available to analyze and other demands on the analyzers' attention, even the best analyzers often lack the time to complete the analysis job or do it well. An expert system that represents a highly skilled expert's understanding of both telephone faults and computer based analysis methods can perform its tasks free from the limitations that hinder analyzers.

ACE's knowledge base and inference engine are written in Franz Lisp [3] and the OPS4 [4] production system language, running on a VAX 11/780. ACE's support routines, including its interface to the database system and the electronic mail that sends output to users, are written in UNIX* shell and C. For a detailed description of ACE see Vesonder et al. [5].

3. Evaluation Methods

ACE has been field tested in several telephone company locations for more than a year. Initially, system performance was tested formally. After that, local cable analyzers were given daily access to ACE results, which they have used for cable repair. These users have been interviewed in depth about the system and have made many suggestions which have been incorporated into ACE. These two procedures are only a part of the evaluations to which a complete project should be subjected.

Evaluation is not a single process. As the recent paper by Gaschnig et al. [6] points out, evaluation occurs throughout the development of an expert system. For instance, each iteration of a rule set is based, in part, on the developers' evaluation of the previous state of the rule set. This paper will focus on the tasks that are specific to evaluating an expert system for a commercial application. There are four major subtasks in the evaluation of such systems.

1. Evaluating the accuracy of the system -- to decide whether the system meets the standard of accuracy, or expertise, at which commercial deployment of the system would be feasible. This is somewhat different than evaluating accuracy in order to improve the rule base, purge it of all inaccuracies, or determine if the software provides an accurate model of human decision making. Commercial systems have to be good enough for their application. As the cost of additional improvements in accuracy begins to rise steeply, some possible improvements may not be made in a commercial system. Additionally, commercial systems need make no claims to mimic human thought processes. They only need mimic correct outcomes of inference processes.

---

* UNIX is a trademark of Bell Telephone Laboratories.

2. Evaluating system sizing and the performance of hardware and software, to find the lowest cost implementation that can provide adequate performance for the application.

3. Evaluating the quality of human/computer interaction. Commercial software can only be deployed successfully if system users are willing and able to work with the software over a long time period.

4. Economic evaluation. Does the action carried out by the system justify the costs of hardware, software, training and maintenance?

The ACE test focused on the first of these four concerns -- proving that a rule based expert system could attain an adequate level of expertise for the application. Since ACE was deployed as a prototype system for testing, it would not have been appropriate to evaluate the other three issues using ACE.

The question then is how to evaluate whether an expert system is accurate enough to allow its being deployed in a commercial application?

Evaluation starts with a critical methodological choice -- the selection of the standard against which the system is to be measured. This is difficult when evaluating expert system accuracy because expert systems are applied to domains in which it is not easy to ascertain correct answers or in which there is disagreement about what the correct answer is. After all, one would not bother to build an expert system in a domain in which problems have straightforward solutions. Even when tests that could evaluate the expert system's answers objectively are possible, the tests are often expensive, time consuming or difficult to perform.

In evaluating ACE, one's ability to do objective tests is limited both by cost and time -- since many hundreds of cables would have to be checked individually -- and by limits on how much the expert system's domain can be manipulated, since the telephone company would object to a wholesale digging up and examining of cables to check whether ACE was right about them. A similar argument can be applied with greater force when medical expert systems are being evaluated.

In the absence of an objective measure against which to gauge system performance, expert system judgements have to be compared with expert judgments. If the judgments of experts in a domain display a high degree of consensus, or if one person who is universally recognized as an expert can be recruited, then the system can be compared against that person. Unfortunately, again, expert systems will tend to be built in domains where experts disagree. One major problem in knowledge acquisition is developing methods to reconcile the conflicting views of domain experts (7).

In a domain where disagreement among experts is the norm, there never will be complete agreement between the judgements made by expert software and those made by a group of disagreeing experts. Additionally, the disagreements among experts point out that the experts themselves are imperfect and at times inaccurate. As a result, the question of what standard to compare an expert system against must be restated to encompass the issue of how accurate does the expert system have to be, given a domain in which inaccuracy -- or at least lack of consensus between experts -- is tolerated?

The solution to these problems that was adopted for testing ACE was to allow the degree of agreement between human analyzers to establish a target for ACE′s accuracy. The criterion established for ACE was that ACE′s agreement with human analyzers should at least equal the agreement between the analyzers themselves. From the customer′s standpoint, expert software meeting this criteria should be indistinguishable in performing a task from a random sample of analyzers presently on the job. If software exceeds the criteria-- in other words by showing a greater degree of overlap with analyzers than is attained between the analyzers themselves-- there would be some basis for assuming that the expert system could outperform the average expert in this analytic task.

4. A Method For Evaluating Accuracy

Accuracy can be assessed by comparing the outcomes from the expert software with the outcomes from live experts in a domain. (For a somewhat different approach to making these comparisons, see [8].) ACE was tested by having ACE and four telephone company analyzers each analyze a monthly body of telephone trouble reports on the same data base. This procedure was repeated for three months. All the experimental subjects were given the same task -- to rank order the most serious candidates for preventive maintenance in several geographic areas each month. The analyzers were instructed to use the database system that stored information on those areas following the procedures they would ordinarily use. They also had varying degrees of personal knowledge of the geographic areas under study. ACE had access to the same database and used a rule base developed to mimic the test analyzers, as well as other analyzers and standard telephone company analysis procedures.

The analysts were given no time or machine limits on how much effort they could put into their analyses. They were told to work on the problem as if they were doing the analysis as part of their normal job function, and their time working on the ACE test was assigned as part of their jobs. (For two of the analyzers, the areas being analyzed were part of their actual analysis job each month.) The analysts had deadlines at the end of each month when they would meet with the system designers to present and discuss their findings. The analysts knew that their findings were being compared with ACE, though they had no access to ACE's results during the test. It was after this three month test period that users started to receive daily ACE output to work with.

There are several ways in which this data collection methodology was less than optimal, but non-optimal research conditions are a way of life in field evaluation. The larger the sample of human analyzers the better, since larger samples give better estimates of actual values for a population. For similar reasons, the longer period of time that data are collected, the better. It would have been preferable to work with analyzers who did not have personal knowledge of the cable plant in the study area. Such human subjects would have been more closely analogous to ACE as an analyzer. In defense of this method, their local knowledge should have given analyzers an advantage in comparison with ACE. In addition, it would have been preferable if analyzers had not known that they were being compared with an expert system -- to eliminate any unforeseen effects from people knowing that they are being compared with an expert system. However, there had to be some explanation for our asking so many telephone company analyzers to analyze the same data, and we never explored presenting any explanation but the honest one.

The statistical analysis of the resulting data is relatively straightforward. Rank order correlations were calculated for each instance where two people, or one person and the expert software provided rankings of the same body of data. It is not necessary to have ranking data. If judgments have been made on an interval scale (such as calculations of trouble seriousness) then product moment correlations can be calculated. Alternately, if the judgment is as simple as whether the same items were selected by different experts, coefficients of association can be used. The groups of person-to-person and of person-to-machine comparisons were then combined, using Fisher's r to z transformation to normalize the data. This provided two average correlations, person-to-person, and person-to-expert system, which could be compared statistically with an ordinary t-test.

The statistical results of the ACE test are proprietary data held by AT&T Bell Laboratories and so cannot presented here. It can be stated that ACE's performance strongly supported the notion that expert system technology could be used in preventive maintenance.

One methodological caveat should be mentioned. When a small sample of analyzers is used, a single person who does poorly can bias results strongly in favor of the software. Consider a test between software (S) and three analyzers (A, B, and C). The machine-person comparisons would be based on three correlations: S-A; S-B; and S-C. The person-person comparisons also would rest on three correlations: A-B; A-C; and B-C. If one of the people were widely divergent, that person would have a greater impact on the person-to-person correlation than on the person-machine correlations, since the person would appear in two of the former, but only one of the latter. This can be corrected for, by watching the data for outliers and analyzing data both with outliers included and excluded to assess the effect such individuals are having on the results.

5. General Considerations

The method described above can, with small adaptations, be used to "prove in" expert systems, at least to the point of testing whether the expert system is competent in its domain. Competence here implies that the system is at least as accurate as well qualified human experts. What does this test imply for the more general realm of expert system evaluation? Consider those tasks mentioned above that have not yet been completed for ACE.

1. Testing to optimize ACE's accuracy and knowledge base. The testing described above demonstrates that an expert system is capable of assuming a place among domain experts. Further improvement of the system requires the type of testing described in (6) -- taking ACE results to the field to find out if they are accurate. When the system proves inaccurate, the software has to be modified accordingly. This iterative process of improving the knowledge base is a major part of building an expert system. A test method such as was used for ACE can provide a basis for deciding when such development efforts can be stopped.

2. The ACE test did not include load or performance tests, nor evaluation of the human interface, because the ACE prototype was not regarded as a system ready for product deployment. An interesting issue is whether these issues can be tested the way they are in other computer systems, or whether special considerations will need to be made for expert systems. The area where this is most likely is the human interface, where users have to be able to understand system outcomes and may require some reassurance about where control of the interaction lies.

3. System economics was not evaluated for ACE. Again, ACE was a prototype not a product, and hence economic evaluation was not appropriate. But the methods used here may provide a basic target that must be attained before an expert system can be proven in economically. The methods for economic evaluation are far afield from the methods described in this paper.

6. Conclusion

The domains in which expert systems prove useful are precisely those in which it is difficult to assess the accuracy of software, because of the lack of means for assessing judgments objectively and the lack of agreement in subjective judgments. This paper describes a method that was used to assess expert system accuracy in such a domain, by using the level of agreement attained by a group of human experts as a target for the agreement with human experts that had to be attained by software. This provides a method for demonstrating the validity of expert software to potential users, and provides data that can be used in other aspects of system evaluation.

REFERENCES

[1] Cantone, R. AI Applications to Automatic Testing. Paper presented to Joint Services Workshop on Artificial Intelligence in Maintenance, Oct. 4, 1983, Boulder, Colorado.

[2] Bonissone, P. AI Maintenance Applications at General Electric. Paper presented to Joint Services Workshop on Artificial Intelligence in Maintenance, Oct. 4, 1983, Boulder, Colorado.

[3] Foderaro, J.K., The FRANZ LISP Manual. Computer Science Department, University of California, Berkeley, 1979

[4] Forgy, C., and McDermott, J. OPS, A Domain-Independent Production System Language, 1977, IJCAI 5, 933-939.

[5] Vesonder, G.T., Stolfo, S.J., Zielinski, J.E., Miller, F.D., and Copp, D.H. ACE: An Expert System for Telephone Cable Maintenance. Proceedings of the Eighth International Joint Conference on Artificial Intelligence, (1983), Karlsruhe, West Germany, Vol. I, 116-121.

[6] Gaschnig, J., Klahr, P., Pople, H., Shortliffe, E., and Terry, A. Evaluation of Expert Systems: Issues and Case Studies, In Hayes-Roth, F., Waterman, D.A., and Lenat, D.B. Building Expert Systems, Addison-Wesley, Reading, Mass., 1983.

[7] Reboh, R. Extracting Useful Knowledge From Conflicting Expertise. Proceedings of the Eighth International Joint Conference on Artificial Intelligence, (1983), Karlsruhe, West Germany, Vol. I, 145-150.

[8] Yu, V.L., Fagan, L.M., Wraith, S.M., Clancey, W.J., Scott, A.C., Hannigan, J., Blum, R.L., Buchanan, B.G., and Cohen, S.N. Antimicrobial Selection by a Computer: A Blinded Evaluation by Infectious Disease Experts. Journal of the American Medical Association, 1979, 242, 1279-1282.

ABOUT THE AUTHORS

Frederick D. Miller is a member of the Artificial Intelligence Systems Group at AT&T Bell Labs, working on design, development, and deployment of ACE. He received his Ph.D. in social psychology from Harvard.

David H. Copp is currently doing AI reserach for the Central Services Organization. He received his Ph.D. in electrical engineering and computer science from the University of California, Berkeley. He has worked on computer performance measurement, microprocessor design, expert systems, and co-authored a high school programming text.

Gregg T. Vesonder is supervisor of the Artificial Intelligence Technology group at AT&T Bell Labs. The group's major responsibility is applying artificial intelligence techniques to integrated information systems. He was one of the chief designers and developers of ACE. Dr. Vesonder received his Ph.D. degree in cognitive psychology from the University of Pittsburgh/Learning Research and Development Center. He is a member of the IEEE Computer Society, the American Association for Artificial Intelligence, and the ACM.

John Zielinski supervises the AI Systems Group at AT&T Bell Laboratories which is responsible for the development of the ACE system. He is a member of the American Association for Artificial Intelligence.

LES: A MODEL-BASED EXPERT SYSTEM FOR ELECTRONIC MAINTENANCE

T.J. Laffey, W.A. Perkins and O. Firschein*

Lockheed Palo Alto Research Laboratory
3251 Hanover Street
Palo Alto, CA 94304

ABSTRACT

Existing Automatic Test Equipment is often inadequate for quickly isolating component failure in large electronic systems. The Lockheed Expert System (LES) has been designed to guide less-experienced maintenance personnel in the fault diagnosis of electronic systems. LES uses not only the knowledge of the expert diagnostician (captured in the familiar form of "IF-THEN" rules), but also knowledge about the structure, function, and causal relations of the device under study to perform rapid isolation of the module causing the failure. In addition to aiding the engineer in troubleshooting an electronic device, LES can also explain its reasoning and actions to the user, and can provide extensive database retrieval and graphics capabilities. In this paper we will discuss the application of LES to a large signal-switching network containing Built-In Test Equipment (BITE). By adding rules, database information, and a few special procedures to the general LES framework, we were able to have a working system in a much shorter time (four man-months) than would have been possible starting afresh.

* Now at SRI International, Menlo Park, California 94025.

1.0 INTRODUCTION

The final report of the OSD/IDA Reliability and Maintainability study [1] emphasizes the importance of developing expert maintenance systems for use where existing Built-In-Test (BIT) and Automatic Test Equipment (ATE) have been inadequate. Existing ATE often use inflexible sequential test programs and BIT systems often produce a large number of false alarms. To eliminate these problems, we have applied LES, a general rule-based expert system, to finding faulty modules in electronic systems. LES is similar to EMYCIN [2], in that it is a framework for building expert systems, but is more powerful in that it makes use of knowledge about the device to aid it in its troubleshooting. Many expert systems, like MYCIN [3], have been constructed from large collections of empirical observations of the expert. It was clear from the beginning of this project that such an approach could be improved greatly by using a detailed model of the structure and function of the device under test, allowing LES to reason about how the device works, and how it fails, in a manner similar to the experienced engineer who would perform the troubleshooting.

Constructing and using a model of this type makes an expert system much more "intelligent" because it is able to provide the system with a more fundamental understanding of the device than is possible using the traditional approach. The importance of LES is that it can reason about electronic devices, understanding how they work and how they fail.

In this paper we will describe how we represent an electronics system in LES, and will indicate how LES in able to combine its knowledge of fault diagnosis (derived from the expert in the form of "IF-THEN" rules) with its internal representation of the electronic device to become a very effective troubleshooter.

2.0 PROBLEM: FAULT ISOLATION IN THE BDS

The electronic device LES is currently being applied to is a large signal-switching network which we will refer to as the Baseband Distribution Subsystem (BDS). It accepts up to 40 baseband input signals and connects them, under computer control, to any one of up to 304 baseband signal output ports. The BDS structure allows connection of any one of its 40 input signals to any one or a combination of all of its 304 output ports with essentially no signal degradation (under normal operation). The BDS consists of 16 equipment cabinets, a terminal, and a line printer.

The BDS also contains Built-In Test Equipment (BITE) which allows the maintenance engineer to break connections and set switches at various points to test for the presence of a signal. This is accomplished by entering operating commands at the local operator's console to control the BDS. One example of such a command is:

TCS,4,N/AM

which tells the BDS to send a test signal from the synthesizer along input line 4, in NO-ADD mode, and give a meter reading. Although BITE is a definite aid in the troubleshooting process, it has several shortcomings. From the above example, one can see that the BITE commands are cryptic (no blank spaces are allowed) and difficult to understand. With approximately 30 commands (each command having four or five different forms), it is extremely difficult for the maintenance engineer to remember even a fraction of these commands. Often, BITE will print diagnostic messages designating a set of components to be checked out. The problem is that it does not designate one component, but usually more than ten. Furthermore, there are often no faulty components in the set designated by BITE. Our expert troubleshooter usually ignores such BITE messages because they give excessive false alarms. Also, BITE fails to identify certain types of problems which occur in the BDS, such as a loose cable. Finally, the major flaw of BITE is that it actually has "bugs" in it which are very difficult to modify, so they are not corrected very often. These problems lead to long maintenance times with the BDS out of action and resources wasted on unnecessary or ineffective maintenance actions.

The purpose of LES is to perform corrective maintenance on the BDS by performing rapid isolation of a faulty printed circuit board or other chassis mounted piece part which caused the failure. The faulty module may be any one or more of the approximately 3000 printed circuit boards, 1000 cables, or other devices which make up the BDS. Such a large collection of components makes the fault diagnosis a very complicated task.

3.0 METHOD USED FOR SOLUTION

In the following subsections we will discuss how LES models an electronic device, how the knowledge of the expert is captured, the goals which the system is pursuing in the solution of the problem, and finally how special problems are handled. In trying to represent the BDS, we generated the block diagram of Figure 1 which shows typical signal paths through the BDS. Surprisingly enough, no such diagram existed previously, and it required numerous discussions with the expert and many hour of studying manuals to obtain it.

SIGNAL FLOW IN THE BASEBAND DISTRIBUTION SUBSYSTEM

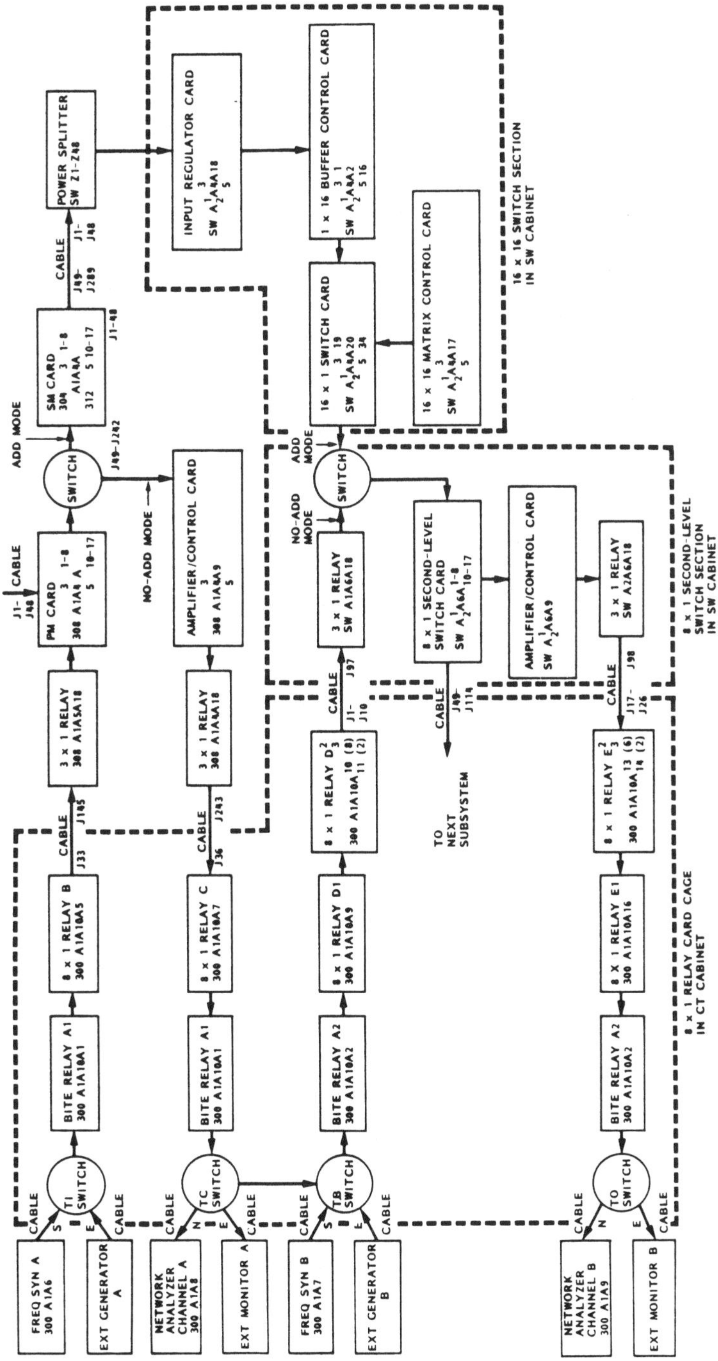

Figure 1

3.1 Modeling An Electronic Device

Obtaining a satisfactory internal representation of the BDS, or other electronic device, requires a complex description. LES represents the structure of the electrical connections and properties of all the components in an "attribute database" (or frame structure) [4-6] with excellent results. This knowledge representation also allows for extensive database retrieval capabilities. The computer system has a distinct advantage over a human repairman in that it can instantaneously list all the components and their locations from a given pair of input and output connections. The repairman, on the other hand, must study wiring diagrams or hope his memory is correct. This is often a time-consuming task and can lead to many wasted hours of valuable personnel.

For the BDS application we chose a set of categories and a set of attributes for each object. Some examples of categories are printed circuit board (card), cable, frequency synthesizer, and spectrum analyzer. Typical attributes of these objects include its name, location, whether a signal passes through it or not, where it gets the signal from, where it sends the signal to, what its supporting components are, whether it's a testable point (i. e. can the user break the connection there and test the signal presence using an analyzer?), its likelihood of being faulty, etc... It is essential that the set of objects and attributes chosen be sophisticated enough to allow LES to use its internal model of signal flow in one direction through a set of nodes (electronic devices) to aid it in its fault diagnosis. Below, we show how a typical object may be represented in LES.

```
(CARD

  (NAME                             '16x1 switch')
  (TYPE_OF                          '16x1 card')
  (LOCATION                         'cabinet 302 A1 A4 A20')
  (FAULTY_LIKELIHOOD                '0.1')
  (SIGNAL_PASSING                   'TRUE')
  (ELECTRICALLY_CONNECTED_INPUT     'CARD(NAME = 1x16 buffer)')
  (ELECTRICALLY_CONNECTED_OUTPUT    'CARD(NAME = 8x1 second-level)')
  (ELECTRICALLY_SUPPORTED_BY        'CARD(NAME = 16x16 matrix)')
  (ELECTRICALLY_SUPPORTS            '')
  (HAS_FAULT_LIGHT                  'TRUE')
  (TESTABLE_INPUT_POINT             'FALSE')
  (TESTABLE_OUTPUT_POINT            'TRUE')
  (GIVES_ALARM                      'FALSE')
  (PURPOSE                          'to accept baseband input signal
                                     from 1x16 buffer card and
                                     connect it to its baseband
                                     signal output')
```

This representation is interpreted as follows: the object is in the card category, it is a type 16x1 card, located in cabinet 302 in section A1 A4 A20, it has a likelihood of failure of 0.1, signals pass through it, its input signal comes from a 1x16 buffer control card, and it sends its output signal to a 8x1 second-level switch card, it is supported by a 16x16 matrix control card, it does not support any devices, and cannot be tested with an analyzer on its input but may be tested on its output.

Each component in the BDS is represented by a similar structure. However, in order to limit the size of our data structure, we represent only those components which could possibly be faulty. This is determined at runtime by the diagnostic messages which are output by BITE when the BDS fails (see sample session). This reduces the number of components we need to represent from approximately 4000 modules to about 100 (see Figure 1).

Using its knowledge that a signal flows through devices in one direction, together with the attribute database, LES is able to identify the set of components along which the signal passes and find appropriate points to test for the presence of the signal. Initial attempts to program a binary search in which a spectrum analyzer tests for signal presence along a signal path was unsuccessful in this application because there were few accessible test points. Instead, the expert used special knowledge for each component, which we encoded in the form of "IF-THEN" rules. In the next section we describe how LES represents the knowledge of an expert troubleshooter in the form of these rules.

3.2 Rules About Fault Diagnosis

The knowledge of the expert at troubleshooting the BDS, is captured in the form of "IF-THEN" rules. There are currently about 50 rules which have been derived by working with the expert, with more being added as the system is checked out. These rules are mostly special cases which allow the engineer to use more knowledge in troubleshooting the system than our simple model allows. Examples are how to set switch positions to troubleshoot more efficiently, which components contain easily recognizable signs of failure such as fault lights, and other similar exceptions to the general case. Other rules involve the necessary BITE commands to obtain test results.

An example of such a special-case rule is: "IF the signal is present at the input regulator card, AND the signal is distorted at the 16x1 switch card, THEN the 1x16 buffer control card is faulty." This rule clearly does not fit our more general model of a component being faulty if the signal passes into but does not pass out of it.

The rules are represented in LES by the "case grammar" format [7].

Although case grammar has been used for representing natural language [8] and for attribute databases, LES is the first system to use this structure for expert system rules. The rule mentioned in the preceding paragraph is represented in LES as follows:

```
IF:    TYPE_ENTRY   'STATE'
       ACTOR        'INPUT_SIGNAL_PRESENCE[CARD(NAME = input regulator)]'
       ACTION_VERB  '='
       OBJECT       'TRUE'
       RULE_NAME    'RULE031'

AND:   TYPE_ENTRY   'STATE'
       ACTOR        'OUTPUT_SIGNAL_PRESENCE[CARD(NAME = 16x1 switch)]'
       ACTION_VERB  '='
       OBJECT       'distorted'

THEN:  TYPE_ENTRY   'STATE'
       ACTOR        'FAULTY[CARD(NAME = 1x16 buffer)]'
       ACTION_VERB  '='
       OBJECT       'TRUE'
       LIKELIHOOD   '100'
```

The case grammar format for rules is consistent with the format of the attribute database. As noted recently by Davis [9], it is desirable to have a few general representations instead of many special representations in order to reduce the problem of translating from one representation to another. Although this structure is more elaborate than that used in other expert systems, it provides greater versatility in describing the relationship between objects under analysis. The information contained in one set of slots is essentially that of one clause (e.g., subject verb object). Ordinary sentence information is, of course, much easier for the computer to understand if it is in the slot format, since the sentence is already parsed.

Variables can also be represented quite easily in this format. For example, the rule: "IF a signal is present at the input to a card, AND the signal is not present at the output of the same card, THEN the card is faulty," is represented in the case grammar format as follows:

```
IF:    TYPE_ENTRY   'STATE'
       ACTOR        'INPUT_SIGNAL_PRESENCE[CARD(NAME = ?x)]'
       ACTION_VERB  '='
       OBJECT       'TRUE'
       RULE_NAME    'RULE001'

AND:   TYPE_ENTRY   'STATE'
       ACTOR        'OUTPUT_SIGNAL_PRESENCE[CARD(NAME = ?x)]'
       ACTION_VERB  '='
```

```
      OBJECT       'FALSE'

THEN: TYPE_ENTRY   'STATE'
      ACTOR        'FAULTY[CARD(NAME = ?x)]'
      ACTION_VERB  '='
      OBJECT       'TRUE'
      LIKELIHOOD   '100'
```

In this rule, "?x" is the variable and can be bound to any object of type CARD. We can bind these variables even tighter by using a form such as:

```
CARD(NAME = ?x & CONTAINED_INSIDE = CABINET(NAME = switch cabinet)).
```

Now the variable ?x can only be bound to a card which is contained inside the switch cabinet. Other systems, such as EMYCIN, have difficulty in cleanly providing such context capability.

In the next section we discuss how LES determines which rules to use in performing its electronic fault diagnosis.

3.3 Reaching The Goal In Electronic Diagnosis

As mentioned earlier, LES is a goal-driven, backward chaining system, like EMYCIN. Instead of a backtracking mechanism, however, the standard AND/OR trees [10] are used to represent goals. Initially, the program sets up several goals (each involving the hypothesis that one of the components along a certain path is faulty) with different priorities. Depending upon the results of tests, which indicate the presence of signals, LES will automatically switch goals by increasing the priority of a goal which looks more promising. For example, if there is no signal present at the first test point, then a rule "fires" which requests the operator to check a specific signal path by setting switch positions. If no signal is present on this path, then finding faulty components along this path becomes the highest priority task.

Each goal has a subject category that defines a set of rules which apply to that goal. Thus, the system uses only the pertinent set of rules when working on a particular goal. For this problem, one set of rules is used for diagnosing and another set for repair.

In the next section we discuss how LES is able to handle the special problems which come up in troubleshooting the BDS.

3.4 Procedures For Handling Special Problems

Extensive calculations or complex processes cannot always be dealt with effectively using rules. These cases are handled better by an ordinary procedure or subroutine. Thus, we have added the capability for LES to call procedures as needed in achieving its goals. Procedure calls are treated as follows: To satisfy a leaf node of the AND/OR tree, the system needs some attribute to have a particular value or range of values. If none of the rules are directly applicable, the program looks for a rule whose "THEN" part states that the value of this attribute "is determined." (The "IF" part will state, "If you call some procedure"). Next the program looks for preconditions (in other rules) which must be satisfied before this procedure can be called. If none are found, the procedure is called. If some preconditions are found, they are added as new leaf nodes on the subtree. (Note that firing of this rule, which involves calling the procedure, is not guaranteed to result in the leaf node becoming "true"). LES continues until it can prove the hypothesis "true," "false," or "unknown."

4.0 SAMPLE SESSION

The following transcript illustrates LES's interaction with a user and the nature of the advice provided. User responses are preceded by "USER:" and annotations are in brackets [].

```
        WELCOME TO THE BDS TROUBLESHOOTING CONSULTANT

        [System starts out with an introductory message
         and a brief explanation of the system which we
         omit to save space]


Enter command (HELP for options)
USER: DIAGNOSE

O.K., let's go isolate the failure in the BDS...

[LES now instructs user to look for some obvious failures,
 then helps him use BITE to set up the test equipment
 properly, which we omit to save space]

[LES now helps user select an input/output connection, so he
 can begin his fault isolation]

Enter "SS" <CR> at the BITE console to obtain the EQUIPMENT OUT OF
SERVICE TABLE.

Examine the set of lines in the INPUT list (not ADD-IN) for lines
which are normally not there.
```

What is the lowest numbered input line which is normally not in the table? (enter HELP for list of lines usually there, enter NONE if none exist)
USER: 4

Enter "SC" <CR> at the BITE console to get the BDM CONNECTION STATUS table.

Enter an output line which is currently not dedicated (i.e. does not show up in table) (0 to 319).
USER: 46

[LES now helps user use BITE to run a test path]

RUN A TEST PATH

You now need to check the Normal Path (through PM, SM and SW).

[See outer path in Figure 1]

Enter "CN4,46" <CR> at the BITE console to connect input 4 with output 46.

Enter "TIS,4/N" <CR> at the BITE console to send the test signal from Synthesizer A along input line 4.

Enter "TON,46/A/M" <CR> at the BITE console to send the test signal along output line 46 to Network Analyzer (channel B).

You must compare the signal detected by Network Analyzer (channel B) at cabinet 300 A1 A8 with that generated by Frequency Synthesizer A at cabinet 300 A1 A6.

If the signal is flowing correctly through the path, the signal detected on the network analyzer should cancel the signal generated by the synthesizer, giving a meter reading in the range -60 to -90 dBm.

Is the meter reading in the -60 to -90 dBm range? (Y or N)
USER: N

[LES suggests another test path to run]

RUN A TEST PATH

You now need to check the Primary Path (through PM and back to CT).

[See top (NO-ADD MODE) path in Figure 1]

Enter "TCS,4/N" <CR> at the BITE console to send the test signal from Synthesizer A through Test Calibrate Path to Network Analyzer (channel A).

You must compare the signal detected by Network Analyzer (channel A) at cabinet 300 A1 A8 with that generated by Frequency Synthesizer A at cabinet 300 A1 A6.

If the signal is flowing correctly through the path, the signal detected on the network analyzer (channel A) should give a meter reading within 5 dBm of frequency synthesizer A's setting of -35 dBm.

Is the meter reading in the -30 to -40 dBm range? (Y or N)
USER: Y

[LES now selects a good test point and asks user to use a mobile piece of test gear, the spectrum analyzer]

USE SPECTRUM ANALYZER

You now need to connect the spectrum analyzer to Input Connector/Regulator Card at cabinet 302 A1 A5 A18 (jack 12) and compare the signal detected with that generated by Frequency Synthesizer A at cabinet 300 A1 A6.

First, you must connect the spectrum analyzer to the input of the Input Connector/Regulator Card.
USER: WHY

[User asks why LES is suggesting this test, and the system explains its line of reasoning]

If we can:
(1) show that INPUT_SIGNAL_PRESENCE of Input Connector/Regulator Card is TRUE;
and
(2) show that OUTPUT_SIGNAL_PRESENCE of 16X1 Switch Card is DISTORTED;

Then it follows from Rule 31 that:
FAULTY of 1X16 Buffer Control Card is TRUE.

Does the signal detected by the spectrum analyzer agree with the generated signal? (Y or N)
USER: Y

NOTE: Please disconnect the Spectrum Analyzer from the Input Connector/Regulator Card at cabinet 302 A1 A5 A18 (jack 12) and secure the old connection.

[LES suggests another test point]

USE SPECTRUM ANALYZER

You now need to connect the spectrum analyzer to 16X1 Switch Card at cabinet 302 A1 A5 A33 and compare the signal detected with that

```
generated by Frequency Synthesizer A at cabinet 300 A1 A6.

First, you must connect the spectrum analyzer to the output of the
16X1 Switch Card.

Is the signal detected by the spectrum analyzer: Distorted, Missing
completely, or Present and good (D, M, or P)?
USER: INFO

[INFO takes the user into the database retrieval mode, where the
 user can type in English type questions which LES will try
 to answer]

What is your question? (enter HELP for options)
USER: WHERE IS SW_16X1_SWITCH CARD?

The 16X1 Switch Card is located at cabinet 302 A1 A5 A33.

Would you like to see a picture of its location? (Y or N)
USER: N

What is your question? (enter HELP for options)
USER: WHAT IS ITS INPUT?

The 1X16 Buffer Control Card is the input to 16X1 Switch Card.

What is your question? (enter HELP for options)
USER: WHAT IS ITS PURPOSE?

The PURPOSE of 16X1 Switch Card is to accept baseband input signal
from 1x16 buffer card and connect it to its baseband signal output.

What is your question? (enter HELP for options)
USER: WHY IS FAULTY OF PRIMARY_MULTICOUPLER CARD FALSE?

[LES can even answer questions about why something is not faulty]

The FAULTY of Primary Multicoupler Card is FALSE because
OUTPUT_SIGNAL_PRESENCE of Network Analyzer (channel A) is TRUE, and
PATH_POSITION of Network Analyzer (channel A) is greater than
PATH_POSITION of Primary Multicoupler Card.

USER: WHERE IS SW_1X16_BUFFER CARD?

The 1x16 buffer card is located in cabinet 302 A1 A5 A12.

Would you like to see a picture of its location? (Y or N)
USER: Y

At what level would you like it displayed?
   (1) Cabinet level,
   (2) Section level,
   (3) Card level, or
```

```
   (4) All of the above
Enter your choice (1 to 4).
USER: 4

[LES now displays 3 figures for the user, which indicate
 where in the BDS the 1x16 buffer card is located. Each
 figure brings him in one level closer. For more details,
 see Figures 2, 3, and 4]

What is your question? (enter HELP for options)
USER: QUIT

We are now leaving INFO and returning to LES. Enter <CR> to help
you remember where you were in your session.
USER:

Is the signal detected by the spectrum analyzer: Distorted, Missing
completely, or Present and good (D, M, or P)?
USER: P

NOTE: Please disconnect the Spectrum Analyzer from the 16X1 Switch
Card at cabinet 302 A1 A5 A33 and secure the old connection.


USE SPECTRUM ANALYZER
---------------------
You now need to connect the spectrum analyzer to cable from Switch
Cabinet to Computer-Test Cabinet at cabinet 302 A3 J98 or cabinet
300 A3 J18 and compare the signal detected with that generated by
Frequency Synthesizer A at cabinet 300 A1 A6.

First, you must connect the spectrum analyzer to the input of the
cable from Switch Cabinet to Computer-Test Cabinet.

Does the signal detected by the spectrum analyzer agree with the
generated signal? (Y or N)
USER: N

[LES suggests another input/output path to try]

We will need to use input line 4 and output line 47 for our next
test.

Enter "SS" <CR> at the BITE console to check if either of these
lines are out of service.

Is line 47 in the OUTPUT or ADD-OUT list of the EQUIPMENT OUT OF
SERVICE table? (Y or N)
USER: N

Enter "CN4,47" <CR> at the BITE console to connect input 4 to output
47 in order to check out path with different 8x1 Second-level Switch
Card but same Switch Amplifier/Control Card.
```

BDS EQUIPMENT CABINET LOCATIONS

Front View

NOTE: The highlighted cabinets are those along the path defined by input line 4 and output line 46.

Figure 2 shows the physical layout of the cabinets in the BDS

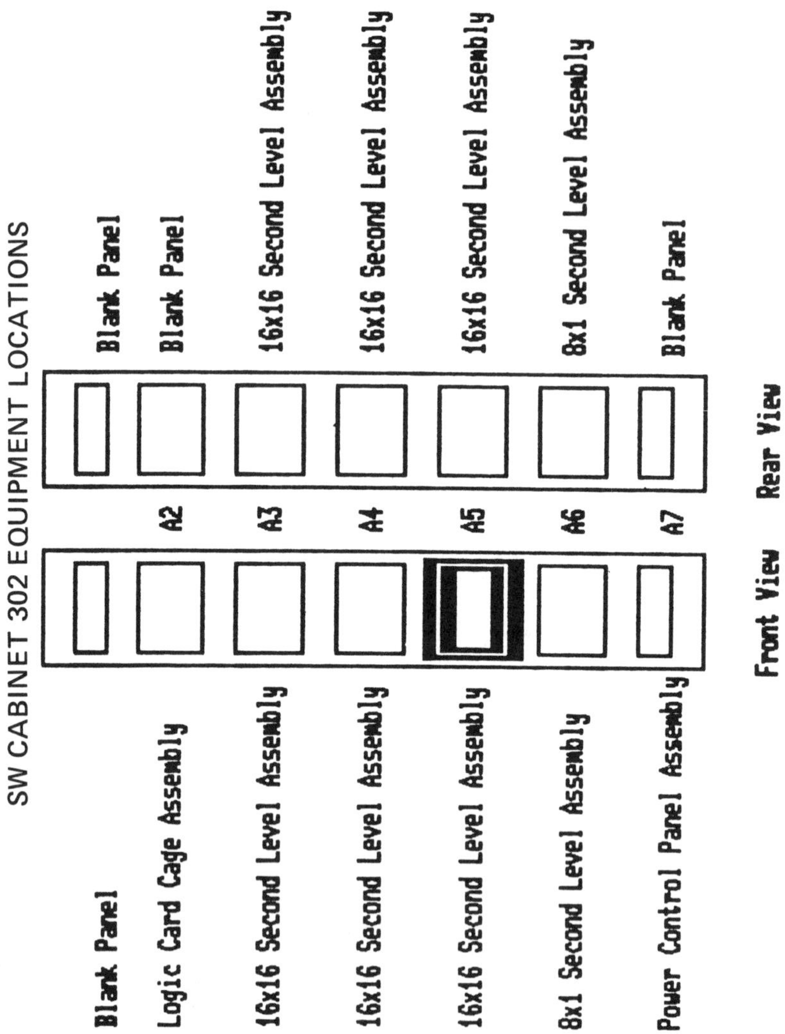

Figure 3 shows how LES highlights the section of the switch cabinet where the designated 1 X 16 buffer card is located

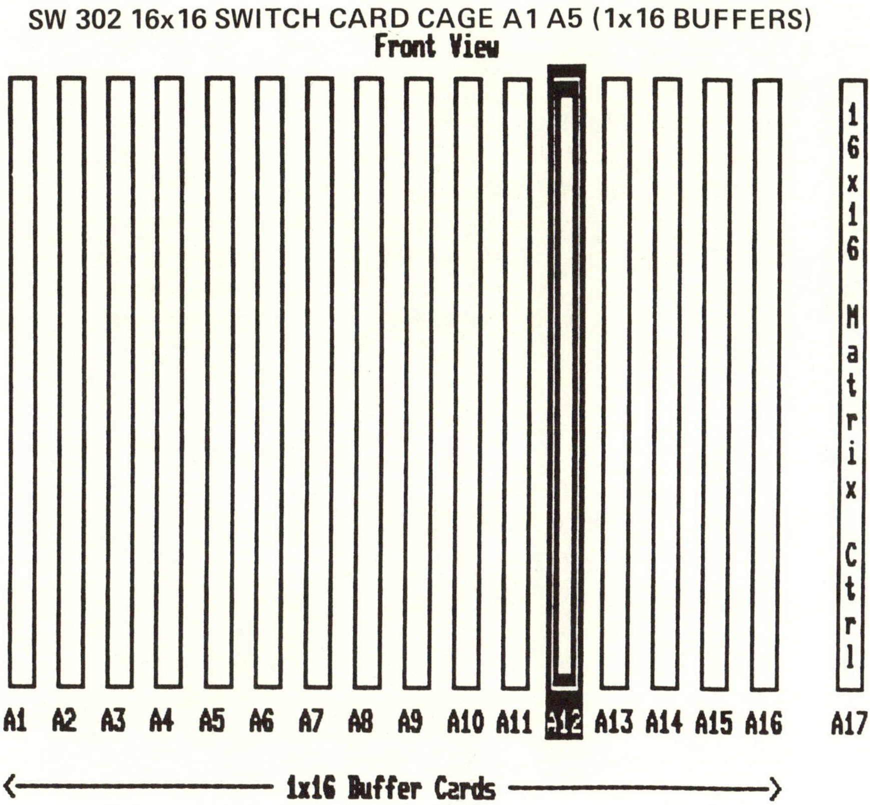

Figure 4 shows how LES highlights the 1 X 16 buffer card which is designated by the user

```
USE SPECTRUM ANALYZER
---------------------

With the spectrum analyzer still connected to cable from Switch
Cabinet to Computer-Test Cabinet at cabinet 302 A3 J98 or cabinet
300 A3 J18 compare the signal detected by the spectrum analyzer with
that generated by Frequency Synthesizer A at cabinet 300 A1 A6.

Does the signal detected by the spectrum analyzer agree with the
generated signal? (Y or N)
USER: WHY

[Again, LES explains his reasoning]

We have established that:
   (1) OUTPUT_SIGNAL_PRESENCE of 16X1 Switch Card is TRUE;
   (2) INPUT_SIGNAL_PRESENCE of cable from Switch Cabinet to
Computer-Test Cabinet is FALSE;

If we can:
   (1) show that OUTPUT_SIGNAL_PRESENCE of path with different 8x1
Second-level Switch Card but same Switch Amplifier/Control Card is
TRUE;
       or
   (2) show that FAULT_LIGHT_SETTING of 8X1 Second-level Switch Card
is ON;

Then it follows from Rule 35 that:
   FAULTY of 8X1 Second-level Switch Card is TRUE.
USER: WHY

[Asking WHY again causes LES to show the components it is presently
 considering as possibly faulty]

If we can:
   (1) show that FAULTY of 8X1 Second-level Switch Card is TRUE;
       or
   (2) show that FAULTY of Switch Amplifier/Control Card is TRUE;
       or
   (3) show that FAULTY of Switch 3x1 Relay Card (test signal output
interface) is TRUE;
       or
   (4) show that FAULTY of cable from Switch Cabinet to
Computer-Test Cabinet is TRUE;

then the goal will have been achieved.
USER: INFO

[Back into the database retrieval mode]

What is your question? (enter HELP for options)
USER: WHAT IS RULE 35?
```

```
Rule 35
-------
(1) Author: T. J. LAFFEY
(2) Date:   JUNE 16, 1983

(3) Author's English: IF THE SIGNAL IS PRESENT AT THE OUTPUT OF
    THE 16X1 SWITCH CARD, AND THE SIGNAL IS NOT PRESENT AT THE
    CABLE FROM THE SWITCH CABINET TO THE COMPUTER TEST CABINET,
    AND THE SIGNAL IS PRESENT ON AN ADJACENT 8X1 SECOND-LEVEL
    SWITCH CARD, THEN THE 8X1 SECOND LEVEL SWITCH CARD IS FAULTY.

(4) LES's Interpretation: If OUTPUT_SIGNAL_PRESENCE of 16X1 Switch
    Card is TRUE, and INPUT_SIGNAL_PRESENCE of cable from Switch
    Cabinet to Computer-Test Cabinet is FALSE, and OUTPUT_SIGNAL_
    PRESENCE of path with different 8x1 Second-level Switch Card
    but same Switch Amplifier/Control Card is TRUE, then FAULTY
    of 8X1 Second-level Switch Card is TRUE.

What is your question? (enter HELP for options)
USER: QUIT

We are now leaving INFO and returning to LES. Enter <CR> to help you
remember where you were in your session.
USER:

Does the signal detected by the spectrum analyzer agree with the
generated signal? (Y or N)
USER: Y

[Finally, LES reaches a conclusion and informs the user]

************************************************************
*                                                          *
* I have reached the conclusion that the 8X1 Second-level *
* Switch Card at cabinet 302 A1 A6 A2 is faulty!           *
*                                                          *
************************************************************


Enter command (HELP for options)
USER: WHY

[LES explains how he came up with his conclusion]

How did I come up with my conclusion(s)?

I said that because:
   (1) OUTPUT_SIGNAL_PRESENCE of 16X1 Switch Card is TRUE,
       and
   (2) INPUT_SIGNAL_PRESENCE of cable from Switch Cabinet to
Computer-Test Cabinet is FALSE,
       and
   (3) OUTPUT_SIGNAL_PRESENCE of path with different 8x1 Second-
```

```
level Switch Card but same Switch Amplifier/Control Card is TRUE.

Enter command (HELP for options)
USER: WHY

[Asking WHY again causes LES to explain how it concluded each of
 the above 3 facts]

How did I come up with my conclusion(s)?

I said that because:
   (1) OUTPUT_SIGNAL_PRESENCE of 16X1 Switch Card is TRUE because
Spectrum Analyzer detected SIGNAL,
       and
   (2) INPUT_SIGNAL_PRESENCE of cable from Switch Cabinet to
Computer-Test Cabinet is FALSE because Spectrum Analyzer detected
NO SIGNAL,
       and
   (3) OUTPUT_SIGNAL_PRESENCE of path with different 8x1
Second-level Switch Card but same Switch Amplifier/Control Card is
TRUE because Spectrum Analyzer detected SIGNAL.

Enter command (HELP for options)
USER: WHY

How did I come up with my conclusion(s)?

I said that because:
   (1) Spectrum Analyzer detected SIGNAL because the user told me,
       and
   (2) Spectrum Analyzer detected NO SIGNAL because the user told me,
       and
   (3) Spectrum Analyzer detected SIGNAL because the user told me.

Enter command (HELP for options)
USER: WHY

How did I come up with my conclusion(s)?

I have given you all the evidence I have.

Enter command (HELP for options)
USER: quit

Exiting program...

[LES gives farewell remarks]
```

5.0 DISCUSSION

There is a urgent need for "user-friendly" computer systems to help in maintenance diagnosis of electronic equipment. As noted in a recent report [1], there are many deficiencies in present BIT and ATE. Unlike existing ATE, LES minimizes the number of tests to find a faulty component. Furthermore, we have discovered several advantages in using an expert system for these applications. First, the existing general expert system program and database structure greatly reduced the time needed to create a working system. Second, the system has user-friendly features (such as the ability to explain its reasoning, ability to answer questions about its database, and only ask for tests as needed in the diagnosis) because they are already built into the expert system.

The accuracy and thoroughness of the computer BDS Diagnostic System should become useful even to the expert. Graphical displays, highlighting the component(s) he is currently working on, have proven highly valuable. The system can tell the user the exact location of faulty or questionable components and remind him of unlikely components (such as cables) which have not been ruled out by the analysis. As rules are added from experience, the system will become able to quickly recognize rare and unusual problems.

For the BDS, encoding some general rules about connected components was somewhat useful in reducing the total number of rules. However, due to practical limitations (such as inaccessibility of many components), the method (tricks) used by the expert were crucial. As LES is tested in the field, we expect more modifications and extensions will be needed.

This case-grammar representation and the attribute-database representation give the system a uniform method for representing the knowledge that is passed between modules of the program. During problem solving, the AND/OR tree goal structure makes it easier for the program and the user to understand the state of the program than a backtracking method in which unsuccessful and completed branches are eliminated or never explicitly created. The system can readily have many goals and subgoals in partially completed states without difficulty. LES can build AND/OR trees in a depth-first or breadth-first manner depending upon a flag setting. However, in practice, we discovered that it worked best if the program tried to work in a depth-first manner but switched temporarily to breadth-first whenever it reached a dead end.

From the dialogue, it is readily apparent that LES is often asking the user to type in BITE commands and for their results. Most of this user interaction could be eliminated if LES were connected directly to BITE and could make its own tests. Future systems should be designed to combine the expert system and BITE.

The interaction between the troubleshooter and the expert system also requires great attention. We are currently integrating voice input/output capabilities into the system in order to allow the troubleshooter the freedom from having to constantly return to the console. Another important capability is to have the expert system adapt to the skill of the user. Different dialogue should be used between LES and an expert, than that between LES and a novice. Much work remains to be done in this area.

REFERENCES

[1] Artificial Intelligence Applications to Maintenance, A report for the OSD/IDA R&M study, Anthony Coppola, Committee Chairman (1983).

[2] W. J. Van Melle, System Aids in Constructing Consultation Programs, UMI Research Press, Ann Arbor, MI (1981).

[3] E. H. Shortliffe, Computer Based Medical Consultations: MYCIN, Elsevier, New York (1976).

[4] W. A. Perkins, "Memory Model for a Robot," Stanford Artificial Intelligence Laboratory Memo. AIM-225, STAN-CS-74-406 (1974).

[5] M. Minsky, "A Framework for Representing Knowledge," in The Psychology of Computer Vision, Ed. by P. H. Winston, McGraw-Hill, New York, pp. 211-277 (1975).

[6] J. S. Aikins, "Prototypes and Production Rules: An Approach to Knowledge Representation for Hypothesis Formation," in Proceedings of the Sixth International Joint Conference on Artificial Intelligence, Tokyo, Japan, pp. 1-3 (1979).

[7] C. J. Fillmore, "The Case for Case," in Universals in Linguistic Theory, Ed. by Bach and Harms; Holt, Rinehart, and Winston Inc., Chicago (1968).

[8] R. C. Schank and C. K. Riesbeck, Inside Computer Understanding, Lawrence Erlbaum Associated, New Jersey (1981).

[9] R. Davis, "Expert Systems: Where Are We? And Where Do We Go From Here," in AI Magazine, Vol. 3, No. 2, pp. 3-22 (1982).

[10] N. J. Nilsson, Principles of Artificial Intelligence, Tioga, Palo Alto, CA (1980).

ABOUT THE AUTHOR

Mr. Thomas J. Laffey is a Senior Scientist at the Lockheed Palo Alto Research Laboratory where he is engaged in the development of the Lockheed Expert System (LES). The LES is currently being applied to the area of equipment diagnosis. Previously, he was employed at General Motors Research Laboratories as a Programmer/Analyst. In 1982, Mr. Laffey received an M.S. in computer science from Virginia Polytechnic Institute where his thesis work was in the area of computer vision and artificial intelligence.

THE APPLICATION OF ARTIFICIAL INTELLIGENCE TO A MAINTENANCE AND DIAGNOSTIC INFORMATION SYSTEM

David R. Antonelli

Boeing Aerospace Company

ABSTRACT

Increasing problems in the complexity of military systems, fault diagnostics, and maintenance training are affecting the readiness of the military services. Expert Systems, a discipline of Artificial Intelligence (AI), appears to offer solutions to many of these problems. However, some problems do exist in present Expert Systems. This paper addresses a different approach to the applications of Expert Systems to logistics in the development of a Maintenance and Diagnostics Information System (MDIS). The MDIS is a multi-domain knowledge acquisition system that supports integrated diagnostics, maintenance, training, data collection and data analysis. Use of systems like these provide each recruit with a computerized expert to aid in the diagnosis and maintenance of system faults.

INTRODUCTION

This paper will discuss the application of Artificial Intelligence (AI) to a Maintenance Information System used in the area of logistics support. It begins with a cursory look at the problems in military systems and maintenance, and problems with present AI approaches. The logistics requirements and the approach used in defining the criteria and design of the Maintenance and Diagnostic Information System (MDIS) are also briefly discussed. The remainder of the paper addresses the MDIS, what it does and how it works. In order to limit the length of this paper, items such as the Inference Engine and the domain details are not discussed.

PROBLEMS

Military Systems and Equipment

The complexity of current and near term military systems is increasing as system design takes advantage of new technology, and multi-mission concepts drive increasing capability requirements into the systems. This complexity puts increasing demands on the already burdened logistics resources necessary to maintain system readiness. Current maintenance aids to support diagnostics and troubleshooting, training and technical publications currently in use fall short in meeting the necessary logistics and readiness requirements.

Consider the problems encountered in diagnosing avionic systems faults. Much of the automatic testing methods in use today such as Built-In Test (BIT) and Built-In-Test-Equipment (BITE), isolate system faults to three or less cards. In some cases, this is acceptable. But, when none of the three cards called out by the automatic test are the cause of the problem, the technician is left to his own devices. If the technician is inexperienced or does not have a high degree of expertise on the equipment, the probable approach is a hit or miss removal and replacement of replaceable units. In other areas removed parts are sent to the depot and returned Retest OK (RTOK). RTOK rates on avionics LRUs average about 30%. (Allen E. Herner, T. M. Miller, Russell M. Genet) Keeping track of these particular RTOK units and obtaining data as to accumulated problems and reasons for removal is all but impossible. Along the same line transient and intermittent faults are as elusive as ever.

Now let's take a different view; the equipment itself. The complexity of both current and near term military systems is increasing as system designers take advantage of new technology. As a result of this increasing complexity, problems are more difficult to diagnose and maintenance time is increasing. In addition the number of technical publication pages required to operate and maintain these systems has dramatically increased. At the same time, the reading and skill level of military recruits is not increasing at the same rate and is putting increasing pressure on both technical publications and training requirements. The requirements for the basic recruit to maintain complex military systems through the use of multi-volume technical publications, often encompassing thousands of pages is directly affecting system readiness and increasing the cost to maintain the current systems. The problems of diagnostics, maintenance and training personnel in these areas are growing at a fast pace.

Artificial Intelligence (AI) as a Possible Solution to the Problem

As recent as a few years ago the military began to look at AI as a possible solution to some of the above problems. One of the AI disciplines that is currently being evaluated is the Rule Based Expert Consulting System, whereby the knowledge of a human expert in a given domain is entered into a computer. This knowledge is used to guide the less experienced user through a specific process. Many of these systems have been used with a high degree of success. A number of people involved with diagnosing problems on physical devices such as electronic and mechanical equipment, looked toward those expert systems developed in support of the medical field as possible applications to physical devices. MYCIN, for example, is an expert system developed to aid medical diagnosis. (W. Van Melle, A. C. Scott, J. S. Bennett, M. Peairs) However, because of the obvious differences between a human being and a physical piece of equipment, medical expert systems didn't quite fill the bill for the diagnostic problems. But even when expert systems were designed and built to diagnose physical systems, many lacked the ability to do a complete job.

A number of problems exist in this area. One of the problems is in extracting knowledge from human experts. In a number of cases, researchers and knowledge engineers have reported bottlenecks in getting the expert's knowledge. The expert starts out with a small knowledge base and builds on that. A system starts out with a few (seventy-five or one hundred) rules, and builds up to a thousand or more rules. In some cases the rule base is never considered complete. Figure 1 illustrates the acquisition of rules in a given system over a period of time. The time required to build present expert systems is from three to five years.

Another problem found in using expert systems is the lack of continuity in the expert's knowledge. Often, in the initial (and sometimes advanced) stages of developing a rule based system, gaps appear in the logic trail. This requires a great deal of rethinking and possibly restructure of the knowledge base. This may account for the large amount of time needed to build an expert system. In addition, in the field of diagnostics and maintenance, the experts knowledge may consist of only those events that occur regularly and in large numbers. Many of the lesser known occurrences go undocumented. A person becomes an expert by working in the field for an extended period of time and through experience accumulates knowledge and a "gut feel" for specific problems. This empirical type knowledge is entered into the rule base. What may not end up in the expert system is the logic and elimination process that a good technician (expert or otherwise) uses when the very uncommon yet very critical problem occurs. Knowledge in the form of production rules is not

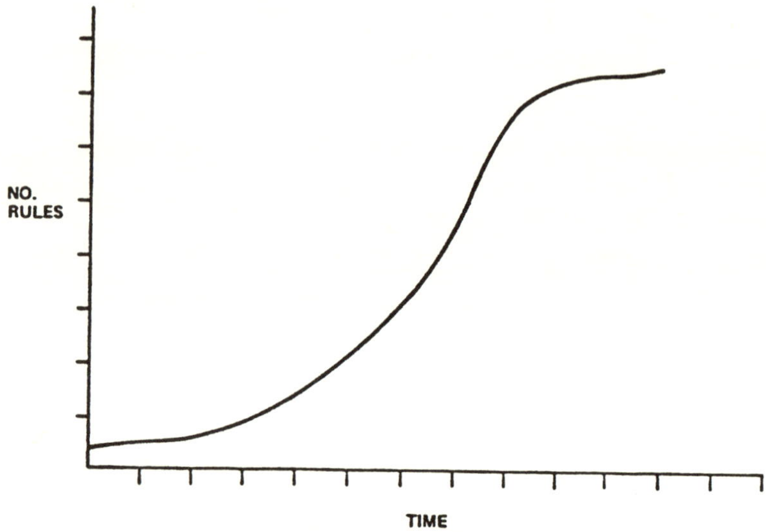

Figure 1. Rules in the Knowledge Base Over Time

enough. In addition to the possible lack of continuity and knowledge gaps, they do not represent the true nature or picture of the equipment being addressed by the expert system.

The single domain approach is another limiting factor in the use of expert systems in today's complex physical systems. It is not only the limited range of knowledge that decreases the effectiveness of expert systems, but the fact that the solution to these problems requires the use of a number of different disciplines. Some of the disciplines are closely related, others seem totally unrelated until they are used in the total solution. This area is discussed later in this paper.

The problems of extracting knowledge from the expert, logic bottlenecks and gaps in the rule base, the extensive time to build an expert system, the need for a single expert and single domain system constraints are the focus of our research in the application of AI disciplines to logistics problems. Some of the above problems with expert systems and others are addressed by William B. Gevarter in the August 1983 issue of IEEE Spectrum; Expert Systems: limited but powerful, pg. 39.

REQUIREMENTS OF A LOGISTICS SUPPORT SYSTEM

In the logistics arena of product support, the requirements for a system encompass a number of disciplines. In terms of fielded systems and equipment, the disciplines of diagnostics, maintenance, training, data collection and data analysis are considered to be of critical importance.

All of these disciplines must be considered if the equipment is to be maintained in a state of readiness. A system addressing these multiple disciplines would offer an effective solution to the problems outlined above. However, if such a system were built to maintain a single item of equipment, the development costs would be prohibitive. Therefore, the ideal system must be a knowledge acquisition system that is essentially generic in nature whereby the user builds many specialized systems from one generic system.

In addition to logistics requirements, two other requirements that directly affect logistics support need to be addressed. Any proposed system that deals with equipment should incorporate integrated diagnostics and be user friendly. The integrated diagnostic concept is supported by the military. Basically it's defined as the most efficient and cost effective mix of failure detection/isolation methods and equipment. Used correctly, this approach coupled with causal reasoning (R. Davis) should go a long way in eliminating the problem of leaving the inexperienced (and sometimes experienced) technician with no resolution when the system in use fault isolates to three cards (devices) and none of them is faulty.

The requirement that a system be user friendly is not only good sense but in a way mandatory. A system is useless unless someone can and wants to use it. Both the system designer and expert can aid in this area. The system must be designed to enable the expert to enter additional "help" where and when it is needed. However, user friendly lies mostly in the hands of the person entering data into the system. It is the expert's responsibility to make sure "help" is in the system. Of all of the concepts and requirements listed above, user friendly is not only the most important, but also the hardest to define. Even though it may be hard to define, some attributes of a user friendly system can be listed. Of course natural language is important, but it is far from enough. The system must be rich in "help"; that is, it must contain additional information and approaches that the expert feels may be needed to supplement a statement or a particularly complex situation. Carrying the concept further, the system could even have the capability of receiving user input describing problems the user is experiencing when using the system. Finally, the system must be built for the intended user. Care must be taken that both the system designer and the domain expert know the capabilities and liabilities of the intended user. Most important in this background is the formal education, skill level, IQ and aptitude for the intended job. Studying the user's needs and the job that the user has to do goes a long way in making the system user friendly and user acceptable.

Probably the most useful attribute that makes a system both user friendly and user acceptable is graphics. Used in conjunction with text it aids in getting the point across and, in most cases, allows for fewer instructions in any given situation. Present state-of-the-art enables animated graphics. If a picture is worth a thousand words, then an animated picture is worth ten thousand words, especially when trying to explain dynamic concepts from the operation of an engine to the Brownian Movement in physics.

The requirement therefore, for a logistics support type of expert system, is a system that covers a number of disciplines. At the same time, it must be able to accommodate many different types of equipment. It must also include in its design the ablity to support integrated diagnostics. But most important, it must be designed and built for the intended user.

APPROACH

Based on a study of a number of expert systems, their functions and domains, and our own expert system, HP1, the following approach to designing and building an expert system was arrived at.

The system designer must consider:

The nature of the problem

The physical composition of the source of the problem

The specific requirements of the Solution

The Expert's ability and skill level

The intended user's abilities and liabilities, and job requirement.

The nature of the problem was stated above and includes the problems of the military (both personnel and equipment), the inherent problems in present expert systems and logistics support problems.

The physical composition of the source of the problem in this case is simply looking at the piece of equipment in terms of its parts and functions. (R. Davis 83a) To stress the point here, let's compare two existing expert systems, MYCIN and DART. (M. R. Genesereth) The physical composition of the source of the problem for MYCIN is a human body, for DART it is a computer. Given the two, the potential for a graphic (tree structure) description, different methods of testing, defining expected output given a specific input, and just general all around probing and removal and substitution of suspected parts is much greater in the computer (DART) than in the human body (MYCIN). Because of this, in the area of research, there is more flexibility in trying out new concepts in diagnostics, freedom to try new testing methods and the effects of failure are less drastic. In addition, physical objects such as computers, engines and the like lend themselves to the application of causal knowledge. (Davis) Causal knowledge can be used to a number of advantages as will be demonstrated later in this paper. It is enough to say that the composition of each source will have its own attributes to aid (or hamper) in building the expert system.

Specific requirements of the solution are shown in the logistics support requirements. Logistics support involves a number of disciplines. Many of these disciplines are synonomous with the possible domains of an expert system. Therefore, the optimum approach to meeting the various logistics needs is the development of a multi-domain expert system. In addition, since the military has many different types of systems and equipment, any proposed expert system must be generic, enabling the experts to build a separate expert system for each different piece of equipment.

In considering the expert, the system must aid the expert in inputing the data in such a way that the bottlenecks and gaps in the logic train are for the greater part eliminated. If this occurs it should speed up the process of building the expert system. In addition, the system must be designed to accept and use causal knowledge.

The intended user's requirements to complete the job include the fact that the user is a maintenance technician who at best will have graduated from high school, be of average intelligence, and have a mechanical aptitude. In the case of equipment the user will need all the help available in diagnosing and maintaining equipment. He will need such information as what parts and part numbers are needed plus what tools are needed to do the job. This must be supported by step-by-step instructions along with graphics. The system must enable the technician with an average skill level to function at a high performance level.

THE MAINTENANCE AND DIAGNOSTICS INFORMATION SYSTEM (MDIS)

The approach to addressing the previously listed problems is the development of a Maintenance and Diagnostic Information System (MDIS). The MDIS is essentially a multi-domain knowledge acquisition system. AI concepts and disciplines are used only where practical and appicable. At this time the MDIS encompasses six domains: diagnostics, maintenance, maintenance training, data collection, data analysis and graphics. Maintenance is divided into repair maintenance and preventative maintenance.

The multi-domain concept presents a number of problems. First, a multi-domain system infers that there will be a number of different experts in different domains entering data into the expert system. This could mean an expert for each domain, although in our case it did not. Another problem is that different experts have different ideas on what constitutes relevant information regarding their specific domain. At first this may not seem much of a problem, but as the system grows, relationships between domains tend to get weaker, especially with a different expert for each domain. Without proper control a multi-domain system could result in a hodge-podge of disjointed bits of information.

In building a system such as this it is important that there be continuity within each domain and a relationship between domains. In order to ensure this, there must be some built-in method of controlling the input by the experts in the various domains. The method used must not only have the physical and functional knowledge of the piece of equipment the expert is talking about, but also knowledge of what previous and related domain data has been input by the various experts during the building of the system. In order to accomplish this, two separate MDIS modules will handle the control, continuity and domain relationship problems. These are the System Description Module and the Builder's Guide.

System Description Module

The System Description Module is used to describe a piece of equipment or a device to the MDIS. Any piece of equipment or device consists of one or more parts. Each part performs a specific function. The sum of the parts are connected or related in such a manner that their combined functions are performed simultaneously and/or in a predetermined and related sequence of events. This total joining of parts and related functions results in a single unit (piece of equipment or device) whose objective is to perform one or more functions. It can also be said that given the specific occurrence of specific input(s) to a given part, its function will produce the occurrence of a specific output called the expected output.

The System Description Module enables a person to describe both the physical (parts) and functional organization (R. Davis 1983b) of the piece of equipment that is to be addressed by the MDIS. The piece of equipment is described in a tree type structure starting with the general form at the top level and progressing to the more detail form as lower levels are described. Each physical part of the equipment and its function must be included. The level of detail in the description is left up to the person describing the equipment. This will of course be governed by the user's needs and the level of domain detail that is desired. Figure 2 illustrates the layout of a system by description levels.

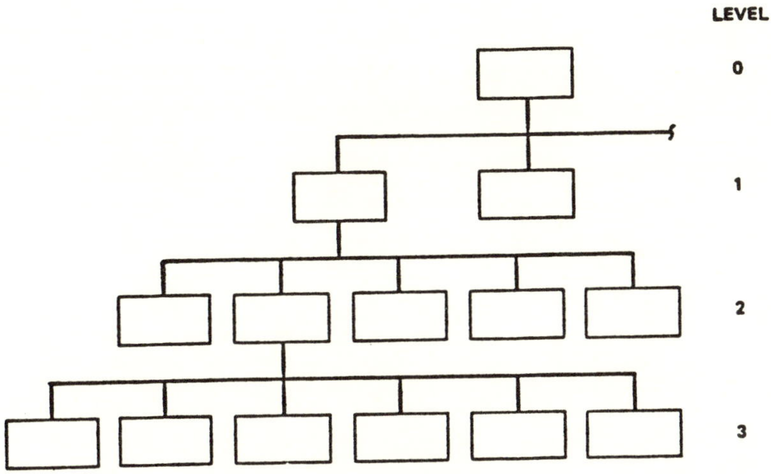

Figure 2. System Description by Level

Care must be taken in describing the equipment. The key is continuity. The System Description Module contains the basic facts that will aid in guiding and controlling the building of the rest of the MDIS. (These facts will also be usd in many of the MDIS domains.) This includes both rule type data and causal knowledge to be entered into the various domains. It is not important that the lowest level of description be reached right away, for lower levels can be added as needed. (In fact levels can be inserted as needed anywhere in the description.) The important thing is completeness of the description during the decomposition (N. Nilsson) from the top level to the lowest level. Figure 3 provides an example of a tree structured physical content for an engine.

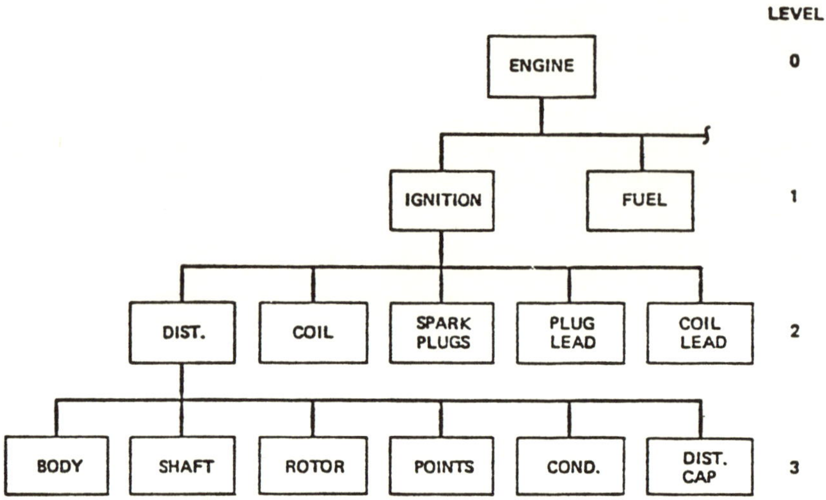

Figure 3. Physical Content of an Engine

Obtaining and entering the physical data is not difficult. A schematic and parts list of the equipment in question will provide the majority of the data that is needed. Of course, the person entering the data must have the ability to enter the data in a complete and logical fashion. The method of entering the data (depth-first or breadth-first) is optional.

Entering the functional data is accomplished in the same manner as entering physical data. For each piece of physical data there must be an accompanying piece of functional data. Functional data can be obtained from the technical description document or one's own knowledge of the piece of equipment. Both physical and functional data are important. They will be used to aid the expert in building the domains of the MDIS and will also be available to the domain expert on diagnostics for use in the diagnostic domain.

The key factors of the System Description are:

1. Any piece of equipment, device or system can be described down to the desired level.
2. The system description must include the physical description and functional operation to the detail required by the domains.
3. Having a complete description will assure continuity. This continuity will aid in solving the problem of logic bottlenecks and gaps when domain experts are entering data into the MDIS. It will also assure the availability of causal knowledge.

Figure 4 provides an example functional description.

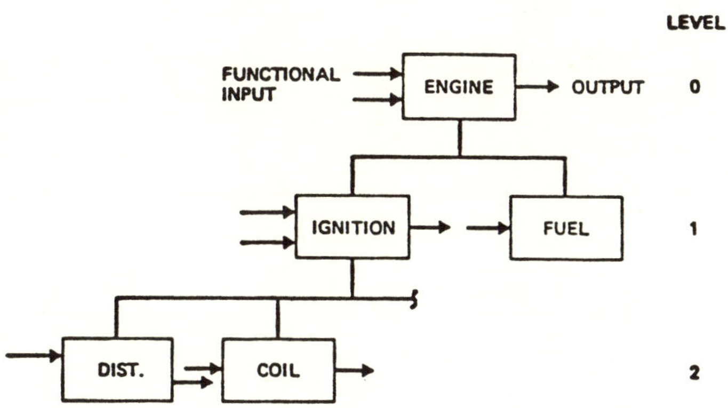

Figure 4. Functional Operation at Each Level

The Builder's Guide

The Builder's Guide uses the system description information to guide the various experts in entering data regarding their domain. It is important to remember that its ability to guide the domain expert is heavily dependent upon the system description. While the system description module aids in continuity within each domain, the Builder's Guide aids in the relationship between domains. (See Figure 5.) It takes all of the description information (both physical and functional) and uses it in aiding in the development of the rest of the MDIS. At this time the domains of the MDIS are diagnostics, repair maintenance, preventative maintenance, maintenance training, data collection, data analysis and graphics. Other domains may be added as our research progresses.

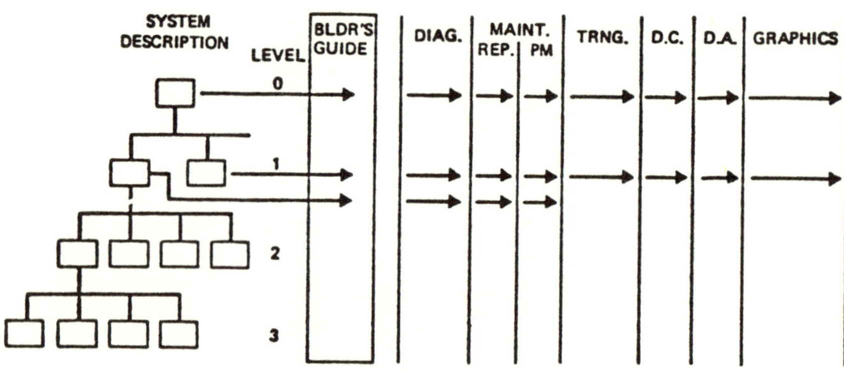

Figure 5. Maintaining Relationships Between Domains

The Guide knows these domains exist and requires that domains be entered in a specific order. The MDIS is somewhat progressive, information in certain domains is used as a guide in building other domains. The order of domain construction is as follows:

1. Diagnostics or Preventative Maintenance must be entered first. Diagnostics must be entered before Repair Maintenance because the Builder's Guide will request a repair procedure for every fault isolation result. It uses the information from both the system description module and the diagnostic domain in aiding to build the repair maintenance domain.

2. Repair Maintenance can be entered only after Diagnostics have been entered. (The diagnostic tells what is wrong; maintenance repair tells how to fix it.)

3. Diagnostics and Preventative Maintenance must also be entered before Maintenance Training.

4. Maintenance Training will be entered only after Diagnostics, Repair Maintenance and Preventative Maintenance have been entered. The training expert will use much of the text and techniques in the previous domains in building the training domain. The training domain will also contain theory. Training information will be requested for every module at each level. The depth and completeness of this domain is left to the expert.

5. Data Collection techniques will have two modes:

   Manual - For both manual and automatic (BIT/BITE) systems. Specific data will be requested from the user but will be entered manually.

   Automatic - For automatic and semi-automatic systems (Integrated Diagnostics). Specific data will be entered automatically.

   Data Collection techniques and specific data needed will be entered after diagnostics, maintenance and training.

6. Data Analysis will incorporate mostly standard statistical techniques and will be entered after data collection.

7. Graphics can be entered on an ongoing basis as each domain is entered, or after the system is complete.

The Builder's Guide performs a number of housekeeping functions before aiding the domain expert in entering data.

First it determines that the system description has been entered and no changes have been made to it. It then gives the domain expert the name of the system or equipment that has been described and shows a breakdown of parts and functions that make up the total system or equipment. Finally it advises the domain expert of what domains are already in the system and what domain or choice of domains it expects next. The Guide uses the graphics capability in describing the above and giving aid to the domain expert.

It starts with the top (level 0) module in the system description and asks the expert for data regarding that module. If this is the first domain being entered (diagnostics or preventative maintenance), then the guide uses only the information in the system description to aid the expert in entering data. The guide will keep a list of those modules in the system description that were not addressed or bypassed by request of the expert. If other domains have previously been entered (diagnostics) and the domain being entered depends on that information (repair maintenance), the guide will use both the system description data and the domain data at that level in aiding the domain expert. An example of this would be if the diagnostic domain were previously entered and the repair maintenance domain was being entered, then both the system description data and diagnostic data at each level would be used in aiding the repair maintenance expert in entering data. The builder continues this in a top down fashion in such a way that specific functions in a piece of equipment are handled individually. When the last module in the piece of equipment is completed, the Guide informs the expert as to which modules were bypassed in the system description and asks the expert to review the logic (continuity) and relationships to other domains, if they are present. An example of verifying the relationships between domains and logic continuity is as follows. The diagnostic domain must be entered before the Repair Maintenance domain. When the repair domain is entered, the guide checks the top system description module and also the diagnostic for that module. A repair procedure must be entered for each description module/diagnostic pair that the Guide shows. If no repair procedure is available, the statement "NO REPAIR PROCEDURE FOR <module><diagnostics> ARE AVAILABLE" is displayed. The Guide checks for other relationships such as the relationship between diagnostics, repair, data collection and data analysis in the same manner.

The MDIS Domains

At this time the MDIS incorporates six domains. Specifications on the contents of each domain and domain relationships have been written. The ability of the Builder's Guide to aid an expert in entering data into the diagnostic domain has been accomplished at a primitive level.

INTEGRATED DIAGNOSTICS

At this point it is important to address diagnostics. Since the MDIS is a piece of software, it can be used in a fully automatic, semi-automatic or completely manual testing mode or any combination of the above.

When used as a part of (or incorporating) integrated diagnostics, parts of the MDIS diagnostic routine would be incorporated in the automatic testing software (in keeping with the integrated diagnostic concept). It will monitor the equipment through the regular BITE and receive input regarding equipment problems from both BITE and BIT. Automatic diagnostics would be supplemented by causal knowledge and manual diagnostics depending on the testability of the given equipment. The data collection domain would also be included in this concept, some data would be automatically input to the data collection module while other data would be manually input. Finally, certain graphics would be portrayed depending on input to the graphics module by the automatic test program. Figure 6 shows the incorporation of integrated diagnostics and MDIS.

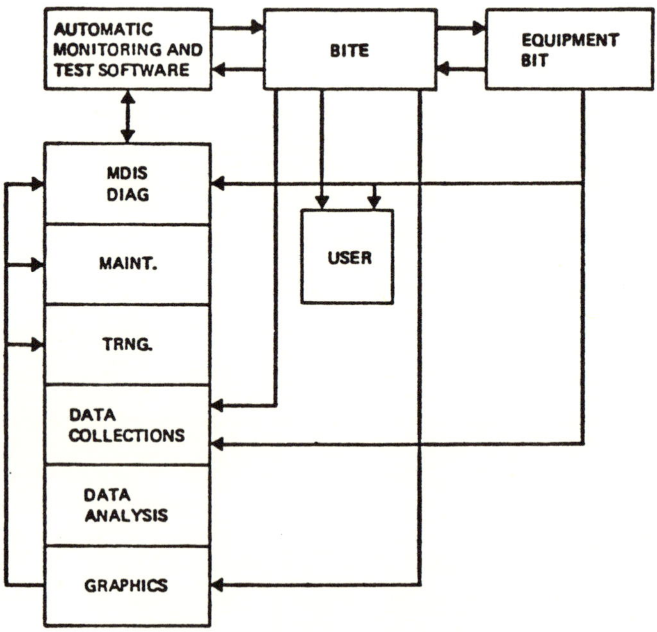

Figure 6. MDIS and Integrated Diagnostics

Military and AI Problems Solved by MDIS

At this stage of the research, it is impossible to state what military or AI problems an MDIS will solve (or create). However, we can state the problems, what solutions an MDIS may offer, and offer remarks as to why a solution might be reached. The anticipated problem solutions are listed on Figure 7.

Projected Use of MDIS

The present use of the MDIS will be in the field only. The data collected by the Data Collection Module and the Data Analysis Module will be dumped and analyzed at a higher level (depot). The information produced from the data can be used in future design, personnel analysis, inventory control and reliability.

In the future we hope to add a learning capability to MDIS. Data from various areas of operation would be analyzed and the results fed back to the MDIS in the field. This would have two advantages. One is that each MDIS could update its knowledge of how it works in its own environment. The other, and even more important, is that each MDIS would know what to expect in different environments. This will make them highly portable and enable them to advise their users of what to expect when a change in environment occurred. This is shown in Figure 8.

Technical Problems

At this stage of the project there are two areas of concern. The magnitude of these concerns won't be known until more information is available.

First there is the natural language interface between the expert and the Builder's Guide and the interface between the user and the MDIS. The expert-builder's guide problem lies only in the input to the Builder's Guide.

PROBLEMS/ REQUIREMENTS	MDIS RESOLUTION APPROACH	REMARKS
High BIT Error Rate	System Description Component Causal Knowledge	Complete equip. description for expert and user.
		Better testing & fault isolation capability.
RTOK	System Description Component Causal Knowledge	Fewer unnecessary removals.
	Data Collection, Data Analysis	Reasons for removal given to MDIS.
		Conditions leading up to and at failure are recorded.
		Effect of different environments and conditions on like component can be analysed.

Figure 7. Anticipated Problem Resolution

PROBLEMS/ REQUIREMENTS	MDIS RESOLUTION APPROACH	REMARKS
Transient Faults	System Description Component Causal Knowledge Data Collection, Data Analysis	Record data leading up to fault. Redesign FI and testing strategy to get more pertinent data regarding fault.
Intermittent Faults	Same as above	Same as above
False Alarms	Same as above	Same as above
Complexity of Equipment	System Description Component Causal Knowledge	Portrays a complete and logical step by step decomposition of the equipment starting at the generalized top level and proceeding to the detailed lower levels.

Figure 7. Anticipated Problem Resolution (Cont.)

PROBLEMS/ REQUIREMENTS	MDIS RESOLUTION APPROACH	REMARKS
Complexity of Equipment	Training	Instructs the user in the desired area at the speed and level controlled by the user.
		Accepts question about the equipment from the user.
		Uses information from the Syst Desc. Comp. the diagnostic domain, maintenance domain as well as training techniques from the training domain.
	Graphics	Complete graphics supports diagnostics, maintenance training and "Help".
Personnel Skill Level	Same as above Data Collection, Data Analysis	Same as above Skill and training requirements of each user are collected and analyzed to determine the type and additional training requirement. System keeps track of level of training requested and type of questions asked. Can also test user.

Figure 7. Anticipated Problem Resolution (Cont.)

PROBLEMS/ REQUIREMENTS	MDIS RESOLUTION APPROACH	REMARKS
Knowledge Bottleneck	System Description Component Causal Knowledge	Complete description of equipment.
	Builder's Guide	Prompts and guides the domain expert when entering data. Questions expert when data regarding specific parts and functions are omitted.
	Multi-domain	Builders Guide ensures relationships between domains at each level. Example; for each diagnostic it requests a repair procedure training data, data collection and analysis methods and proper graphics.
	Data Collection, Data Analysis	Expert has an opportunity to review users problems as system is in use.
Build Time	System Description Component Builder's Guide	Will shorten build time.
		Data from like equipment can be used with modification.

Figure 7. Anticipated Problem Resolution (Cont.)

PROBLEMS/ REQUIREMENTS	MDIS RESOLUTION APPROACH	REMARKS
Single Domain	Multi-domains	
Ambiguous FI	Syst Description Component Causal Knowledge	More in depth fault isolation
	Data Collection, Data Analysis	Failure data can help restructure the system. User problems can be analyzed.
Must Be Generic	Syst. Description Comp. Builder's Guide	Use of Flavovs and Builder's Guide software enables the description of most systems or equipment.
Use Causal Knowledge	Uses Causal Knowledge	

Figure 7. Anticipated Problem Resolution (Cont.)

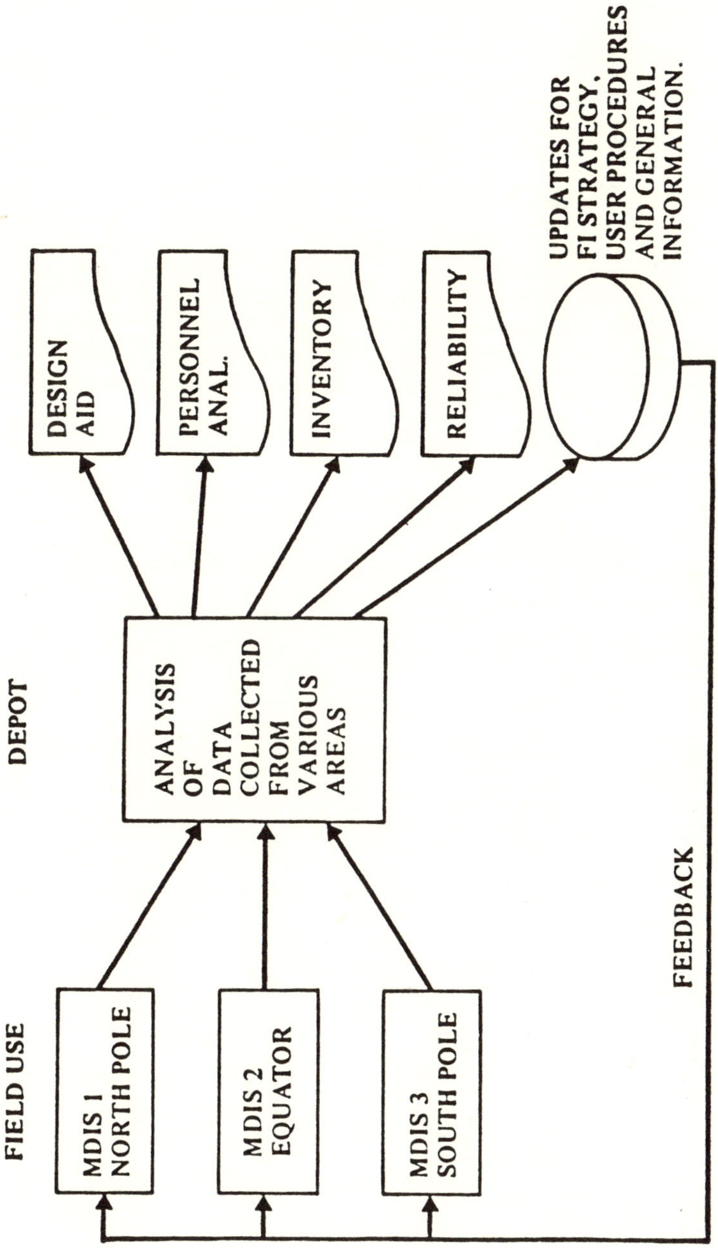

Figure 8. Projected Use

We do not feel that the expert will have a problem understanding the output from the guide because, as the designers, we can control the output with a limited vocabulary. In the case of the user - MDIS, the problem lies both in the input and output. Only the expert building the domains can control those, and as the designers of MDIS we have little control over this.

Another problem may be the management of building the system by the customer. An empty MDIS will have the capability to describe a piece of equipment or system and after it is described, aid domain experts in updating data. To what depth this will be taken, who will make the decision and who inputs the data has not been addressed yet.

Conclusion

The System Description Module was built that described both the physical and functional operations of a four cycle, internally reciprocating engine. Only the ignition system was described to the lowest level of detail. The ignition system was chosen because it encompasses both mechanical and electrical parts and functions. At this time this module is used only to aid the domain experts in building their domains. The system description module is programmed in Franz Flavors (Wood 82) and runs under UMLISP (Allen 82).

The Builder's Guide was built and programmed in OPS5. At this time it is able to use the data from the System Description Module (level one only) to guide an expert in building the diagnostic domain. Both modules operate, but only at a primitive level. No attempt was made at building other domains such as repair maintenance or preventative maintenance. At this time the MDIS is not considered operational. But even at this early stage of this phase of the research, some conclusions can be drawn.

First, when designing the system the total concept should be looked at and documented before starting. What domains are to be included, the objective of each domain, what activities must occur to reach the objectives and the relationship between domains is important. This information will govern the design and detail of both the System Description Module and the Builder's Guide. Without this knowledge of what has to be done within the domains of the MDIS, the system will be limited to only the information that the System Description Module can produce and the ability of the Builder's Guide to access and use that information in guiding the domain experts

Another conclusion was drawn about the System Description Module itself. If one physical operation, that is one part, is left out, then its function will probably be left out. However, continuity can be achieved anyway, but this is false continuity, and will result in problems in building the domains. An example of this is the engine that was used in the System Description Module. The condenser was left out of the system description, therefore its function was left out. The Builder's Guide did not know a condenser and its function was missing and proceeded to aid the diagnostic domain expert based on what it knew. Because of the flexibility of Flavors, the physical and functional data on the condenser could easily be added to the system description. The Builder's Guide detected this and advised that an update to the System Description Module was made and that the diagnostic domain should be updated.

REFERENCES

1. Allen E. Herner, T. M. Miller, Russell M. Genet: "Diagnostic Errors and Human Factors in Built-In Test (BIT), Air Force Human Resources Laboratory (LRLA), April, 1981.

2. W. Van Melle, A. C. Scott, J. S. Bennett, M. Peairs: "The Emycin Manual," Stanford University, October 1981.

3. R. Davis: "Expert Systems: Where Are We? And Where Do We Go From Here," The AI Magazine, Vol. 3, No. 2, Spring 1982, pp. 3-22.

4. M. Genesereth: "Diagnosis Using Hierarchical Design Models," Proceedings of the National Conference on Artificial Intelligence, August 1982, pp. 278-283.

5. R. Davis: "Diagnosis Via Causal Reasoning: Paths of Interaction and the Locality Principle," Proceedings of the National Conference on Artificial Intelligence, August 1983, pp. 88-94,

6. N. Nelsson: "Principles of Artificial Intelligence," Tioga Press, 1980.

ABOUT THE AUTHOR

Mr. David R. Antonelli is currently conducting full-time research on the application of AI to diagnostics at the Boeing Aerospace Company. He has also served as an Instructor of diagnostic software and hardware used in the electronics of the E3A Sentry Program. In earlier associations, he has completed studies on the use of failure rate data for predicting reliability of newly designed aircraft components. Mr. Antonelli received his B.S. degree in statistics and industrial management from New York University in 1962.

INTELLIGENT INFORMATION RETRIEVAL FROM ON-LINE TECHNICAL DOCUMENTATION

Arthur F. Griffin

Support Systems
Hughes Aircraft Company
Long Beach, CA 90810

ABSTRACT

Computerized maintenance manuals contained in massive, on-line text and graphics data bases require an intelligent facility for information retrieval. An unsophisticated user must be able to easily find specific facts, procedures, etc. without having to specify precisely the information he seeks. Hughes is developing an intelligent retrieval approach based on semantic network knowledge representation. Because conventional serial computers are too slow for large semantic networks, we have designed and prototyped special purpose, parallel processing hardware called Associative Loop Memory (ALOOP). ALOOP also dynamically organizes a knowledge base in a manner that imitates human memory.

Introduction

The growing complexity of defense systems coupled with the decreasing skill levels of military maintenance personnel have greatly complicated technical documentation for training and on-the-job use. To address this problem, the armed services have produced fully proceduralized, step-by-step documents such as the Army's Skill Performance Aids (SPA). However, this approach increased the volume of required data by three to five times, as compared to conventional manuals, thus creating problems with document size and cross-referencing.

In 1978 Hughes began investigating computer techniques to reduce SPA data handling problems. We are currently developing an integrated on-line document authoring and presentation system, sponsored in part by the Army and the Navy. Figure 1 characterizes our system.

Paralleling these contracts, Hughes has an IR&D program to examine longer range technical information problems. We focused our 1982 and 1983 efforts on indexing and cross-referencing; i.e., given a voluminous set of computerized technical manuals, how does a user find a particular piece of information? Conventional information retrieval techniques were found wanting [SIGIR, 83], so we started exploring an Artificial Intelligence (AI) approach.

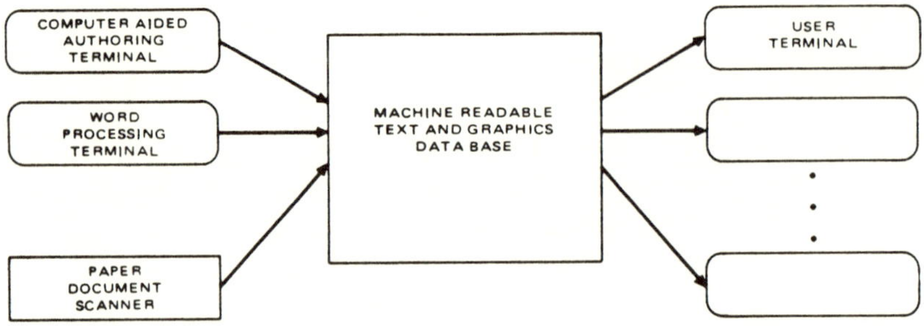

Figure 1. Full Text, On-Line Data Bases.

In 1982 we began developing a knowledge base structure called Associative Loop Memory (ALOOP). ALOOP lets a user search for information he cannot specify precisely. This search is done through an associative semantic network of key words. These key words and the relationships between them are extracted from ordinary, human readable text.

ALOOP is implemented for real time use in a parallel processing architecture ideally suited for Very Large Scale Integrated (VLSI) circuits. We have demonstrated the feasibility of this memory concept with a hardware prototype and a software emulator, both currently operational in our laboratory.

Defining the Information Retrieval Problem

From the beginning of this project, we were aware that the current state of the art in AI presented serious size and speed limitations for practical applications requiring large knowledge bases. However, we believed that these limitations could be overcome in the near future by making some judicious tradeoffs between automated AI functions and functions that human users do well with seemingly little effort. Extending this line of thought to information retrieval, we assumed that although the user may not know exactly what he was looking for, he would recognize it when he saw it. If the user performs this recognition function, then the job of the automated system is to provide an intelligently guided browsing facility. To begin, the system must rapidly guide the user through a large collection of on-line documents to sections that are likely to be relevant.

The system also has to present those sections in a way that allows the user to judge relevance quickly. If the retrieved sections are not relevant, then the system must suggest alternate search paths. Further, the system is required to dynamically organize its knowledge in response to user queries so that it can react more intelligently to similar queries in the future. Finally, the system must minimize the bottleneck of knowledge acquisition that characterizes many current AI systems; i.e., the system has to extract index words and relationships from the text data base automatically to avoid the costly, laborious task of human intellectual indexing.

Semantic Network Approach to Text Browsing

Our approach to intelligently guided browsing is based on semantic networks, a form of knowledge representation found in many AI systems. Semantic network representation was originally proposed as a model of human memory by M. R. Quillian in the late 1960's. Quillian asserted that human memory behaves as though concepts were stored as complex networks of semantic associations. Recall is accomplished by traversing the network's associative links [Ratcliff, 81; Brackman, 79].

We use a semantic network memory model to index and search a text data base. The following figure exemplifies a network that links together key words extracted from the text of a maintenance manual. This segment of network was retrieved in response to the query "torque meter" identified by "**" in the figure. The other links in this example are text page numbers on which two words co-occur in close proximity, indicating words that are likely to be semantically related. Network links can also indicate inferential relationships; e.g., part-of, instance of, and type-of. Further, links can be used to attach procedural information such as IF-THEN rules popular in expert systems.

The network can be thought of as a key word road map through the data base. The user can quickly traverse the network in any direction to browse the text. If the user reaches the edge of the network, he can grow additional nodes and links in any direction.

Semantic networks interest us for two purposes: (1) representing knowledge in computer memory and (2) displaying knowledge graphically to a user. We are struck by the power of semantic network diagrams to present complex associations and interrelationships in a way that is easy to understand. We see the potential of interactive network displays as a simpler alternative, or adjunct, to natural language interfaces for both input and output.

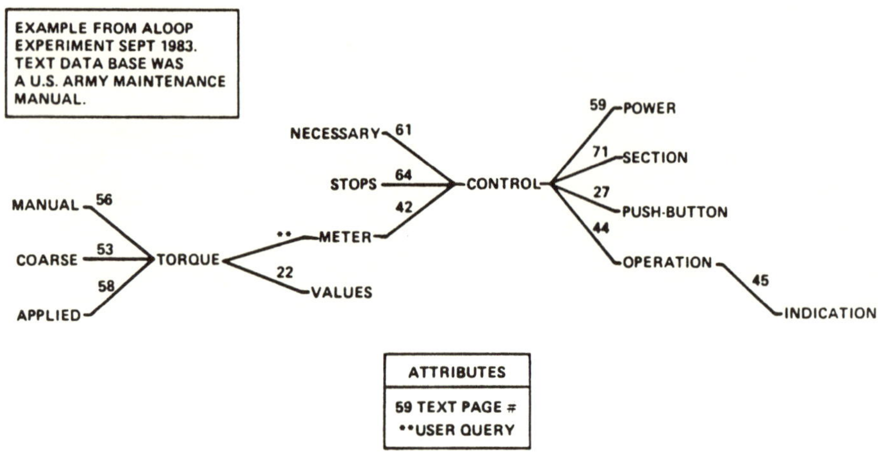

Figure 2. Associative Network Display as a Text Data Base Index.

ALOOP Parallel Processing Hardware

Semantic networks must be very large to index multidocument text data bases. The problem is that conventional serial computers cannot move through these networks fast enough. W. Daniel Hillis has done some impressive work at MIT on non-conventional computer architectures for AI applications. He points out that today's AI programs running on serial computers manipulate a few hundred facts and make decisions in minutes that would take only seconds for a human. For many real world AI applications, we will need to scale up the knowledge data base to a few million facts, and decisions would take years using serial computers to manipulate a data base of this size [Hillis, 81].

To cope with this speed problem, we are implementing the ALOOP concept as special purpose, parallel processing hardware. Segments of a semantic network are stored in a large number of independent circular queues or memory loops, shown as circles in Figure 3. All memory loops are searched simultaneously in parallel, rather than serially searching through the semantic network. In searching each loop, matched pieces of the network are passed up to successively higher levels in the hierarchy of loops. When matched pieces of the network move up, they displace nonmatched pieces that move down. Figure 3 shows this exchange as compare/transfer (C/T) boxes. Network pieces from different loops are combined as they move up and ultimately reach the top level loop. The contents of the top loop are displayed to the user as the key word roadmap, mentioned earlier.

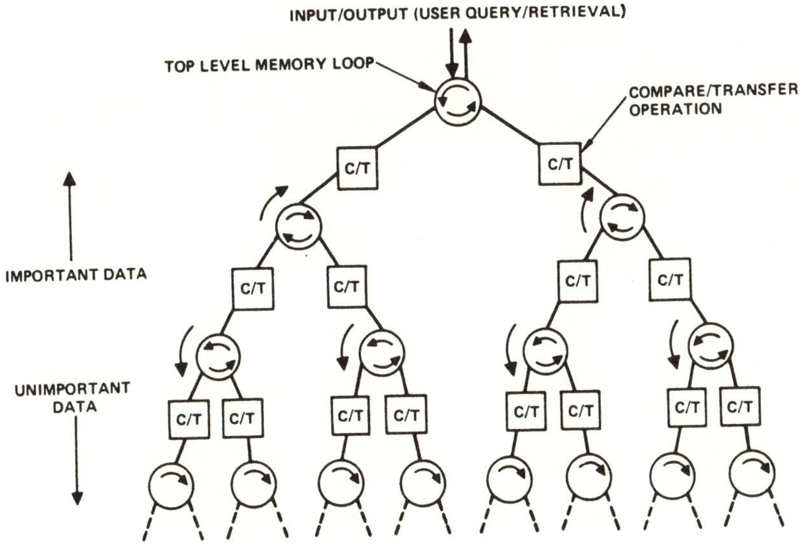

Figure 3. Associative Loop Memory (ALOOP) Architecture.

Dynamic Memory Organization

In addition to having speed, ALOOP dynamically organizes its knowledge base in a manner that imitates human memory. Roger Shank's cognitive modeling research at Yale suggests that human memory dynamically organizes itself so that people are automatically reminded of the appropriate knowledge from past episodes as required to process current experiential inputs [Shank, 82]. This kind of dynamic organization occurs in ALOOP due to three cummulative effects of the segment exchange mechanism described above: (1) all queries to memory and the associations resulting from the retrieval process become an integral part of the knowledge base, (2) "important" associations are brought to the more accessible top levels, where they are easily remembered; and (3) "unimportant" data are pushed down into less accessible lower loops where they are gradually forgotten. The meaning of "important data" and "unimportant data" changes as the user requires, because the browsing paths he selects control the contents of the top level loop. In turn, the entire contents of each loop act as queries to the loops one level down in the hierarchy.

Loosely Coupled Knowledge Representation

We call the key to ALOOP's dynamic memory behavior "loosely coupled knowledge representation." Semantic network segments are stored and manipulated as a collection of n-tuples, the simplest case being object-attribute-value triples. The value of one triple can be the object of another triple. Object-object, object-value, and value-value links are also permitted. In this way, these associative links can chain triples to form arbitrarily complex networks.

Here is an example of three triples chained through a value-object link, ROBIN:

```
NEST-----57------ROBIN
                 ROBIN-----ISA-----BIRD
WORMS----103-----ROBIN
```

The attributes of the first and third triple are page numbers of the text on which ROBIN, NEST, and WORMS, respectively, co-occur in close proximity. The attribute of the second triple, ISA, indicates that ROBIN "is a" subset of the set BIRD.

The networks formed by these triple chains are not static; i.e., they are not always repeatable, as in other inference systems. During normal processing, chains continuously fragment and recombine with other chains. Why would one want a scheme for knowledge representation and manipulation that appears so chaotic? To answer, consider the similarity of this scheme to human remembering, which can also be a very chaotic process. At times, thoughts seem to enter and leave human consciousness at random. As Donald Norman, cognitive psychologist at the University of California, San Diego, has succinctly expressed:

> ". . .The various phenomena [repeated errors humans make] I have described plus others imply that the parts of action sequences are neither strongly ordered nor tightly coupled. That is, I think the biological system is structured to use ambiguous information for memory search, to allow itself to be responsive to multiple sources of information, to combine and overlap data paths, and to deliberately intermix what one would have thought to be independent processing streams.

Although these properties can lead to errors, I believe that they are also exactly the sort of thing that gives us much of the power of human creativity and judgment, to allow us to be tolerant of noise and error, to behave flexibly, to respond in imaginative and creative ways to novel events, and to be able to shift our strategies and behavior when the situation shifts." [Norman, 81].

We believe that building this loosely coupled quality of human cognition into AI systems is a promising approach to achieving the flexibility required for truly intelligent behavior.

Progress, Current Status, and Future Plans

In 1982 we designed and constructed a hardware prototype of ALOOP. As Figure 4 shows, the prototype was controlled by a host computer. User interface software running in the host, a VAX 11/780, sent queries to the prototype. The result was successful retrieval and display of loosely coupled semantic knowledge stored in the ALOOP hardware.

We constructed the hardware prototype by modifying five single board microcomputers (Z-80) and linking them together in the parallel processing architecture described in Figure 3. Each loop was implemented in separate yet identical modules, each having its own local memory (RAM and ROM). We wrote assembly language firmware for the compare/transfer operation and added electronics to each board, so triples could be transferred between neighboring loops through dedicated high speed input/output (I/O) ports. We demonstrated that a very large memory array could be constructed by replicating our single type of module.

Additionally, we developed a simple, initial version of automatic text analysis software to address the problem of costly intellectual indexing. The program reads text, extracts key words, and converts them to object-attribute-value triples for ALOOP. We have shown that this software can generate triples to create very large knowledge bases. Currently, the program's understanding of relationships between words is limited to text proximity, but we plan to incrementally increase the level of language understanding as ALOOP matures.

Our ALOOP work has continued in 1983. Recently, we completed sentence/page retrieval software that allows true on-line text browsing. Following a four-step process, the user:

1) enters the initial key word query via keyboard;

2) examines the resulting triples display and grow network in the direction of interest;

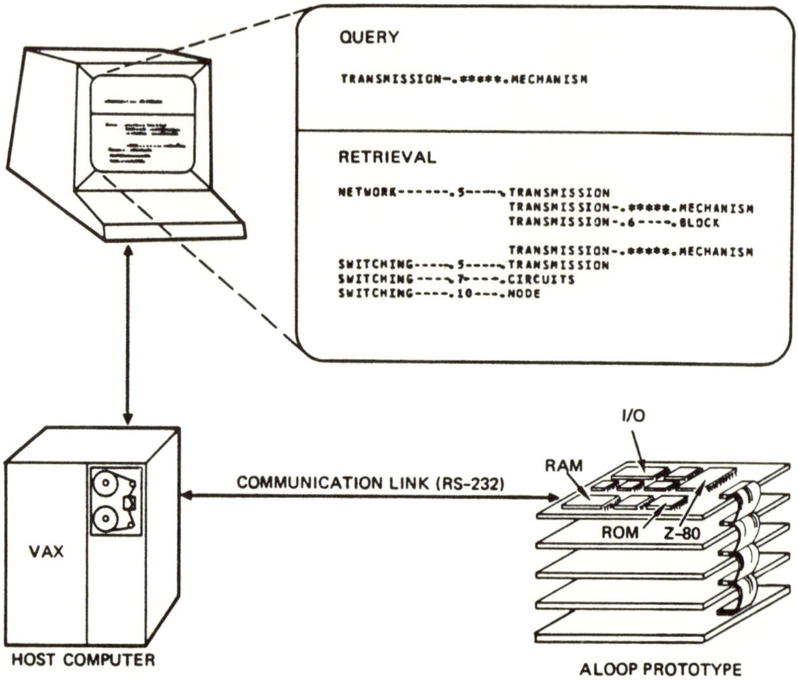

Figure 4. Associative Loop Memory (ALOOP) Hardware Prototype Demonstration.

3) indicates with a cursor the key words that seem relevant (text sentences are displayed from which the key words were extracted); and

4) expands the display to a full text page, provided that the sentence appears relevant.

The user can switch back and forth between any of these steps to quickly browse a text data base.

We are using an ALOOP software emulator to run a series of non-real time experiments in 1983. Good progress is being made towards understanding how to control loosely coupled knowledge so that a human user can easily interact with the top level contents of the ALOOP. We are also experimenting with loop architectures other than the tree structure in Figure 3.

By the beginning of 1984 we will have in place all of the basic components to manipulate a large text knowledge base. We will then begin to incrementally increase the inferential and language understanding aspects of ALOOP. We are beginning work on a set of procedures that will dynamically replace word proximity relationships with semantic primitives such as PART-OF and INSTANCE-OF. Disambiguating word meaning will be part of these procedures.

We will also begin design of an advanced hardware prototype with much larger memory capacity than that in our feasibility demonstration. The design will support a knowledge base containing a loosely coupled mixture of n-tuple relationships (e.g., frames) as well as triples.

Finally, we will develop an interactive graphics display for networks containing both semantic primitives and proximity relationships. We will then experiment with the display to navigate through and browse a multi-document text data base.

ACKNOWLEDGEMENTS

Thanks go to Wally Tao and Linda Hissam for their initiative and their continuing hard work on the Associative Loop Memory project.

References:

[Brachman, 79] Roland J. Brachman, "On the epistemological status of semantic networks," in Nicholas V. Findler (ed.), Associative Networks: Representation and Use of Knowledge by Computers, Academic Press, New York, 1979.

[Hillis, 81] W. Daniel Hillis, "The connection machine," MIT Artificial Intelligence Laboratory, A.I. Memo No. 646, September 1981.

[Norman, 81] Donald A. Norman "A psychologist views human processing: Human errors and others phenomena suggest processing mechanisms," invited paper, IJCAI-81, pp. 1097-1101, Vancouver, B.C., Canada, 1981.

[Ratcliff, 81] Roger Ratcliff, "Parallel-processing mechanisms and processing of organized information in human memory," in Hinton, G.E. and Anderson, J.A. (eds.), Parallel Models of Associative Memory, pp. 265-283, Erlbaum Associates, Hillsdale, N.J., 1981.

[Shank, 82] Roger C. Shank, Dynamic Memory: A Theory of Learning in Computers and People, Cambridge University Press, 1982.

[SIGIR, 83] "Proceedings of the sixth annual international ACM SIGIR conference on research and development in information retrieval," ACM, Bethesda, Md., 1983.

ABOUT THE AUTHOR

Arthur F. Griffin is a Senior Staff Engineer for Hughes Aircraft Company Support Systems. He is responsible for developing test and training applications of artificial intelligence. He is the originator of the associative loop memory concept (ALOOP) and is the principal investigator of two projects that apply this AI technique to information retrieval. Previously, he led an effort that developed an interactive graphics system for displaying technical documentation.

ON THE REQUIREMENTS OF EXPERT SYSTEMS FOR FAULT ISOLATION

Jeffrey Van Baalen

Martin Marietta Aerospace
Mail Stop 0570
P.O. Box 179
Denver, CO 80433

I. INTRODUCTION

Martin Marietta Denver Aerospace is involved in applications oriented research and development in artificial intelligence. The charter of the group is to augment Martin Marietta's existing technology base with artificial intelligence (AI). Our research and applications work is integrated in the sense that they drive each other in an iterative fashion. That is, DOD and NASA applications have led us to pursue research into our AI software tool set. This enhanced tool set has, in turn, made new applications of AI possible.

Three areas of AI form our main research and development thrusts: expert systems, natural language understanding, and planning. Our experience has shown that applications require a mixture of techniques from these different areas. For example, it is often appropriate to utilize a natural language front end in expert systems applications. Also, for some planning problems, we are employing an expert system approach.

II. EXPERT SYSTEM DEVELOPMENT TOOLS

We have found, as have many other groups involved in expert system construction, that it is crucial to have a sophisticated development environment. After establishing the requirements of anticipated NASA and DOD expert system applications, we found that available tools did not meet our needs. This convinced us to design and develop a rule-based system called HAPS.

HAPS (the Hierarchical, Augmentable Production System architecture) is a sophisticated tool designed to allow the rapid construction of rule-based systems in real-world environments--that is, in uncontrolled environments which require the use of tremendous amounts of both knowledge about the application domain and expert knowledge about problem solving in that domain.

One of the major advantages that this system has over the traditional production system implementations is the notion of goal directedness. HAPS has a separate memory structure called goal memory, which contains a hierarchy of goals which the system must achieve. All rules must apply in the context of some goal; thus, HAPS rules are expressed in the form:

IN some particular goal context,
IF a given set of conditions is true
THEN perform this set of actions.

The system is initialized with a top goal, and the overall system objective is to achieve this goal. On each cycle, a set of modifiable Goal Selection Strategies are used to select the current goal, which becomes the system's focus of attention for that cycle. When a rule is applied towards achieving a goal, it can declare that goal to be a success or a failure, or it can cause the goal to sprout subgoals.

Another characteristic of HAPS is the ability to construct hierarchically structured levels of working memory. Data items can be declared local to a particular goal. This means that they are available for the solution of that goal and its subgoals. When a goal is achieved, there is no longer any need to keep the local data associated with that goal. Thus, working memory does not clutter up with data items that are no longer needed. Also, this scheme allows each goal to have its own world model. This permits the simultaneous pursuit of multiple problem solutions which might ordinarily interact with each other to produce inconsistencies.

In a similar fashion, HAPS introduces the notion of production hierarchies. Under this scheme, a rule set can be loaded into the system at runtime and declared local to a particular goal. This rule set is available for the pursuit of that goal and its subgoals. Furthermore, these rule sets can be loaded in by another rule, allowing the production hierarchy to be extremely dynamic. The major advantage of this scheme is that it allows HAPS to function without a decrease in level of performance in very large expert systems, since only a small fraction of the entire rule base needs to be processed at any given time.

HAPS is provided with a modifiable set of Goal Selection Strategies (used to select the current goal) and Conflict Resolution Strategies (used to choose between competing rules). Making these strategies modifiable allows the user to tailor the needs of the system to individual applications. Also, these strategies can be changed by rules in the rule base, allowing the system to modify its behavior in response to changes in its environment.

Finally, HAPS is equipped with a set of Alternate Memory Structures, which can be used to store data items in the same way as standard working memory. Examples of types of alternate memory structures are tables and arrays. These structures make HAPS easier to interface to other existing software systems. Also, the operations performed on these structures (for example, pattern matching) are designed to allow HAPS to more easily interface to real-time changing data.

In summary, the HAPS system is equipped with many features which make it applicable to the development of large, sophisticated expert systems in real-world domains.

III. EXPERT SYSTEM FOR FAULT ISOLATION

Using the HAPS programming language, we are developing two expert systems for potential use on Space Station. The task of these two systems (in concert) is to automate power system related functions beyond the capabilities of traditional automation. More specifically, when married with traditional automation techniques, these systems will significantly reduce the burden of flight support decision making. In addition, they will allow timely reaction to changing parameters of future complex missions (e.g., Space Station).

One system's task is to monitor a spacecraft power system, identify parameter changes that indicate a potential fault, isolate the fault, and, if possible, suggest appropriate workaround procedures. It is the second system's task to adjust a spacecraft mission timeline (which dictates which loads are activated when) in reaction to changing power system capability. Depending on the situation, these systems may work together or separately. If a fault occurs in the power system, the fault isolation system activates. Following the fault isolation process, load management (the job of the second expert system) may be required. If the identified fault cannot be worked around and the fault decreases the power system capability then load management is necessary. However, if the fault can be worked around, then the load management expert system need not be notified. There is also the possibility that the load management system could work alone. This happens anytime a change in the mission effects the power system capability (e.g., if a portion of the power system needed to be taken offline for unscheduled maintenance). The load management and fault isolation expert systems are now described separately.

The load management system supplements the activities of a spacecraft flight operations director. This individual is faced with a variety of questions in maintaining the health and function of a spacecraft during its mission life. Examples of these questions with respect to the power system are:

> "In response to a degraded power generation capability, how should the mission timeline be altered?"
>
> "What changes can be made to the mission timeline to extend the life of the batteries?"
>
> "When is a preferable time to take specific batteries offline for reconditioning?"

Current technology requires that all timeline generation or alteration be performed by human experts on the ground. These activities are extremely man intensive. This expert system is intended to decrease the man-intensive nature of (and time required to) modify mission timelines. It is our belief that the reasoning process necessary to modify a mission timeline is similar to the reasoning process required to construct the original timeline. Therefore, the system's utility with respect to premission timeline construction is also being investigated.

The fault isolation expert system operates in reaction to changes in the behavior of a spacecraft power system. It must be capable of isolating faults not only in the power generation and storage system but also in the power busses. It has control of the power system and load control switching network in order to test hypotheses about fault locations.

The expert system approaches fault isolation in a top-down fashion, attempting first to isolate a fault within large portions of the system. To do this, it considers the system as composed of a small number of complex elements. Each of these elements may, in turn, be composed of many distinct components. The complex components are considered "black boxes" by specifying their functional behavior and their relation to each other. Isolating a fault in this way allows the system to consider the interaction of a small number of elements. Once the faulty element is identified, its components are considered in isolation from the rest of the power system. Some or all of these may themselves be complex elements. This allows the system to work with progressively smaller and more detailed portions of the power system. At each step, the system considers the interaction of only a small number of elements, significantly simplifying the fault isolation process. At any step in this process, the system may propose several possible fault locations. Then it will modify the configuration of the power system or one of the power busses in order to determine which of its propositions are true.

To support the following discussion, consider Figure 1 which is a diagram of the power system under consideration. Basically, there are several power generation channels, each designed to produce the same amount of power. Each channel has solar arrays for daytime power generation and batteries for nighttime. Part of the power generated during the day is used to charge the batteries for subsequent nighttime power generation. The power channels each feed the main power bus, which, in turn, distributes this power to the load busses. Each load bus distributes power to potentially many loads which are connected to it. A switching network enables any power channel, any load bus, or any load to be isolated. There is also some switching capability in each power channel for isolating portions of the solar panels, the batteries, etc. The following two examples illustrate the fault isolation process. They are intended to illustrate the top-down isolation approach as well as many other features that will be explained.

Suppose that the switching transistors of a regulator on one of the power channels open circuit during a heavy load period at the beginning of daylight. This will cause the output of this channel to drop to zero. Since this is a heavy load time, the load bus voltages will be drawn out of specification. Thus, the fault will be manifested initially as out of specifications on the load busses. The expert system now considers the power system as composed of a power generation element, a main power bus, and a load element. Upon investigation of the input/output parameters of these three elements, one of two possibilities may arise. If the current flowing through the load element does not appear unreasonable, then the expert system hypothesizes that the fault is in the power generation element. It now proceeds to a more detailed level of analysis of the main power bus element. Now it considers this bus to be composed of several sections--each corresponding to a power channel. The system now utilizes the switches between the main power bus sections to isolate each channel systematically. If one of these channels does not return to normal, then the fault has been isolated to that power channel and analysis can continue into that element to determine that the regulator is at fault.

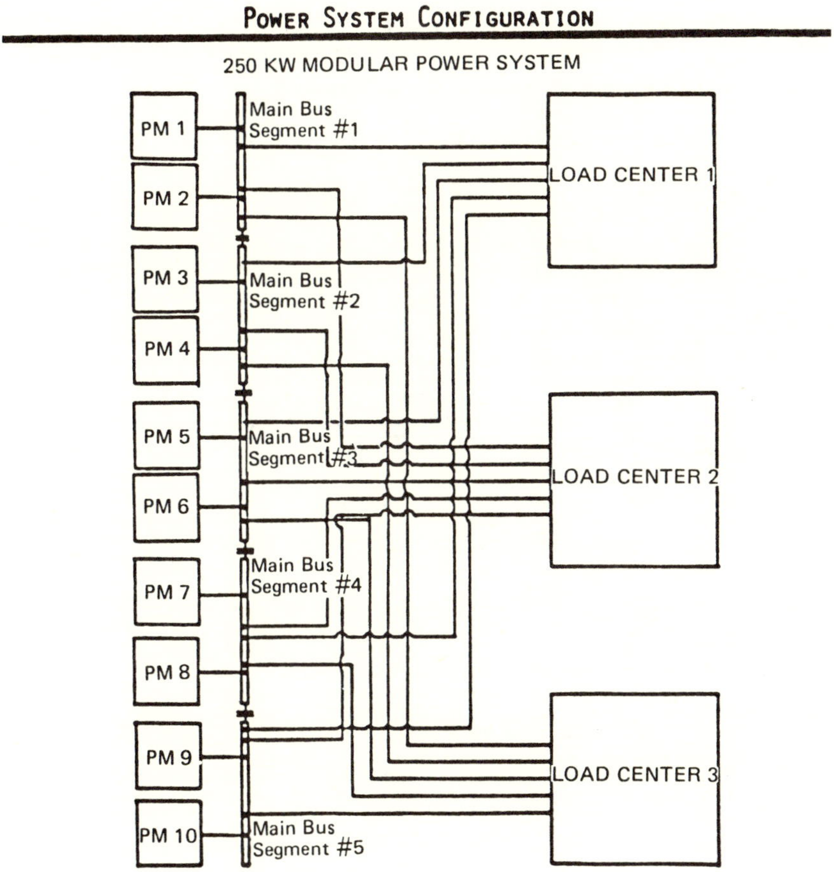
POWER SYSTEM CONFIGURATION
250 KW MODULAR POWER SYSTEM
PM 1
PM 2
PM 3
PM 4
PM 5
PM 6
PM 7
PM 8
PM 9
PM 10
Main Bus Segment #1
Main Bus Segment #2
Main Bus Segment #3
Main Bus Segment #4
Main Bus Segment #5
LOAD CENTER 1
LOAD CENTER 2
LOAD CENTER 3

Figure 1.

Power System Configuration (Continued)

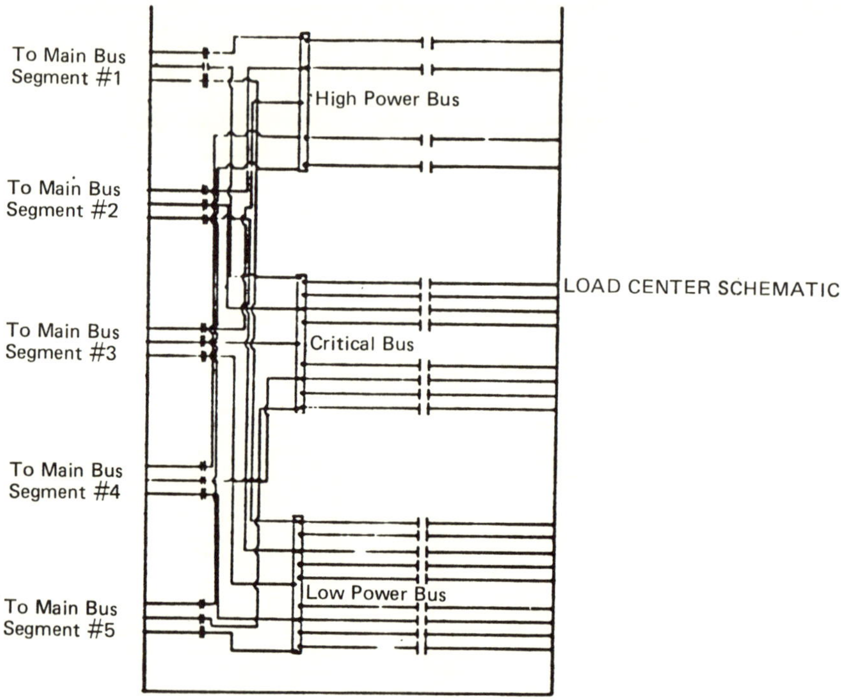

Figure 1 (cont.)

Suppose, however, that no problem can be found with any power channel. Then the current readings for the load element are assumed to be wrong and analysis proceeds to consider each of the load busses(the load element in more detail). Finally, the suspect load bus is considered in more detail and the fault is isolated to a load or cabling on that bus. If a faulty load is present, then the expert system can halt fault propagation by switching the load off. If cabling is at fault, then fault propagation can be halted by switching to redundant cabling.

As a second example of the expert system's capabilities, consider its actions when it detects two battery measurements which are out of range. The current is very low and the voltage is very high. The indication is that the battery is open circuit. In this example, the ability to measure these parameters has allowed the expert system to bypass some of the top-down process. However, it continues to employ this process to consider the cause of this situation. Inspecting a more detailed model of the relevant power channel, the situation could be caused by one of two things--the isolation diode could have failed open, or the cabling could be open circuited. The expert system can now propose a test to determine which possibility is the case. It proposes to close the charging relay, knowing that if the measurements return to within specification, then the isolation diode is the failed element. In this case, the system has already identified a workaround. Otherwise, there is a cabling fault requiring a replacement of cable.

To see how the expert system is capable of this type of analysis, it is necessary to briefly discuss its organization. It has access to a hierarchical model of the power system. The model supports the top down fault isolation process. At each level, the model consists of "black boxes" and connections between them. Each box is described functionally and the connections between them are described as supporting information flow. That is, each box is viewed as a functional element with a description of how it effects the information flowing in to create the information flowing out. This technique has been shown to be sufficiently general to characterize any system for fault isolation purposes. During its operation, relevant portions of levels of the hierarchy are read into the HAPS working memory to support the expert system's reasoning process.

The reasoning mechanisms of the expert system are, of course, encoded in the HAPS rule base. There are two classes of rules used by the system: generic fault isolation rules, and rules specific to the type of power system. These rules have been extracted from power system experts. The model and rule base are embedded in the framework of HAPS to yield the expert system depicted in Figure 2.

IV. APPLICATION OF EXPERT SYSTEMS TO FAULT ISOLATION AT THE DEPOT

The techniques being developed for the fault isolation expert system are sufficiently general to apply to a variety of fault isolation problems. In particular, we have considered use of such a system in conjunction with conventional ATE for fault isolation at the depot. We believe that an ATE system augmented with an expert system of the type previously described could significantly increase throughput at the depot. In fact, the time that each

FAULT ISOLATION EXPERT SYSTEM CONFIGURATION

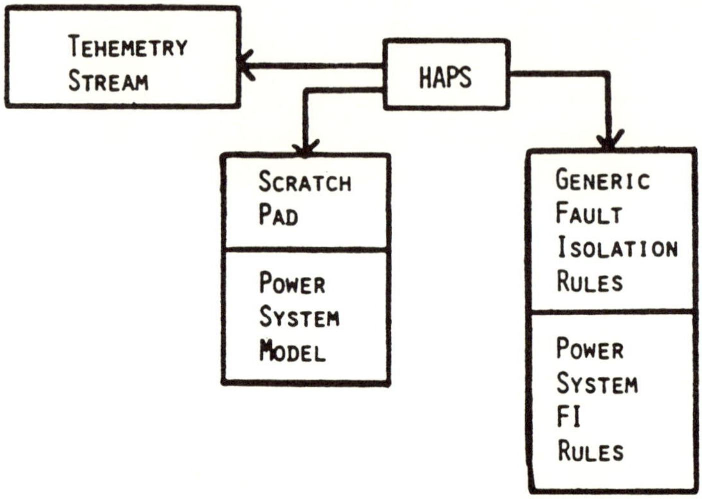

Figure 2.

system under test would have to spend at the depot would be increased in two ways. First, it can easily be shown that the top-down fault isolation technique will find the fault in a failed unit in far less time than performing a brute force battery of tests (as is done by current ATE systems). Second, and perhaps more important, the additional diagnosis step that requires a human diagnostician could be virtually eliminated. As in the expert system described above, an ATE expert system could go beyond simple fault detection to perform much of the diagnosis that currently requires a human diagnostician at the depot. Furthermore, in extreme cases where the expert system fails to completely isolate a fault, the system could explain its analysis to a human diagnostician. This could significantly decrease the time a human diagnostician would need to spend in subsequent analysis.

An expert system with these desired attributes would be similar to the power system fault isolation system previously described. This expert system would be imbedded in a hardware system, including a computer and a device with capabilities similar to existing ATE. Existing ATE software would be replaced/augmented by the expert system. The expert system's knowledge base would contain a specification of the general capabilities of its ATE front end, a specification the system under test, and a specification of the ATE connector. Its rule base would include fault isolation rules extracted from the diagnostician. Some of these would be general rules concerning the fault isolation process and others would be specific to the system under test(see Figure 3). This system could iteratively identify a test to be performed on the SUT, perform the test, and analyze the results (thereby determining the need for additional tests).

The above discussion identifies two important advantages of the described expert system approach to fault isolation at the depot. It could significantly increase the throughput at the depot by decreasing the time to identify a fault and by decreasing the necessary involvement of diagnosticians. Also, in instances where a diagnostician needs to consider a fault that the expert system is unable to find, it is able to explain its analysis in the expert's terms. This capability has implications with respect to a tutoring. These explanations can serve in some situations to assist a novice diagnostician in techniques he is unfamiliar with. However, much additional work must be done not only on explanation but also on other issues in the realm of computer aided instruction before this type of system can be used as an effective tutor.

There are additional benefits realized with the expert system approach that could significantly decrease certain costs and manpower currently incurred at the depot. Some of these are now discussed. First, once an ATE expert system has been developed employing the described approach, it will become extremely cost effective to add new SUTs. This is due to the fact that one need only construct a hierarchical model of the device(most of the information for which comes from design documentation) and replace the device specific rule set. All of the generic fault isolation rules can be maintained for all devices. Second, if changes need to be made to the logic of the expert system or to its model of a device, this can be done very rapidly at the depot. Virtually eliminating expensive software modification costs. This is principally due to the user friendly nature(high level) of this data. Just as rules are an extremely understandable representation of the logic of the expert system, so the model is an understandable representation of the SUT.

ATE EXPERT SYSTEM

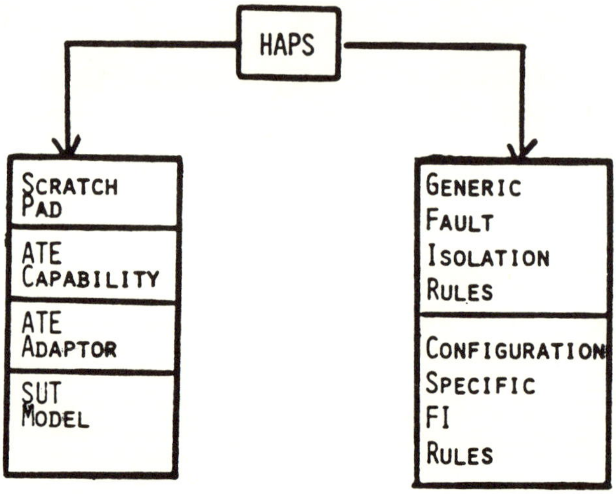

Figure 3.

V. Conclusion

This paper discusses one route to introduce expert system technology into the area of device maintenance. It relates the experience of Martin Marietta Denver Aerospace's artificial intelligence group in its attempts to build expert systems for complex, real world problems. Based on our experience, we found it necessary to develop a rule based system tool called HAPS which extends the expert system paradigm in several ways. Using HAPS we are developing a number of expert systems. One of these systems performs fault isolation on a spacecraft power system. We believe that this problem is closely related to the maintenance problem.

The paper proceeds with an example of how to extend the expert system currently under development for fault isolation at the depot. The potential benefits of the application of expert systems are described. These include:

- increased throughput at the depot,
- decreased cost to add new SUTs to the expert systems diagnosis repertoire,
- decreased cost to change the system's logic or SUT model,
- and an explanation capability.

ABOUT THE AUTHOR

Jeffrey Van Baalen has headed the Artificial Intelligence Group in the Advanced Automation Technology Section of Martin Marietta Denver Aerospace since its inception in 1980. Under his direction, the group has begun the construction of an integrated environment for the development of AI software systems. A number of natural language interfaces have been developed and a number of expert systems are under development, notably an expert system for satellite fault isolation. Mr. Van Baalen has also initiated research in natural language understanding and in the use of meta knowledge in decision making systems.

Other Noyes Publications

COST-EFFECTIVE MAINTENANCE MANAGEMENT
Productivity Improvement and Downtime Reduction

by

Frank Herbaty
Frank Herbaty & Associates
Maintenance Management Consultants
Bolingbrook, Illinois

An approach to the optimization of maintenance management and the reduction of overall maintenance costs, with particular emphasis on the aspects of productivity improvement and downtime reduction, is described in this concisely written text.

The cost-effective operation of any plant or manufacturing facility is greatly dependent on the maintenance management staff and the efficiency with which it performs. Optimization of maintenance is the art of performing maintenance in a manner that best achieves a company's goals. It involves the delicate balancing of sums spent on maintenance labor and materials against production loss costs due to inadequate maintenance. Timing is obviously extremely important.

Few books exist on this subject, and this is a first to emphasize maintenance optimization and to differentiate between the most important and the more trivial functions of a maintenance manager and his staff. It presents a practical system for concentrating corrective effort where it will reap the highest rewards.

The book is based on the author's extensive experience and, in all cases, he has selected for discussion the methods he personally has found to work best. Numerous colorful case studies are used to illustrate items in point.

The book is presented in four parts. Part I defines maintenance management and how its cost is measured, taking into account company goals, safety, environmental impacts, and product quality. Parts II and III detail downtime reduction and productivity improvement, considered by the author to be the two most important areas of maintenance management. Part IV addresses maintenance support systems such as materials, engineering, labor relations, purchasing, and accounting, etc.

A condensed table of contents listing **part and chapter titles** is given below.

ISBN 0-8155-0953-7 (1983) **260 pages**

Other Noyes Publications

ROBOTICS APPLICATIONS FOR INDUSTRY
A Practical Guide

by

L. L. Toepperwein, M. T. Blackmon, W. T. Park
General Dynamics Corp.
Fort Worth, Texas

W. R. Tanner
Productivity Systems Inc.
Farmington, Michigan

W. F. Adolfson
Advanced Technology, Inc.
McLean, Virginia

This book provides an in-depth introduction to the basic concepts and techniques pertaining to the use of robotics technology for manufacturing and industrial applications. A special section is devoted to robotics in motor vehicle manufacture.

In an era when cost-effective technology and increased productivity are of prime concern, these studies should be of value in many decision-making processes. There is little question that computer aided manufacturing is going to become the technology of choice in coming years, and one of its first major U.S. applications has been in motor vehicle manufacture.

The book contains two parts. Part I details the basic concepts of robotics technology—robot configuration, sensors, tooling, work station integration, current application information, and future trends. It provides an approach to the implementation of the technology, a means of determining implementation costs, and a review of documentation of available literature. Part II covers robotics use in motor vehicle manufacture. Patterns of usage and current robot populations are given for the worldwide auto industry. New technology development requirements are identified and current research efforts described.

A condensed table of contents listing **part, chapter, and selected subtitles** is given below. An outstanding glossary of terms is included in Part I.

ISBN 0-8155-0962-6 (1983) **326 pages**

FLEXIBLE MANUFACTURING SYSTEMS HANDBOOK

Prepared by the Staff of the

Automation and Management Systems Division
The Charles Stark Draper Laboratory, Inc.

Flexible manufacturing systems (FMSs) represent a relatively new method for increasing productivity. Originated in the 1960s, the technology is now proven and increasingly available. FMSs are particularly attractive to manufacturers producing in middle volume ranges—between mass production and one of a kind. The book is designed to answer the following questions:

- Why an FMS?
- Will an FMS best serve your application?
- What problems might be encountered?
- How do you design an appropriate system?
- What is required to operate a system?

A flexible manufacturing system is defined as a "computer-controlled configuration of semi-independent work stations and a material handling system designed to efficiently manufacture more than one part number at low to medium volumes." Three essential components of an FMS are 1) standard numerically-controlled machine tools, 2) a conveyance network, and 3) an overall control system. Flexible manufacturing technology can provide direct hardware/software solutions to various management challenges facing today's manufacturer, such as low-cost methods for quick product start-up, adaptability and responsiveness to changes in demand, and capacity to readily resurrect out-of-production designs.

The book is presented in four parts. Part I is intended to help answer broad policy questions at corporate levels. Part II contains detailed descriptions of the subsystems that make up a typical FMS as well as descriptions of several operational FMSs. Part III is designed to serve as a detailed guide to planners at corporate and plant levels, and Part IV contains a sample request-for-proposal, a proposal, and other technical material.

A condensed table of contents listing **part and chapter titles** is given below.

ISBN 0-8155-0983-9 (1984) **392 pages**

Other Noyes Publications

HIGH TECHNOLOGY INTERNATIONAL TRADE AND COMPETITION

Robotics Telecommunications Computers Semiconductors

Edited by J.K. Paul

This book presents an overview of the current international competitive situations in four high technology industries—robotics, computers, telecommunications, and semiconductors. It is based on research by the *U.S. Dept of Commerce, International Trade Administration* and the *U.S. Congress, Office of Technology Assessment*. The "high tech" industries have contributed significantly to U.S. economic development in the past two decades in terms of economic expansion, employment opportunities, and national productivity. This same growth in high technology industries is also evident in other industrialized countries, and, as a result, there is an intensifying international competition in most high tech fields and an increasing awareness of problems which may result from so-called "targeting" practices of other governments.

The book is divided into two parts. Part I provides profiles for each industry as well as the text of papers given by industry speakers at a series of DOC meetings. The industry profiles present brief assessments of each industry, its international competitive situation, important competitive issues. and options for addressing the issues. Part II covers international competition in the electronics industry from four different perspectives—structure and trade, competitiveness, financing, and national industrial policies.

A condensed table of contents listing **part and chapter titles and selected subtitles** is given below.

ISBN 0-8155-0988-X (1984) **394 pages**

Other Noyes Publications

ARTIFICIAL INTELLIGENCE EXPERT SYSTEMS, COMPUTER VISION AND NATURAL LANGUAGE PROCESSING

by

William B. Gevarter

National Aeronautics and Space Administration

An overview of artificial intelligence (AI), its core ingredients, and its applications is presented in this volume. AI is a field with over a quarter century of history; however, it wasn't until the 1980s that AI received economic and popular acclaim and went through the transition from a primary research area to potential commercial applications. The full impact of AI's transition has yet to be felt. Recently, AI was made the basic thrust of Japan's Fifth Generation computer research effort. Success in this venture could project the Japanese into a dominant position in information sciences in the 1990s. Similar importance has been placed on AI by the U.S., Great Britain, and France.

The real payoff for AI will be in applications. Intelligent computer programs are now emerging from the laboratory into practical applications. This book presents overviews of key application areas—expert systems, computer vision, natural language processing, speech interfaces, and problem solving and planning. Basic approaches to these systems, the state of the art, existing systems, participants, and future trends are detailed. The book should be useful to engineering and research managers, potential users and others seeking a basic understanding of the rapidly evolving area of artificial intelligence and its applications.

A condensed table of contents listing **part and chapter titles and selected subtitles** is given below.

ISBN 0-8155-0994-4 (1984) 226 pages

Other Noyes Publications

HANDBOOK OF TOXIC AND HAZARDOUS CHEMICALS AND CARCINOGENS 1985 Second Edition

by Marshall Sittig
Princeton University

"Sittig's book is an important addition to the literature on toxic chemicals . . . . a valuable desk reference . . . . Protecting against potential public health hazards requires widespread knowledge about commercial chemicals."—from the Foreword by *U.S. Senator Bill Bradley of New Jersey.*

The vastly expanded *Second Edition* of this Handbook presents concise chemical, health and safety information on nearly 800 toxic and hazardous chemicals and carcinogens (up from nearly 600 in the previous edition). The addition of carcinogens to the Handbook increases its value considerably over the previous edition. It enables responsible decisions to be made by chemical manufacturers, safety equipment producers, toxicologists, industrial safety engineers, waste disposal operators, health care professionals, and the many others who may have contact with or interest in these chemicals due to their own or third party exposure. The book will thus be a must for industrial and medical libraries.

Included in the book are:

- **all** of the **EPA Priority Toxic Pollutants,**
- **all** of the substances whose allowable concentrations in workplace air are adopted or proposed by **ACGIH,**
- **all** of the substances considered to date in the Standards Completion Program of **NIOSH,** and
- **most** of the chemicals classified as **EPA "hazardous wastes,"**
- **most** of the chemicals classified as **EPA "hazardous substances,"**
- **most** of the chemicals reviewed in **EPA "CHIPS"** documents, and
- **most** of the chemicals reviewed in **NIOSH Information Profiles.**

In addition, this Second Edition includes:

- **all** of the carcinogens identified by the **U.S. National Toxicology Program,**
- **many** of the chemicals profiled by the **Dutch Association of Safety Experts**, the **Dutch Chemical Industry Association,** and the **Dutch Safety Institute,**
- **most** of the chemicals described in the **ILO** *Encyclopedia of Occupational Health and Safety* (1983), and
- **most** of the chemicals in the **United Nations'** *IRPTC Legal File* (1984).

Essentially the book attempts to answer six questions about each compound (to the extent information is available):

(1) What is it?
(2) Where is it encountered?
(3) How much can one tolerate?
(4) How does one measure it?
(5) What are its harmful effects?
(6) How does one protect against it?

The chemicals are presented alphabetically and each is classified as a "carcinogen," "hazardous substance," "hazardous waste," and/or a "priority toxic pollutant"—as defined by the various federal agencies, and explained in the comprehensive introduction to the book. Data and citations are furnished, to the extent currently available, on any or all of these important categories:

Chemical Description
Code Numbers
DOT Designation
Synonyms
Potential Exposure
Incompatibilities
Permissible Exposure Limits in Air
Determination in Air
Permissible Concentration in Water
Determination in Water
Routes of Entry
Harmful Effects and Symptoms
Points of Attack
Medical Surveillance
First Aid
Personal Protective Methods
Respirator Selection
Disposal Method Suggested
References

ISBN 0-8155-1009-8 (1985) **950 pages**